Humphrey Carpenter

Humphrey Carpenter began his career working for the BBC and throughout his life continued to broadcast regularly for Radio 3 and Radio 4. He wrote many best-selling, award-winning biographies with subjects including J. R. R. Tolkien, C. S. Lewis, Ezra Pound, W. H. Auden, Benjamin Britten, Dennis Potter and Spike Milligan. He was a prolific author of children's books, a skilled jazz musician and a highly innovative director of Cheltenham Literary Festival from 1994 to 1996. He died in January 2005 with the 'Seven Lives' near completion. It has been edited, with additional material, by Candida Brazil and James Hamilton.

Praise for *The Seven Lives of John Murray*:

'Humphrey Carpenter's history of the firm, completed by other hands after his death in 2005, is an evocation of a vanished age' *Daily Telegraph*

'A treasure trove of fascinating information paced into Humphrey Carpenter's riveting history of the world's longest surviving publishing house . . . Terrific' *Daily Mail*

'A masterpiece of sympathetic biography' *Herald*

'Experience suggests that histories of publishing houses are not the first place to look for entertainment, but here's one to make us think again' *Sunday Times*

'Engrossing' *Choice*

'[A] delightful history' *Country Life*

'Continuously lively and interesting, with vivid and perceptive character sketches of the successive members of the dynasty. It tells a remarkable story' *Scotsman*

'[A] jolly romp of a publishing histo

D1328996

Also by Humphrey Carpenter

The Angry Young Men

W. H. Auden: a biography

Benjamin Britten: a biography

The Brideshead Generation

The Envy of the World: fifty years of the BBC Third Programme and Radio 3

The Inklings: C. S. Lewis, J. R. R. Tolkien, Charles Williams and their friends

Jesus (Past Masters series)

Spike Milligan: the biography

The Oxford Companion to Children's Literature (with Mari Prichard)

Dennis Potter: a biography

A Serious Character: the life of Ezra Pound

Robert Runcie: the Reluctant Archbishop

Secret Gardens: the Golden Age of Children's Literature

That Was Satire That Was

J. R. R. Tolkien: a biography

EDITED

The Letters of J. R. R. Tolkien (with Christopher Tolkien)

The Puffin Book of Classic Children's Stories

FOR CHILDREN

The Mr Majeika series

Shakespeare Without the Boring Bits

The Joshers

The Captain Hook Affair

The Seven Lives of John Murray

The Story of a Publishing Dynasty
1768–2002

HUMPHREY CARPENTER

Edited by Candida Brazil and James Hamilton
with additional material by James Hamilton

JOHN MURRAY

First published in Great Britain in 2008 by John Murray (Publishers)
An Hachette UK Company

First published in paperback in 2009

1

A CIP catalogue record for this title is available from the British Library

ISBN 978-0-7195-6533-5

Typeset in Monotype Bembo by Servis Filmsetting Ltd, Stockport, Cheshire

Printed and bound by Clays Ltd, St Ives plc

John Murray policy is to use papers that are natural, renewable and recyclable products and
made from wood grown in sustainable forests. The logging and manufacturing processes are
expected to conform to the environmental regulations of the country of origin.

John Murray (Publishers)
338 Euston Road
London NW1 3BH

www.johnmurray.co.uk

I cannot express it better than by proposing the toast of 'Albemarle Street'. I do not know what other name to call the toast by. (*Hear, hear.*) Amongst ourselves we always allude to the firm as Albemarle Street, and I daresay you know what that means. (*Applause.*)

John Murray IV speaking at the coming-of-age dinner
for his son, John Murray V, 9 October 1905

Contents

CONTENTS

Illustrations

All images are taken from the collection of John and Virginia Murray.

Preface

As a young author my husband Humphrey Carpenter once joined a group of writers and publishers walking round London publishing houses for charity. A cask of beer, installed for the day, awaited them at each destination. Many of the London publishers' offices then still displayed their venerable origins and Humphrey, not himself a Murray author, visited the fabled 50 Albemarle Street for the first time.

When this book was commissioned in 2002, Murray's was one of the last remaining in its ancestral home, but that was about to change. Murray's had been sold and the publishing business was soon to leave 50 Albemarle Street. Invited to Murray's for the launch of a friend's book, in the room where Byron's memoirs were burnt, Humphrey enquired about the Murray Archive. Always ready to seize the moment, he was soon asking Virginia Murray, the archivist wife of the seventh John Murray, whether anyone was now using the archive to write the firm's history. 'We've been looking for somebody for months' was the answer, and before long John Murray joined the conversation. A few weeks later Humphrey had made his case to the family and to Roland Philipps, head of the 'new' John Murray under Hodder Headline, and he began work. He often said he became a biographer because he loved reading other people's letters; now he was in the same house as an incomparable collection of them, and sometimes read them at a desk in the drawing room, with Byron's portrait above the fireplace.

Humphrey had delivered a first draft, and begun revising, when he died suddenly of a heart attack in January 2005, aged fifty-eight. He had left some gaps to fill, and planned further interviews. Having sometimes dramatised episodes in previous biographies, he had also written imaginary scenarios for three points in the Murray book where he thought they could change the pace, give an alternative viewpoint, and entertain. But he hadn't yet quite convinced his publisher, and it was left for later decision. So the book was both near to and, without him to do it, far from completion.

Felicity Bryan, Humphrey's agent, then brought to it her incomparable energy and focus, and ensured that two people took on the task with enthusiasm. Candida Brazil, for whom Humphrey had developed huge respect when she edited two of his previous books, covered the first stage of editing and filling gaps. Working on the book when the Murray Archive finally left the house, she describes that departure. Candida was succeeded by James Hamilton, biographer of J. M. W. Turner and Michael Faraday, and author of *London Lights*, an account of intellectuals, scientists, artists and engineers rubbing shoulders in nineteenth-century London. He filled out the book's account of Murray's nineteenth-century scientific, art and travel publishing, and dealt, in lieu of the author, with the remaining tasks. Since Humphrey's dramatisations always divided readers, James proposed a solution: one of them remains in the main text, but 'Scenes from a Silent Movie' (with gorilla) and another suggested scene were banished to the Appendix.

The editors' (and author's) acknowledgements follow. I have a different sort of gratitude: to everyone mentioned above for their role in bringing the book to publication, and to other friends who read the text in the first months after Humphrey died, to Bob Osborne and Jeremy Lewis, and to Andrew Nicholson and Bill Zachs who combined friendship with deep and relevant scholarship.

Humphrey could not have written the book without goodwill and unfailing help from Virginia and John Murray. They knew his choice of material and opinions would be independent, and without expecting always to agree with him they gave him every kindness and made his days at 50 Albemarle Street a delight.

Mari Prichard
January 2008

Editors' Acknowledgements

IT HAS BEEN a tough but fascinating business editing Humphrey Carpenter's buoyant and boisterous typescript for publication. His voice was there throughout, his laughter, his caprice, his lightly carried erudition, and it was this that carried us along when the work of a stuffier dead author might have given cause for boredom or rebellion. Errors, now, are more likely to be ours than Humphrey's.

We would like to thank, both on Humphrey's behalf and on our own, these who agreed to be interviewed, or who generously gave advice or access to published and unpublished research: Bruce Barker-Benfield, Jim Belben, Jane Blackstock, Jane Boulenger (Mrs Moore), Janet Browne, Gill Clack, Peter Cochran, Robin Darwall-Smith, Paul Douglass, Debbie Gill, Peter Gilliver, Tim Hely-Hutchinson, Linda Kelly, Fiona MacCarthy, Warren McDougall, Grant McIntyre, Don Mackean, Andrew Nicholson, Richard Ovenden, Nick Perren, Gail Pirkis, Judith Reinhold, Nigel Reynolds, William St Clair, William Thomas, Nick Utechin, Yvonne Ward and William Zachs. At the National Library of Scotland Ruth Boreham, Iain Brown, David McClay, Rachel Thomas and their colleagues were unfailingly helpful with our enquiries, and have demonstrated that the John Murray Archive has landed in exactly the right place. For permission to make quotations we would like to thank Maggie Hanbury and the Estate of Kenneth Clark, Magdalene College Cambridge, Dervla Murphy, John R. Murray, the Royal Geographical Society, and the *Daily Telegraph*.

At John Murray's repositioned publishing house in Euston Road we thank Roland Philipps, Rowan Yapp and Peter James. We have been given endless support by them and by Mari Prichard and Felicity Bryan, but most warmly of all we thank Diana Murray, Hallam Murray, John R. Murray and Virginia Murray who by their generosity and hospitality have shown how the Murray sense of enterprise, community and public spirit has reached even unto the seventh generation.

Candida Brazil
James Hamilton
January 2008

Prologue

From the *Daily Telegraph*, 11 May 2002:

LAST CHAPTER AS OLDEST PUBLISHER IS BOUGHT OUT

By Nigel Reynolds

John Murray, the oldest independent book publisher in the world and the last of London's 'gentlemen publishing houses', has been forced to sell out to an *arriviste* rival because it says it is too small to survive in a fiercely globalised industry.

The deal with Hodder Headline, part of the W. H. Smith group, is said to be worth up to £20 million and caused shock and surprise in the book world yesterday. The Murray family said it was the only way to save the firm.

The Murray name will live on as separate division of Hodder, though in the long term there are fears that its identity could disappear.

John Murray, founded in 1768, is one of the most revered names in British publishing with a long and colourful history. It is regarded as the last survivor of a gentler time when authors and editors would sit around a fire plotting books with no thought given to the bottom line.

John Murray's authors read like a list from a companion to English literature. It published Jane Austen, Lord Byron, Charles Darwin, Arthur Conan Doyle and John Betjeman.

Remarkably, it has always been run by a John Murray. The current chairman is John Murray VII who is in his fifties.

He said yesterday that his two grown-up sons, Octavius and Charlie, were not interested in taking over the firm and it had no future as an independent publisher. He blamed literary agents for driving up authors' advances and said the family firm, which made a profit of £367,000 in 2000 and has annual sales of only £8 million, could no longer bid for major books ...

In the gentle days, Mr Murray said yesterday, many of the writers had private incomes, and advances and profits were seldom discussed, nor did they matter.

He went on: 'The family has never made any money. We had salaries, that's all. Everything went back into the firm. It had to. It was the only way of carrying on.'

Mr Murray's father, John 'Jock' Murray VI, was delighted when someone described him as 'the only publisher in whose company a failed author could sit at ease'.

PART ONE

1768–1811
32 Fleet Street

I

Blockheads making fortunes

———

IN *A PUBLISHER and his Friends*, his book on the Murray family and firm published in 1891, Samuel Smiles begins as follows: 'The publishing house of Murray dates from the year 1768, in which year John MacMurray, a lieutenant of Marines, having retired from the service on half-pay, purchased the bookselling business of William Sandby, at the sign of the "Ship", No. 32, Fleet Street, opposite St. Dunstan's Church.'[1] Thus, in Smiles's evocation, the first John Murray strides on stage like a character in a novel, the man who is going to get the heroine in the end. He is decent and honourable, with a geniality that conceals romantic depths that the girl will plumb in the final pages. What's more, he has an ancestry. John MacMurray was descended from the Murrays of Athol. His uncle, Colonel Murray, was 'out' in the rising of 1715, under the Earl of Mar, when being 'out' meant rebelling against the Hanoverian monarchy. Colonel Murray served under the Marquis of Tullibardine, the son of his chief, the Duke of Athol, and led a regiment in the abortive fight at Sheriffmuir. After the rebellion against the Hanoverian dynasty had been suppressed, Colonel Murray retired to France, where he served under the exiled Duke of Ormonde, who had attached himself to the Stuart Court.

The Colonel's brother Robert followed a safer course. He prefixed the 'Mac' to his name, settled in Edinburgh, adopted the law as a profession, and became a writer to the Signet.[2] But according to William Zachs, who wrote about the early Murrays a hundred years after Smiles,[3] these adventures more likely happened to Robert Murray's uncle, rather than to his brother, who would have been a teenager in 1715.

Smiles's agenda, apparent from the first page of his book, is to elevate the Murray family, socially and intellectually. Hence he gives us 'Colonel Murray', presenting him as a man who hobnobs with Scots aristocrats in France, rather than the angry young man wearing a torn kilt with a dirk thrust into his stocking-top, straight out of the pages of *Kidnapped*. Even the Colonel's pedestrian brother Robert, the father of the first John Murray, has a grand title, 'writer to the Signet'. All this meant was that he was qualified to issue warrants and writs.

Clearly Smiles would like the Murrays to have been related to the Duke of Athol. Though Smiles seems not to have known it, Murray was the family name of the second Duke, the one involved in the 1715 rebellion, but there is no evidence to show that the Duke was related to the publishing Murrays, whose origins seem to have been entirely humble. 'Murray' is one of the commonest Scottish surnames, alleged variously to derive from Moravia, and from no further away than Ireland. What's more, our story starts not with the romantic–aristocratic Jacobite rebellions, but on some farmland near Edinburgh.

Robert Murray, the father of John Murray, was born in 1698, the son of the tenant of Eastmains farm on the Dalhousie estate near Dalkeith, seven miles south-east of Edinburgh. Scotland did not deny a proper education to such people: after a parish schooling, Robert matriculated at the University of Edinburgh on a four-year course, and though he studied there for only two years, from 1716, this was enough to get him apprenticed to a lawyer. The Murrays were on the way up.

Five years later, Robert McMurray, as he now spelt his name, set up as a lawyer in Edinburgh. He and his wife Jean, daughter of James Ross of Dundee, lived on the first floor of a crowded tenement overlooking Baillie Clerk's Land, a small courtyard off the Royal Mile. Smoke from the shop beneath filtered through the floorboards, water had to be carried up from the ground floor, and foul smells betrayed the lack of sanitation. On New Year's Day 1737, in the midst of the celebrations, Jean McMurray gave birth to her seventh child, their only son to survive. He was christened John.[4] The child had scarcely turned five when his mother died, worn out by a life of continual pregnancy. Aged only forty, Jean had given birth to nine children, of whom five had perished.[5] An aunt moved in to look after the survivors.

'As the only son,' writes Zachs, 'John was given every advantage his father's means allowed . . . At an early age he would have been enrolled in one of the town's private academies to receive a basic grounding in Latin, English and arithmetic.'[6] Later, he attended the High School, and at the age of fifteen enrolled at Edinburgh University. But his time there was even briefer than his father's. 'He was not a bookish person,' writes Zachs. Bookselling and publishing do not necessarily involve the intellect or the imagination; the story of the Murrays is not chiefly about the life of the mind. The first John Murray was undoubtedly a man of action.

Like many sons of Edinburgh, John McMurray wanted to break free from that exquisite but often stifling settlement. We do not know how he occupied himself between leaving university and his mid-twenties, but in 1762 he was commissioned into the 34th Company of Marines as a second lieutenant. He went to Portugal, and would later note with regret that he had had the 'misfortune never to have taken one trip to India.'[7] Scarcely had he been commissioned than the Seven Years' War with France was over, won by the British, and as a result, in February 1763, Lieutenant McMurray found himself at the naval base at Chatham, trying to live on half-pay. At this point he met a seventeen-year-old local girl Nancy (really Ann) Weemss, and fell in love. Her father, a retired naval captain from Brompton near Chatham, was deeply suspicious of the twenty-six-year-old McMurray, and as it turned out was right to be so. Captain Weemss was certain that the young man was after his daughter's dowry of £700, the equivalent of nearly £60,000 in the early-twenty-first century, and withheld it until McMurray was in gainful employment. In March 1763 he reluctantly allowed the marriage to go ahead. Having few contacts in England, McMurray went back to Scotland to look for work. Through an uncle he found a post as private secretary to Sir Robert Gordon, of Gordonstoun, Morayshire, now the spartan public school. Duties included looking after the library, one of the best stocked in Scotland, a task that may have given McMurray a taste for handling books. Initially, however, he saw potential in taking the Gordon estate's salmon to sell in London, but nothing came of this, and Gordonstoun became a dead end. In October 1765 he drifted back to Edinburgh. It was now that McMurray began to keep a letter-book, a habit that remained with him all his life.[8] This was a diary of outgoing correspondence, in which each letter sent was summarised, a regular practice of eighteenth-century businessmen, but rare among private individuals. In one entry, McMurray noted that he was 'going to London in January; perhaps sooner. Was very melancholy, owing to unlucky accidents &c.'[9] A week or so later he recorded a plan of 'going to London some time next month upon chance', and needed the help of the Gordon family in getting him recommendations 'to introduce me at first into business'.[10]

London was a challenge for McMurray, as for any Scot of his day. After the failure of the 1745 rebellion, the Scots had gradually begun to colonise England peacefully, an immigration unpopular with many English. The English labelled the Scots 'North Britons', and claimed they were dirty, lazy and ill educated, clannish and in league against honest English tradesmen. Samuel Johnson's contempt for the Scots, and James Boswell's plea, 'I am a Scot, but I cannot help it,' was typical of the time. Not surprisingly, John McMurray's plans were delayed. Letters arrived from Nancy in Chatham imploring him to come back to her and get himself a job. John's response was chivalrous. 'I was resolved to support her as my wife while I had one sixpence in the world,' he wrote.[11] But, as the weeks passed, he failed to leave Edinburgh.

Maybe he should go abroad? He wrote to Archy Paxton, a friend he had made at university, to ask 'if he could procure me to be appointed Superintendent over any of the new purchased lands in Grenada'.[12] To placate his father-in-law, he even considered going back to sea, perhaps as a purser in the merchant navy. In April 1766 McMurray pulled himself together and sailed on a trading boat from Leith to Great Yarmouth, where he took a coach to London. He promptly developed smallpox, and was ill for three months. Although he had no job, he took control of Nancy's income, which, beside the £700, drew a small rent from a farm in Kent. With Nancy's money in his pocket, John settled in London, and tried to get into business.

He considered trading in china cups and plates; he considered being a novelist. In May 1767, soon after his thirtieth birthday, he noted that he had 'begun a work . . . in the literary way', but had abandoned it because he could not think of an ending.[13] Nevertheless, only six months later McMurray's tale *The History of Sir Launcelot Edgevile* was published in five instalments in the *Court Miscellany*, November 1767 to March 1768. In his biography of John Murray, William Zachs is tough on *Sir Launcelot Edgevile*, which he describes as:

> typical of the undistinguished mass of sentimental fiction produced at the time . . . poorly characterised, didactic in tone . . . It relates a few curious episodes in the life of the eponymous hero, a cosseted twenty-five-year-old who begins to make his way in a turbulent world. Most eighteenth-century fiction of this kind ends hastily, but 'Sir Launcelot' has no ending at all, at least not one that appeared in the *Court Miscellany*.[14]

Yet there is real feeling in the story's harsh satire on the immorality of high society, expressed with a good deal of illicit sex. The cast includes a jeweller who has pimped (or 'p——p'd', as the printed text has it) for an unscrupulous countess, and a mistress who compensates for her foppish lover's impotence by going out into the street and seducing the first attractive young man who passes by. The author definitely wants us to think he is a man of the world, but the story's weakness is that after five episodes it simply stops – McMurray seems to have had too many other things on his mind. He did not regard himself as in any way an intellectual. 'Look about you,' he wrote in his letter-book, 'and see who it is that thrives most in the world. It is the industrious and plodding no matter how illiterate and not the abstracted man of sense & learning.'[15]

McMurray regained control of his life, and in May 1767 applied successfully to rejoin the Marines on full pay. He and Nancy set up home together in a rented house near Chatham a year later. His first duty as a marine was to be a policeman at the dockyard. Unfortunately his own behaviour disqualified him for the job, as he tells in his letter-book: 'as I came home from the Crown in Rochester where I had accidentally got much in liquor … I was beset in Chatham by 4 or 5 stout shipwrights on account of some gallantry I was foolishly showing to a girl.'[16] In other words, he was drunk and chasing a skirt. The shipwrights knocked him down and beat him up – four or five Englishmen to one Scotsman – so that 'every part of my face, head & temples, was cut and mangled'.[17]

The fact that McMurray had largely brought the attack on himself by being drunk did not prevent him from writing an indignant complaint to the Chatham dockyard authorities, nor from warning an acquaintance about the evils of drink: 'Overcome your inclination for liquor and every thing with you will prosper.'[18] As to women, it was during this period that he fathered an illegitimate son. McMurray does not seem to have been troubled by a conscience. Although he was a churchgoer, religion played little part in his life. Observing that 'the spirit of dissipation and diversion prevails … in the present age',[19] he seemed happy to participate in the general degeneracy of the times.

Despite the financial security of his naval commission, McMurray was still on the lookout for business opportunities. There was, after all, his wife's £700 to be invested. Early in October 1768 he learnt that a bookselling business run by William Sandby at 32 Fleet Street in the City of London was for sale. The shop bore the sign of a ship, a symbol that McMurray would take over on his stationery, and appropriately so, considering the number of books he would come to distribute by water. The house was a four-storey building, erected after the Great Fire of 1666, leased by the Worshipful Company of Cordwainers.[20] McMurray had no experience of bookselling. In his letter-book he records what happened next:

> Oct. 9th. Wrote to Mr A. Paxton that I could not be in London before Tuesday; that I was yet fond of going into Mr Sandby's business, and if he continued to approve would certainly carry that project into execution; that Mrs McMurray would cheerfully contribute every thing to assist me &c.

Wrote to Mr Wm. Kerr[21] that I had some thoughts of going into the bookselling business which was approved of by my friends, particulars of the scheme I sent him. That it would require £1000 to buy the stock &c and as I could not raise all that money myself asked if he would assist me with £400 &c.

Wrote to Mr Sandby that I would be in town on Tuesday – that I proposed to examine the catalogue on Wednesday morning and give an answer to the proposals that day or next &c.[22]

A week later, McMurray wrote to another friend, William Falconer, the author of the popular poem *The Shipwreck* (1762), inviting him to invest in the business: 'Many blockheads in the trade are making fortunes, and did we not succeed as well as these, I think it must be imputed only to ourselves.'[23] In other words, any old fool could be a bookseller. McMurray had a lot of learning to do.

2

Beer to Bengal

B LOCKHEADS OR NO, there was a huge amount of competition in the bookselling trade in London, and it was increasing. By the end of the 1760s there were around eighty booksellers in the capital; by the end of the century this number approached three hundred, including another John Murray who had a shop from 1783 in Princes' Street, Leicester Fields.[1] One of McMurray's first actions, once he had arranged a mortgage to buy Sandby's shop and business, was to change his surname to Murray, jettisoning what a friend called 'the Wild Highland Mac'.[2] This was an evident precaution against anti-Scots feeling.

Murray was entering a trade that had until recently carried considerable danger for its practitioners. The invention of printing had initiated a running battle between authority and its critics which had continued for more than two centuries. As late as 1719 one John Matthews had been hanged for publishing a pamphlet in which he asserted that James Stuart, the 'Old Pretender', was the rightful king of England. There had been no lack of tough campaigners for free speech: John Milton had called for it in *Areopagitica* (1644), and in the 1760s John Wilkes was making a pest of himself to the government by daring to criticise the royal speech to Parliament. The mechanism of censorship was still securely in place to drive Tom Paine, author of *The Rights of Man*, out of the country in 1791, and as late as 1810 William Cobbett would be thrown into jail and fined heavily for objecting in print to the army's use of flogging. In general, however, by 1768 the authorities' paranoia about books had subsided, and the trade in words was both brisk and relatively safe.

At the end of October, John and Nancy Murray packed up their house near Chatham, left Brompton, and moved into 32 Fleet Street, occupying rooms above the shop. They were surrounded by their competitors. The heart of the London book trade was in shops and offices around St Paul's Cathedral, but its activities were moving slowly but steadily westward, and many proprietors had set up business in Fleet Street. In *The Godwins and the Shelleys* (1989) William St Clair surveys the London book trade a few years after Murray's arrival:

> Business was booming. Besides the seven or eight hundred new books produced each year – four times the number of twenty years earlier – there were several monthly periodicals and an immense output of pamphlets, broad-sheets, textbooks and ephemera. Although many books were still financed by patronage or subscription the economics of the trade were altering rapidly. Entrepreneurs found that they could sell direct to a growing and increasingly literate public both at home and abroad. Already more books were published in London in a single year than in the whole century in Spain.[3]

St Clair adds that many of the newcomers to the business were Scots with experience of other trades, who challenged traditional cartels and restrictive practices, and found new markets for books: 'As yet there was no clear distinction between publisher and book-seller – the bookseller made the financial arrangements with the author, commissioned the printing, and sold the books both direct to the public and to the country booksellers.'[4] The bookseller was thus doubly influential, and his shop became a centre of literary life, the precursor of gentlemen's clubs of the nineteenth century. Benjamin Disraeli, whose family was to become much involved with the Murrays, recalled the situation: 'In those days, when literary clubs did not exist, and when even political ones were extremely limited and exclusive in their character, the booksellers' shops were social rendezvous. Debrett's [in Piccadilly] was the chief haunt of the Whigs; Hatchard's, I believe, of the Tories.'[5]

While booksellers began to organise themselves, professional writers remained rare birds. To write for money was socially *infra dig.*

This played into the hands of the booksellers, who tried to pay as little as possible for copyright. Royalties as we know them today were virtually unheard of, and the best an author could expect was a half-share in the profits of a book. The bookseller of course could deny that there had been any profit. Many title pages were without an author's name, a situation that made it difficult for a writer to claim his or her due, and without the stimulus of recognition and return literature tended to stagnate. The literary world was waiting for an entrepreneur who was prepared to take financial risks with new books: John Murray was not a likely candidate.

Murray began by confidently advertising his arrival: 'John Murray sells all new Books and Publications. Fits up Public or Private Libraries in the neatest manner with Books of the choicest Editions, the best Print, and the richest Bindings. Also, Executes East India or foreign Commissions by an assortment of Books and Stationery suited to the market or purpose for which it is destined: all at the most reasonable rates.'[6] The reality, when he opened the shop for the first time on Saturday 20 October 1768, was somewhat less glamorous. Murray's first two customers, Lord Wentworth and the Dean of Durham, bought books on account. The Dean took six months to pay, and Wentworth never paid at all. A third customer paid cash, but only a few pence for stationery. As a tradesman, Murray had to show an obsequious respect to the aristocracy. After Murray had been running the shop for a year and a half, Lord Wentworth cancelled his subscription to the *Critical Review*, a journal published by a friend, as he had engaged another bookseller. Etiquette dictated that Murray had to make an ingratiating reply despite this loss of business: 'I submit to your Lordship's inclination and I am with the utmost respect your Lordship's most obedient servant.'[7] Bills were not always settled in the orthodox fashion. The ledger entry for a Mr Garden, who bought a history of England, a dictionary and a copy of *Peregrine Pickle*, records that he paid part of his account with a cheese, deemed to be worth one guinea, nearly twice as much as the novel. Conversely, Murray obtained his candles and coal by paying with books.

Dealings with other booksellers usually involved notes of credit and other paperwork rather than an exchange of cash. Thomas Constable writes of his Edinburgh publisher father Archibald:

> Money, in its metallic form, appears to have been entirely in disuse by 'the trade' in their dealings with one another. It floated ethereally in bills and promissory-notes from man to man, calling at the banks for transmutation . . . That the whole system was a vicious and ruinous one is shown by the number of men I find suddenly writing to my father from the Abbey – a sanctuary for debtors in the neighbourhood of Holyrood Palace.[8]

Nevertheless, Murray's cashflow gradually improved. On 11 November a customer bought Johnson's *Dictionary*, at a hefty £4 10s, the equivalent of more than £350 today. By now the first fruits of John Murray's embryonic career as a publisher were beginning to form, as other booksellers purchased a regular stream of copies of the fifth edition of Lord Lyttelton's *Dialogues of the Dead*, albeit at wholesale rates. This was Murray's first publication, its rights taken over from Sandby. The title page declares: 'Printed for J. Murray Successor to Mr Sandby'.

The *Dialogues* are imaginary conversations, in the manner of the classical writer Lucian, between the shades of Addison and Swift, Ulysses and Circe, and an English duellist and a North American Mohawk Indian, Bloody Bear, who finds the Englishman's admission that he has killed a friend in a duel deeply shocking. This was a popular form with writers: Isaak Walton had adopted it in *The Compleat Angler* (1653), and Humphry Davy would do so in *Consolations in Travel* which Murray came to publish in 1830. The retail price in the shop of the *Dialogues* was 5s 6d, but Murray offered it to the trade for 2s 11d, provided each purchaser bought a minimum of six copies. The prices were the equivalent of about £22 and £12 today.

Murray had himself to understand the craft of printing, and to decide how many copies he should have bound. Binding could cost as much if not more than the book itself. His edition of the *Dialogues* was a fine start to his career as a publisher, set handsomely as it was in a large clear typeface, with good spacing between lines. To sell books abroad, especially to the British in India, Murray began to coax his naval contacts. Parcels took nearly six months to reach India, and as a result he was obliged to offer extended credit. He gradually built up a lucrative trade with India, as he did with Edinburgh and Newcastle, two other markets served by water. As the sailing boats crawled up the coast they were vulnerable to piracy, attacks by enemy vessels in times of war, and always to shipwreck. Meanwhile some of Murray's grander London customers continued to take advantage of him. The Bishop of Carlisle, who regularly came into the shop, helped himself to books and left without paying: 'His Lordship called on me today . . . He has taken from me Robertsons Hist[ory] of Charles 5th and Sherlock's discourses in 5 vols.'[9] Murray began to wonder if he would ever 'reap some advantage from this method of His Lordship taking books from me . . . I never solicited it.'[10]

He was also upset that Sandby had not kept his promise to add Murray's name to the title page of Lord Lyttelton's *History of Henry II* when this was next reprinted, which would have ensured that Murray got a share of the income. The *History*, in three quarto volumes, sold for three guineas, the equivalent of about £250, thus allowing the bookseller a substantial profit. Despite the fact that Lyttelton was still alive, he had sold his copyright to Sandby, in line with the common practice in which copyrights of successful books changed hands lucratively within the book trade. One nice little earner was the copyright of *Paradise Lost*, owned by Jacob Tonson, whose successors claimed he had bought it from Milton. Tonson was also regarded as the proprietor of Shakespeare, though it seems unlikely that the playwright himself had ever shaken hands on the deal. Sandby and Murray eventually settled their dispute, though not before Murray had brought his lawyer into it. Murray had 'a litigious and disputatious nature',[11] and would head for a law-court at the slightest whiff of controversy.

One of the causes for which Murray battled in the late 1770s has a thoroughly modern relevance. The Rev. William Mason began a lawsuit against Murray in 1778 for including in his popular edition of Thomas Gray's poems three short verses, the copyright of which Mason claimed Gray had bequeathed to him. Murray published a pamphlet in which he defended himself vigorously on the grounds that Gray had not cared about copyright, and had 'made a present of his poems to the public'.[12] If Mason were to win, Murray argued, 'he shuts the door against extracts of all kinds ... If fifty lines are property, one line is property'. Nevertheless, Mason won the case, obtaining an injunction to stop the sale of Murray's edition. Much of the literary world, led by Samuel Johnson, seems to have been on Murray's side. 'Johnson signified his displeasure at Mr Mason's conduct very strongly,' wrote Boswell, describing the amount quoted as 'only fifty lines'.[13] It is tempting to regard Murray's attitude as a campaign for freedom of speech, but Mason was not being entirely partisan when he described Murray as exemplifying his profession's determination to get something for nothing. Mason wistfully observed that it would be nice to have an act of Parliament 'in favour of authors, and prevent the piracy of booksellers'.[14]

Far-flung customers of the Murray shop included the Rev. Jacob Duché, minister of a church in Philadelphia. Duché was a would-be author, and sent Murray some essays and sermons, receiving in return what was the firm's first rejection letter. Murray's report on the book read: 'I confess that the Spirit of Dissipation & Diversion prevails too much in the present age for any one to expect that a work of such a serious Nature as yours will be generally read.'[15] He softened the blow a little by suggesting that the style be pepped up in the manner of Addison's *Spectator* or Johnson's *Rambler*. He ended encouragingly: if Duché would finish the book, Murray would read it again and give 'my candid opinion'. Duché did as he was advised, but took the book to another publisher. He found success latterly, publishing letters and sermons, including one which perhaps showed that he would not be put off by rejection letters, *The Duty of Standing Fast in our Spiritual and Temporal Liberties* (1775).

Murray paid close attention to the quality of his authors' writing, and sometimes upset them by his editing. He criticised one writer's 'want of urbanity', which caused offence,[16] to which he responded that it was better to be honest. He passed on tips to authors: 'If you are able to entertain the Ladies your business is done.'[17] Here is Murray's advice on how to write a saleable history book: 'It should be addressed to the Mob of Readers, the literary Amateurs, & to smatterers in taste. Hume, Gibbon, Robertson & now Ferguson have derived most part of their success & reputation from this very circumstance by adapting their History to slender as well as to profound capacities.'[18] Further, he was tactful when telling authors that their manuscripts had been edited out of recognition. To Archdeacon John Gast, author of *The History of Greece from the Accession of Alexander* (1782), he wrote:

> You will occasionally observe some small Variations from your Modes of expression. This was suggested to me by a few learned Friends who approved of the intrinsic Merit of the performance, but recommended, *as indispensably necessary*, a little more polish to be made in the Style in order to accommodate the Work to the Taste of the Times.[19]

Murray was always on the lookout for customers who might become authors. When his wife's young sister Hester's writing master purchased slates, pencils, paper and spelling books from the bookshop, Murray told him: 'Should you chuse to form a Spelling book of your own I shall willingly print it for you.'[20] To Lieutenant Stephen Payne Adye, serving in America with the Royal Artillery, he wrote: 'As American affairs are supposed with us to be critically situated, so I would be obliged to you for an account of some parts of them as they occur.'[21] Murray's invitations to tyro authors were two-edged swords, as the author might find he ended up paying the costs of printing and publication.

Lieutenant Adye, whom Murray had known in Edinburgh, had already written and published a book on courts martial in America. Murray had two hundred copies of this book *A Treatise on Courts Martial: Also an Essay on Military Punishments and Rewards* shipped to England and sold under his own imprint. Adye bore the expenses, including the cost of a handbill advertising the book, which is as dull as the subject would suggest. The appendix on military punishments, however, is somewhat livelier: 'The Lacedaemonians punished a coward, by clothing him in womans apparel, and making him stand every third day in the market or other public place, which was looked on by men of spirit as worse than death.'

Then, as now, authors complained of inadequate advertising. 'There is no possibility of getting an advertisement inserted in the *St James's Chronicle* at a short notice,' Murray advised one of them. 'I have had an advertisement of my own for that paper lying in the printers hands for these 6 weeks past and not yet appeared.'[22] He believed in the power of advertising: when he published a book on the peerage of Britain, he sent a handbill to every member of the House of Lords. He regularly spent up to a third of the cost of publication on advertising, and cut out and pasted his advertisements into an album. Murray also occasionally resorted to reviewing his own books in the *Critical Review*, edited and printed by his friend Archibald Hamilton. But no amount of advertising could shift a book that was published at the wrong time of year: 'it is very seldom that Large Volumes are published at this dead season,' he wrote in June 1772. 'Two Guineas Advertising will hardly move such a book, unless it can blaze of itself like a comet.'[23]

Although he was fast acquiring experience and skill in publishing and bookselling, he remained interested in other forms of trade. He corresponded with a Glasgow brewer, John Cunningham, about selling beer in London and perhaps also in India: he referred to the exercise as 'Beer to Bengal'. Eventually a consignment of over seven hundred bottles was despatched by sea, but while it was en route Murray sampled some bottles that had been held back in London, and found that the beer had deteriorated: 'three Bottles, one after another, all bad', he complained to Cunningham. 'I should imagine that the Disease proceeds from the Corks which were every one of them Mouldy.'[24] The venture came to an acrimonious end, and Cunningham tried to get Murray to pay for the beer he had drunk himself. Other commodities in which Murray traded included partridges and woodcock, 'fever powders', paste jewellery, lottery tickets and Irish linen: general trading of this kind was common among eighteenth-century London booksellers.[25] The paste jewels, reproductions of antique gems, were the work of James Tassie, a Scottish sculptor living in London who also made relief portraits in profile. Many of these are now in the Scottish National Portrait Gallery.

Meanwhile Murray was always looking, as is any modern publisher, for a bestseller such as *Robinson Crusoe* or *Tom Jones*. He failed, and instead got a book on courts martial, which stubbornly refused to sell. He tried again with John Millar, Professor of Law at Glasgow University, who had written *Observations Concerning the Distinction of Ranks in Society* (1771). This describes the rise of what would now be called the middle class, the bulk of Murray's customers: 'people of low rank are gradually advancing towards a state of independence', while 'at the same time ... old families will often be reduced to poverty and beggary'. This 'fluctuation of property' is 'observable in all commercial countries'.[26] Middle class and aristocracy mingled in Murray's shop. Like many booksellers, he gave regular dinners, partly as sales technique, but largely because of his convivial nature. Not everyone was impressed by the guest-list; the Scottish historian Thomas Somerville gives a scathing picture of Murray literary soirées during his first visit to London in 1769:

> I met with ... several authors of inferior note, at the house of Mr Murray, bookseller, Fleet Street, to whose attention and civility I was indebted ...The extravagant self-sufficiency of his guests, their barefaced reciprocal flattery, and the contempt which they expressed for the most esteemed living authors, often provoked my indignation.[27]

But when were literary gatherings not like that?

3

Lewd women and anatomical views

IT WAS NOT long before Nancy Murray's father's suspicions began
to prove justified. One of John Murray's uncles had died in 1769,
leaving an estate at Mount Ross, near Belfast. Murray undertook
to sell it on behalf of the eight heirs, of whom he was one. This
necessitated three trips to Ireland, between 1771 and 1775, to
untangle the legal position. During the first trip he met Jane Ann
Burgess, with whom he had an affair, and to Archy Paxton's amaze-
ment Murray proposed that she should join the Fleet Street house-
hold. 'How absurd!' Paxton wrote, 'to think that Mrs Murray could
possibly be happy with having a person in the house, who had
formerly and still seems to make an impression on your heart.'[1]
Paxton adds that he had told Nancy 'that you could not possibly be
sober when you wrote it'.

A root of the trouble seems to have been that Nancy could not,
or would not, have children. Murray refers to this sourly in a letter
of 1775: 'I pray for your success in begetting all Legitimate Children.
I would not be churlish though unsuccessful my self.'[2]

Murray had however already produced an illegitimate son, Archy,
named after Archy Paxton, born early in 1770. Archy lived for his
first nine years with a married couple in London, who sent Murray
regular bills of twelve guineas per year for the upkeep of 'the Boy
Archibald Murray'.[3] Rather surprisingly, Samuel Smiles mentions
Archy several times, referring to him politely as the second John
Murray's 'half-brother Archibald Murray'.[4] A handwritten note in
the Murray family copy of Smiles's memoir, written probably by
John Murray III, states: 'Archibald – an elder son – was illegitimate;
but in continual intercourse with the family, & in after life a trusted

adviser to his brother.'[5] Murray concealed the identity of the mother, though William Zachs suggests that she was a 'kept mistress', or may have been his sister-in-law Hester Weemss, who would in due course become his second wife.[6] Certainly Hester wrote flirtatiously to Murray, while her father made sharp remarks when she wanted to come to London and stay with John and Nancy. 'Sir,' he wrote to Murray in July 1770, shortly after the birth of Archy,

> I am informed that you are very desirous of Hett to accompany you to London: the properest method would have been for you first to ask my consent, I am still her father notwithstanding you[r] endeavour to perswade her to believe otherwise. She shall always find a parent while I live notwithstanding I stand accused [of] having no money left of my own but what belongs to your wife & her I have not spent all thank god on lewd women.[7]

While this may allude to the illegitimacy, Weemss could scarcely have written it if Hester, who was still at boarding school, had just given birth to Murray's child. Nor do Weemss's letters to Nancy, or Hester's to Murray, contain any references to Archy. Murray would visit the boy several times a year, and Archy came to 32 Fleet Street for Christmas and family celebrations. Meanwhile Nancy, who was clearly miserable, fell ill.

In February 1774 the House of Lords, considering the case of an Edinburgh bookseller named Donaldson who had allegedly pirated a book, ruled that copyright was not perpetual and could not be sustained after the twenty-eight years stipulated by the 1710 Act. The Lords wanted to make books cheaper, by limiting the occasions on which copyright had to be paid. The aim was to promote free trade, and Murray himself gave evidence to the Lords that established booksellers had operated a cartel which excluded newcomers like himself from buying stock and copyrights. One consequence of the Lords' decision was that it was no longer always necessary for booksellers to form syndicates to share the cost of copyright. Murray observed that 'the public is not fond of seeing many names to a new publication'; also, it was better for a book if there was just one backer: 'Tho but the simple publisher, he is elated or depressed in the fate of his work, little short of the author himself.'[8] Nevertheless, of the approximately one thousand books that bear the name of the first John Murray on the title page, nearly 40 per cent are co-publications, many of them with Joseph Johnson and Thomas Cadell, two of the best-known London booksellers of the day. There were different types of co-publication: 'Murray might be an equal shareholder, or he might act merely as a selling agent either for another bookseller or for the author.'[9]

Shares in books were auctioned to booksellers at the Queen's Arms in St Paul's churchyard: 'Dinner will be on the Table at Two O'Clock Precisely.'[10] Catalogues were issued in advance. For two guineas a bookseller could secure a quarter-share in the copyright of *The Art of Tormenting*,[11] or for twenty pounds a sixty-fourth share in Chambers's ever lucrative *Dictionary*.[12] Some co-publications Murray planned and financed himself, then offered shares to other booksellers. An example is Thomas Beddoes's *History of Isaac Jenkins* (1793), an instructional chapbook about the dangers of alcohol for the poor, a typically banal moral tale of fatuous simplicity: as Roy Porter puts it, 'the staple admonitory pap of the times'.[13] At the other extreme of cost and complexity in co-publication is the enormous and lavishly illustrated treatise *The Anatomy of the Human Gravid Uterus Exhibited in Figures* (1774) by William Hunter, the pioneer physician and Professor of Anatomy at the Royal Academy. With its almost life-size engravings of the female torso sliced open to reveal the womb and the child within it, this was a milestone in medical publishing. The genitalia are also depicted in great detail, but Hunter writes: 'The thighs and pudenda require no explanation.' The book originated in Birmingham in 1774; Murray bought copies from Hunter himself at £5 7s each, and sold them for £5 18s.

Surprisingly, in the light of his private life, Murray could be prudish in sexual matters. He was offered by Charles Elliot the chance of co-publishing a book on a cure for venereal disease, *The Syphilitic Antidote*, but turned it down because 'the nature of it might affect with modest people the character of my shop'.[14] He added: 'At London, however, you cannot fail of finding a Vendor not so nice.' Later, he realised that this genre had its market, and in 1787 published an account by Thomas Brand, *The Case of a Boy, who had been Mistaken for a Girl*, which included 'three anatomical views of the parts before and after the cure'.

Many co-publications in which Murray had a stake did not involve him in more than paying his share and selling the book in the shop. The pamphlet *Lunardi's Grand Aerostatic Voyage through the Air* (1784) describes a balloon flight which had just been made by an 'enterprising Foreigner' from London to Ware in Hertfordshire. His passengers were a dog, a cat and, initially, a Mr Biggins, who had to get out of the basket because he was too heavy. The Prince of Wales was among the spectators at the launch, and shook hands with Lunardi as he set off. The balloonist, described as 'the flying conjuror', attempted to steer by means of an oar, and afterwards claimed he had ascended to a height of three miles. Baron Munchausen could not have done better.

As happens in publishing today, some proposals for books arrived at 32 Fleet Street as completed manuscripts, others as synopses, perhaps with sample chapters. Naturally Murray was more comfortable when taking on a book by an established author than one by an unknown or novice writer. Various people acted for him as readers, one in particular being Gilbert Stuart, another Edinburgh expatriate who practically lived at 32 Fleet Street, and advised Murray constantly on what to sign up and what to reject.

Described by the *Critical Dictionary of English Literature* as 'a sot, grumbler, scold and literary Ishmaelite',[15] Stuart had been educated at the University of Edinburgh, and was intended by his father, a university professor, to become a lawyer. Although Stuart drank and whored away his student days, he read widely in jurisprudence and constitutional history, and published his first book, *An Historical Dissertation Concerning the Antiquity of the English Constitution* (1768), when he was twenty-five. This won him an Edinburgh doctorate of law, with which he set off for London, where he became friends with Murray. Stuart was a prodigy; he could, and often did, write very well, and very fast, when drunk; and he would boast of having turned out two reviews of the same book, one a panegyric, the other virtually libellous in its abuse, both of them beautifully shaped. He was without principle as a reviewer: if the author was a friend, or Murray had published the book, Stuart gave it what we would now call a rave.

Stuart was a stereotypical hack, and yet he complained about the state of books and publishing: 'Literature, in the present age, seems to be reduced to a manufacture ... books multiply, without serving the purposes of information or taste.'[16] He himself, however, wrote books, published by Murray, that were of doubtful purpose, such as *A View of Society in Europe, in its Progress from Rudeness to Refinement* (1778). Encouraged by Murray he planned to write a life of Smollett, but like so many biographers he was censored by his subject's family, and nurtured plans of revenge: 'they will deserve all I can say'.[17] Meanwhile Murray hired him to translate books from the French. Stuart reviewed one of them, anonymously of course, and praised his own handiwork.

Murray could not afford the inflated prices that his rivals paid to the most popular authors, and would not bid for books in the market place. He usually asked an author to name his own price, and if he thought the sum named was not too great he would settle on the spot, or would talk it down if he reckoned it was excessive. Sometimes he would pay the entire sum upon the receipt of the manuscript, but more often he and the author agreed that nothing would be paid until three months after publication. As with all publishers, Murray was sometimes dismayed by the unprincipled behaviour of authors, complaining that they were not in haste to 'practice their own Rules'.[18]

Murray's print-runs were small by modern standards. 'I have constantly seen repentance follow from printing a larger number, but *never* from printing a small one,' he wrote in 1779 to a prospective author, the Rev. Mr Lothian.[19] He advised Lothian to finish his book, offer the MS to the trade and if it was declined to print 250 copies privately: 'Everything would depend upon printing no more than the *250 copies* ... I know you would be enticed to print a larger number.' Five hundred copies was a typical run for a book that

Murray guessed would sell well, and 250 for a work on medicine or politics. Printers charged less per copy for short runs, because on long runs the type wore out and had to be replaced.

If he liked a book, or an idea for a book, but thought it would not make any money, Murray would propose what we would now call vanity publishing, in which the author pays the costs. This was usually feasible because most of his authors were not full-time writers depending on a literary income, but clergy, academics, physicians or military men. Another method that Murray adopted was to publish by subscription, raising cash in advance to ensure the commitment of a certain number of readers. Johann Kasper Lavater's *Essays on Physiognomy* (1789) was issued by Murray to subscribers part by part. In spring 1775 Murray felt his achievement after six or seven years as a bookseller and publisher had been disappointing: where were the bestsellers? He wrote to the Rev. Whitaker: 'Commend me . . . to a saleable Book such as the *Pilgrims progress* or *Robinson Cruso* that will please the Million. What signifies a learned and ingenious Book to me which there are not learned and ingenious men enough to buy?'[20]

Murray spent much of 1775 in Dublin, in the final stages of sorting out his uncle's bequest. Eventually, he came away £2,000 the richer, and this transformed his business. In 1772 he published only a dozen books, but by 1778 this figure had risen to over forty. Nancy, who was left in charge of the shop together with an assistant, William Weed, hated his being away, and with good reason. The diary Murray kept during the trip reveals what he got up to. On 23 April 1775 he set off in the Manchester coach. The journey, with several nights in inns, took him through the Peak District, and then on by boat from Liverpool to Dublin. He bought a picnic hamper for the voyage: cold roast beef, a loaf and 'a couple bottles port wine'.[21] It should have been a brisk crossing, but the wind was contrary, and the boat made little progress. Murray passed the time lying in bed, writing poetry about his wife:

> A zone of flowers I fondly placed
> Around my Nancy's beauteous waste! [sic]
> But by her cruel hands unbound
> Sudden she threw it on the ground.

In his imagination he offers her other adornments, but she rejects them all, declaring that the only gift she wants is 'my Husband's heart'.[22] He is feeling guilty already. When they came in sight of the Irish coast, Murray noted the uniformity of the whitewash on every building – 'from the sea they appear somewhat like snowballs scattered upon the shore'.[23] In Dublin, he put up at the Old Cross, 'a bad Inn ... chosen ... on acco[un]t of its cheapness', and discovered that his attorney had just died, leaving him in a 'lonely situation'. But Irish hospitality was soon lavished on him – he complains that the drink is virtually forced down his throat – and he was invited by the doyen of the Dublin booksellers, George Faulkner, to Sunday dinner. During the nine courses and four wines, his host name-dropped shamelessly, recalling his acquaintance with the great Dean Swift and with Alexander Pope, making out that Pope was 'of great importance with them'.[24]

Murray rented two rooms in Dublin for 10s 6d per week, and continued to enjoy himself: 'Past the Evening ... at a public house.'[25] On another evening he went to a 'brilliant' performance of *The Beaux' Stratagem* given by army and navy officers.[26] The next night there was some 'hard drinking' at dinner with Mr and Mrs Vickers,[27] followed by a puppet show – again 'brilliant'. The evening ended in a pub with 'a potched egg & brandy & water'. Murray was rarely without company, even at breakfast. 'Dined w[ith] Mr David Ross ... And we made a day of it. For we drank six bottles claret & one of Frontiniac. Were very happy.'[28] This gave Murray a massive hangover, but nevertheless he was at it again two nights later: 'At 4 dined at Ranelagh ... Had a fine dinner, consisting of boiled chickens boiled neck of mutton roast ducks quarter of lamb, ham sallad pease & asparagus ... Drank about six bottles claret – had tea & walked home at about 9 at night ... and before I went home had a frolic of my own which if not attended with ugly consequences I shall be happy.'[29] Despite this fear of venereal disease, Murray frolicked again with the women of Dublin a month later:

> Drank six bottles of wine, which it seems intoxicated me uncom-
> monly. At twelve o'clock I went away in a chair, but broke from it in
> Essex street & ran after some girls in Crampton Court ... I rambled

in the streets for 2 hours, at which time I discovered that my watch was gone. This event brought me a little to my senses. But I had no remembrance where I lost it. I went into no house. So that in all probability it was picked from my pocket on my first sally into Crampton Court.[30]

Murray advertised in the newspaper for the return of his watch, which was brought to him by a soldier who had visited a prostitute that same evening – evidently Murray had been with her too.

Despite his outrageous behaviour in Dublin, Murray wrote to Nancy accusing her of having an affair while he was away. Her reply is painful: 'D[ea]r John, I have this moment a letter which I can only know to be yours by the handwriting and that I wish from my soul I could proswade my self that some Demon had imitated, to put a final end to my miserable existence.' He had complained that Nancy had not answered his letter, but she thought he would already be on his way home: 'Good god your ungenerous Letter kills me, & strikes deep to the heart that never yet deceived you or was since your absence otherwise employed than in my attention to your shop & house … Days Hours Weeks have I pass'd alone & all the return I have meet with from you is … such a Letter … I did not think you capable of penning.' She signs herself 'the Most Unhappy woman that breaths'.[31]

Back home in London, Murray continued his whoring habit, perhaps in the company of Joseph ('Joey') Johnson, the bookseller with whom he made his greatest number of co-publication deals. In a letter of September 1775 Murray disclaims knowledge of the 'I-ch' that Johnson is alleged to have caught, and of the 'bountifull Lady' who bestowed it upon him.[32]

One of Johnson's and Murray's most lucrative partnerships was their co-publication of the English translation of Johann Kaspar Lavater's *Essays on Physiognomy*. Lavater was a Swiss physician who formulated the 'science' of physiognomy, which purported to divine character from facial expression and the shape of the head, a forerunner of phrenology. The illustrators of *Essays on Physiognomy*, who included James Gillray and William Blake, produced hundreds of engravings to make this a very expensive book which had to be financed by subscription, and issued in forty-one parts over ten years. Murray and Johnson, however, eventually made about £1,000 profit each, the largest sum that Murray ever accumulated from a single book.[33]

As Murray's rate of publication rose, he acquired a warehouse in 1774, and regularly issued catalogues. His stock also included many antiquarian and second-hand titles. Meanwhile Nancy's health was deteriorating, and it became clear that she had consumption (tuberculosis). Misery was undoubtedly also a cause of her decline. The end came on 22 September 1776: 'At a quarter before nine o'clock at night my virtuous and innocent wife expired.'[34] Murray declared himself stricken by her loss. A year and a half later he married her sister.

4

A sad accident

━━◆━━

Aᴌᴛʜᴏᴜɢʜ ᴍᴀʀʀɪᴀɢᴇ ᴡɪᴛʜ a deceased wife's sister was no
longer illegal by the 1770s, it remained frowned upon. Samuel
Smiles, writing as late as the 1890s, was clearly uncomfortable about
it, since he does not say whom John Murray took as his second wife,
merely that he 'married again'.[1] Murray's second marriage seems to
have been far less stormy than his first, and Hester brought him the
children he badly wanted. The first, a boy, was born on 27 November
1778, exactly nine months after the wedding. This suggests that the
relationship between John and Hester had been proper, or perhaps
fortunate, before they were married. Once again, Murray named the
child after an old friend, this time a naval chum, John Samuel. Both
his names were given to the boy. It is not clear whether the 'John'
mattered particularly to Murray. There is certainly no evidence that
he had a succession of Johns in mind, running the business down
the decades.

Six more children followed, of whom two girls survived: Jenny
and Mary Anne. Both married clergymen. Care for his children
undoubtedly changed John Murray, but he continued to have a
guilty conscience. When a client and former schoolfriend, Samuel
Bagster, called at 32 Fleet Street to terminate a deal, Murray was
absent. 'Finding you out – I decline your offer, S.B.,' Bagster wrote
on a blotter on Murray's desk. A few hours later a hot and flustered
Murray turned up at Bagster's house: 'Pray Sir! What have you
found me out in doing?' he demanded. On being told he had got
the wrong impression, Murray melted away.[2] Nevertheless he seems
to have been frank about his propensity for 'frolics', since he joked
in a letter to Mrs Thomas Faulkener in Dublin that, when Hester

went to the country for a week, if anything 'wrong' happened it would be her fault for deserting him.[3] There were no more trips to Dublin, and fewer six-bottle nights: Murray began belatedly to look after his health. But some damage was already done, and in May 1782, at the age of forty-five, he suffered a stroke. 'A deplorable alteration has taken place respecting my health,' he told James Gilliland, his brother-in-law:

On Friday last whilst I was standing in my own Shop at midday I was seized with a swimming in my head & sleepiness in my left limbs. After sometime I retired to my bed where after a passing of 24 hours, my fate was announced in its horrors and I was left in a Palsy, the power of my left side being totally, or very near to it, taken from me. I have already had my feelings upon this melancholy event: and shall no doubt not-withstanding all the philosophy I possess have more & more. To bewail my calamity however is fruitless, it is now certain in its nature, & will, no doubt, tho perhaps not abruptly prove fatal in its consequences. It is better if it can be done to bear it with fortitude, & to conduct my business with patience & attention for the benefit of my family; for it is of moment now that I lose as little time as possible.

After this dark side of the picture let me inform you that I am comforted with some hope. Dr Pitcairn & his Nephew my physicians thinks more favourable of me than I do of myself, and a variety of living instances have been adduced of patients much older than my self prevailing over the same disorder. These things in my favour I hear with a stragling hope, but without foolishly flattering myself that I shall ever be a man again.[4]

Murray made a good recovery, taking exercise to restore the full use of his legs, but the discipline to restrain himself from the kind of excess that had caused the stroke was beyond his reach. His energy and determination were such that while recuperating from the stroke he set up the *English Review*, which began publication the following January. 'Nothing is easier in theory,' he wrote a year after the stroke, but went on to admit that looking after his health was 'too little attended to'.[5]

Murray's illegitimate son Archy was now at boarding school, pre-paring for a naval career that turned out to be an unorthodox success.

Encouraged by his father, Archy set up the first-ever printing press at sea, and made his reputation as a correspondent for naval newspapers. He spent a large portion of his naval officer's salary on books, having a four-thousand-volume library by 1811. A contemporary considered his 'disposition naturally grave, and his manners ... particularly gentle and attractive'.[6] Affectionate and loyal as he was to Archy, Murray inevitably lavished special care on his legitimate son. Young John was sent to a series of boarding schools which, one by one, failed to come up to the standard required by his father. With hindsight, one assumes that the boy was intended for the book business; but Murray was frequently impatient with his trade, and may well have also considered the navy as a career for his legitimate offspring. In a 1776 diary entry, he expresses the desire to throw his shop out of the window.

Young John's schools were not always chosen for the best reasons. Initially, he was sent to study with a clergyman, the Rev. Dr John Trusler of Cobham, Surrey. A Murray author and a progressive schoolmaster, Trusler was inclined to educate his pupils in subjects such as French and German rather than Greek and Latin, thus preparing them for a life of business rather than schoolmastering. From Trusler, young John went briefly to the Rev. Dr William Rutherford's Academy in Uxbridge, before travelling to Edinburgh to try to get in to the High School. This plan failed when the boy was rejected on account of a slowness to learn. Murray sent his son back to Rutherford, in whose care he took a severe blow to the head, which put him in bed for several days. He was then despatched for sea air to Margate in Kent, where the headmaster, a third clergyman, the Rev. Christopher Wells, had opened a seminary for young gentlemen whose health required sea air and bathing. Here, young John made excellent academic progress, despite poor spelling.[7] Aged thirteen he moved on again, to the Naval College at Gosport kept by Dr William Burney. Here, he met with another accident, a far more serious one.

John Murray had by now had several successes as a publisher. His series *Shakespeare's Remarkable Characters*, a group of essays on individual characters in which the author, William Richardson, described them as if they were real people, ran from 1774 to 1793. Richardson was typical of Murray's authors in that he wrote for fun rather than profit. 'I find it amusing,' he told Murray, 'it is my hobby horse.' He even offered to reimburse Murray for any losses, an arrangement which suited Murray very nicely.[8] One of the attractions of the medical books in which he increasingly specialised was that their authors held lucrative positions as doctors and did not expect substantial payments from their publisher. There was also an increasing market for history books. Murray began to specialise in these also, early titles including a vindication of the Catholic Mary Queen of Scots by the Rev. John Whitaker, a Church of England clergyman. Whitaker also wrote a history of Manchester which sold badly. When Murray was in Manchester in 1775 on his way to Dublin, he was given a guided tour of the city by Whitaker which he found spectacularly boring.

Very little of Murray's list consisted of works of new fiction, and none that he published has endured. The only serious money he made from novels was by buying shares in, and reprinting, the works of such authors as Fielding, Sterne, Smollett and Defoe. In 1783 he bought a one-sixteenth share in *Robinson Crusoe*, and joined a syndicate to reprint it the next year. He did better with poetry, one success being a pastoral fantasy *Armine and Elvira*, by the Rev. Edmund Cartwright, the inventor of the power loom. Despite its jingly rhymes, *Armine and Elvira* went into seven or more editions and was praised by Walter Scott in the introduction to his *Minstrelsy of the Scottish Border* (1802). Nevertheless it made less than £100 profit. Another of Murray's notable shareholdings was a twenty-fifth share of one of the greatest literary works of his time, Samuel Johnson's *Lives of the English Poets*. This was originally published as prefaces to the series *Works of the English Poets* (1779–81). Murray and Johnson had probably met, and in a letter to Whitaker on the day of Johnson's funeral, 20 December 1784, he wrote: 'Poor Dr Johnson's remains passed my door for interment this afternoon . . . He was about to be buried in Westminster Abbey.'[9]

The elder John Murray's greatest publishing achievement was the creation not of any book, but of a journal. As early as 1769, Gilbert

Stuart had recommended him 'to connect yourself with . . . some review or periodical work',[10] and in the years that followed Murray attempted to make his mark in this field. He was involved with Stuart's own *Edinburgh Magazine and Review*, which ran for three years and provided Stuart with a vehicle for vitriolic criticism. There were other Murray magazine ventures, but it was not until 1783 that he got the formula right, with the launch of the monthly *English Review*. By this time however he had enjoyed a decade of success with *Medical and Philosophical Commentaries*, a specialist quarterly review of the latest books and developments in medicine. Under the editorial eye of an Edinburgh physician, Andrew Duncan, this contained vividly written reports on such cases as that of a ten-year-old boy whose head had been gored open by a bull, with the brain protruding through the wound: 'The substance of the brain I dressed with dry lint . . . It soon began to skin over at the edges; and . . . suppurated, and dropt off in pretty large pieces. In two months it was completely skinned over, and the boy perfectly well. He still continues so.'[11] Each number of *Medical and Philosophical Commentaries*, founded in 1773, sold around a thousand copies, giving Murray a decent profit.

Before Murray launched the *English Review* there were two other literary reviews in London: the Whig *Monthly Review* and the Tory *Critical Review*. Murray's aim was to be less obviously political, and more focused on literary trends. Gilbert Stuart was closely involved, but he could not live comfortably with other people's success in the literary world, and in the columns of the *English Review* his name came to be a byword for vituperation. While the *English Review* was running, Stuart wrote playfully to Murray: 'I have a bad name, & so will not subscribe this note . . . Yours till death XXXXX.'[12]

There was a clear statement of purpose at the beginning of the first issue, in January 1783, of Murray's magazine:

I. It is proposed, that *The English Review* shall contain an account of every book and pamphlet which shall appear in England, Scotland, Ireland, and America.

II. It is proposed to give occasional accounts of literature in France, Italy, Germany, and Spain.

III. As there is a necessary connection between eminent men and their writings, this work will frequently comprehend original memoirs [that is, biographies] of celebrated authors. And in this department an extreme care will be exerted to attain the truth.[13]

The issue begins forbiddingly, with a thirteen-page review of a grammar of the Bengali language. This reflects Murray's considerable interest in India as a source of trade, made more pertinent by his shareholding in the East India Company. Next comes a lively review of *Cecilia, or Memoirs of an Heiress, by the Author of 'Evelina'*; a discussion of a translation of Linnaeus, which had been undertaken by 'a Botanical Society at Lichfield'; and a witty judgement on the posthumously published works of a bishop: 'What has been so often said is here again repeated. Surrounded with Greek and Latin sages, we tread the wonted round; and the old beaten track brings us to the end of our journey.'[14] Equally condescending treatment is dished out to the notorious radical Tom Paine, for his *Letter Addressed to the Abbé Raynal on the Affairs of North America*: 'Mr Paine's writings are ingenious, and profound . . . But he speaks of Britain with the highest degree of prejudice and acrimony; while he magnifies the virtues of his [American] countrymen, with a passionateness of expression, that bespeaks the partisan rather than the philosopher.'[15]

One would have expected Murray to publicise his own books favourably in the *English Review*; but the first issue includes scarcely a mention of them, while the second contains a bad review of a Murray novel, *Adventures of a Rupee* by Helenus Scott: 'It is in vain, that we have endeavoured to discover any traces of merit.' The issue concludes with articles on the theatre and politics. The theatre article was written by Thomas Holcroft, a former strolling actor turned playwright and novelist, whose escapades included pirating Beaumarchais' *The Marriage of Figaro* by means of attending performances night after night until he and a friend had committed the entire text to memory.

Murray edited the *English Review* himself, taking on the burden of finding eighty pages of good copy for each issue. He stipulated that a monthly political article should be handed in by the 25th of each month, only a week before publication, so that it would be up to date. Reviewers were paid generously; sometimes Murray would accept an article in lieu of money owed to him. Beside Thomas Beddoes and Gilbert Stuart (the latter was suspected of being the brains behind the magazine), regular contributors included William Godwin, who reviewed books and took his turn at writing the political article which concluded each issue. Murray allowed Stuart to indulge in his usual vituperation. 'His manner is diffuse and feeble,' Stuart wrote (anonymously, of course) in a review of a fellow Scot, 'he is often incorrect and ungrammatical.'[16]

Many of the authors who wrote for the *English Review* were denizens of Grub Street. In his picaresque novel *Modern Times*, of which Murray published an edition in 1785, the Rev. Dr John Trusler, an energetic writer as well as the clergyman schoolmaster of young John Murray, describes his downwardly mobile hero Gabriel Outcast as working for a review much like Murray's. Gabriel is told that authors of new books often write their own reviews, thus saving the proprietor money. Outcast has to write against the clock: on one occasion a huge five-volume book is delivered to him at night, with the instruction that his review must be in 'by nine tomorrow morning'.[17] He learns of a mythical reviewer who in two hours could turn out as much on 'poetry, mathematics and physics . . . as would employ four compositors to set up for two days', despite the fact that he knew next to nothing of the subjects. This star of the journals, he learns, has now disappeared from the literary scene, having been deported to a penal colony in Jamaica for some unmentioned crime.[18]

William Godwin, then aged twenty-seven, had been employed in Suffolk as a dissenting minister, but had fallen out with his congregation because of his radical views. He now emerged into literary London, in the hope of earning his living by writing. His work for the *English Review* was his main source of income, but after a couple of years Murray could no longer tolerate his radical politics: 'I must release you in future from the trouble of the Political Article,' he wrote to Godwin in November 1786. 'Our Ideas will never meet . . . As sole proprietor of the English Review . . . I cannot admit matter foreign to my sentiments . . . No doubt you will think it impertinent in an illiterate fellow of a bookseller to attempt in any shape to control or to dictate in these matters.' He asked Godwin to send him a bill for all work done, and concluded: 'You will do me justice to believe that I wish not to offend.'[19]

Murray himself was no diehard Tory. He favoured political reform to give public opinion and a free press a role in the parliamentary process, but abhorred the violence of John Wilkes's supporters. Wilkes had been a thorn in the flesh of Parliament and the monarchy for twenty years, and was Lord Mayor of London while continuing to make a nuisance of himself with his revolutionary demands.[20] To be fair to Murray, Wilkes's mob had a particular prejudice against Scotsmen living in London, and sometimes beat them up. Murray's political outlook reflected his concerns as a businessman. The American War of Independence moved him to lament that 'a Revolution has taken place much to the prejudice of our business'.[21] When a bill to abolish slavery in the British West Indies was being debated in Parliament in 1788, Murray published contributions to both sides of the argument. And when the French Revolution broke out in 1789, he saw it as an opportunity to sell books, and was soon reissuing the works of Rousseau.

Nevertheless the Revolution and the subsequent war with France did no good to the book trade, and at the end of 1791 Murray told a client he was 'seriously *much* distressed for money'.[22] To another, he wrote: 'I continue to vegetate, wishing to retire but not able to accomplish it.'[23] And to a third, who was going abroad: 'Whether we shall ever meet again is a matter not easily determined. The stroke by which I suffered in 1782 is only suspended; it will be repeated, and I must fall in the contest.'[24] On paper, the Murray business was in profit, as William Zachs notes. 'The problem was his customers – the trade in particular – were not paying. Time and again he wrote angry letters of demand, some so severe that he thought better and redrafted more tactful ones.'[25]

Murray's handwriting in the letter-books often grows shaky, reflecting his health and state of mind. Meanwhile his right-hand man and drinking companion Gilbert Stuart had already succumbed to drink, jaundice, asthma and dropsy, dying in the summer of 1786 aged forty-two. It was during 1793, when things were already at a low ebb in Murray's life, that fourteen-year-old John, at school in Gosport, was the victim of a freak accident. Samuel Smiles tells the story:

> The writing master was holding his penknife awkwardly in his hand, point downwards, and while the boy, who was showing up an exercise, stooped to pick up the book which had fallen, the blade ran into his eye and entirely destroyed the sight. To a friend about to proceed to Gosport, Mr. Murray wrote: 'Poor John has met with a sad accident, which you will be too soon acquainted with when you reach Gosport. His mother is yet ignorant of it, and I dare not tell her.'[26]

The boy was taken to London to see an oculist, but the cornea had been too much damaged, and little could be done. John Murray II remained blind in that eye to the end of his life. Smiles is here quoting a letter begun on 19 March 1793, which is in fact to Archy. Murray does not tell him exactly what has happened, but does report: 'It has disturbed my sleeping and waking hours – yet his health is out of danger.'[27] There is also a letter to Sempil, a surgeon in Gosport: 'He has been under the care of Mr Ware ever since he returned from Gosport, who says that his eye is evidently much better, the inflammation is gone and it is much clearer. Mr Ware has also some expectation that the sight of it may in some degree be recovered. But . . . it would be vain for me to indulge improper or vain hopes.'[28]

Young John, removed from Gosport, was sent to Loughborough House School in Kennington, run by the Rev. Dr William Roberts. But the accident proved to be the last straw for his father's health. At the end of August 1793, Murray was attacked by severe pains and was ordered to bed. His shopman, Samuel Highley, explained to creditors a month later that Mr Murray was suffering from 'a severe fit of illness which has now confined him to his bed these five weeks past'.[29] Murray was able occasionally to dictate letters and give instructions to Highley. In mid-September he made his will; his wife Hester was to take charge of the business. On 6 November 1793 he died, aged fifty-six. Three days later he was buried in the north vault of St Dunstan's Church, just across the road from his bookshop.

Financially, Murray's book business was a success.[30] At his death the value of stock was nearly £9,000, and syndicate shares and other property a further £3,300. The firm's annual turnover was in excess of £6,000. Though creditable, these figures were not nearly so high as those of other London publishers such as William Strahan, who was worth nearly £100,000 at his death in 1785. But Murray, who had started in business with practically nothing but his charm, guile and enthusiasm, did better than most of his competitors.

Archy Paxton and two old friends, the Rev. Donald Grant and George Noble, were appointed trustees to look after the future of the shop, while Hester handed over the day-to-day running of the business to Highley, 'my faithful shopman' as Murray had described him in his will, when leaving him £10.[31] As for young John, still recovering from his accident, his school career had now ended, and, at the age of fifteen, he was indentured for seven years as an apprentice to Highley. The trustees did their best to collect money owed to Murray. One Dublin bookseller had owed nearly £600 for the past four years. Several authors whose books had failed to make profits hoped that their debts would now be forgotten; but this was not to be. Bills were sent out for the production costs, 'regretting want of success in the sale of them'.[32] Hester began bravely to publish under her own name, but the risks she took were few. The *English Review* carried on under the editorship and proprietorship of one of its contributors, William Thomson.

A year after Murray's death, Hester married Henry Paget, a retired army officer, and a few months later moved out of Fleet Street to settle at her new husband's home in Shropshire. Young John, who had just turned sixteen, was left in London as an apprentice, largely at the mercy of his guardian, Archy Paxton. Writing to his half-brother Archy in late April 1795, John hoped that Paxton would find him some more 'eligible situation'.[33] Had Paxton known of this, he might have removed John from the book business altogether. John's status was raised in November 1795 when he was made a partner –

though, until he came of age, Highley would continue to be answerable for the business to the trustees. Highley opened a new set of letter-books and ledgers for the partnership, and the imprint now read: 'J. Murray and S. Highley (Successors to the Late Mr Murray').[34]

The business began to grow again, specialising in medical books and reprints of past successes. But John and Highley still failed to hit it off, and in July 1800, uncertain about the future, the twenty-one-year-old John wrote plaintively to Archy: 'I wish my Father was alive.'[35] The partnership was renewed for a further eight years, but after eighteen months John and Highley had had enough of each other. Highley pulled out of 32 Fleet Street and established his own business a few doors away where he became a successful publisher of medical and scientific books. Eventually he moved back into the old Murray premises, John having taken Murray's to a new, smart address in the West End.

5

Serious plans as a publisher: John Murray II

'THE TRUTH IS', John Murray II wrote in March 1803, at the age of twenty-four, 'that during my minority I have been shackled to a drone of a partner; but the day of emancipation is at hand. On the 25th of this month I plunge alone into the depths of Literary Speculation.'[1] This letter, to the playwright George Colman, is the second entry in the younger John Murray's first letter-book of his reign over the firm. He chose a larger format than his father's letter-books, 32 by 20 centimetres, bound handsomely in green tooled leather. Murray wrote in a copperplate hand smaller and more delicate than his father's, offering to publish Colman's work: 'I am . . . honestly ambitious that my first appearance before the public should be such as will at once stamp my character for respectability.' The younger John Murray had learnt the art of flattery from his father, apologising to Colman for intruding:

at a moment when you must be engaged in Theatrical Bustle & surrounded by the compliments & congratulations of your friends. I was present during the representation of your admirable Comedy [*John Bull*] on Saturday evening & I felt in common with all around me the delight & fascination which could not fail to be produced by the union of wit, sentiment & humour. I should consider it a very high honour if I was so fortunate as to become your publisher.[2]

The 'drone' continued to annoy young Murray:'He advertises himself as "successor to the late John Murray", who died not less than ten years ago, with the intent to make the public believe that I, his son, am retired from business, or am dead. That this wicked insinuation has had this effect, I have the letters of two or three persons to prove.'[3] Murray nearly lost his shop when the partnership with Highley broke up, and, agreeing to draw lots for the house, Murray had the good fortune to win.[4] This may be family legend, but he and Highley did have to resort to arbitration to untangle their differences, and this must have been expensive. Murray reported to Edmund Cartwright: 'It has cost me so much more than I could well afford to pay, to retain the house of my father that I am not over rich at present.'[5] Meanwhile, the threat of invasion from France was depressing the trade: 'I sell no books but such as are upon medical & scientific subjects.'[6] He had intended to pay a visit to Edinburgh, 'but my *military duties*, and the serious aspect of the times, oblige me to remain at home'.[7] Murray was among thousands of young men who had volunteered for military training to protect the country from the Napoleonic threat, and was accepted despite his blind eye. As his nephew Robert Cooke remarked, 'Mr Murray could see sharper with one eye than most other people can with two.'[8]

Despite the distractions and worries, Murray started to build his own list. In 1798 Murray & Highley had been one of the three booksellers who published a breakthrough medical work, *An Inquiry into the Variolae Vaccinae*, in which a country doctor from Gloucestershire, Edward Jenner, described his method of vaccination against smallpox by using cow pox. Jenner's discovery was not immediately accepted by the sceptical medical profession, but the book became the talk of the town, with some odd ideas circulating: one doctor argued that if people were infected with cow pox they would develop bovine characteristics. Murray, whose parents had both had smallpox before he was born, wrote in 1803 to one of Jenner's colleagues assuring his correspondent that he was 'a Medical Bookseller', and proposed to publish a cheap edition of *An Inquiry*. This had originally been lavishly produced in large format, with two-colour illustrations showing the various poxes bursting out on the human arm in sepia and rosy pink. 'At present its size & price preclude it from general circulation . . . I will undertake at my own cost to print a large impression in a popular form . . . I have considered the cause which I should serve and the honour of being Dr Jenner's publisher, rather than my own immediate emolument.'[9]

While this idea seems to have come to nothing, the letter reveals how rapidly the young Murray has mastered the language of publishing, claiming to follow high principles while at the same time getting himself a bargain. But to publish medical books was to follow directly in his father's footsteps, and Murray was not inclined to do that too closely. When Henry Dewar, a military surgeon from Northumberland, offered him *Observations on Diarrhoea &c*, he briskly turned it down: 'the subject ... is more likely to raise yr own reputation in your profession than to prove advantageous to a Bookseller'.[10] The route Murray followed in breaking new ground was to dabble in exposé. His response to the threat of invasion was to publish in late 1803 an English translation of a book satirising the main characters of the French Revolution, *The Revolutionary Plutarch*, by — Stewarton. He explained to the Dublin booksellers Gilbert & Hodges that it had been 'written with a view of exhibiting to the minds of the wavering, a true portrait of the villainies of the present rulers of the French Republic'. Since the first edition, it had been 'rendered more attractive by the insertion of the names of the Buonaparte family'.[11]

The essay on Napoleon accuses him, when a schoolboy, of torturing his dog to death because it had stolen part of his supper; and, at the age of fifteen, of getting a washerwoman's daughter pregnant and then causing her death by medicine intended to produce a miscarriage: 'On the day that his poisoned mistress had been buried, he began to court her younger sister.' This was a dangerous accusation to come from the house of Murray.[12] Before publishing *The Revolutionary Plutarch* Murray had it vetted by one of the first authors with whom he built up a personal friendship, Isaac Disraeli, or D'Israeli as he preferred to spell his name, father of the future Prime Minister. D'Israeli thought the book was too long, especially the section on the Bonapartes: 'the reader will be satiated by so much of this filthy family'.[13]

Isaac D'Israeli was twelve years older than Murray. His son Benjamin claimed that the family was descended from Sephardic Jews who had been forced to emigrate from Spain to Venice in the fifteenth century, adopting their invented surname in gratitude to

God for saving them. This was the stuff of legend; more prosaically, Isaac's father had been a merchant who had come to London to sell Italian produce, but later became a stockbroker. Isaac wanted to be a poet, but his mother scorned the idea and threatened him with having to go into business. He wrote a poem condemning commerce, and sent it to Samuel Johnson, who was ill and failed to read it. Eventually, Isaac was allowed by his father to pursue a literary career. When he was twenty-five he inherited his grandmother's fortune and became independent.

In 1791 his first substantial book, *Curiosities of Literature*, was published anonymously by the elder John Murray to whom D'Israeli had given the copyright. It sold well and was reprinted and enlarged several times, eventually running to six volumes. *Curiosities of Literature* is an ironic survey of the literary world past and present, organised by topic, such as 'Biblomania' (defined as 'collecting an enormous heap of books without intelligent curiosity'),[14] 'Literary Journals' (said to be the work of 'puerile critics and venal drudges'),[15] 'Prefaces' ('I have observed that ordinary readers skip over these little elaborate compositions'),[16] and 'Men of Genius Deficient in Conversation' ('Descartes . . . was silent in mixed company; it was said that he had received his intellectual wealth from nature in solid bars, but not in current coin').[17]

Robert Southey claimed that his fellow poet Samuel Rogers had described Isaac as having 'only half an intellect', but he amused Byron.[18] D'Israeli produced other books of the same sort, including *Calamities of Authors*, published by Murray in 1812, a compendium of 'the misfortunes of literary men', a work designed to persuade the reader that 'to devote our life to Authorship is not the true means of improving our happiness or our fortune'.[19] There is more bombast here than anecdote, though D'Israeli gives an amusing account of the political writer James Drake, who 'dared every extremity of the law' in the sedition that he penned, and used 'a masked lady' to deliver his manuscripts to the printer. *Calamities of Authors* is not a book that the elder John Murray would have published. It mocks 'literary Scotchmen, who have perished immaturely in the metropolis . . . and [have] scarcely left a vestige of the wrecks of their genius',[20] and picks specially on Gilbert Stuart: 'The celebrity of . . . other Scottish writers diseased his mind . . . He confined all his literary efforts to the pitiable motive of destroying theirs.'[21] Stuart is reproved for using 'the frenzied language of disappointed wickedness',[22] and D'Israeli implies that he is one of those who drank themselves to death in 'an obscure corner of a Burton ale-house – there, in rival potations, with two or three other disappointed authors, they regaled themselves on ale they could not pay for, and recorded their own literary celebrity, which had never taken place'.[23]

When Murray became independent from Highley, his acquaintance with D'Israeli soon ripened into a close friendship. Letters and scraps of paper in the Murray Archive 'testify to the constant, almost daily communication which was kept up between them, for D'Israeli . . . very soon became the literary adviser to his friend'.[24] He was a very different sort of publisher's reader from Gilbert Stuart. 'It is a most disagreeable office to give opinions on MSS,' D'Israeli wrote to Murray. 'One reads them at a moment when one has other things in one's head – then one is obliged to fatigue the brain with *thinking*.'[25] Actually he gave clear advice: 'I have read the 2nd sheet[26] with great pleasure,' he told Murray of *The Revolutionary Plutarch* in October 1803, 'the style of the translation is much superior to what you thought. It is very clear, & requires only occasionally a word more or less. My advice (not worth much certainly) generally *sins* on the side of Prudence. If you are prudent therefore print 750 and charge 9s/- – if you are Enterprising print 1000 . . . The Writer is not of the middling Classes.'[27]

D'Israeli seems to have felt that he was the junior partner in the relationship, signing one of his letters: 'Your humble and affectionate nephew.'[28] Yet he was capable of taking the avuncular role. After Murray had been away from Fleet Street on business, D'Israeli advised him: 'be assured your *presence is absolutely necessary* in and about your shop'.[29] Smiles points out that Benjamin Disraeli's memoir of his father, in his introduction to a reprint of *Curiosities of Literature*, omits the episode of *Flim-Flams! or, the Life and Errors of my Uncle*, an attempt to emulate Sterne's *Tristram Shandy*. In an early chapter there is some mockery of Lavater's *Physiognomy*: the uncle invents a machine with which philosophers can measure their own heads, to decide whether they are geniuses. But, compared to Sterne, most of the humour fails to ignite. *Flim-Flams!* was published in 1805, and D'Israeli, who had persuaded himself that the world would die laughing at it, was badly bruised by the reviews and tried to persuade Murray not to issue a second edition. He thought he had bungled the writing: 'Whatever real merits may be in the work are entirely outnumbered by the errors of its author.'[30] Then he changed his mind: 'I begin to think the book is *not half so bad* as some choose to think.'[31] The second edition went ahead with a new introduction by the author. 'My father', writes Benjamin Disraeli, 'was very impulsive, and indeed endowed with a degree of volatility which is only witnessed in the south of France.'[32] He could, however, be serious. Murray & Highley had been part of the syndicate which published his novel *Vaurien: or, Sketches of the Times* (1797), which contains some striking remarks about Jews: 'Christianity is nothing but improved Judaism . . . It is imagined that the Jews are distinguished by a national countenance . . . The Judaic visage we sometimes ridicule is frequently the countenance of his Spanish Majesty . . . The Hebrews, who have no spot on earth their own, include all the varieties of the human species.'[33]

John Murray soon had marriage in mind. A substantial part of his father's business was with booksellers in Edinburgh, in particular with Charles Elliot of Charlotte Street, who, with the elder Murray, had co-published more than fifty titles since 1774. Smiles notes that Elliot 'was one of the first publishers in Scotland who gave large sums for copyright. He gave William Smellie a thousand pounds for his *Philosophy of Natural History*, when only the heads of the chapters were written.'[34] Elliot died in 1790, leaving, on paper, more than £30,000. He was badly let down when an employee he had sent to Philadelphia to start an American branch of the business failed to repay a loan. Worry over this probably shortened his life. The journey from London to Edinburgh was arduous for John Murray, but there were compensations to be found in the northern capital: principal among these was Anne Elliot, Charles Elliot's daughter.

On 15 October 1806, Anne wrote a letter to John Murray in reply to an advance from him. She maintains a careful balance between encouragement and caution worthy of the Jane Austen heroine whose name she was, eventually, to supply:

'Sir, The very serious purport of your letter, would require much more time for reflection, did not the flattering expressions contained in it, demand instant acknowledgement, – permit me therefore, to return you my warmest thanks for the very favorable (but undeserved) opinion you are pleased to entertain of me, and believe I shall ever retain a grateful sense of the honor which you have conferred.

You must be sensible that in an engagement of such moment a much longer acquaintance is necessary, (than we can boast of) so as to know perfectly each others temper and disposition, for the qualities required in so close a union must be very different from that of an acquaintance – suffice it to say that from what I have seen, I have every reason to think myself fortunate in the acquisition of your acquaintance.

My Mother is so indulgent as to leave every thing to my own determination, from the very favorable opinion she has formed of you, her approbation may be looked upon as granted, but my Uncle must also be consulted, and I have not yet seen him, accustomed as I have ever been to regard him as a father; (for I may say I scarcely had the happiness of knowing any other) his opinion cannot be dispensed with, and from the great attention I have always experienced from Mrs Sands and him, I owe them every respect and confidence – I am certain that whatever they consider as conducive to my happiness, will meet with their hearty concurrence. – And I remain.

With the sincerest Esteem and Respect, Anne Elliot.'[35]

By comparison with his father, Murray was a sober young man who would have had little difficulty persuading the Elliot family of his respectability. There were, however, elements in Edinburgh society who took pleasure in tempting him off the path of righteousness. On his expeditions to the Scottish capital he had become friends with another young publisher and bookseller, Archibald Constable, who was nearly five years his senior. This became a profitable business relationship, but also one beset with alcoholic hazards. The son of a Fife nobleman's land steward, Archibald Constable had been inspired to join the book trade by a childhood fascination with stationery sold in a country bookshop. He served an apprenticeship with the Edinburgh bookseller Peter Hill, a friend of Robert Burns, married a printer's daughter, and set up on his own when he was only twenty-one. At first he specialised in Scottish history and literature, and his Edinburgh shop became a popular meeting place with young writers, including Walter Scott. He was one of the publishers of Scott's *Minstrelsy of the Scottish Border*, which began to appear in 1802, and in the same year his was the name on the title page of the new and daring *Edinburgh Review*. This journal, unconnected with the one of the same name run by Gilbert Stuart some years earlier, not only made its reputation instantly with a shocking brand of trenchant criticism, but paid its contributors many times the going rate. Murray wrote tentatively to Constable in April 1803, saying he was looking for an Edinburgh co-publisher for several books, 'but . . . I presume that you have already sufficient business upon your hands & that you would not find mine worth attending to. If so, I wish that you would tell me of some *vigorous* young Bookseller, like myself just starting into Business, upon whose probity, punctuality, & exertion you think I might rely.'[36] Constable told him to look no further, and a friendly partnership began. The London publisher of the *Edinburgh Review* was Longman,[37] but Murray persuaded so many of his own customers to take out subscriptions that in 1805 the editors replaced Longman with Murray as the London distributor. Meanwhile Murray was also selling large numbers of new books by Walter Scott, for which Constable had paid unheard-of advances: a thousand guineas for *Marmion*, without even seeing a line of the manuscript. Scott himself later described this as a price 'that made men's hair stand on end'.[38]

This financial flamboyance possibly came about because Constable's partner Alexander Gibson Hunter was a wealthy man, the son of a landowner. During one of Murray's Scottish visits, Hunter carried him off to enjoy the perilous hospitality of the Forfarshire lairds, which meant bouts of heroic drinking in a whole string of great houses.[39] Smiles adds that Murray took part 'much against his will', and that he found the well-behaved society of Edinburgh New Town 'more congenial'. Hunter describes the goings-on to Constable in a letter in which he reports that 'poor Murray' has so far 'escaped' the worst of the binges, but will 'get a bellyful' when they have 'a *go* at the red Champagne'.[40] Sure enough, a few days later:

> What think you of seven of us drinking thirty-one bottles of red Champagne, besides Burgundy, three bottles of Madeira, etc etc?. . . of all this Murray contrived to take his share . . . He has since paid for it very dearly. He has himself principally to blame, having been so rash as to throw a challenge to the Scots from the Englishmen . . . He has since been . . . very unwell; but yesterday I got him physicked, and today we dine with Major Ramsay at Kelly – from which God send us a happy deliverance.[41]

Meanwhile Murray was being vetted by the Elliot family's solicitor. He said he had £5,000 in capital, but intended to make 'far more considerable' amounts.[42] He also told Hunter that he had 'serious plans as a publisher'.[43] The solicitor gave his clearance, and the wedding was arranged for early March 1807. Anne wrote to Murray: 'I have been taking all the good lessons I can, from my Mother, concerning the management of a house, but the method will be so different in London that I will require all your assistance in teaching me what is proper, and I expect you will make many allowances for me at first.'[44] Anne need not have worried. Among her fiancé's current publications was a book that told her everything she needed to know: *A New System of Domestic Cookery; formed upon Principles of Economy, and adapted to the use of Private Families. By a Lady.* The lady in question was a family friend of the Murrays, Maria Elizabeth Rundell, the widow of the Bath surgeon Thomas Rundell. Murray published the first edition in 1805, without paying Mrs Rundell anything. Later, when he had started to remunerate her, she wrote to him that she had 'never had the smallest Idea of any return for what I considered, & which really was, a free Gift to one whom I had long regarded as my friend'.[45] She says the same in the introduction to a later edition of *Domestic Cookery*: 'as she will receive from it no emolument, so she trusts it will escape without censure'.[46]

This introduction explains that the book was intended for 'the families of the authoress's own daughters'. Smiles claims that 'previous cookery books . . . had been written by French cooks chiefly for tavern use',[47] but this is not true: cookery books for domestic use had been appearing at least since the sixteenth century, and more recently *The Art of Cookery Made Plain and Easy* (1747) by Hannah Glasse had been a bestseller. Mrs Rundell was not a pioneer, but she was bringing a well-established science up to date: hers for example was the first cookery book to give instructions in making coffee. The book reflects the rise of the middle class. The old social classes, aristocracy and tradespeople, were being remade by what Mrs Rundell, following Daniel Defoe, calls 'those in a middle line', who did not have armies of servants to do the cooking and keep house. On the other hand, the recipes were not intended for the poor, or for those of a delicate constitution, judging by the amount of eggs and cream that go into the plainest dishes. The book contains such advice as:

An excellent plain Potatoe Pudding

Take eight ounces of boiled potatoes, two ounces of butter, the yolks and whites of two eggs, a quarter of a pint of cream, one spoonful of white wine, a morsel of salt, the juice and rind of a lemon; beat all to a froth; sugar to taste. A crust or not, as you like. If wanted richer, put three ounces more butter, sweetmeats and almonds, and another egg.[48]

The style of the food is formidably English: the book begins with instructions in carving a joint, and only a few recipes have French titles. Yet the modern world of convenience foods and takeaways is not so remote. From India there is 'Chicken Currie', flavoured with ready-made 'currie-powder',[49] though the 'Indian Pickle' to accompany it is to be made with garlic, vinegar and mustard seed.[50] In the 1811 edition there were recipes for kebabs and Chinese food,

'Mutton kebobbed' and 'China Chilo', the latter made of minced lamb flavoured with cayenne pepper and served on a bed of rice. The influence of America is also perceptible:

New-England Pancakes

Mix a pint of cream, five spoonfuls of fine flour, seven yolks and four whites of eggs, with very little salt; fry them very thin in fresh butter, and between each strew sugar and cinnamon. Send up six or eight at once.'[51]

6

Quarterly

———

THE MURRAY ARCHIVE has a copy of the 1811 edition of *Domestic Cookery* inscribed 'Anne Murray'. On 28 March 1807, Mrs Rundell wrote to John Murray to congratulate him on his marriage: 'my sincere good wishes that the late event may be productive of every thing that can make yourself & Mrs Murray happy'. But she nevertheless complained that the second edition of *Domestic Cookery* had been filled with mistakes by whoever prepared it for the printer. 'He has made some dreadful blunders such as directing rice pudding seeds to be kept in a keg of lime water, which latter was mentioned to preserve eggs in.'[1] The errors did not, however, harm the book's growing reputation, and by September 1808 it had sold so well that Murray gratuitously sent a payment to Mrs Rundell of £150 – the equivalent of about £7,500 today. She told him she was embarrassed to pocket it: 'your persuasion of its being honourable to my poor abilities, is *really necessary* to make me believe I do not err in accepting it'.[2]

In late February 1807, Murray went by mail coach in appalling weather to Edinburgh for his wedding. The journey took six days.[3] He and Anne honeymooned in Kelso, after a journey full of incident. 'On our road here,' Murray wrote to Constable,

> our horses & driver both indifferent were thrown down and rolled over & over with an appearance so horrible that the least of the misfortunes which we expected to have resulted from this accident were a broken leg to the post boy & an inability [illegible] to proceed . . .
> But with the help of messengers all was reinstated in little more than half an hour without any hurt or other inconvenience than the delay.[4]

Once he and Anne were back in London, Murray wrote to Constable that he was immensely happy: 'Neither my wife nor I have any disposition for company or going out.'[5] Only a month later, however, he and Constable were on the road together. Murray was on his way to visit his mother and stepfather at Cann Hall, Bridgnorth, while Constable was hoping to recover at least one serious debt. They stopped in Oxford and Birmingham, and continued to Lichfield, where they met the poet Anna Seward, whose grandfather had taught the young Samuel Johnson. Anna Seward spoke enthusiastically of the poetry of Walter Scott, but less so of her late neighbour Dr Erasmus Darwin with whom she had quarrelled. Reporting all this Murray concluded his letter to Anne: 'thy faithful & loving husband John Murray'.[6]

John Murray does indeed seem to have been both faithful and loving. He had not inherited his father's talent for night-life: a single bottle of claret was enough to make him unable to work the next day. A letter to his wife, now called 'Annie', of July 1809, when they had been married for two years, reveals the depth of his affection and indeed his fidelity. 'I have been out no where,' he declares, 'my thoughts are very constantly with you and I make many fervent resolutions of being more uniformly kind and attentive to a truly dear wife.' As to living it up: 'I generally breakfast by 8 & am always in bed before Eleven.'[7]

Anna Seward's opinion of Scott was typical of the times: the young Walter Scott's name was on everybody's lips. *Marmion: a Tale of Flodden Field*, famous even before publication for its four-figure advance, came out in February 1808, a year after Murray's marriage. Murray's name was among those on the title page. Scott himself had visited Murray in London in March 1807, shortly after the publisher had returned to the capital with his new wife. 'He appears very desirous that Marmion should be published by the King's birthday,' noted Murray.[8] This deadline could not be met, but Murray told Constable he regarded it as 'honourable, profitable and glorious to be concerned in the publication of a new poem by Walter Scott'.[9]

Constable had first met Scott around 1800, when Scott was a twenty-nine-year-old lawyer. He had been among the co-publishers of his first book, *Minstrelsy of the Scottish Border* (1802–3), and similarly participated in the publication of Scott's first major work, *The Lay of the Last Minstrel* (1805). Then came the spectacular advance for *Marmion*, in which Murray had a quarter share of £250. Sales of the poem justified the advance – in three years it sold around 28,000 copies, and was reprinted many times. It has had devotees ranging from John Ruskin, who considered Scott's depiction of Flodden to be the finest description of a battle in the literature of the world, to A. N. Wilson, who has praised the 'high light verse' in which most of it is written.[10] The plot, which includes such scenes as Marmion's discarded mistress being walled up in a convent on Lindisfarne, is as colourful as any Scott novel. Nevertheless, *Marmion* was given a largely hostile notice in the *Edinburgh Review*, by the magazine's trenchant editor Francis Jeffrey. Scott had been an enthusiastic supporter of the *Edinburgh Review*, and was 'rather proud' of the way in which it 'kept authors and literary men up to the mark . . . though it crushed the seemingly weak, it stimulated the strong'.[11] However, when it was his turn to feel Jeffrey's lash, 'Judge Jefferies' as the literary world had nicknamed him, Scott ceased to see the joke.

The same number of the *Edinburgh Review* (April 1808) also included an article on 'foreign politics' which clashed with Scott's own political outlook. It branded the current war against France as 'disastrous . . . deplorable', and suggested that Britain was the aggressor.[12] Scott's biographer and son-in law, J. G. Lockhart, described Murray as saying to himself, on reading the article: 'Walter Scott has feelings, both as a gentleman and a Tory, which these people must now have wounded; the alliance between him and the whole clique of the *Edinburgh Review* is now shaken.'[13]

Meanwhile Murray had to some extent retracted his friendship with Constable on account of the latter's financial unreliability. On 12 March 1808 Murray wrote to Constable, pointing out that only a year before he had had no hesitation in making Constable a trustee of his wife Anne's marriage settlement: 'two bonds of a thousand pounds each'. To his dismay, Constable had withheld half this money on feeble excuses, and when Murray had asked for it, prevaricated over payment. 'This behaviour, Mr Constable,' wrote Murray, 'does not appear to me to be reconcilable either with friendship or business.' There had been similar delays in the payment of other sums due from Constable, and Murray was often left to settle Constable's London debts for him.[14] Then, towards the end of 1808, Constable opened his own premises in London to sell his books and the *Edinburgh Review*, and this widened the breach still further. Murray was set free to pursue his own schemes which, not surprisingly, involved the author of *Marmion*.

Scott and Murray had roots in common. Scott's father, like Murray's grandfather, was an Edinburgh lawyer, and Scott had followed him into the profession. He was now a principal clerk to the Court of Session in Edinburgh, which gave him a steady income without his having to practise as an advocate, and allowed him time to build his literary portfolio. He was also able to divide his time between Edinburgh and Ashestiel on the River Tweed, where he eventually built his country house, Abbotsford. Murray knew that the way to sign up Scott was to approach James and John Ballantyne, two brothers with whom Scott had been at school, and who were now his printers. James Ballantyne and Murray met in Yorkshire in October 1808 to discuss Scott projects. Their conversation was sufficiently encouraging to make Murray decide to continue travelling north, to meet Scott himself on the banks of the Tweed.

'Mr John Murray of Fleetstreet ... paid me a visit,' reported Scott, describing his visitor as 'a young bookseller of capital and enterprise & who has more good sense and propriety of sentiment than fall to the share of most of his brethren ... I found his ideas most liberal & satisfactory.'[15] For his part, Murray never forgot the scenery of the Tweed and the hospitality of Scott and his young French wife, Charlotte Carpenter. Samuel Smiles describes them climbing the local hills, Murray on foot and Scott, who had been lame since contracting polio in infancy, riding his Shetland pony, constantly stopping to tell Murray about local legends and pointing out from the hilltop the sites of Borders battles against the English. Murray had two schemes to put to Scott, both of which involved editing rather than original writing. The first would use Scott's name to promote the sales of books which Murray already owned or in which he could acquire a share of the copyright. It was to be an extensive series of the work of British novelists, organised historically, to begin with Daniel Defoe, and to proceed to the present day. Scott would contribute biographical prefaces and explanatory notes, and Murray drew up thirty-six titles to begin with.

The manically energetic Scott, who had been known to write 120 pages in a day, albeit legal documents rather than fiction, was delighted by the idea, and offered to do it for nothing should it prove to be unprofitable. He asked Murray to send him 'an old catalogue of a large circulating Library' to jog his memory about authors and titles.[16] A project of this magnitude did not daunt him in the least: he was already editing the complete works of Dryden, and was about to tackle Swift, both of them for the Ballantynes. He did not tell Murray that he had signed a secret partnership agreement with the brothers. This would eventually ruin him financially.

Murray's second proposal to Scott was that he should start a new literary and political magazine, with a Tory bias in opposition to the Whiggish *Edinburgh Review*, and that Scott should be closely involved. Murray had timed this proposal very well. Scott had mostly got over his irritation with Francis Jeffrey for the review of *Marmion* back in April, but a new number of the *Edinburgh* had just come out which included a political article by Jeffrey, 'Don Cevallos and the Occupation of Spain', which Scott thought contained intolerable implied criticism of the British monarchy. He wrote at once to cancel his subscription, and turned to Murray's proposal.

Scott had already been talking in senior Scottish circles about the need for 'counter measures against the *Edinburgh Review*', which seemed to him to be doing 'incalculable damage' to the country with its prophecies of a 'speedy revolution' on the French model.[17] Unfortunately it was also the only literary review worth reading. Murray may have been considering offering Scott the editorship of his rival journal, as Scott's name would increase the circulation. Word went round in Edinburgh circles that Scott had been offered the job, but had turned it down because he was too busy, and because he felt the editor would need to live in London.[18] However, Scott's correspondence gives no indication that any such offer was made. Writing to Murray and others, he saw his role as giving advice and commissioning authors. In this capacity, he told Murray, he could 'work like a horse'.[19]

In the next few weeks Scott wrote pages of advice on the new magazine in his practically illegible handwriting. He felt it must not be overtly political, though it was important to launch a counterblast to the 'disgusting' views of Jeffrey and his treacherous gang.[20] He did not want to put the clock back to the pre-*Edinburgh* style of reviewing, which had passed blandly approving judgements on 'everything that reached even mediocrity'.[21] And he told Murray that the new journal should emulate the *Edinburgh* in one crucial respect: everyone should be paid. 'Each contributor should draw money for his article, be his rank what it may.'[22] He did not say why he thought this was important; but he may have felt that it created an air of professionalism, saving the journal from the gentleman amateur on the one hand and from the unprincipled hack on the other.

The editor, Scott continued, would have to be ruthless. Inevitably, some contributors would send in articles of 'stupefying mediocrity'; only a shrewd editor could save the day: 'he renders it palatable by a few lively paragraphs or entertaining illustrations'.[23] Meanwhile Murray had begun the search for such a shrewd editor. He had had the idea for the journal a full year before he approached Scott, because in September 1807 he had written to George Canning, the Foreign Secretary. Canning had himself run a satirical weekly newspaper, the *Anti-Jacobin*, which promulgated Tory values in revolutionary times, and Murray thought he might have advice to offer. Canning did not reply directly, but through his cousin, Stratford Canning, recommended that Murray approach the satirist William Gifford.

Why was Murray, who sprang from a line of at least mildly rebellious Scots, throwing in his lot with the English Tory establishment? A cynic would say that he was a publisher, and publishers will turn anywhere within reason for business. But it runs deeper than that. Writing to George Canning, Murray laid out his political credentials:

'Permit me, Sir, to act as the person who addresses you is no adventurer, but a man of some property, and inheriting a business that has been established for nearly a century.'[24] This was a bit of an exaggeration, 1768 to 1807 is not even a half-century, but Murray clearly felt the weight of family history. He may already have thought himself to be a member of a dynasty, for when his and Anne's first child was born on 16 April 1808, there was no question as to what name to give the boy.

William Gifford, Canning's recommendation as editor of the new journal, was born at Ashburton in Devon in 1756. He wrote that he 'derived nothing but a name' from his family,[25] though claimed that they were among the most ancient and respectable in the West Country. His father, Edward Gifford, had run away from school, travelled with a gypsy king and worked as a plumber and glazier before inheriting land. He was later involved in an attempt to incite a riot in a Methodist chapel, and ran away to sea to avoid prosecution. Edward Gifford died of drink before he was forty; his wife soon followed him to the grave. William was then eleven. The boy, who had a dwarfish stature, may have been deformed from birth, a misfortune compounded when he was injured after a table fell on him, leaving him hunchbacked and crippled. The American scholar George Ticknor, who met Gifford in 1815, described him as 'a short, deformed, and ugly little man, with a large head sunk between his shoulders, and one of his eyes turned outward, but withal, one of the best-natured, most open and well-bred gentlemen I have ever met'.[26]

William Gifford's godfather, keen to get him off his hands, found him a place as a cabin boy on a Devon coaster. But life at sea was too tough for him. His was not an easy childhood; nor was his younger brother's, who, apprenticed to a farmer at the age of seven, fell and broke his thigh. William, who had tried to teach his little brother to read and write, then encouraged him to go to sea, but this failed, and the child died about a year later. 'Gifford was now alone in the world,' writes his biographer Roy Benjamin Clark.[27] He resumed his schooling, doing so well that there was some talk of his succeeding the headmaster, who was overdue for retirement. His guardian, however, dismissed the idea, took him away from school and apprenticed him to a shoemaker. From this disputatious Presbyterian, Gifford picked up tricks of oratory, such as how always to avoid a plain word for a complex synonym, and thus silence an ignorant opponent.

Gifford hated the cobbler's trade, and managed in secret to cultivate a life of the mind, with the assistance of the Bible and a few books and magazines. His only writing implement was an awl, with which, having no ink, he scratched on offcuts of leather. Although he had scarcely heard of poetry, his first literary attempts were in verse, and he earned a few pennies by entertaining friends with rhymes. When the cobbler discovered this, and banned him from writing, the boy's spirit was broken, and he sank into depression. His luck changed when a local doctor recognised Gifford's potential and raised a subscription to send him to school, generosity which he rapidly justified by translating the *Satires* of Juvenal.

Gifford went up to Exeter College, Oxford, in 1779, at the age of twenty-two. There he proved to be a brilliant mathematician, and was soon teaching undergraduates himself. After taking his degree, he acquired the patronage of Lord Grosvenor, tutoring his son and travelling abroad with the boy. Grosvenor supported him for many years, during which time Gifford continued to translate Juvenal and to write verse satires and criticism, including *The Baviad* (1791) and *The Maeviad* (1795) which attacked literary fashions. His Juvenal translations were published in 1802. In 1797 George Canning and his Tory friends enlisted Gifford as editor of the *Anti-Jacobin*. He did so well that Canning awarded him a pension of £1,000 a year.

Gifford lived in some style, with his housekeeper Nancy, in a house near Green Park. His health was precarious, as on top of everything else he suffered from asthma and jaundice. He wrote of himself as having:

> one eye not over good,
> Two sides that to their cost have stood
> A ten years' hectic cough
> Aches, stitches, all the various ills
> That swell the dev'lish doctor's bills,
> And sweep poor mortals off.[28]

Naturally, as a satirist he made enemies. One of them, Leigh Hunt, described him as 'the satirist who could not bear to be satirised – the denouncer of incompetencies, who could not bear to be told of his own'. Hunt recalled him as 'a little man with a warped frame and a countenance between the querulous and the angry'.[29] But he was the obvious choice for the job that Murray needed to fill.

Murray made an unusual financial arrangement with Gifford. On publication of each number of the *Quarterly Review*, as the new journal was called, Gifford would receive 160 guineas. It was up to him to decide how much to pay contributors and how much to keep for himself. Murray also paid him an annual salary of £200. These sums added up to an amount which Murray admitted was far more than he could expect the magazine to earn 'for the first year at least',[30] but he told Scott that he felt it was important to pay Gifford properly: 'the success of the publication must depend in a great measure upon his activity'.

It was essential to hit the public hard with the first number, especially as the whole enterprise was a secret until the last moment. This was both because Murray was anxious that they might not get the contributors they wanted, and because he planned to keep the *Edinburgh Review* in the dark about its new rival for as long as possible. Jeffrey sensed that something was up, announcing that he was keeping party politics out of the *Edinburgh* in future, but Scott assured Murray that their plans still had not been discovered.

Napoleon had just put his brother on the Spanish throne, and so the conspirators agreed that the first issue should open with an article on Spain, in response to Jeffrey's polemic. Gifford offered the commission to the poet Robert Southey who had travelled in Spain; but Murray told Scott that this was a misunderstanding: 'It is true that Mr Southey knows a great deal about Spain . . . but at present *his* is not the kind of knowledge which we want, and it is, moreover, trusting our secret to a stranger, who has, by the way, a directly opposite bias in politics.'[31] Southey was indeed known as a radical; but one of the spectacles to be offered by the *Quarterly Review* would be his transformation, in its pages, into a Tory. Southey declined to write on Spain, and provided an article on missionaries instead. So Gifford found himself with an unwanted article on missionaries – thus are magazines run – and the Spanish piece was taken on by George Canning himself. He and Gifford closeted themselves with George Ellis, who had been a contributor to the Anti-Jacobin, and after four days the article emerged.

Names of reviewers came and went. The novelist and playwright Elizabeth Inchbald agreed to write on theatre and fiction; and then got cold feet. Even Gifford showed signs of anxiety, pleading poor health and a chronic dislike of society as his excuse for failing to get the first issue together by Murray's deadline. Murray himself must have been waking in the night and contemplating the enormous bills that the project was running up. Only Scott was unflagging, turning out one article after another for the first number at such speed that, once they were posted, he claimed to have no recollection of what they were about. 'I seldom read over my things in manuscript,' he told Murray, explaining that he did his revision when the proofs came.[32] Scott contributed four lengthy articles to the 240-page first issue: on Burns, whom he calls a 'wonderful man',[33] on Southey's translation of the Spanish epic El Cid, 'a most entertaining volume',[34] on a book on the early life of Swift, whom he admires, but finds guilty of 'coarseness',[35] and on Sir John Carr's Caledonian Sketches. Scott considered this Englishman's view of Scotland to have been lazily researched. Other contributors included Isaac D'Israeli, on Sir Philip Sidney, while Gifford wrote on an absurd historical–romantic novel, Women; or Ida of Athens by Miss Owenson, and on Public Characters of 1809–10, a collection of cartoons of contemporary figures. When another lady novelist, Alicia T. Palmer, heard that her Daughters of Isenberg: a Bavarian Romance was to be reviewed by the Quarterly, she 'had the temerity to send three £1 notes', Murray reported to Scott.[36] Gifford passed the bribe to charity.

Scott felt he could have written even more for the first number of the Quarterly Review, or the Quarterly as it soon became known, if he had been able to work in London. 'In London,' he assured Murray, 'I could soon run up half a sheet of trifling articles with a page or two to each, but that is impossible here [in Scotland] for lack of materials.'[37] Meanwhile it became clear that the first issue, January 1809, was not going to be in the shops during that month. James Ballantyne, who would be publishing it in Edinburgh, blamed Gifford: 'Would G. were as active as Scott and Murray!'[38] Nevertheless, Gifford was attentiveness itself when it came to checking proofs. He had an eagle eye that noticed the smallest typographical blemish. Writing to Murray he announced:

> In Southey's article there are two slight alterations which, if it falls in your way, you might make. Sieks is in one place mispelt Seeks: and Persic should be printed instead of Persian. Having no proof (which is wrong) I cannot point out the pages, but the latter error is when the Translations of the Bible are first mentioned. I hope you will see that the corrections of the Proof are all made. The Printers, you see, cannot be relied on.[39]

The first number eventually appeared in the last week of February. 'I received the *Quarterly* an hour ago,' Ballantyne reported to Murray on the 28th. 'It looks uncommonly well.'[40] But there was an air of talking it up, rather than wild enthusiasm. George Ellis said he was not discouraged by what they had produced, though he could not help remarking that the most recent number of the *Edinburgh Review* was the best so far. Ballantyne enjoyed the 'high spirits' of Scott's articles, and thought his piece on Robert Burns, while lacking the 'elaborate eloquence' of Jeffrey's *Edinburgh* criticisms, was 'more original'.[41] Neither Scott nor Murray concealed their mild disappointment. Murray sent a critique of the first issue to Scott, who replied: 'I see the faults you point out, but hardly know how to prevent them at this distance.'[42]

Sales were promising: the first print-run of four thousand copies sold out, much of it to customers in Edinburgh, and though Murray complained that so far he was 'considerably out of pocket'[43] the plain fact was that they were less than three thousand behind the circulation of the *Edinburgh*. 'I find that, upon comparison with the *E.R.*,' Murray wrote to George Canning's brother Stratford, 'we are thought to want spirit, and we require a succession of novelty to attract public attention.'[44] Stratford Canning was now a diplomat in

Turkey, and Murray suggested that one possible novelty would be for him to get hold of foreign journals, and send them on to London for review. Stratford Canning felt that this would be impossible: 'Literature neither resides at Constantinople nor passes through it ... We are entirely insulated. The Russians block up the usual road through Bucharest, and the Servians prevent the passage of couriers through Bosnia.'[45]

Murray decided that he needed Scott to come south and help him sort out the *Quarterly*, and offered him expenses of up to £100 if he could not get them paid in his capacity as an official of the Scottish law courts with business in England; he could.

For the second issue, Scott wrote the lead article on 'Gertrude of Wyoming' and other new poems by Thomas Campbell, and a review of a novel, *John de Lancaster* by Richard Cumberland. Other contributors included Southey on Portuguese literature, Gifford ('Translation of Persius'), Isaac D'Israeli ('Periodical Papers' under the pseudonym 'Nathan Drake'), and George Canning, who co-wrote 'Austrian State Papers' with the historian Sharon Turner. According to Smiles, Murray rather than Gifford was the energy behind the *Quarterly*, persuading new writers to join the team, picking books for review and choosing reviewers. But as an editor Gifford could not be bettered, and Murray was lucky indeed to have his services. We have seen how attentive he was to the texts, and this asset was enhanced by his understanding of authors, and his patience:

> There is always so much vivacity, and so much striking ingenuity in Mr D'Israeli (I speak, as you will know, with perfect sincerity) that I am always desirous of his writings. Unfortunately, his pencil marks are so loose & imperfect, that I cannot discover, with any certainty, what he means to omit, nor where the connection falls in. What do you think of requesting him to draw his pen across what is now to be omitted; and setting up the rest in a slip or two? It will make a very interesting article, & I will correct it with all my care.[46]

Nevertheless, Gifford was utterly unbusinesslike. The second issue was even later than the first, and in May 1809, when it was already two months overdue, Murray wrote to Gifford that he was in a state of 'complete misery' when he contemplated the chaos in which

Gifford worked.[47] Gifford replied good-humouredly that the trouble was largely non-communication, and uncertainty as to who was in charge: 'You have too many advisers, and I too many masters.'[48]

Gifford was certainly not going to work all hours just because Murray was anxious about losing money. When he finally delivered the second *Quarterly* to the printer, Gifford went off for several weeks' holiday in the Isle of Wight, where 'a fortnight's complete abstraction [from] all sublunary cares has done me good, and I am now ready to put on my spectacles and look about me'.[49] He also told Murray that he had lost his copy of Horace somewhere on the journey to Ryde and could not do without it, so could Murray get him a replacement? The second *Quarterly* emerged in late May 1809, and George Ellis sent Murray a critique. It was 'incomparably better' than the first number, but Ellis had found a long article on the New Testament, by George D'Oyley, 'very tedious'. However, the issue as a whole was, he felt, much better than the *Edinburgh*,[50] and Gifford remarked that their Scottish rival was now copying the *Quarterly*'s seriousness of manner.

They could be too serious; Ellis judged the third issue, which was as late as its predecessors, to be appallingly dull. He could not find anybody willing to read and comment on the articles on Greek grammar and Gothic architecture, and felt they probably needed a larger team of accomplished contributors. Isaac D'Israeli reported to Murray that nobody in Brighton, where he was staying, had heard of the *Quarterly*, though the *Edinburgh* was in the shops. But he added: 'My son Ben assures me you are in Brighton. He saw you! Now, he never lies.'[51]

Worry about the *Quarterly* began to give Murray stomach pains. 'If I am over-anxious,' he wrote to Gifford, 'it is because I have let my hopes of fame as a bookseller rest upon the establishment and celebrity of this journal.'[52] When he reproached Gifford for the continuing delays to each issue, which were putting at risk the money he was pouring into the project, Gifford threatened to resign. Murray grumbled to his wife that Gifford did not even appreciate that all the books they reviewed must be new ones. The rest of the Murray business was by and large healthy. In the spring of 1809 his medical list consisted of nearly thirty useful titles – handbooks of midwifery, general surgery, tropical fevers – while his general books included a new ten-volume edition of Defoe, a nautical handbook for fledgling naval officers and the *Edinburgh Encyclopaedia*, which had reached the fourth volume. Old favourites such as Isaac D'Israeli's *Curiosities of Literature* and Mrs Rundell's cookery book jostled with an illustrated biography of Michelangelo in which the artist's poetry had been translated by Southey and Wordsworth.

The *Quarterly* slowly began to establish itself. Its constant failure to appear on time became a hallmark rather than a drawback, and it soon produced its first profitable spin-off for Murray. The fifth issue (February 1810) included a review of four recent biographies of Nelson, by Robert Southey, who poured scorn on all of them, including the life by the Rev. Stanier Clarke, self-styled 'authorised biographer'.[53] Southey then supplied his own thirty-eight-page account of the life of the hero of Trafalgar. Southey was ashamed of himself for taking on such hackwork, but Murray could see its potential, and persuaded Southey to expand it into a two-volume biography, telling him it would 'become the heroic text of every midshipman in the Navy'.[54] Southey complied, with the result that his Nelson earnings eventually totalled £300. We can be certain that Murray's made a good deal more than that, for the book remained in print throughout the nineteenth century and into the twentieth. It perpetuated all the colourful myths about its hero, with scant regard for truth.

Walter Scott's *Lady of the Lake* was reviewed by George Ellis in the issue of May 1810. 'No poet of the present day has acquired the same celebrity as Mr Scott,' he wrote,[55] judging that the new poem won him 'a place amongst the greatest masters of his art'.[56] Ballantyne, with whom Murray was now falling out over finance, had failed to offer Murray a share in publishing the *Lady*; Constable, who had been similarly excluded, suggested to Murray that she 'will probably help to drown them!'[57]

Another poet got much rougher treatment. In the issue for November 1810, the opening piece was a review, said to be by Gifford but not in his style, of the new narrative poem *The Borough* by George Crabbe. The reviewer judged Crabbe to have 'greatly misapplied great powers' with his determination to portray 'low life' with complete realism.[58] The review quotes from, but makes no comment on, the section of the poem that would eventually immortalise its author, the story of the fisherman Peter Grimes and the fate of his boy apprentices.

In the issue for March 1812, George Ellis gave an enthusiastic review to another new narrative poem, which had set fashionable London on fire. This was *Childe Harold's Pilgrimage* by Lord Byron, and John Murray was its publisher. Its arrival signalled the beginning of the most colourful and dramatic period in Murray's personal and professional life, and of one of the most intense relationships between publisher and author in the history of literature.

PART TWO

1811–1824
Letters to Lord Byron

7

Lord and Master

B YRON FIRST CROSSED Murray's threshold at a difficult time for the firm. 'Mr Murray is really so very poor at this time that He trusts you will excuse his sending again his Account. Mr Murray desired me to say He will feel very happy if you will occasionally favour him with an order.'[1] There was a cashflow problem. Printers' and binders' bills had to be settled before significant income had come in from booksellers, and then there were the bad debts to contend with. Some consignments, sent off on a wish and a prayer by sailing ship from the Pool of London, could not possibly expect financial return for a very long time, if ever. Not only was Murray trading by sea with Newcastle, Edinburgh and India, but his books were pioneering the trade routes even as far as Australia. Shortly after a ship left bearing books to the Senior Chaplain in New South Wales, another sailed away bearing the invoice: 'Sir, The Ship Clarkson, Captain Clarkson, being upon the eve of departing for your Colony, inclosed I beg leave to hand Invoice & Bill of Lading for the School Books shippd on our Account amount with insurance £206.18.2, which I hope will arrive safe with you.'[2]

There was packing and wrapping to contend with, a task which, before sending £415 3s worth of books to the Dublin bookseller C. P. Archer, occupied 'the whole of yesterday in packing them'.[3] A consignment worth somewhat over £400 would have consisted of at least five or six hundred volumes, perhaps half a ton of books. In July 1812 Murray drew up his 'Country Accounts', which revealed sums owing to the publisher of up to £77 6s 10d, and sent them out to twenty-four booksellers all around the country, from Newcastle and North Shields in the north-east, to Exeter and Fowey in the south-west.[4] Murray's now were a company with a truly national influence.

In May 1811 John Murray, 32 Fleet Street, published his list of 'Books lately published, in the press, or publishing'.[5] By any standard of measurement this is a gargantuan list: there are ninety-four titles. In English literature there are volumes on the works of Ben Jonson by William Gifford, and on John Ford and Beaumont and Fletcher by Henry Weber, poetry by Thomas Campbell and James Hogg, and Mrs Dorset's *The Peacock at Home*. There is a history of the County of Rutland 'with many plates', and books on astronomy, chemistry, botany, medicine and nosology, the classification of diseases. *Observations on the Utility and Administration of Purgative Medicine in Several Diseases* by James Hamilton MD is there, as is *Hints to the Bearers of Walking Sticks and Umbrellas* (third edition, with eleven plates and woodcuts, anonymous – in fact by John Shute Duncan). John Murray shows very successfully in this list that he is a friend to all disciplines and subject to none. It was shrewd of him to corner a market in publishing medical books, physicians then as now being competitive and assiduous in promoting and gaining knowledge of new developments in their profession. The army's interests were covered by *Sketch of the Campaign in Portugal* and *Observations on the Movements of the British Army in Spain*; and armchair travellers by *Some Account of New Zealand* by John Savage.

Murray knew how to speak to niche markets, advertising *Analecta Graeca Minora* with the words: 'Ad Usum Tironum Accommodata. Cum Notis Philologicis, quas partim scripsit, ANDREAS DALZEL A.M. S.R.S. Nuper in Academia Jacobi VI Scotorum Regis Lit. Gr. Prof. Eidemque, a Secretis et Bibliothecarius.' He maintained an eye on the Edinburgh market, with J. Stark's *Picture of Edinburgh*, illustrated with a map and thirty wood engravings, and with Andrew Duncan's *Edinburgh New Dispensatory* and the *Edinburgh Annual Register for 1809*, to be published in May 1811.

It is clear from this list that, while John Murray spread his printing orders round many printing companies, his prime task was to keep the books moving, and to get them out into shops and into the world. Without proper warehousing, distribution and outlets, he would have been smothered by *Woman: A Poem* (by Eaton Stannard Barrett), or crushed under tottering piles of *Paganism and Christianity Compared* and *Queen-Hoo-Hall: A Legendary Romance*, by Joseph Strutt.

Soon, however, he was to have in his portfolio an author who not only would become an intimate friend, but whose works would transform his business into one of the most successful and prestigious in the history of publishing. In mid-July 1811, a young man in an open-necked shirt, with a pronounced limp, checked in to the small but expensive London hotel, Reddish's, in St James's Street. His trunks and boxes gave evidence that he had been in eastern parts of the world. The poet Lord Byron had returned from abroad, where he had spent the past two years travelling in Greece, Turkey and Asia Minor, and other parts of the Mediterranean and the Levant. He had come back to England with the intention of arranging his embarrassed affairs and settling his debts, and visiting his mother at Newstead Abbey in Nottinghamshire, before setting out on his travels again. Things were to turn out rather differently, however.

He was already known to the public as the author of a juvenile production *Hours of Idleness* (1807), and of a biting satire in response to its critics *English Bards and Scotch Reviewers* (1809), which had recently entered its fourth edition. He had brought back with him the manuscript of a long poem written in Spenserean stanzas, describing the various countries he had passed through and the sites and scenes he had witnessed. *Childe Harold's Pilgrimage*, as it was to be called, was a sort of diary or travelogue of the kind of Grand Tour that young noblemen then took after leaving university. Byron, however, had been to unusual places such as the Ionian Islands and Albania, because, quite apart from his exotic tastes, the Napoleonic Wars had made the conventional routes impossible. Byron had completed two cantos of an extraordinary soliloquy, delivered by a new kind of hero: sexually experienced to the point of world-weariness, shrewd and ironic in his judgement of contemporary politics, and a melancholic exile basking in his own romantic isolation. Though Byron himself denied it, few were convinced that Childe Harold was not a self-portrait.

He first offered the poem to William Miller, with whom he had an outstanding debt, who was one of the foremost publishers of the day, and whose premises in Albemarle Street Murray was to purchase a year later. Miller, however, objected to various passages, and in particular to those in which Byron railed against Lord Elgin as the plunderer of the Acropolis marbles. Elgin was a Miller author, and Miller could not accept slighting words against him, so he declined it. Undismayed, Byron determined to find another publisher.

Among the friends and acquaintances who had come to visit him soon after his return to England was an elderly and impoverished relative by marriage, Robert Charles Dallas, who had first approached him in January 1808 after reading *Hours of Idleness*, and had subsequently made himself useful in seeing *English Bards and Scotch Reviewers* through the press. Byron, having other more important and pressing matters to attend to, placed the poem in Dallas's hands to take to Murray, now the publisher of the increasingly successful *Quarterly Review*. Being urgently called away to Newstead where his mother lay dying, he accepted Dallas's offer to act as mediator between them.[6] Here, again, though, there was the possibility of offence: for Byron had given Murray a mocking mention in *English Bards and Scotch Reviewers*, singling him and Miller out as the publishers of Scott's *Marmion* (1808), of which he had written scathingly:

> And thinkst thou, SCOTT! by vain conceit perchance,
> On public taste to foist thy stale romance
> Though MURRAY with his MILLER may combine
> To yield thy muse just half-a-crown per line?[7]

But Murray was immediately taken with the poem – his enthusiasm for it being no doubt encouraged by the favourable opinion of William Gifford, on whose judgement he depended. Byron, however, had strictly enjoined Murray not to show the manuscript to Gifford: he admired Gifford as a satirist and had praised him in *English Bards and Scotch Reviewers*, but he did not wish to be seen as courting his applause (or censure). Nevertheless, when Dallas wrote to Byron he told him that Gifford had pronounced the poem to be not only the best thing he had done so far, but equal to anything that was currently being written. His only criticism was that it stopped abruptly, unfinished, at the end of the second canto.

Murray himself, in his first letter to Byron, was full of compliments and admiration. Without alluding to Gifford in any way, he echoed his sentiments, but was concerned about certain political and religious opinions Byron had expressed, which, he said, 'may deprive me of some customers amongst the *Orthodox*'. He begged Byron to revise the poem and complete it: 'Your Fame my Lord demands it – you are raising a Monument that will outlive your present feelings, and it should therefore be so constructed as to excite no other associations than those of respect and admiration for your Lordships Character and Genius.'[8] Byron's reply was playful yet firm. He accepted Murray's compliments with good grace, but refused to make any alterations to please the 'Orthodox', and emphasised that it is 'a *political* poem & written for a *political* purpose', though he did not say what he meant by this.[9] He did however make it perfectly clear in his maiden speech in the House of Lords a few days before publication of *Childe Harold* that he was no Tory. He spoke eloquently against the Tory government's bill which made it a capital offence for weavers to damage the machinery which was depriving them of employment, and followed this with a powerful poem, published anonymously in the *Morning Chronicle*, attacking the sponsors of the bill for implying that men's lives were less valuable than machines.

Childe Harold contains nothing quite as revolutionary as this. Nevertheless there was plenty in it to keep Murray worried about the feelings of his Tory customers. Byron emphasises the futility of war, a contest in which the only winner can be death;[10] while, as to religion, he describes a Spanish crowd praying to the Virgin, and tartly observes that she is probably 'the only virgin there'.[11]

The first edition of *Childe Harold*, a lavishly produced quarto volume, was advertised for 1 March 1812, but actually appeared on 10 March. Three days later, all five hundred copies were sold. This had been achieved partly through one of Murray's 'trade dinners' at the Albion Tavern five days before the official publication date. Hatchard's, who were already established in Piccadilly, took fifty copies, and Longman's twenty-five; but the rest of the trade showed no more than a mild interest, with orders in single figures. This was despite the fact that Murray was offering the edition at cut price. However, a month later he went ahead with a cheaper octavo edition, launched with another dinner. This equivalent of a paper-back, reduced for the trade from 12s to 8s 6d, was snapped up: Longman's took two hundred, trade sales during the dinner reaching a spectacular total of 1,330.

According to the ledger, Murray paid £525 for 'the whole Copyright' of the first two cantos of *Childe Harold*, and recorded it in the ledger.[12] Byron, however, was frequently short of cash and had given the copyright to Dallas in January 1812.[13] Besides lining his pocket with this very substantial sum, Dallas had also written Murray a begging letter: 'An unexpected misfortune has happened ... The fact is, I have been arrested.' Could Murray 'lend me twenty guineas for a couple of months?' The arrest was presumably for debt, and Murray reluctantly complied, with the words 'vexatiously inconvenient to me'.[14]

Meanwhile the fan-mail had begun. It was generally anonymous, and many of the writers sent Byron their own poetry. One of the earliest such offerings inspired by *Childe Harold* was in obsessively neat handwriting: 'Turn not from this address because the writer is anonymous. I am only deterred from declaring myself by the fear of being ridiculed should you receive it with feelings uncongenial to those which actuate me ... Most earnestly do I entreat you to read this book with serious attention.' Presumably she enclosed a collection of poems.[15] Another was from a lady calling herself Echo: she too sent verses ('Oh, Byron! thou hast known enough of pain'), and solicits a clandestine meeting: 'Should curiosity prompt you, and should you not be afraid of gratifying it, by trusting yourself *alone* in the Green Park at 7 o'clock this evening you will see Echo ... Be on the side of the Green Park that has the gate opening into Piccadilly.'

Whether Byron kept this particular appointment we do not know. Nor do we know when Byron and Murray themselves first met. Yet Murray too, as is clear from the earliest letters, succumbed almost at once to the poet's spell. Ten years older than Byron, Murray could if he chose play the wise uncle or even father to the glamorous young man, but in the event he wrote to Byron as if he too were a conquest. In a series of letters he addresses Byron with a respect that quickly modulates into adulation – 'My Lord'; 'My most dear Lord'; 'My dear Lord – & Master'.[16] At the slightest hint of irritation or disapproval from the poet in this first correspondence he is reduced to abject apology and the wheedling tones of a rejected lover. In one note, apologising for a misunderstanding among his staff, Murray writes of 'the misery I suffer at receiving a Letter from your Lordship without one word of that kindness which has made all the former ones so dear'.[17]

Partly, of course, it was the tradesman's fervent reverence for an ennobled client. Murray had plenty of members of the House of Lords among his customers and indeed his authors; and yet he tried to communicate with Byron across a social gap that seemed to frighten him by its breadth and depth. This does not, however, sufficiently explain Murray's strength of feeling. Another letter, dated 30 December 1813, is beyond belief as a communication from a publisher to one of his authors:

> My Lord
>   I feel nearly as little able to write to you, as I was to speak – without motive, or object, & merely from caprice, to place me at the mercy of one, whom your Lordship told me, but a few days ago, would *never forgive* me – were an act of consummate Cruelty which I can not conceive it possible for you seriously to meditate – but it has produced the entire effect upon me – for I never felt so bitterly unhappy than at this moment – If you really meant to give the Stab you gave to my feelings, may God harden my heart against man, for never, never will I attach myself to another.[18]

This might be a letter from a lover, so passionate it is, and illuminates the strong personal cast that this partnership developed.[19] The intimacy was strengthened by one of the most important decisions Murray was to take in his life. Within seven months of the publication of *Childe Harold* he was moving from Fleet Street into William Miller's old premises at 50 Albemarle Street, just up the road from

St James's Street where Byron was living. Byron was delighted to hear that they would be 'nearer neighbours'.[20]

Murray was following the general drift of booksellers from the City of London to the West End. As he explained to a correspondent, Albemarle Street was well placed for selling books to the smart set, 'peculiarly favourable for the dissemination of any work of eminence among the fashionable & literary part of the Metropolis'.[21] The move seems also to have earned him the resentment of some of his rivals. Writing to Hobhouse a few years later he told him that James Ridgway, who had his premises in Piccadilly, was 'jealous of my migration to this end of the town'.[22] The price of the house was nearly £4,000, but Miller gave Murray extended credit, with three of Murray's most valuable copyrights as guarantees: Mrs Rundell's cookery book, his quarter share in Scott's Marmion, and the Quarterly Review. A surprising absentee from the list, perhaps, is Childe Harold. However, though Byron's poem earned Murray a profit of £2,500 during its first five years in print, evidently not much of this had come in before he transferred his business across town.

The move was traumatic. 'I am distracted at this time between two houses,' Murray wailed to Byron on 22 October 1812. Nevertheless he found time for another booksellers' dinner, at which nearly a thousand copies of Childe Harold had been sold. According to Murray, this was the fifth edition: he had been making small alterations in the contents of the book, so that new editions could be announced regularly. The ruse was successful. By the time his family had settled into the former Miller house, Murray could tell Byron that sales had been 'unprecedented': 4,500 copies in less than six months, a massive figure by the standards of 1812.[23]

Murray felt thoroughly pleased with himself, so much so that he decided to remake contact with his half-brother Archy, illegitimate son of his father, and now a purser in the navy. He proudly announced to Archy that he was 'not far from the top of the first rank in my profession', and mentioned his recent appointments as bookseller to the Admiralty and the Board of Longitude,[24] which he said brought him 'something more solid'.[25] And he told Archy about the house.

8

The highest honour and emolument

———◆———

ALBEMARLE STREET RUNS from Mayfair into Piccadilly at the midway point between Berkeley Square and the Royal Academy. An alder tree marks the junction with Piccadilly. Named for the Duke of Albemarle, the street was laid out at the end of the seventeenth century to provide houses for both the burgeoning professional classes and the aristocracy. Numbers 48, 49 and 50 were built speculatively by Benjamin Jackson, a master mason in royal employment, who bought the land and presumably designed the houses.[1] Standing four storeys high, number 50, built c.1715, was a private house until William Miller set up his bookselling business there around 1804.

Arriving at 50 Albemarle Street is always something of a ceremony. However much one may have been shuffling or slouching along Piccadilly, the moment one turns the corner one starts to feel a spring in the step and a sense of elegance and occasion. The front door generally stands ajar, with the big brass plate worn by two hundred years of polishing – *Mr. Murray No. 50*. The visitor still announces himself or herself to the receptionist in the wood-and-glass kiosk, which sits in the entrance hall like a lift whose wires have been cut. Then, sent politely down the hall to a neat little waiting room with its spectacular glass dome dating from about 1812, the visitor would sooner or later risk a cough or a 'hello' just to sample the mini-echo produced by the dome. The echo is extraordinary and precisely localised: you have to stand directly below the centre of the dome, and then merely whisper. Your practically silent words come back as a private shout, but for your ears only. It is like hearing your own thoughts, or, from decades ago, the thoughts of an earlier visitor caught at random and allowed to escape. This is the room in which

77

Lady Caroline Lamb lingered hopefully for Byron, usually with little success.

The staircase is lavishly wide for the size of the house, yet beautifully proportioned, leading first to a half-landing with a bust of Byron and a window looking down on the exterior of the dome, then carrying onward and upward in style to the glory of the house – the main drawing room, known now as the Byron Room. This room, which gives off a golden glow from the mellowed gilding of the Japanese wallpaper chosen to mimic Spanish wallpaper, runs the whole width of the house. Two tall French windows lead to balconies overlooking the street. One might reasonably expect to see Paris outside, rather than Mayfair, as the room would fit just as easily into French salon life as it has for decades into the milieu of the London literary world.

The portraits look down at the visitor; and there are yet more in the next room, the middle drawing room. Pride of place is given to Byron, but there is also his plump little mother: 'Mrs Byron', it says on the frame. Robert Southey is there, as are George Crabbe, looking oddly like the singer Peter Pears, who played Crabbe's Peter Grimes on the operatic stage, and the first and second John Murrays. John Murray II, by Henry Pickersgill, holds a pensive pose which hides his damaged eye. In the background the bust of Byron displays an unByronic expression of stoicism.

In the Murray Archive we can trace the fitting out of this marvellous pair of rooms: the middle drawing room is no mere annexe to its larger sibling, but a handsome little chamber in itself. The joiner David Reid and his assistant Mr Sneezum itemised work done for Miller before Murray and his family moved in and could enjoy the improvements:

April 25th 1812
To First Floor to Elagant book Cases fixed at both ends of the room & five book Stands under ditto with Mahogany Tops & all ornamented with Paintings & 2 other Book Stands.[2]

The pride of the paintings arrived two years later. The 1814 exhibition at the Royal Academy included two portraits of Byron by

Thomas Phillips, one in Albanian costume and another, a half-length with an open-necked shirt, known as the 'cloak' portrait. Byron promised one of them to Murray, who in the event got the 'cloak' portrait. Later, in 1835, Murray commissioned from Phillips a copy of the Albanian portrait.

In the climb to the second floor, the staircase sheds not one inch of size or dignity, even though it is heading for quarters less grand than the *piano nobile*. The rooms are smaller on the second floor, and it does indeed begin to look like a family home. John Murray VII recalled that when he first came to Albemarle Street as a child, 'you could tell which had been the children's bedrooms, because they still had children's books on the shelves'.

On the fourth and final floor Murray recalled how, as late as the 1960s, the priceless archives – the letters from Byron and Jane Austen and Darwin and vast numbers of other people – were kept in the laundry cupboard in the attic.

> There wasn't even a safe. And we did have a burglary. I then had to sleep here for a few nights, and all night long heard a noise, like people walking round the house. It was tempting to regard it as the ghost of Lady Caroline Lamb, but the oak stairs were compressed during the day, with so many people going up and down – about forty-five worked in the building until 2002. So at night the treads all slowly creaked back to their normal positions.

The Murray account-books refer to setting up a shop somewhere on the ground floor. Murray's was a bookshop as well as a publisher when the family came over from Fleet Street in 1812. The shop was clearly situated on the ground floor, apparently divided into front and back sections by a sash window. According to the joiner's list things were just as 'elagant' here:

> To Counting House to Elagant Mahogany Writing Table Fixed in Window & fitted up with large Mahogany Drawers under ditto & Divided and Locks & Handels Compleat.
>   To 2 Seprate Book Stands between Colloums and Glass Sash on top to face Both Shops fitted Compleat
>   To 2 Stuffed Counting House Stools with leather Covers.[3]

John Murray VII vividly remembers the accounts clerks sitting on high stools in his childhood: the stools finally went to the Museum of London. But the location of the dining room remains a mystery: a letter from Robert Browning in 1886 contains a description of dining at Murray's, 'in the room which, in Byron's time, was the front-shop: the present drawing room being then the dining room'.[4]

Down the staircase to the basement is a warren of subterranean rooms including the old wine cellar (now holding ledgers) and the coal cellars under the road, now converted to storage space. 'In the old days,' John Murray VII remembers, 'we needed a lot of coal. It was like stoking a battleship. We had a wonderful Irish stoker called Mr Stafford.'

Browning must have been mistaken about the dining-room, judging by John Murray II's letter to Archy written in August 1813, nearly a year after the move to Albemarle Street. Murray describes his pleasure and pride in his new house:

> I have lately . . . ventured upon the bold step of quitting the old establishment . . . and have moved to one of the best in every respect that is known in my business, where I have succeeded in a manner the most complete & flattering. My House is excellent – it would surprise you – and I transact all my department[s] of my business in an elegant library, which my drawingroom becomes during the morning, where I am in the habit of seeing Persons of the very highest rank for Literature & talent such as Canning – Frere – Mackintosh – Southey – Campbell – Walter Scott – Mad. de Stael – Gifford – Croker – Barrow – Lord Byron &c &c &c – leading thus the most delightful life with the means of prosecuting my business with the highest honour and emolument.'[5]

John Murray's enjoyment of his business led him naturally into a habit of dropping names. This same self-satisfaction pervades his letters to Annie a year later, when she is visiting her family in Scotland. Murray is fussing that their Fleet Street carpets look too shabby for the new surroundings. But Murray's name-dropping does provide a cast-list of the men and women who populated the pristine drawing-rooms, and thereby established a literary legend. Many of the names are now forgotten, but some still echo through British political and literary history. Canning, a Cabinet minister until he resigned as Foreign Secretary over a policy disagreement, was also a poet and a literary parodist. John Hookham Frere was another Tory MP, who had been a close friend of Canning's since they were at Eton together; he was closely involved with the *Quarterly* and frequently gave Murray advice. Sir James Mackintosh, Scottish physician, philosopher and historian, had started out as an advocate of the French Revolution, but later recanted, and accepted a knighthood from the Tories along with an appointment as a judge in India. Campbell was the popular poet Thomas Campbell, whose *Gertrude of Wyoming* had been a Murray bestseller in 1809.

Another guest at the soirées was Mme de Staël, a free-thinking Swiss-Frenchwoman who had been hounded out of Europe by Napoleon. She had accompanied Sir James Mackintosh to a soirée, and soon Murray began to negotiate publication of her book in praise of German culture, *De l'Allemagne*. In discussing this book, which had so infuriated Bonaparte when it was first published in French in 1810, Mme de Staël sent Murray comically bilingual notes: 'Voilà la preface, my dear Sir, avec les corrections de Sir James ... Il y a bien longtemps que je n'ai été chez vous, c'est a dire in the headquarters of Mr Canning.'[6]

Gifford thought that she suffered from verbal diarrhoea. 'Madame de Staël', he remarked to Murray, 'will write and print without intermission.'[7] Byron nicknamed her 'Mrs Stale'.[8]

Croker and Barrow, the penultimate names on the list that Murray proudly sent to Archy, were senior civil servants at the Admiralty who contributed regularly to the *Quarterly Review*. That brings us back to the last name, Byron. Murray soon realised that by acquiring this glamorous young author he had also acquired his camp followers, girlfriends and boyfriends as well. They did not behave themselves. Letters like this tended to be left lying around:

> These flowers have no Hope of pleasing you they come trembling with fear in case you should be offended at their being sent is it possible that you looked kindly on me at Miss [illegible]'s I durst not

believe it – but my heart felt your goodness though it was my duty to you & to all not to show it thank you also for not having spoken ill of me to Hobhouse – his noticing me the other night made me ready to cry – when any friend of yours speaks kindly to me – I dread what they must think of me – for I am almost ready to fall at their feet.[9]

This is Lady Caroline Lamb, sobbing at her rejection by Byron after a few weeks in bed with him. The pile of her letters to Byron, which he left with Murray when he went abroad, includes a small manila envelope labelled 'Caro Lamb hair'. What the envelope contains is one of the tresses which poor Caro hacked off, and presented to Byron, when she attempted to make herself look like the Cambridge choirboy whom Byron had lately seduced. That at least is what he claimed, claiming also that the boy was the love of his life. The hair is light brown, and could pass for blonde in a favourable light. There was also an envelope of clippings of Caroline's pubic hair, but this has now vanished, destroyed perhaps by the third or fourth John Murray.

Murray probably first became aware of Caroline Lamb when she turned up at Albemarle Street in January 1813 with a letter supposedly from Byron, in which he asked Murray to hand over to Caroline a miniature portrait of himself. She longed to have it: 'as to his refusing you the Picture – it is quite ridiculous – only name me or if you like it shew but this note & that will suffice'.[10] At the end of the letter, Byron has written: 'This letter was forged in my name by Caroline L. for the purpose of obtaining a picture from the hands of Mr M.'

Murray was taken in: Caroline's forging of Byron's handwriting was creditable, and Byron wrote immediately to object: 'She is a woman (& of rank) with whom I have unfortunately been too much connected ... be more cautious in future & [do] not allow anything of mine to pass from your hands without my *seal* as well as signature ... The *delinquent* is of one of the first families in this kingdom.'[11] Murray responded by warning Caroline that forgery might get her into trouble with the law, but she loved the idea of penal transportation, and she signed her reply, 'Horatio Nelson & Lady Hamilton'.

Nelson's enduring relationship with his mistress summed up what she wanted to be to Byron: 'You have known him as a friend [and] as a Patron,' she wrote to Murray, 'I knew him as more – were he now to turn grand foe – to laugh at you openly – to make you his jest his scorn – it would wound you – but oh for one moment think what it is for a Woman to bear.'[12]

Murray seems to have sent her some books by other authors he was publishing. 'I . . . could not like the *Paradise of Coquettes* – you were not I hope angry at this,' she wrote to him after dipping into a long poem by the Scottish philosopher Thomas Brown. Her letters are often frantic, and tend to begin without a capital letter: 'is there any thing I can do to serve you – if there is name it', and punctuation often vanishes: 'will you be at home if I call tomorrow at half past eleven & do not have Bishops'. This was an allusion, presumably, to the grandeur of what Byron referred to as Murray's Synod now to be found in the Murray drawing room.[13]

Caroline offered Murray one of the paintings she had commissioned for Byron, showing herself as a pageboy. Murray seems to have been nervous of what the bishops might think of it, as Caroline then wrote: 'As the Pages Picture cannot be put up in your room, put what I send you to ornament your Chimney – it is a Lamb & a Page can any thing be more appropriate to remind you of me.'[14] This particular subject is not in the archive; the miniature that is there shows Caroline not with a lamb but with a black dog nuzzling at her black and gold page's jacket.[15]

As far as we know, Caroline Lamb did not actually appear uninvited at the Murray salon, but if she had been lurking in the glass-domed waiting room she may have pounced on people as they came downstairs. There is no mention of Caroline in the account of the salon by George Ticknor, who was at Albemarle Street on an ordinary day in the spring of 1815. This young American had come to London with a letter of introduction to Gifford, who proved to be charm itself. He carried Ticknor off to 'a handsome room over Murray's book-store, which he has fitted up as a sort of literary lounge, where authors resort to read newspapers, and talk literary gossip'.[16] This is not quite the way Murray would have wished to have it described, and the day that Ticknor attended only minor celebrities were in attendance – 'Elmsley, Hallam ... Boswell, a son of Johnson's biographer'.

Another American, Washington Irving, who came to Albemarle Street a few years after Ticknor, adds some details of how the salon worked: 'The hours of access are from two to five. It is understood to be a matter of privilege, and that you must have a general invitation from Murray.' Like Ticknor, Irving was particularly struck by Gifford's fragile physique: 'He is generally reclining on one of the sofas, and supporting himself by the cushions, being very much debilitated.'[17] Writers had congregated in London coffee houses for many generations: Dryden and Addison favoured Will's in Covent Garden, and other professions and allegiances had their favourite haunts: Tories went to the King's Head, city stock traders to Jonathan's in Lombard Street, aristocrats to Evans's in King Street, Covent Garden, and so on.[18] Gentlemen's clubs of various types were becoming a well-established feature of the capital: the Club, Samuel Johnson's cabal, had been founded in 1764. Murray was the first London publisher to hold daily soirées like this; it was one of his characteristic experiments, as he explored possibilities in his newly emerging profession.

Ticknor was unlucky in his timing: only a few weeks later, he could have witnessed an introduction which Murray had long been trying to engineer. 'This day,' noted Murray on Friday 7 April 1815, 'Lord Byron and Walter Scott met for the first time.'[19] Murray's son, the third John Murray, by now nearly seven, claimed to remember the meeting very well. What caught the boy's eye was the extraordinary fact that the great men both limped. 'Lord Byron's deformity in his foot was very evident,' the third of the Murrays told Samuel Smiles many years later, 'especially as he walked downstairs. He carried a stick. After Scott and he had ended their conversation in the drawing-room, it was a curious sight to see the two greatest poets of the age – both lame – stumping downstairs side by side.'[20] If that sounds a little too polished a reminiscence from a very old man, there is a note by John Murray III in the archive: '1815/April 7 W Scott & Ld Byron met first at No 50 Albemarle St & were introduced to each other by JM. They conversed together 2 hours.'[21]

Scott and Byron had presents for each other: a Turkish dagger for Byron, an urn full of Greek bones for Scott. Murray had a case made for the urn of bones. Scott found Byron mild compared to his reputation: Byron had insulted Scott in *English Bards*, but that was forgotten. Scott, who referred to the Albemarle Street salon as his 'four o'clock friends',[22] was now metamorphosing into a novelist. 'Pray read *Waverley* which is excellent,' Murray had written to Annie on 22 August 1814, a month after it had been published anonymously. Byron and Scott 'continued to meet in Albemarle Street nearly every day', John Murray III assured Smiles years later, 'and remained together for two or three hours at a time'.[23]

A less rosy picture of the Albemarle Street atmosphere is painted by James Hogg, the Scots countryman poet and novelist who was known as 'the Ettrick Shepherd' because he had once tended sheep in the Ettrick Forest in the Scottish lowlands. Murray, who was now publishing Hogg, travelled to Edinburgh where he met the poet with Scott. Hogg was not seduced:

> The only time that ever his [Scott's] conversation was to me perfectly uninteresting was with Mr Murray of Albemarle Street London. Their whole conversation was about Noblemen Parliamenters and literary men of all grades every one of which Murray seemed to know with all their characters and propensities which information Sir Walter seemed to drink in with the same zest as I did his highland whisky toddy. And this discourse they carried on for two days and two nights with the intermission only of a few sleeping hours and there I sat beside them the whole time like a stump and never got in a word. I wish I had the same chance again.[24]

9

A civil rogue

THE GLORIOUS REPUTATION of being Byron's publisher soon began to bring its obligations. By the time of Waterloo, everyone wanted to be published by Murray. As Smiles puts it, he was 'inundated with poems and novels from all parts of the country'.[1] An early 'hopeful' to approach 50 Albemarle Street was a forty-year-old unmarried parson's daughter from Hampshire, whose novels of middle-class life were beginning to build up a cult following: the Prince Regent was reliably said to be among her admirers. So far, however, she had not been lucky in her publisher.

Sense and Sensibility was published in 1811 by Egerton's of Whitehall, who printed it very badly at the anonymous author's own expense. It sold out and was reprinted, and the author pocketed a modest profit. *Pride and Prejudice* (1813) was a huge success, but *Mansfield Park* (1814) a comparative failure commercially: Egerton postponed the second edition. Meanwhile Jane Austen pressed ahead with her next novel, which she decided to offer to Murray. The manuscript of *Emma* arrived at Albemarle Street in the early autumn of 1815, and it could easily have been rejected out of hand, or even lost. Smiles records that Murray and his staff could hardly cope with the unsolicited flood. However, Miss Austen's reputation was big enough for her to get special treatment, and *Emma* was immediately redirected to Murray's oracle. Gifford had been asked to assess Miss Austen's commercial potential, and he began with *Pride and Prejudice*, which he had never read. He was impressed by its avoidance of the Gothick: 'No dark passages, no secret chambers, no wind howling in long galleries, no drops of blood upon a rusty dagger,' he reported.[2] Indeed no; Miss Austen had already satirised such things in *Northanger Abbey*, completed in 1803, but still unpublished. Gifford's task was to report on the new novel. 'Of *Emma*, I have nothing but good to say,' he told Murray. The manuscript had a few errors and infelicities of expression which he offered to deal with: 'I will readily undertake the revision.'[3] When the time came, Jane Austen, of course, would not let him do any such thing.

Acting as his sister's literary agent, the banker Henry Austen began negotiations with Murray to rescue Jane from Egerton. Murray's first offer seemed inadequate to the Austens. 'The Terms you offer are so very inferior to what we had expected,' Henry Austen told Murray. 'The Sum offered by you for the Copyright of Sense & Sensibility, Mansfield Park & Emma, is not equal to the Money which my Sister has actually cleared by one very moderate Edition of Mansfield Park.'[4] Jane, writing to her sister Cassandra, names the sum Murray had offered, £450, and comments: 'he is a Rogue of course, but a civil one'.[5] Murray, of course, had no notion that he was bidding for an author whose popularity and sales would eventually become even greater than Byron's. He followed his father's policy and kept his distance from novels as a publisher, although as a reader he loved them. His catalogue for February 1815 included what was in effect one specimen of the genre, *The Journal of Llewellin Penrose, a Seaman*, but this was advertised as non-fiction.[6] It was the work of John Eagles, landscape painter, critic and author, who claimed to have based it on the reminiscences of a Welsh sailor, William Williams. John Hookham Frere thought it almost as good as *Robinson Crusoe*, and Byron, to whom Murray lent the manuscript, said it had kept him awake until the small hours: 'I never read so much of a book at one sitting in my life.' The 1815 list also included poetry – Murray may have been hoping he would stumble across another Byron, but the next catalogue (no date, but 1816) featured *Emma* on the front page, and advertised no other novels. Jane Austen, on account of her growing reputation, was being given very special treatment.

On 3 November Jane wrote to Murray, reminding him that the manuscript of *Emma* was still in his hands, and suggested that he call on her at her brother's house in Hans Place in the hope that they might come to a decision. An important point emerges from this:

she is inviting *him* to call, like the tradesman she considered him to be.[7] We do not know exactly what passed between Murray and the Austens, but it was evidently agreed that Murray would publish *Emma* on commission. This meant Jane Austen would bear the financial risk of publication, but would pocket the profits, less a 10 per cent commission for Murray, if the book was a success. Much the same arrangement had been made with Egerton, but the difference was that she trusted Murray to make a better job of printing and advertising.

So Jane Austen's *Emma* went ahead as a Murray book. It was typeset at lightning speed, with a different team of compositors handling each of its three volumes. Even so, in a letter of 23 November 1815, Jane expresses her irritation at delays in her clear, expressive handwriting:

> Sir,
>
> My Brother's note last Monday has been so fruitless, that I am afraid that there can be little chance of my writing to any good effect; but yet I am so very much disappointed & vexed by the delay of the Printers that I cannot help begging to know whether there is no hope of their being quickened. – Instead of the Work being ready by the end of the present month, it will hardly, at the rate we now proceed, be finished by the end of the next, and as I expect to leave London early in Decr, it is of consequence that no more time should be lost. – Is it likely that the Printers will be influenced to greater Dispatch & Punctuality by knowing that the work is to be dedicated, by Permission, to the Prince Regent? – If you can make that circumstance operate, I shall be very glad. – My Brother returns *Waterloo* with many thanks for the Loan of it. – We have heard much of Scott's account of Paris; – if it be not incompatible with other arrangements, would you favour us with it – supposing you have any set already opened? – You may depend upon its being in careful hands.[8]

Murray knew how to flatter his latest author by lending her and her brother the pick of his current books. Jane told Cassandra that Murray was now being overwhelmingly polite: there were delays with *Emma*, but he explained that the printers had been short of paper, and the supplier had promised that there would be no further hold-ups. Murray also arranged for the proofs to be delivered directly to and from the printers, Roworth's of Temple Bar, who were handling volumes one and two, and J. Mayes of Hatton Garden, volume three. This was to save the Austens from having to bring the proofs back to Albemarle Street. 'In short,' wrote Jane, who was proofreading all three volumes, 'I am soothed & complimented into tolerable comfort.'[9]

The second of the two letters from Jane Austen that survive in the John Murray Archive, dated 11 December 1815, deals with the business of dedicating *Emma* to the Prince Regent. Jane had been encouraged to do this by the Prince's librarian, the Rev. James Stanier Clarke, whose letters recall those of the obsequious Mr Collins in *Pride and Prejudice*, and who had the presumption to suggest that a character much like himself should be the hero of Jane Austen's next novel. In her letter Jane asks that the royal dedication should appear on the title page, and requests Murray to send the three volumes to the Prince Regent, by way of Clarke at Carlton House, ahead of publication. This was to take place on Saturday 16 December. Murray did this, and more: he had the royal copy bound in morocco leather, at the author's expense, and put the dedication on a page to itself as was the custom. Austen was embarrassed at her ignorance of protocol; she said she had never noticed the proper place for dedications. In the event, nothing came of this approach to royalty; no financial reward, no social preferment. Murray may have been cynical about the dedication from the outset. He had already expressed his opinion of the Prince Regent in a letter to Byron written from Brighton a few years earlier: 'The Prince Regent's appearance or behaviour either prevented from coming or drove away from the Place – all respectable people – he was more outrageously dissipated the short time he was here than ever – & has sunk into the vilest of his former associates.'[10]

Austen sent Murray a list of friends and family to whom she wished to give complimentary sets of *Emma*: about two dozen in all. One set went to the British Museum, which acquired all published books by law, free of charge, as the British Library does now. Meanwhile Murray put the novel on sale to the trade, reducing the price as usual. Longman's responded enthusiastically, and took fifty copies, but the smaller firms were cautious, averaging half a dozen each. Meanwhile Murray spent a lavish £50 on advertising the book.

Emma was in the shops just in time for Christmas 1816 – publication date was given as 1816, which was standard practice. At first it looked as if it was going to be a bestseller: Murray broke his rule of not puffing his own books in the *Quarterly Review*, and suggested that Walter Scott might like to write a piece about it. Scott responded magnificently with an article in the autumn issue of the *Review*. He did not name Austen, since she had never yet been identified on a title page, but said that *Sense and Sensibility* and *Pride and Prejudice* had been recognised by the reading public as far superior to the usual novels, 'the ephemeral productions which supply the regular demand of watering-places and circulating libraries'.[11] Scott identified Austen as one of the innovators who was turning her back on sensationalism and portraying the 'middling classes' as they really were: 'keeping close to common incidents . . . she has produced sketches of . . . spirit and originality . . . In this class she stands almost alone.'[12] Murray sent Scott's review to Austen, who was pleased, but nonetheless regretted that there was no mention of *Mansfield Park*, soon to be published by Murray in a second edition. She reported to him, with some amusement, that the Prince Regent had described the book as 'handsome', a compliment to the publisher rather than the author.[13]

As the excitement of publication died down, it became apparent that *Emma* was not going to be Austen's commercial breakthrough. Murray had had two thousand copies printed, but after twelve months only 1,248 had been sold. This was enough to put the book into profit, but, when the loss sustained by the Murray edition of *Mansfield Park* was set against it, it resulted in a net earning for Austen of only £38 18s 1d. A cheque for this amount was sent to her in October 1816, nearly a year after publication. This was the firm's general practice: Murray's promissory notes, that is his cheques in payment to authors, were variously dated three, six and twelve months after publication. Murray's clerk misspelt her name, and when she endorsed the cheque on the back she felt obliged to repeat the mistake, to make it conform: 'Jane Austin'.

Jane Austen was finally named as the author of her books when Murray published *Northanger Abbey* and *Persuasion* as a single four-volume title in 1818. But by then she was dead. 'I am printing two short, but very clever Novels – by poor Miss Austen – the author of Pride & Prejudice,' Murray wrote to Lady Abercorn.[14] *Persuasion* paid Murray the pretty compliment of giving its heroine the maiden name of his wife, Anne Elliot. Ironically, sales picked up, and in February 1819 Murray was able to tell Cassandra Austen that £500 had accrued for Jane's estate. Twelve years later, he asked if Cassandra would sell the copyrights of all her sister's novels. Cassandra refused, but agreed that, with Egerton dead, it was time for new editions. However, Murray did not publish these, and another forty years would pass before the full-scale Jane Austen cult began.

If there had ever been a Coleridge cult it was well and truly over by the time the poet approached Murray with a thinly disguised plea for help in 1812. Samuel Taylor Coleridge was just turning forty, but he could already be described as a burnt-out case. It was fourteen years since his revolutionary verse-tale about the albatross and its unfortunate murderer had opened the Wordsworth–Coleridge *Lyrical Ballads*, and sadly the Ancient Mariner's tale had proved to be a prelude not to popular literary success, but to a life scarred by drug addiction. Coleridge's other masterpiece, 'Kubla Khan', remained unpublished. Coleridge called often at 50 Albemarle Street, but always being told that Murray was out he wrote a letter proposing the sort of book that causes publishers to take fright: a collection of his favourite epigrams from German, Spanish and Italian literature. As Coleridge put it to Murray:

> I wish to have *your* opinion concerning the *physiognomy* of a Work, which Mr Mason Good and one or two other literati think promising. In the huge cumulus of my Memorandum & common place Books I have at least two respectable Volumes, the nature of the Contents of which I can perhaps convey to you in part by the proposed title-page:

'*Exotics naturalized*, ie impressive Sentiments, Reflections, Aphorisms, Anecdotes, Epigrams, short Tales and eminently beautiful passages from German, Spanish and Italian works . . . Collected, translated and arranged by S. T. Coleridge.'

. . . I dare venture to say, that it will be one of the most *entertaining* Books in our Language.'[15]

Murray, of course, ducked it, and for a couple of years Coleridge left him alone. Then in August 1814 he was back, saying that Charles Lamb had told him that Murray was looking for an English verse translation of Goethe's *Faust*, although in fact he hoped that Murray would take him over altogether, and relaunch him as another Byron.[16] To Coleridge's mortification, Murray offered a mere £100 for *Faust*: 'humiliatingly low', moaned Coleridge.[17] Although he accepted reluctantly, the job was never done.

A further year passed, until Coleridge swallowed yet more pride and made an approach to Murray via Byron, who had sneered at the older poet in *English Bards and Scotch Reviewers*:

> Shall gentle COLERIDGE pass unnoticed here,
> To turgid ode and tumid stanza dear?'[18]

Byron could now afford to be more generous. Although he judged 'Kubla Khan' to be meaningless word-music, Byron liked what he saw and heard, and encouraged Murray to publish Coleridge. Murray responded warily – 'Coleridge is . . . fanciful & will make much talk'[19] – and sure enough, the moment he began to show interest, Coleridge flooded Murray with ideas. There should be a magazine reviewing *old* books; the *Quarterly Review* should publish a series of articles by Coleridge; Murray should issue a Collected Coleridge; and so on, and so on, till Murray grumbled in dog-Latin that Coleridge was '*Summum Borium*', the greatest of bores.[20] Meanwhile Murray paid Coleridge some very modest sums, including £20 for non-exclusive rights to 'Kubla Khan', which duly appeared in *Christabel and Other Poems* during 1816.

Initially, it looked as if Murray had a Coleridge revival on his hands. The first edition of 1,500 copies sold out, and second and third editions followed swiftly. But the book was savaged in the

Edinburgh Review where it was described as 'utterly destitute in value', and that 'not one couplet was real poetry'.[21] The *Quarterly Review* ignored it altogether, and sales languished. Murray thereafter took no further interest in Coleridge, with one curious exception: he commissioned a portrait of him from Thomas Phillips, and it still hangs among other portraits of the literati of Byron's day in one of the Albemarle Street drawing rooms. It shows Coleridge looking content and prosperous, fleshy if not actually fat, and not at all like a victim of laudanum and other forms of opium. Did Murray guess that posterity would put Coleridge in the literary pantheon? Did he have a sneaking suspicion that 'Kubla Khan' would one day be seen as a *sine qua non* of the Romantic movement?

Murray was exceedingly careful to ensure that his letters to authors were absolutely clear. One of his hopeful authors in 1815 was the Rev. William Beloe, a one-time librarian at the British Museum who nine years earlier had been sacked for carelessly allowing a thief to ingratiate himself and steal dozens of prints from the Reading Room.[22] 'It is a rule with me,' Murray told him, 'from which I never deviate, to arrange finally the terms of every engagement before I make any payment.' Even though John Murray had only one eye, he would not let anybody get away with pulling the wool over it. His contract with the inventor and engineer James Watt was as precise as Watt's own engineering drawings:

> I inclose my notes at 12, 18 & 24 mos. from this date amounting in all the sum of Five Hundred Pounds for the entire and perpetual Copyright of the System of Mechanical Philosophy consisting of the article written by Professor Robison in the Encyclopaedia Britannica & in the supplement thereto & for the MSS of the continuation of the Elements of Mechanical Philosophy the first part of which was formerly published and I promise further to pay the sum of Three Hundred Pounds at Six, Twelve and Eighteen Months date from the day on which I shall publish a second Edition of the works above specified, making in all with the bills I now inclose 500£ and three other Bills for 100£ each ... making in all the sum of Eight Hundred

Pounds for the intire and perpetual Copyright of the works & notes above enumerated.'[23]

Working with such a shrewd and realistic man as James Watt must have been a pleasure compared to trying to make arrangements with with an author as tricky as Madame de Staël, whose son, Baron de Staël, offered terms for a novel which Murray found easy to refuse: 'You are not aware I fancy', Murray told him,

> of the great changes which have taken place in the sale of every thing in the country which is operating to the destruction of speculations of any kind ... One Thousand Pounds for one edition of the work in French and one in English, we paying the translation, each to consist of fifteen hundred copies ... You have no conception of the total alteration since we have had the opportunity of emigrating to Foreign Countries, and I could not have made you this slender offer unless Messr Longman had agreed to take half the risque.'[24]

Nearly five years on from moving to Albemarle Street, Murray's business was developing a firm commercial foundation, with a constantly growing network of customers. But it was not long before the flaws in the deal that he had struck with Miller when he purchased number 50 became clear. Murray spoke his mind to Miller in August 1813:

> Your Good Will and Business for which I paid so liberal a sum comprised all your customers generally and particularly with such exceptions only as were either specified in our contract or mutually agreed upon afterwards ... The fact is – Miller – I have never received from you any one act of friendship since I purchased your house, where you appeared to leave me to my fate, never entering the door, as was remarked even by the common porter in my shop, except for your own service. Your Good will has never produced me an Hundred pounds – & the books, which you said 'were you upon our deathbed, as my friend, you would advise me to take of you' will prove a considerable loss. There are heavy disadvantages and such as must have prevented me, were it not for my own connexions and ulterior views, *forever* from realizing even your kind, but scanty wish, 'every prosperity which I could *reasonably* look for.'[25]

Nevertheless, business was, in general, going well. At Midsummer 1812 Murray sent out invoices to twenty-four country booksellers; five years later his clerk had to despatch accounts to fifty-seven booksellers, including seven in Ireland – Dublin, Waterford and Cork.[26] Occupying the prominent position in London literary and social life that he did, Murray found himself at risk of being drawn into dealings that would be against his own interest. He acted quickly and firmly when an arrangement entirely unsuited to his business was proposed by the Scottish social reformer Robert Owen:

> As it is totally inconsistent with my plans to allow my name to be associated with any subject of so much political notoriety & debate as your New System of Society – I trust that you will not consider it as any diminution of personal regard if I request the favour to cause my name to be immediately struck out from every sort of advertisement that is likely to appear upon this subject. I trust that a moments reflection will convince you of the utter impropriety of my receiving the Books of registery which I understand you talked of sending to my house.'[27]

Given the extreme care Murray took in making his business arrangements, it is puzzling that he spent a fortune on George Crabbe. Murray's involvement with Crabbe began, rather than ended, with a portrait. Crabbe had been popular for years, with his old-fashioned moral tales in rhyming couplets about the lives and tragedies of working people, firmly based on experience. Crabbe had had a dual career as a physician and a parson, and had spent his early years at Aldeburgh in Suffolk. His stories included the misadventures of Peter Grimes, fisherman and boy-murderer, and the tragic tale of Ellen Orford. By the time of Waterloo, Crabbe was in his sixties, and one of yesterday's men in the literary world. Thus he was surprised to find himself taken up by the fashionable publisher of Byron. While he was in London in 1817, Crabbe wrote to a friend:

> Among other claims upon me, was one of Mr Murrays to whom tho' we have no other Connection, I engaged to sit for my Picture & Mr Phillips a painter well-known (in George Street Hanover Square) has

succeeded in taking not only a good Likeness but he has also made an excellent picture. It is intended for Mr Murray Albemarle Street & will soon be taken thither & placed with those of Mr Scott, Lord Byron, Campbell, Rogers etc.'[28]

The portrait, which hangs in 50 Albemarle Street near Coleridge, shows Crabbe with his hands nervously clasped. He was by now vicar of Trowbridge, Wiltshire, where he cultivated the manner of a countryman who cannot quite cope with city life. His notebooks, preserved in the Murray Archive, are full of pressed wildflowers, and there is even a dragonfly which has survived almost intact. Crabbe liked to reminisce about how he had been nearly destitute when trying to make a living as a young writer. His understanding of the book business, however, was far from naive: he had been published by Hatchard's, but felt that they did not promote his books properly. As a consequence of the portrait, his eye was on Murray, to whom he wrote: 'I confess that I should love to have my books presented to the public in an advantageous and respectable manner.'[29]

He had a new book on the stocks, *Tales of the Hall*, a country-house *Arabian Nights*, with stories-in-verse in his old manner. This was a book that the previous generation might have snapped up, but no one was going to go wild over it in this era of Regency sophis-tication. So why did Murray offer Crabbe an advance far bigger than any paid to Byron? Crabbe was so astonished that he did not dare to mention the sum that Murray had named to him: a letter to Murray refers coyly to 'the Day in which I accepted the offer you did me the Honour to make me'.[30] The amount was no less than £3,000. It was to include all Crabbe's copyrights, but even so Sydney Smith alleged that the sum was too vast for Crabbe to comprehend: 'All sums beyond a hundred pounds must be to him mere indistinct vision – clouds and darkness.'[31] It became reality when, in June 1819, the contract was signed and Crabbe received three promissory notes of £1,000, to be paid in six months. 'He was in a high state of excite-ment,' writes his biographer Neville Blackburne, 'refusing all efforts to part him from this tangible evidence of his worth.' Friends urged him to bank his notes, 'but he set off for Trowbridge still clutching them'.[32]

Tales of the Hall got some good reviews, but after the initial rush sales dried up. The ledgers in the Murray Archive do not tell the story clearly. There is a tangle of sales figures, confused by the inclusion of copies taken over from Hatchard's, but there is no escaping the grim numerals '£3000'. Clearly a black hole has appeared in Murray's accounts.

'Tell me if Mrs Leigh & your Lordship admire *Emma*?' Murray asked Byron at Christmas 1815. He had sent copies to Byron, who does not seem to have read it,[33] to Caroline Lamb, and to Byron's half-sister Augusta Leigh.[34] (Augusta was the daughter of Byron's father's first wife; she and Byron had been brought up apart.) Murray was probably not aware of Byron's incestuous relationship with Augusta, conducted in her marital home near Newmarket, while her husband went to the races. 'I hope that Mrs Leigh & the family are well,' wrote Murray, while Byron was staying there.[35] Murray regularly supplied Byron with the books and journals he wanted. Indeed, so much of his time was taken up with attending to Byron's needs that other Murray authors sometimes felt they were lacking his attention. 'I have had such a letter from Mrs Rundell – accusing me of neglecting her book,' Murray wrote to his wife in September 1814, adding of the cookery writer: 'her conceit surpasses any thing'.[36] Rundell's letter has not survived,[37] but it is evident that Murray, perhaps tactlessly, tried to keep her sweet by sending her the latest Byron books. The *Childe Harold* triumph of spring 1812 had been followed by more bestsellers. These were poems which only committed Byronists read nowadays, but which caused hysteria in their day. Murray's ledger shows that *The Giaour*, a title that nobody then knew how to pronounce, and cannot still, made him a profit of £1,256. *The Corsair* made a further £3,660, almost enough to buy 50 Albemarle Street all over again. 'I sold on the Day of Publication, a thing perfectly unprecedented, 10,000 copies,' Murray told Byron of *The Corsair*, 'and I suppose Thirty People who were purchasers (strangers) called to tell the people in the Shop how much they had been delighted & satisfied.'[38] A week later he told Byron: 'You can not meet a man in the Street – who has not read or heard read the Corsair.'[39]

Although there was still a shop on the ground floor of 50 Albemarle Street, Murray no longer saw himself chiefly as a bookseller. By 1816 he was signing himself to Byron: 'Your faithful Publisher'.[40] He spoke proudly of 'my Authors',[41] and assured Byron that it was always open house for them at Albemarle Street: 'I am *At Home* – for the remainder of the Season & until the termination of All Seasons.'[42] Byron, meanwhile, contributed to Murray's change of role by learning to accept comments from the man he had treated as a tradesman. He told Murray, when *The Giaour*, a tale of passion set in Turkey, was being prepared for a second edition: 'as you will see I have attended to your Criticism & softened a passage you proscribed this morning'.[43] Murray called the revisions 'admirable'.[44]

Murray's changing position in the book business was accompanied by increased social status. Byron now signed his letters to him 'Ever yrs, B'. He even began to allow that Murray was a busy man, with many other calls on his time. 'I shall be very glad to hear from you or of you when you please,' Byron wrote almost humbly, 'but don't put yourself out of your way on my account.'[45] A real trust had grown up between them. Byron, who was still doubtful about earning cash from authorship, suggested that Murray should delay in making him a financial offer for another Turkish melodrama, *The Bride of Abydos*, until it had been published. They could see how it had sold. On his side Murray was keen to pay generously and without delay £1,000 for *The Bride*, *The Giaour* (for which he had already paid once) and a group of miscellaneous poems. He congratulated Byron on the size of this copyright payment, which he claimed was even more than Walter Scott had been offered. This was not so: twice as much had been paid for *The Lady of the Lake*. Byron refused to be bullied. 'It is too much, though I am strongly tempted,' he wrote in his journal.[46] Murray's later lavish payment to George Crabbe, seen in the light of this argument with Byron, now begins to look like showing off to the literary world that he can afford to pay an author £3,000.

Murray was distressed when, in December 1813, a row broke out between him and Dallas. The latter, alleging that he needed cash to support his soldier nephew, claimed that Murray owed him money for the later editions of *Childe Harold*. Murray's refusal to pay up led

Dallas to complain to Byron, who told Dallas he could not only have the copyright of his next poem, *The Corsair*, but could take it to another publisher where he would very likely get more money. Murray felt crushed by this disloyalty, and it was now that he wrote the passionate letter in which he averred that his whole faith in human nature had been toppled: 'If you really meant to give the Stab you gave to my feelings, may God harden my heart against man, for never, never will I attach myself to another.'[47] Dallas was contemptuous of this letter, which was indeed more characteristic of Caroline Lamb than of the entrepreneurial publisher of Albemarle Street. But it certainly worked with Byron, who told Dallas they must stick with Murray and did his best to soothe Murray's feelings.

The next instance of conflict was over politics. Just before publication of *The Corsair*, another Turkish story, with pirates, Byron asked Murray to add to the book his short poem 'Lines to a Lady Weeping'. First published anonymously in a newspaper two years earlier, the poem describes the Prince Regent's daughter regarding her father with disgust:

> Weep daughter of a royal line,
> A Sire's disgrace, a realm's decay.

Byron was now prepared to identify himself as its author, but Murray, anxious that it would 'disturb the political feeling' – in other words, offend his Tory friends – suggested that Byron slip it among the miscellaneous poems in the next edition of *Childe Harold* where nobody would pay it much attention. '[It] does not accord with your character.'[48] Byron refused to make the change. 'I care nothing for consequences,' he told Murray, adding that he himself could not '*torify* my nature'.[49]

There followed a fine farce, with Murray-the-Tory deciding to remove the offending poem from *The Corsair* and tuck it out of sight in the reprinted *Childe Harold*, and Murray-the-businessman putting it back into *The Corsair*,[50] and enjoying the lengthy attacks on Byron in the Tory press. He did not actually say to Byron 'All publicity is good publicity,' but the thought must have crossed his mind. What he did admit to Byron was, 'My *sordid* propensities got the better of me,' adding that he was convinced that *Childe Harold* was 'certain of becoming a Classic'. [51]

Byron was furious with Murray for attempting to censor him: 'You have played the Devil – by that injudicious *suppression* – which you did totally without my consent.'[52] He was also upset that printers' errors were not being corrected in the heat of reprinting. It was in this context that misunderstandings started to develop between Murray and Byron about money, made worse by the intervention of the poisonous Dallas. Not surprisingly, there began to be disagreements about exactly what had been paid for and what had not. Byron made suspicious noises to Murray, who responded by suggesting that it was unworthy of his Lordship to interest himself in such things. Just when they should have been celebrating the great success of *The Corsair*, things turned sour. But after a few days Byron poured cider on troubled waters, offering Murray a hogshead of it, fresh from Worcestershire. The offer was accepted gracefully.[53]

Byron was now playing with Murray's feelings, as he habitually did with his lovers. He announced to Murray that he was giving up poetry, and told him to stop advertising and destroy all remaining copies of his books. Murray objected, of course: he would 'go to the worlds end' to serve Byron, so why did his Lordship want to cause him 'so much misery of Mind'?[54] Having achieved this desired effect, Byron backed off, telling Murray it was business as usual, and promising that one day he would explain why he had behaved like that. He never did.

When in April 1814 news came that the Napoleonic Wars were over, Murray passed it on to Byron: 'Buonaparte has either solicited or accepted a retirement upon a *Pension* in the Island of Elba – He has formally abdicated . . . Boulogne is opened . . . A Fine Subject for an Epic,' he suggested to Byron, who obliged with an ode on the downfall of Napoleon.[55] Murray now had enough confidence to criticise Byron directly, rather than passing off his comments as Gifford's: 'the closing lines are not good . . . I think any degrading notice of Kings should not be in a poem which will otherwise find universal admirers.'[56] Byron meekly did as he was asked. 'All your alterations appear to me great improvements,' Murray told him.[57]

By the time of *Lara* (1814), the last of his Turkish tales, Byron was flattering Murray about his literary abilities, passing on a compliment from Augusta: 'I have just read to her a sentence from your epistle – and her remark was "how *well* he writes" – so you see – you may set up as Author in person whenever you please.'[58] He encouraged Murray to visit him at Newstead, his family seat, though when Murray called in October 1814 Byron was absent. Murray was disappointed in the place. 'My notions had been raised to the romantic,' he told Annie, but the building was 'now fast crumbling to dust'. Moreover 'Lord B's immediate predecessor stripped the whole place of all that was splendid or interesting.'[59]

This letter to Annie comes at the end of a fascinating series written when she and Murray were separated for two months. She had taken the children to her family in Edinburgh, and John intended to profit from his temporary bachelor state by going to Paris with Isaac D'Israeli, France now being 'open' following the fall of Napoleon. In the event, he never got further than Brighton. Whereas his father would probably have frolicked with some ladies of the town, or at least had a few six-bottle evenings, the younger John Murray led an exemplary life. He seemed scarcely to know how to enjoy himself, and was the victim of a debilitating ennui which lay just beneath the surface of this ambitious businessman.

'Did you leave me any *Tea* – & where is the Key of the Sugar?'[60] a somewhat petulant Murray asks his absent wife. One of the children has walked off with his penknife; he does not know how much to pay the cook while the family is away; he is sleeping badly, kept awake by riotous noise from Green Park; he is anxious that Isaac D'Israeli will prove an irritating travelling companion. Moreover, if he leaves for Paris after staying with the D'Israelis in Brighton, it will mean a fourteen-hour crossing to Dieppe, as opposed to a mere three hours from Dover to Calais. He wishes he was going to Scotland instead; in fact he wishes he was going nowhere. He cannot cope with packing: 'I have hardly yet begun to prepare a single thing & I don't know how to set about it – my mind is overgrown with weeds & I have not courage to pluck them out.'[61]

His body is bothering him too. 'I have got a complaint in my bowels which troubles me a good deal and induces me to keep the house but Dr Black thinks it is nothing.'[62] He has been reading 'all the Novels of tolerable reputation that I could lay hold of.' Meanwhile Annie has been proposing that young John should eventually go to boarding school in Scotland. Murray is against it, on the grounds that he will pick up a Scottish accent, an indication of how English the Murrays had become in only two generations, though presumably Annie spoke with an Edinburgh accent.

As the days pass without his wife, Murray begins to sink into lethargy and self-pity: 'I am really a sad Landlord for any one to live with & I have neither society amusement or good nature to render them comfortable – being absolutely an unsociable & outrageous being.'[63] However, he is finally starting to pack for Paris, via Brighton, or at least he has asked for his suitcases to be set out, so he can choose which to take. He now thinks that Paris 'will be the essential & perhaps only thing to rouse me from the lethargy into which "thy cruel absence" has plunged me'.[64]

Eventually he gets to Brighton, putting up in the Ship Inn, because the D'Israelis' rented holiday house is full. 'I have now finally settled not to go to France.'[65] He is still having bowel trouble, and the Brighton lifestyle soon begins to pall: 'we . . . do nothing but lounge about'.[66] A week of the place is more than enough for him, and he heads back to Albemarle Street. The plan is to go on to Scotland to rejoin the family, but 'I must set all my machinery at work for my winters market before I leave town.'[67] To his bowel trouble Murray has now added a bad cold, plus an inflamed nostril, 'from my indiscretion in extracting a Hair'.[68] And Byron is back in town.

More than that, Byron has summoned Murray to impart some astonishing news. Murray reports it to Annie as if it were a play.

'Can you keep a secret?' Byron asked Murray.
'Certainly – positively – my wife's out of town,' Murray joked
  edgily.
'Then – I am going to be *married*!!!'

Murray's response was quick and witty: 'The devil! I shall have no poem this winter, then?'

'No,' answered Byron.
'Who is the lady, then, who is to do me this injury?'
'Miss Milbanke, do you know her?'
'No, my Lord,' admitted Murray.

Byron looked satisfied. 'So here is news for your Mrs,' he told Murray complacently.

Murray's comment to Annie was: 'I fancy the lady is rich, noble & beautiful – but this shall be my days business to enquire.'[69] Byron had confided in Murray as if they were social equals, and Murray added to Annie that Byron anticipated trouble from Caroline Lamb, whom he described as 'the fiend who interrupted all his projects – & who would do so now if possible'.[70] In fact the marriage to Annabella Milbanke was to unravel speedily without Caro's assistance. Caro had been quite calm when she heard he was betrothed, and had written to Murray: 'I trust in God Byron will be most happy – he has chosen one who is good & sensible & who deserves well of him – it is his best chance of keeping clear of all that has too often led him astray.'[71]

He was marrying Annabella in the hope of persuading a gossiping nation that he was innocent of incest. Yet he was soon writing *Parisina*, a verse-tale of incestuous love. It is proof of the honesty that now existed between Byron and Murray that the latter admitted to being sexually aroused by his first reading of it: 'I tore open the packet you sent me and have found in it a Pearl – I am really writing to you before the billows of the passions you have excited are subsided.'[72] Murray offered Byron a thousand guineas for *Parisina* and another new poem, *The Siege of Corinth*. As usual, Byron declined, but he liked the suggestion made by Sir James Mackintosh that he should take the money and give it to the penurious William Godwin, whom he admired. Murray was furious:

> Your Lordship will pardon me if I cannot avoid looking upon it as a species of cruelty . . . to take from me so large a sum – offered with no reference to the marketable value of the poems, but out of personal

friendship and gratitude alone – to cast it away ... upon persons who have so little claim. . . It is actually heartbreaking to throw away my earnings on others. I am no rich man. . . but [am] working hard for independence.[73]

Byron was equally angry, and withdrew the poems from Murray. Eventually they were reconciled, and the two poems were published in February 1816. 'You are a Strange Man,' Murray wrote cheekily to Byron, adding: 'I write with the Room full – & hope you will excuse my haste & impudence.'[74] By this time, Annabella had gone back to her parents, the marriage was rapidly over, and Byron was reassuring Murray that it was better that way: 'You need not be in any apprehension or grief on my account.'[75] But the failure of the marriage, which, said some, was the consequence of Byron's prefer- ence for anal sex,[76] had refuelled the gossip, and Byron had decided to escape it by resuming the foreign travels that he had broken off five years earlier. Among his preparations was the selling off, in April 1816, of many of his books. Murray bought a large number of them himself.

Some time during that month, Murray wrote his last extant letter to Byron in England. This he ended with an allusion to Byron's farewell lines to Annabella: 'Fare *Thee* well J. Murray'. Then Byron was gone, and poor Caroline Lamb, who still turned up from time to time at Albemarle Street, wrote Murray a predictably melancholy letter: 'My visit to your House today has made me miserable ... your room speaks of him in every part of it – and I never see you without pain – yet ... you have been a sincere upright and manly friend ... If ever you are grieved send for me – for I am yours in my heart and soul.'[77] But, as time passed, she dried her eyes. Indeed, she seemed to be transferring her affections to Murray. 'I wish', she told him, 'to know what yr plans are will you come to Paris with me for a fortnight?'

10

A certain poem

B Y THE TIME he received Caroline Lamb's invitation, John Murray had already been to Paris, having left England on 15 July 1815 and returning a fortnight later. His travelling companion was Isaac D'Israeli's wife's nephew, George Basevi, a quiet and sensible young architect. Annie Murray remained at home in Albemarle Street, looking after the business and the children, and naturally John wrote her a full account of what he saw on this trip, his first abroad.

It was a year later than he had intended, but by now the Battle of Waterloo had been won, and Napoleon was gone for good. Murray had the impression that the French were glad to see British tourists, though some of the local troops looked sullenly at their former enemies. He and Basevi crossed from Dover to Calais in only two and a half hours, and though they had both been seasick they immediately went sightseeing on arrival. For the first time in his life, Murray was able to inspect what he called 'the Superstitions of Catholicism', a church 'studded with Pictures & Carvings . . . of Saints, Christs, Virgins', and 'boxes for Auricular Confession', with 'the operation actually proceeding'. He and Basevi tried to hear what was being confessed, but were prevented from coming near enough.[1] To get them to Paris the pair hired for the equivalent of five pounds 'an ill looking Vehicle resembling an old-fashioned one Horse Chaise'. Despite trundling along at seven miles an hour, and only achieving that through 'bribes of Money and flattery', they reached Paris in less than three days, on account of the excellence of the roads. Murray was astonished by the vastness of the cornfields: 'I am sure that we saw more Corn during our way to Paris alone than is grown in the whole of England.'[2]

Renting rooms in the Hôtel des Etrangers in the Rue Vivan, they plunged into the inimitable life of the capital. 'Paris is certainly far more extraordinary – wonderful – than any description that I ever heard or read.' They felt like Gulliver's Lilliputians come to gaze at Brobdingnag. An early port of call was the Palais Royal, 'equal to which we have *nothing*', though its colonnade of shops reminded Murray a little of Covent Garden and Berkeley Square. They put their lives at risk merely by walking the streets, with 'every possible description of Vehicle tearing along so as to frighten one to death'. There was no pavement, and the traffic drove 'smack up to the Houses'. This may make Murray sound feeble, but a month earlier he had survived a mugging in the north London fields, on his way home after dining with the D'Israelis, when he was knocked down and robbed by two thugs. A lesser man might have used this as an excuse not to go to Paris. Murray kept running into London acquaintances in the streets of Paris. 'If one wishes to meet ones friends,' he informed Annie flamboyantly, 'Paris is the only Place.' And what did she make of his report that he and Basevi had visited one of the celebrated cafés chiefly to inspect its well-known 'beautiful Bar Maid', who did indeed prove to be 'very handsome'? And was she disturbed by his passing remark that at night the Palais Royal became 'the concentration & Sink of all that is dissipated'?[3] He assured her that on his next visit she would come too.

This was a business trip, and Murray introduced himself to the Paris bookseller Barrois, who invited him and Basevi to dinner, though Murray's grasp of French was hardly up to professional matters. Life became a merry round of visits to the opera and to expensive tourist restaurants, though they refused to be impressed by French cuisine. The Louvre was almost too much for Murray, who felt 'quite lost' amid the wealth of paintings.[4] As the two weeks drew to a close, his letters to Annie became filled with work concerns: money to be collected from creditors, arrangements to be made with printers, and he was glad to be going home. Nevertheless he told her that 'we propose to come again'.[5]

Murray might have recommended Paris to Byron, but when the poet left England the following spring he headed instead for Venice, via the Alps. At first, letters flew as frequently between publisher and poet as they had when no sea divided them. At the end of June 1816, Byron reported: 'I have finished a third Canto of Childe Harold ... in some parts – it may be – better.'[6] Murray asked a City businessman named Brown to collect it when passing through Switzerland, but in the end a copy was brought to England by Percy Bysshe Shelley, with whom Byron had been staying.[7]

Murray received the poem on 12 September 1816, and immediately took it to Gifford, in bed with jaundice, who read it delightedly at a sitting. Murray told Byron he proposed to pay 1,200 guineas for it, directly into Byron's bank account, this sum also to cover the purchase of the original manuscript 'with every scrap belonging to it'.[8] He had already begun to preserve Byron manuscripts, having them copied, sometimes by members of his family, rather than sending the original to the printer. When he had read the new canto himself, Murray increased his offer to 1,500 guineas, but Byron's friends pressured him to add another five hundred. Byron had written to Douglas Kinnaird:

> I believe Murray to be a good man with a personal regard for me. But a bargain is in its very essence a hostile transaction ... Do not all men try to abate the price of all they buy? – I contend that a bargain even between brethren – is a declaration of war ... I have no doubt that he would lend or give freely what he would refuse for value received in MSS.[9]

Murray did agree to the extra sum, but seems to have been nervous about paying so much, since he added to Byron: 'and now the Lord (Not you) have Mercy upon me'.[10]

Byron accepted the money, though he told the publisher that nothing would upset him more than Murray being out of pocket. However, poor sales of a Byron poem seemed unlikely, while by his own admission Murray was no longer haemorrhaging money over the *Quarterly Review*. 'My Review is improving in sales beyond my most sanguine expectations,' he told Byron in September 1816. 'I now sell nearly 9,000,' he boasted, adding that a friend 'says the Edinb Rev is going to the Devil'.[11] Half a year later, the circulation was still increasing: 'I printed 10,000 of the last Q. Rev & the Number of the next is 12,000.'[12]

As well as carrying such professional news, Murray's letters did their best to amuse Byron with anecdotes about mutual acquaintances: 'Mr Frere ... came to me whilst at breakfast this morning and between some Stanzas wch he was repeating to me of a truly Original Poem of his own – he said carelessly – by the way about *half an hour ago* I was so silly (taking an immense pinch of Snuff & priming his nostrils well with it) – as to get *Married*!!!'[13] Byron reciprocated confidentially, telling Murray that he had begun an affair in Venice with the pretty young wife of his landlord, a girl named Marianna. Murray the respectable family man was philosophical. 'You do what all so wish,' he told Byron, 'but want the *power* to do.'[14]

Canto III of *Childe Harold*, even more of an instant travelogue that its predecessors, appeared in the London shops on Monday 18 November 1816, followed on 5 December by Byron's *The Prisoner of Chillon and Other Poems*. Murray told Byron he had sold 'Five Thousand Pounds Worth of thy Poetry' at an Albion dinner,[15] but the literary world was now all a-buzz with the mystery of the authorship of a new anonymous Scottish novel, just published by Ballantyne. This was *The Black Dwarf* and was announced as the first volume of *Tales of my Landlord*. 'Every One is in Extacy about it,' reported Murray, who seems not to have realised that it was yet another product of Walter Scott. He believed at this stage that Scott's brother Thomas had written it; whereas Augusta Leigh became convinced that the mystery author was no less than Byron.[16]

Scott had written a highly complimentary review of *Childe Harold* Canto III in the *Quarterly Review* for October 1816, and Murray hoped that Byron might have the next canto ready for publication in the autumn. Byron replied that he had no plans to resume the Childe's travels at present. Murray was now really more interested in the cash value of Byron the celebrity than in publishing his latest poetry; he told him that if he would 'keep an exact Journal of all you see' there would be money in it: 'I will use nothing without your positive permission.'[17] If there was to be more poetry, let it be kiss and tell: 'a good Venetian Tale ... call it *Marianna*'.[18] Byron eventually bit on this one, though he called it *Beppo*.

Murray also recruited Byron as a talent scout for Albemarle Street: 'Pray if your Lordship stumble upon any curious MSS &c – think of me.'[19] In return, he acted as Byron's postman. Letters sent out to Venice through Customs in Venice and London often failed to reach Byron, who suspected that some over-zealous Whitehall clerk thought it his Tory duty to prevent the poet from receiving such necessities as his favourite red tooth powder. It became Murray's job to buy the tooth powder for Byron, and to find somebody going out to Venice who could take it. It was essential to wrap it in several layers, otherwise disaster would strike: on one occasion a friend reported that books and other packages for Byron from Murray had been received safely, 'except the damage they have sustain'd from being well powder'd with the red dust which you had intended for his Lordship's teeth'.[20]

Murray wrote his letters to Byron in the main drawing room at Albemarle Street, under the gaze of the 'straight' Thomas Phillips portrait of Byron. Unsolicited poetry was still pouring in. 'Shoals of MSS Poems,' Murray told Byron. 'Two three four a day – I require a Porter to carry – an Author to read – and a secretary to write about them.'[21] Among the books he did publish at this time was what purported to be Napoleon's autobiography, *Manuscrit venu de St Hélène d'une manière inconnue*, which arrived, apparently from Napoleon's place of exile, without explanation. Murray believed it to be genuine, or at least to be the work of one of Napoleon's henchmen, but it turned out to be a fake, cooked up by Jacob Frédéric Lullin de Chateauvieux, a friend of Madame de Staël. Nevertheless Murray's English translation, *Manuscript Transmitted from St Helena by an Unknown Channel*, went into several editions, prefaced with the sensible disclaimer that its genuineness was for the reader to judge. Napoleon himself is said to have been amused by it, though the style is disappointingly wooden. 'I might have gone to America,' the book concludes, 'but after having reigned over France, I could not think of debasing her throne by seeking glory elsewhere ... I have nothing now to defend but the reputation History is preparing for me.'[22]

Caroline Lamb was still haunting Albemarle Street, fondling the sword Byron had acquired from the Waterloo battlefield. 'Oh – I wish I could run it through his body,' she told Murray.[23] She had already assaulted Byron with words, writing a sensational novel, *Glenarvon*, about their affair,[24] just after Byron had gone abroad. Its eponymous hero is a shrewd and devastating portrait of the poet: 'So fair, so young and yet so utterly hardened and perverted'.[25] Murray must have been thankful that Glenarvon is not a professional poet but an Irish revolutionary leader, and consequently no publisher makes an appearance in Caroline's novel. Despite his famous expletive 'God damn!'[26] on reading *Glenarvon*, when the Italian translation of the novel was held up because the censor insisted on Byron's consent, Byron immediately obliged. He told Murray: 'I did not recognise the slightest relation between that book and myself – but ... *I* would never prevent or oppose the publication of *any* book in *any* language, on my own private account.'[27]

Yet there were now some unpleasant developments in the area of Byron and money. When Murray had received the first act of Byron's Alpine drama *Manfred*, he promised him 300 guineas for the whole play. Byron's attitude to literary earnings had now changed radically, chiefly thanks to the cost of foreign travel, and he started to bargain with Murray. He asked for 600 guineas for *Manfred* and another manuscript, *The Lament of Tasso*, telling the publisher: 'I won't take less than three hundred g[uinea]s for anything.'[28] In response, Murray wrote that the third act of *Manfred* did not seem to him and Gifford to be up to scratch. 'You must not publish any thing that will not set the town in flames now,' he warned.[29]

Byron realised that Murray was reading selected passages from his letters to the gatherings at Albemarle Street. Sending some satirical verse, which turned out to be an early fragment of *Don Juan*, he warned Murray: 'You may show these matters to [Thomas] Moore and the *select* – but not to the *prophane*.'[30] Rather later, Murray read out a letter in which Byron describes falling in the Grand Canal on his way to a tryst. Moore was shocked not just by Byron's sexual activities, but by the fact that Byron had told the story to somebody who was his social inferior: 'Murray, the bookseller – a person so out

of his [Byron's] caste & to whom he [Byron] writes formally, beginning "Dear Sir".'[31] Moore was far from being a member of Byron's
caste himself: his father had been a Dublin grocer. But he and Byron
had painted the town red together in the past, and had become close
friends. It may be that Moore, a five-foot-nothing sparrow of an Irish
Catholic with an outstanding poetic gift, was already lining himself
up to be Byron's biographer – though he was nine years older than
his friend, and there was no certainty that he would survive Byron.

The fourth Canto of *Childe Harold's Pilgrimage* was now delivered,
and Murray offered 1,500 guineas. 'I won't take it,' Byron answered.
'I ask two thousand five hundred guineas . . . if Mr Moore is to have
three thousand for Lallah.' This was indeed what Tom Moore had
just been promised by Longman's for his planned but not yet written
Lalla Rookh, what was to be an oriental romance in verse.[32] Byron
also pointed out that Murray still owed him money according to
previous agreements. Murray gave way, though he got *Beppo* into
the bargain, while protesting at the tone Byron was now beginning
to use with him, treating him 'as if I were your Taylor'.[33] He also
reported that *Manfred* was not popular with 'the general reader'
through lack of plot.[34] Meanwhile, reporting the activities of the
firm, Murray mentioned that he was publishing 'Two new Novels
left by Miss Austen – the ingenious Author of Pride & Prejudice –
who I am sorry to say died about 6 weeks ago'.[35] Byron reports in
July 1818 that he has a 'ludicrous' composition 'not yet finished – &
in no hurry to be so'.[36] This was the beginning of *Don Juan*. He is
also at work on his memoirs, which began as a proposed preface to
a planned collected edition of his works: 'some memoirs of my life
to prefix to them'.[37] Soon however they outgrew the original plan,
and Byron told Moore that he could publish them when he, Byron,
was 'cold'.[38]

Simultaneously, Murray wrote to ask Byron for something of
exactly this kind:

> May I hope that yr Lordship will favour me with some work to open
> my Campaign in November with – have you not another lively Tale
> like Beppo – or will you not give me some prose in three Volumes –
> all the adventures that you have undergone . . . with your reflections

on life & Manners – to tell me that I may at any rate expect something by the end of September.[39]

Unknown to Byron, Murray had already promised £500 to John Polidori, a young doctor who had been a member of Byron's entourage at the beginning of his European trip. This payment was an advance on the rights to the diary he would keep describing Byron's doings and behaviour.

Murray went to stay with Walter Scott at Abbotsford in the late summer of 1818. Scott had still not acknowledged authorship of his novels, though 'no one doubts' that they were his work.[40] Murray, who had taken a half-share in *Blackwood's* the previous month, sent Byron 'a number or two of Blackwoods Edinburgh Magazine ... I think that you will find in it a very great Share of talent & some most incomparable fun & as I have purchased half the Copy right of it I shall feel very much obliged if you would occasionally send me some anonymous (if you please) fun to add to it.'[41] Byron, however, had other ideas. On 24 September 1818 he told Murray: 'I have written the first Canto (180 octave stanzas) of a poem in the Style of Beppo.'[42] Writing to his close friend John Cam Hobhouse in London, Byron gave him some idea of what was in store for readers of *Don Juan*. The new poem would begin with 'a dedication in verse ... to Bob Southey ... The Son of a Bitch ... said that Shelley and I "had formed a League of Incest".'[43] Continuing to Murray, he wrote: 'I maintain that it is the most moral of poems – but if people won't discover the moral that is their fault not mine.'[44] Byron's language was beginning to get more hard-boiled; he now spoke of 'the bitch my wife'.[45]

Don Juan is Byron's masterpiece. Unlike most of his major poems it is totally accessible and enjoyable to present-day readers, and attempts to recapture the broad satirical comedy of earlier, less hypocritical ages. Although its events may be bawdy – the sixteen-year-old Juan being smothered between his mistress's breasts in Canto I while she hides him from her husband – or horrific – the cannibalism following the shipwreck in Canto II – this sensationalism is always balanced by the ironic voice of Byron himself. He usually uses the last two lines of the *ottava rima* to tease out a world-weary little *bon mot*:

> What men call gallantry, and gods adultery,
> Is much more common when the climate's sultry. (I, 53)

> If *you* think 'was philosophy that this did,
> I can't help thinking puberty assisted. (I, 93)

> Let us have wine and women, mirth and laughter,
> Sermons and soda-water the day after. (II, 178)

To show the rhyme-scheme at work in a complete stanza, here is Byron's wonderful anatomy of how a marriage can auto-destruct:

> Some take a lover, some take drams or prayers,
> Some mind their household, others dissipation,
> Some run away, and but exchange their cares,
> Losing the advantage of a virtuous station;
> Few changes e'er can better their affairs,
> Theirs being an unnatural situation.
> From the dull palace to the dirty hovel;
> Some play the Devil, and then write a novel. (II, 201)

We have to thank Caroline Lamb for inspiring that last line, but the idea of using the Italian rhyme scheme for comic effect came from another member of the Murray circle, John Hookham Frere, who pioneered it in his Arthurian satire *Whistlecraft*, published by Murray in 1818. *Whistlecraft*, which takes its name from its narrator, a Suffolk harness-maker, was a commercial failure. Murray complained in June 1818 that he still had not sold five hundred copies of the first part. The work is lumpy compared to *Don Juan*, but there are occasional moments of charm. 'I've a proposal here from Mr Murray,' the poet tells his muse at the opening of Canto III,

> He offers handsomely – the money down;
> My dear, you might recover from your flurry
> In a nice airy lodging out of town,
> At Croydon, Epsom, any where in Surrey;
> If every stanza brings us in a crown,
> I think that I might venture to bespeak
> A bed-room and front parlour for next week.[46]

Byron had delegated the future of *Don Juan* to John Cam Hobhouse, telling him to take the advice of such London acquaintances as Frere and Moore. Byron feared that his publisher might lose his nerve over such racy stuff: 'the damned Cant and Toryism of the day may make Murray pause – in that case you will take any Bookseller who bids best'.[47] He was now taking a hard-headed attitude to money, telling friends: 'What I get by my brains I will spend on my bollocks.'[48] Byron actually writes 'b––ks', so he might equally have meant 'books', of course.

At first Murray was keen to go ahead: there is a gap in his surviving letters to Byron, so we do not know his reaction when he read the first canto of *Don Juan*. Hobhouse, however, and particularly Frere, felt strongly that open publication should be avoided. While Hobhouse wondered if Frere was jealous of Byron taking over his *ottava rima*, Byron himself affected indifference. As far as he was concerned, Murray could publish openly, 'or you may publish anonymously – or *not* at *all* – in the latter event print 50 on my account for private distribution'.[49] On 27 December 1818 Hobhouse wrote in his diary that Murray had called on him, wanting to advertise *Don Juan* at once. Hobhouse responded that he was 'not sure'.[50] Murray was bringing out a collected edition of Byron's poems, and told Byron that 'the appearance at this time of a popular original work from you would render me the greatest possible service'.[51] On the other hand he wished Byron would write a major work 'worthy of you', even if it took 'some Six or Eight years'. Byron was scornful: 'I'll try no such thing ... "Seven [*sic*] or eight years"! God send us all well this day three months ... since you want *length* you shall have enough of *Juan* for I'll make 50 cantos.'[52] What really concerned him was the prospect of censorship: Gifford and Murray had taken the occasional snip at his poetry since 'The Lady Weeping'. 'There shall be *no mutilations*,' he warned Murray. 'You sha'n't make *Canticles* of my Cantos.'[53]

Murray began to send proofs of what he archly called 'a certain poem' to Venice at the end of April 1819.[54] He told Byron there was a public waiting for it – 'the enquiries after its appearance are not a few' – but he requested Byron to 'wrap up or leave out certain approximations to indelicacy'.[55] Byron laughed at this circumlocution, but protested: 'There is *no indelicacy* ... For my part I think you are all crazed.'[56] However, Murray had his blue pencil sharpened, and wrote on 28 May asking Byron to 'modify or substitute' various details such as a line mocking Sir Samuel Romilly (I, 15), who had cut his throat after the death of his adored wife, and the line (II, 10) 'She taught them to suppress their vice and urine.' More seriously, he felt that 'the Shipwreck is a little too particular & out of proportion'. Yet he had to admire 'the power which you alternately make ones blood thrill & our Sides Shake'.[57]

These contradictory comments infuriated Byron, who described them to Hobhouse as Murray's '*fear* to have *any opinion at all* – till he knows what the Public think'.[58] He was also upset by Murray's failure to offer a fee for the poem: Byron demanded that a sum be named at once, else they would take it to the highest bidder. When Murray asked if he meant to finish *Don Juan*, Byron snarled back: 'what encouragement do you give me ... with your nonsensical prudery?'[59]

The first two cantos of *Don Juan* were published in a single volume, a generously spaced quarto, on Thursday 15 July 1819, priced at a guinea and sixpence. There was no author's or publisher's name on the title page, but only 'PRINTED BY THOMAS DAVISON, WHITEFRIARS', and the epigraph from Horace: 'Difficile est proprie communia dicere.' This translates as 'It is difficult to speak of what is commonplace.' The proposed dedicatory verses to Southey had gone, and a number of lines in Canto I had been removed and replaced by asterisks. These included the Romilly stanza (I, 15), and a passage beginning with the last two lines of I, 129 which referred to syphilis, although Byron is actually talking about the discovery of vaccination. Murray did not tell Byron about these cuts when he sent news of the book's reception from an address that may have made Byron laugh: 'Wimbledon Common'. Murray had bought a country retreat, 'a little place', he told Blackwood.[60] Caroline Lamb got wind of it: 'I wish to see yr little Cottage at Wimbledon – could I do so *today* or tomorrow.'[61]

Murray admitted to Byron that it was quite literally a retreat: 'Having fired the Bomb, here I am out of the way of its explosion.' People were calling at Albemarle Street to express disapproval that Murray had 'had any thing to do with it'.[62] In fact he had thrown himself into the project with far more commitment than Byron had given him credit for. On the three days leading up to publication, *The Times* had carried front-page advertisements: 'ON THURSDAY, DON JUAN'. Not knowing this, and fearing the worst, Byron complained: 'Of Don Juan I hear nothing further from *you* – you chicken-hearted – silver-paper Stationer you.'[63]

Murray was no coward when it came to the sensational. Caroline Lamb's letters to him make it clear that he seriously considered publishing *Glenarvon* before letting it go elsewhere, and his eventual decision to reject it was probably motivated more by a desire not to offend Byron than by a fear of public disapproval. Hobhouse wrote in his diary that Murray would publish *Fanny Hill* if Byron had been its author. He offered Byron 2,000 guineas for Cantos I and II of *Don Juan* and another poem, *Mazeppa*. Byron said it was too much if the poem failed, too little if it succeeded; but he accepted.

Murray promised to send Byron 'all the Abuse & all the Commendation of Juan which I can gather'.[64] There was plenty of both. The first comment to reach Murray, who instantly passed it on to Byron, was from Francis Cohen, the historian later known as Francis Palgrave, who wrote occasionally for the *Quarterly Review*.[65] Cohen told Murray that *Don Juan* was 'an extraordinary performance', and though he disliked much about it, particularly the juxtaposition of the bawdy and the beautiful, a frequent complaint from reviewers, he was certain it would sell, on the grounds that everyone likes 'to read about naughty people'.[66] Murray described these comments to Byron as 'very fair'.[67]

The Murrays were expecting their sixth child, and Cohen wrote: 'Tell Mrs Murray that if she presents you with a boy, you must christen him Don Juan.'[68] But Annie had a miscarriage, and nearly died; two years later another baby was stillborn. 'I can not expect to go through the world with out participating in the Misfortunes of all around me,' Murray wrote to Byron. Four children, John, Christina, Hester and Maria, were to survive him.[69]

In the wake of Cohen's letter and Gifford's comments, Murray asked Byron to consider making a 'few slight alterations' when the cantos were reprinted: removing allusions to the pox,[70] and dropping the parody of the Ten Commandments.[71] 'Fill up these & with something better & let us put forth the New Edition with your Lordships name.'[72] Otherwise, Murray was full of praise of the poem – 'such prodigious power of Versification ... so much wit' – and asked Byron how long it had taken to write: 'Will you let me have Any fragments of your first design which I should like amazingly to see & keep.'[73] Byron responded that doubtless all his critics were right, and he was wrong, 'but do pray let me have that pleasure ... don't ask me to alter for I can't – I am obstinate and lazy'.[74] As to the use of his name, he told Murray: 'Continue to keep the *anonymous* about "Juan" – it helps us to fight against overwhelming numbers.'[75]

Six weeks after publication, Murray reported that there was still 'a great outcry – but every body reads [it]'. His eldest son John, now at school at Charterhouse, went up a notch in his schoolfriends' estimation when they discovered that his father published the bawdy epic. However, sales were disappointing: 'I have 300 left out of 1,500 printed – it was published late in the season.'[76] And: 'Its sale would have been universal if some 20 Stanzas had been altered & wch by preventing the book being shewn at a Ladys work table – have cut up my Sale.'[77] On the other hand the bookseller J. Onwhyn thought it worth publishing a pirate edition. Murray castigated him as an audacious villain and took legal advice, but was warned not to put his head, and Byron's, above the parapet for such a precarious project.

Murray now admitted that cuts had been made in the first edition without the author's knowledge or consent. He sent Byron 'the leaves which have the Asterisks', inviting him to 'fill them up' as he liked, providing he avoided 'allusions to a certain disease', syphilis.[78] Byron had already seen the asterisks, in extracts printed in *Galignani's Messenger*, an English-language newspaper printed in Paris, and he sneered at these 'pains taken to exculpate the modest publisher'.[79] He said he would write a preface that would exonerate Murray, 'but at the same time I will cut you all up (& *you* in particular) like Gourds'. In reality, his mind was almost entirely occupied with his latest mistress, Teresa Guiccioli.

Murray, meanwhile, was convinced that Byron might reform. 'If you would only condescend to keep in the line,' he wrote to him exasperatedly, 'every one will gladly yield to you the head of it.'[80] He was starting to complain about the position Byron had put him in – 'I did not want unnecessarily to give my name to a publication that I knew would be liable to such an outcry',[81] – but at the same time he was asking if Byron could send him 'two Cantos more of Don Juan' in time for the Christmas market.[82]

'Outcry' was perhaps an exaggeration. Certainly there were reviewers who declared themselves shocked: the *St James's Chronicle* wrung its hands over 'the utter absence of moral feeling',[83] and the *Blackwood's* critic called it 'a filthy and impious poem'.[84] Murray lashed out in response to this. 'You must know that Blackwoods – commonly called Blackguards – Magazine is a scurrilous publication,' he told Byron, adding that he had pulled out of his shareholding, though it had cost him £1,000.[85] But, for every prissy complaint, there was an expression of wild enthusiasm. 'Never was English festooned into more luxuriant stanzas,' declared the *Literary Gazette*.[86] Francis Jeffrey in the *Edinburgh Review*, despite grave reservations, described Byron as a genius. Nobody doubted for a moment that the author was Byron, nor the publisher Murray.

It was just as well that the virtues of *Don Juan* were attracting as much attention as its supposed vices. The French Revolution, the fear that it might happen in Britain, the rise of evangelical Christianity and a general disgust with the licentiousness of the Prince Regent were just four of many factors combining to replace the relaxed liberalism of the eighteenth century with what hindsight perceives to be a prelude to Victorianism. As Murray put it in a letter to Byron, 'the character of the Middling Classes in the country – is certainly highly moral'.[87] And in another letter he wrote: 'The Comedies of Charles Seconds days are not tolerated now – and even in my own time I have gradually seen my favourite Love for Love [by Congreve] absolutely pushed by public feeling from the stage.'[88] Yet Murray felt it was a good thing that the moral belt was being tightened: 'real progress and the result of refinement'. Byron snorted contemptuously at this: 'You talk of *refinement*, are you all *more* moral? – are you *so* moral? – No such thing.'[89]

A few months after Cantos I and II of *Don Juan* reached the shops, in the wake of the massacre in St Peter's Fields, Manchester, which rapidly became known as 'Peterloo', Parliament passed an act by which blasphemous or seditious publications could be seized, with banishment for reoffenders. Byron had already banished himself, but Murray may well have feared the policeman's knock.

Byron's friends had been unanimous in their recommendation that *Don Juan* should remain in manuscript. Thomas Moore's journal records them meeting at Albemarle Street in January 1819, and agreeing that Byron, having been out of the country for so long, had lost his sense of literary decorum.[90] They were particularly unhappy at Byron's caricature of Annabella Milbanke, in the guise of Juan's mother. Among the victims of the new legislation was Byron's friend Hobhouse, who spent some weeks in Newgate jail accused of the authorship of a seditious pamphlet. Murray thought he was foolish to have got into this predicament: 'I am certain that he has no *tact* in politics – no more than I have to be a Sculptor.'[91] On his part, Hobhouse, a political radical, suspected that Murray might be in league with the government. In some ways this was a curious notion, considering that he had just published a supposedly seditious poem; yet it was true Murray had many friends in high Tory places. 'Do not write any thing to Albemarle Street you do not wish to be seen by all the public offices,' Hobhouse warned Byron. 'The man does not mean to do you a mischief – but he is vain ... and for the sake of a paragraph with "my dear M[urray]" in it would betray Christ himself.'[92] Murray visited Hobhouse in Newgate, and the prisoner noted in his diary: 'Murray was entertaining – but told all the secrets of all his friends – and abused them practically one after the other.'[93]

Murray himself refused to believe that seditious writings destabilised the country. 'It is much more probable that Italy will be overwhelmed with Lava', he wrote to Byron, 'than that we shall have a revolution here.'[94] But he resorted to bribery in the hope of getting Byron to clean up *Don Juan*: 'Will you revise it & send me another Canto & I will send your Lordship a Thousand Guineas.'

Meanwhile the stress was getting at Murray. In November 1819 he made a surprising confession to Byron: his failure to write long letters to the poet was, he claimed, caused by:

> the distraction wch I have two years ago undergone from the numbers of people ... most of uncertain use to me, who have been introduced to my Drawing Room – until at length I can endure it no longer for it unhinges my mind so compleatly from all or any connected thought that I can not carry on my business and I have this moment refitted my house & shall confine this meeting to some dozen persons with whom I have actual business.[95]

There is no record of anyone being thrown out of, or barred entry to, the Murray salon, but it seems that the habitués got the message that they were no longer always welcome whenever they cared to turn up. Within five years, a new club, the Athenaeum, intended for men of literature, art and science, opened in Waterloo Place, performing the same function albeit with more formality, as Murray's soirées. J. W. Croker, a Murray regular, was a chief initiator of the Athenaeum, other founder members including Thomas Campbell, Francis Palgrave (Cohen), Samuel Rogers and George Canning. Murray himself soon became a member, and when John Murray III was admitted, the elder Murray presented the club with a copy of every book on his current list.

By the beginning of 1820, Byron, who was now in Ravenna, was finding it hard to continue with *Don Juan*. 'The outcry has not frightened but it has *hurt* me,' he wrote.[96] Murray felt equally uncomfortable, lapsing into the lethargy and 'Melancholny', as he invariably spelt it, which always threatened to engulf him. He procrastinated over answering Byron's letters, leaving Byron in suspense. When he did write, it was to say that he and Byron's friends thought Canto III and IV were 'by no means equal' to their predecessors.[97]

Shortly before he received this letter, Byron informed Hobhouse that he had had enough of Murray's non-communication. Hobhouse was to take the new cantos to Longman's, or to 'any respectable publisher who will undertake them'.[98] Murray and he would remain friends and correspondents, 'but as publisher *that* leaf of his ledger will close for ever'. It was not Murray's lack of enthusiasm for *Don Juan* that infuriated Byron, 'but because he *hesitates* and *shuffles*'.

When Murray's letter effectively rejecting the new cantos reached him, Byron was almost more relieved than angry. At least he now knew where he stood. He wrote to Murray that he would change publishers if he did not answer his letters. 'You must not treat a blood horse as you do your hacks otherwise he'll bolt out of the course.'[99] Learning from Hobhouse how upset Byron had been by his non-communication, Murray wrote to apologise for 'my long & Stupid silence ... I am most sincerely grieved at this but I could not induce myself to write about any thing at once so delicate & disagreeable.'[100] If Byron wanted to publish Cantos III and IV, he would be glad to oblige, and reported additionally that Caroline Lamb had been to a masquerade as Don Juan, attended by 'the Devils from the Theatre'.[101] He ended the letter in his most abject manner: 'I entreat you to send me a Letter of forgiveness.'[102]

Murray had been despatching new books from his list to Byron, in the hope of getting enthusiastic quotes for publicity. 'Do give me a paragraph on the more important of the books,' he begged.[103] Byron ignored most of them and was rude about one: 'too stiltified, & apostrophic – & quite wrong'.[104] This was *The Sceptic* by Felicia Dorothea Hemans, a versified warning against scepticism which Murray published in 1820. Byron, who was the sort of sceptic Mrs Hemans had in mind, made the obvious pun, referring to her as 'Mrs Hewoman'.[105] He was equally abusive about Keats, whom Murray did not publish, and referred to Wordsworth as 'Turdsworth'.

All businesses in London, including publishing, went into an economic trough in the second half of 1820. This was caused in part by the public scandal over Queen Caroline, wife of the Prince Regent, who had now become king on the death of his father George III. Caroline had been living abroad, separated from the Regent, and on her return to England she was accused of adultery and put on trial. However, public support for her was so great that the legal proceedings were abandoned. Murray reported these goings-on to Byron, adding sanctimoniously: 'The Times are sadly out of Joint,'[106] and passing on gossip about the failure of Tom Moore's latest book: 'They tell me that his "Rhimes on the Road" were so dull that after setting up Six Sheets they were obliged to distribute them[107] & give up the publication.'[108]

Meanwhile attention shifted away from *Don Juan* to the uncontroversial historical verse-drama that Byron had just completed, *Marino Faliero, Doge of Venice*. He was now anxious that if he owned up to the authorship of *Don Juan* he might forfeit his rights as parent of Ada, born to Annabella just before the collapse of the marriage. Nevertheless, by Christmas 1820 he had finished the fifth canto. 'If it be equal to the *Fourth* it will be grand,' Murray wrote to him, but reiterated that he and Byron's friends all found the third canto dull.[109] Nevertheless, Murray continued, the moment he received the fourth 'I will instantly publish – I have announced it – with a very extraordinary collection a list of which I inclose.'

Murray's list for 1821 occupied a couple of pages in the trade journal the *Monthly Literary Advertiser*. The forty-five books which Murray advertised, easily outdoing other publishers in quantity, give a vivid picture of the range of his output, and are a timely reminder that he did not just publish Byron. As a modern publisher might, he begins the advertisement with political biographies and memoirs: a life of William Pitt, a book on political quarrels in the 1750s, and *Memoirs of the Last Nine Years of the Reign of George II* by Horace Walpole. This manuscript had been found at Walpole's death in 1797. There is a life of a very mad George III by Edward Hawke Locker, and the beginning of a series of lavishly illustrated travel books, in which the text was often no more than an excuse for the engravings. For a book on Italy, Murray had engaged J. M. W. Turner to enliven the original drawings by the architect James Hakewill. Turner, who had not yet been to Italy, nevertheless improved Hakewill's drawings with confidence.

Illustrating books was a very expensive, frustrating and time-consuming business. While the rate of work of typesetters could be calculated and charged precisely, the production of an engraving depended heavily on the complexity of the image to be engraved, the size of the plate required and the talent of the individual engraver. It was time for Murray to make himself clear again. He wrote firmly to James Hakewill to say that he would not be paying for engravings he had not himself commissioned:

> It is necessary for me to say explicitly, that I will not be answerable in any way for any drawings, engravings or other expense that you may choose to incur for the Views in Italy without my positive consent being first given in writing.
>
> That it was never my intention to extend this work beyond twelve numbers unless after making a reasonable trial of a portion of the said twelve numbers I found the sale of the work to prove sufficiently advantageous: for these twelve numbers sufficient preparations has been already made and it is not my intention to give out any other drawings to the engraver except those of Mr Turner.
>
> If you have of your own accord without my concurrence given orders for any other drawings or engravings it is at your own expense and risque and it is for this reason I advise you if you have done so, to order them to be immediately stopped.[110]

An engraver whom both Turner and Murray employed was the entrepreneurial Charles Heath. It appears that Heath lulled Murray into a sense of false security over another commission, from which, almost too late, Murray was just able to extricate himself with one of his firm, sharp letters:

> The cause of my suffering myself to be persuaded by you to engage in a new set of plates for Ld Byron's works which I neither wanted nor contemplated – was your dwelling on the cheapness, dispatch, ability & absence of all trouble even as to payment with which they would be executed. The Drawings were to be done for 10£ or Guineas and the engravings in no instance to exceed £20 or Guineas. I was not to be asked for a shilling until the whole should be completed and put into my hands for publication & then you were to take a lazy bill which at the least would extend to six months ... You may have said differently – but if so it is the last transaction I ever will enter into with you. The whole of these engravings were to have been

executed at least Eight months ago, & you now send me home only six that are finished & asked me to give you £300 . . . Upon what principle of common justice do you expect your demand to be attended to the moment it is made when you set the example of such shameless deviation from all punctuality yourself – to say nothing of the gross indelicacy of making so instantaneous a demand at a period of the year in which my man of business is doing his books. I want no long letters – if my statement agrees with yours write.[111]

The costs of the project with Hakewill and Turner were in danger of getting out of hand, and when Murray realised that the book would lose money he sold Turner's drawings to recoup costs. Some of them were eventually bought by Ruskin, who praised Turner's lightness of touch.[112] The Hakewill–Turner book on Italy was in monochrome, but some of Murray's travel books had hand-coloured illustrations. One of the finest of these, published two years after the *Monthly Literary Advertiser* list, is an account of polar exploration by John Franklin, who died in 1847 while trying to find the North-West Passage to India and China. The hand-colouring makes the polar landscapes seem threatening and dramatic.

For all the fame that he acquired as Byron's publisher, it may be that John Murray's greatest contribution to the advancement of knowledge and of human understanding of the world was his commissioning and publishing of dozens of books of travel. Murray's travel writers and artists went all over the globe: the advertisement includes books on Germany, Syria, Athens, China, the Cape of Good Hope, the interior of South America, and North Africa. Not for nothing was John Murray II a founder member of the Royal Geographical Society. After Waterloo Britain had a large navy unused to the arts of peace, and, as Secretaries to the Admiralty, J. W. Croker and John Barrow had to find the navy something constructive to do. With the post-war expansion of scientific endeavour and the continuing search for new trade routes and political alliances, opportunities for global exploration developed. These in their turn led to publishing opportunities which Murray was quick to exploit. In 1816 Lord Amherst led an embassy to China to try to establish a trading agreement. Although this failed, it did find success in the volume that Murray published on the return. In Henry Ellis's *Journal of the Proceedings of the Late Embassy to China . . . Interspersed with Observations upon the Face of the Country, the Polity, Moral Character and Manners of the Chinese Nation* (1817) a new insight into the extraordinary nature of Chinese society was offered, introduced by the words: 'An Embassy to China is so rare an event in the history of Europe, that a correct narrative of the occurrences attending it possesses a degree of interest, almost independent of the mode in which the narrative itself may be executed.'[113]

This paragraph, which is styled an 'Advertisement' – it would nowadays be known as a blurb – leads the reader to expectations of the strange and the exotic. There are few passages in *Journal of the Proceedings of the Late Embassy to China* more exotic than the account of the interminable negotiations which Amherst and his staff undertook with the Mandarins of the Chinese court on how the Emperor should be approached. Lord Amherst was not prepared to *ko-tou* (that is, kow-tow, which required him to lie prostrate in front of the Emperor), but would bow low and give the same obeisance as he would give his own sovereign:

> His object was to combine a proper manifestation of respect to his Chinese Majesty with the duty he owed his own Sovereign, and the positive commands he had received on the particular point; that whatever might be the particular ceremony performed, the respect he felt in his heart for his Imperial majesty could not be thereby augmented.[114]

The compromise agreed upon with the Mandarins was that rather than prostrate himself Amherst should bow to the Emperor nine times. Despite the fact that the embassy failed in its task of establishing new trade agreements, it did endorse a publishing phenomenon which pointed the way to the firm's greatest mid-nineteenth-century achievement, the creation of the series of Handbooks for Travellers. In the meantime, other books whose texts and illustrations took the reader out of his armchair and into the furthest-flung parts of the world included John Franklin's *Narrative of a Journey to the Shores of the Polar Sea, in the Years 1819, 20, 21, and 22* (1823) and

Major Dixon Denham and Captain Hugh Clapperton's *Narrative of the Travels and Discoveries in Northern and Central Africa in the Years 1822, 1823 and 1824* (1826).

An idea of the richness and colour instilled into the narratives can be drawn from a story told later in his life by Sir George Back, one of Franklin's travelling companions. 'Do you see this cloak?' Back asked John Murray IV when leaving a dinner at Albemarle Street. 'It was once lined with fur, but when our provisions ran short in the Arctic regions, I had the fur stewed, and we lived off it for several days; then we made soup of my boots, and found them very good. When they were done, I tried my shot-belt; but that was of good English leather, and my digestion has never recovered from that attempt.'[115] Coloured in the telling though this story probably was, it was the detail and tone of the travel accounts published by Murray throughout the nineteenth century that inspired countless adventure-story titles for boys, and kept the thrill of adventure fresh for a new generation.

Poetry also inspired Murray's illustrated books. The 1820 list of published books includes a set of engravings based on George Crabbe's poems, and another to illustrate Byron. Science books feature strongly in the advertisement: a book on astrophysics, *Elementary Illustrations of the Celestial Mechanics*, a manual of chemistry, and John Robison's book on 'Mechanical Philosophy', physics, which includes 'a copious Article on the History and Operations of the Steam Engine' with its revisions by James Watt, which made it 'the only account which can be relied upon'.[116]

The literary items in the advertisement include a biography of Sheridan by Thomas Moore, which proved to be a practice run for his eventual life of Byron. There is also an American work, a new edition of *The Sketch Book of Geoffrey Crayon, Gent.*, by Washington Irving, published anonymously. Irving, sometimes referred to as the first American short-story writer and man of letters, had arrived in England in 1815 to run the Liverpool branch of a family business. Aged thirty-two, he had already published a couple of books in America, and on the strength of this entered the Murray circle on visits to London. Murray asked him to watch out for any of his

(Murray's) books that might be worth republishing across the Atlantic.[117] Walter Scott encouraged Irving, and he began to write the *Sketch Book*, a series of stories including 'Rip Van Winkle' and 'The Legend of Sleepy Hollow'. Murray initially turned it down, but on Scott's persuasion he changed his mind, and it was a huge success. Murray had paid Irving only £200 for the copyright, but in the light of excellent sales he doubled this voluntarily. In the preface to a revised edition of the *Sketch Book*, Irving calls Murray 'the Prince of Booksellers'.[118] Considering the volleys of abuse he was getting from Byron, Murray would have appreciated this.

I I

Torn and burned before our eyes

———

IT WAS DURING January 1821, the month that he placed a prominent
advertisement for his books, that Murray first got wind of another
Byron work which might prove tricky. 'I am going to Lady Davys
tonight to whom Moore has, I understand, lent your MSS Memoirs
when at Paris,' Murray reported to Byron, adding: 'is this Right I have
not seen them yet.'[1] Hobhouse reported the same to Byron: that Tom
Moore had lent 'your life & adventures' to Lady Davy, when she was
in Paris, and he, Hobhouse, wondered whether Byron had meant
Moore to be quite so liberal with this manuscript.[2]

In fact Byron was happy that his Memoirs should be read. He told
Moore that he wanted people to have the opportunity to 'contradict
or correct me'. Moore was welcome to lend the original manuscript,
providing that '*one* correct copy' was made and deposited 'in honourable hands, in case of accidents happening to the original'.[3]
Byron also suggested that Moore might try to make some badly
needed money for himself out of the Memoirs, and that he might
ask Murray or Longman's, Moore's publisher, for a cash advance
against publication after Byron's death. Moore duly wrote to Murray
late in 1820 making such a proposal, and Murray agreed to pay him
2,000 guineas, on condition that, if he survived Byron, Moore would
edit the Memoirs for publication.

Murray reported this to Byron, and suggested that Byron might
from time to time make additions to the text, to keep the book up
to date. As its future publisher he also felt that, from now on,
'Moore should not *shew* the Memoirs to any one.'[4] And in September
1821 he wrote to Byron secretively, saying: 'Moore is in town &
incog[nito] – I have the precious Memoirs.'[5] Moore, trying to avoid

his creditors, took to wearing a false moustache in London. Murray drew up a contract, had Moore sign it, and forwarded it to Byron for his signature.

Meanwhile the third, fourth and fifth cantos of *Don Juan* were published anonymously in August 1821, and, rather late in the day, Murray offered Byron a thousand guineas for them. Byron was furious. 'He offers me for *all* – the sum he once offered for two cantos . . . I will accept nothing of the kind,' he wrote to Douglas Kinnaird.[6] He was convinced that Murray was paying some authors more lavishly, and when a copy of the new *Don Juan* arrived in Italy, he was outraged by its omissions and inaccuracies. Worse still, the erratic pace of the mail meant that often Murray seemed to be ignoring his complaints, even though he tried to answer Byron's letters by return of post. Murray increased his offer, but another layer had been stripped from Byron's patience.

Byron's name still sold books – Samuel Smiles records the Murray family tradition that Albemarle Street was so crowded with buyers for the new *Don Juan* cantos that copies had to be handed out of the windows. But the old relationship of trust between Byron and Murray was wearing thin. Byron began to fling abuse at Murray calling him 'shuffling' and 'timeserving'.[7] The denouement came when, in the autumn of 1822, Leigh Hunt's radical brother John turned up at 50 Albemarle Street to demand that Murray hand over to him the latest Byron manuscripts for publication in the Hunt brothers' paper the *Liberal*. Murray, who had been at Harrow parish church stage-managing the funeral of Byron's five-year-old illegitimate daughter Allegra, wrote an outraged letter to Byron, describing how John Hunt had behaved like a bailiff or an assassin. Murray's chief clerk now had orders that Hunt was not to be received if he came to the house again. Byron now blamed Murray, quite unfairly, for some tittle-tattle about little Allegra's funeral that had got into the press. In response, Murray turned pathetic, pleading with Byron in his most fawning, spaniel-like persona: 'I beseach you not to set me down for such an incurable Blockhead as not to think of you . . . as far superior as a Man of Genius to any man breathing . . . *Every day of my life* I sit opposite to your Lordships Portrait.'[8]

They had been down this road often before, but this time Murray played a family card: 'I have had to pay £16,000 for an insane brother-in-law ... I can never hope to have One Pound of it repaid.'[9] This was William Elliot, a constant drain on Murray's resources, not clinically insane but adept at soaking up other people's money. On this occasion, Murray had foolishly financed William's scheme to make a fortune by speculating in foreign markets. He may have felt a residual loyalty to William, because he first came to know Annie through him. Byron had no intention of ending his working relationship with Murray, and sent three more cantos of *Don Juan*. But Murray was so upset by the accompanying letter, now disappeared, that he returned the cantos unopened. Douglas Kinnaird had in fact already read some extracts to Murray, who wrote to Byron to say that they were so 'outrageously shocking' that he could not publish them. He had stopped fawning, and was trying to upset Byron with the news that 'even your former works are considerably deteriorated in Sale'.[10] Meanwhile Byron told Kinnaird that he did not mind people suggesting minor cuts in the new cantos, 'but I *wont* be dictated to by *John Murray Esqre*'.[11]

As usual, Byron's anger with Murray eventually dissolved into his natural good humour; and if Byron had survived, their partnership might have resumed in full. On 21 February 1824, Byron wrote Murray a letter from Greece which was perfectly sunny – 'You will perhaps be anxious to hear some news.'[12] But, before Murray could reply, Byron's story was over.

The terrible news was sent to Murray in an eccentrically spelt but deeply moving letter from Missolonghi, where Byron had spent some weeks supporting the Greeks in their war of independence against Turkey:

> Sir, Forgive me for this Intrusion which I now am under the Painfull Necessity of wrighting to you to Inform you of the Mallancolly News of my Lord Byron whom his no more he Departed This Miserable Life on the 19 of April after an Illness of only 10 Days ... W Fletcher Valet To the Late L. B. For 20 years. PS I Mention My name and Capacity that you may Remember & forgive this when

A determined pose, in which John Murray I presents himself to the world as a canny and successful publisher in David Allen's portrait, c.1777

John Murray II's damaged right eye is neatly hidden by the downcast gaze in Henry Pickersgill's portrait of early 1830s. Thorwaldsen's bust of Byron stands in the background

Thomas Moore, the Irish-born poet and diarist, and friend of John Murray II and Byron, painted by Sir Thomas Lawrence, 1829

A copy by Thomas Phillips RA, commissioned by John Murray II, of Phillips' celebrated portrait of Lord Byron in Albanian Costume which encapsulated the poet's exotic romanticism

Drawing room, 50 Albemarle Street, 1907

Right: 32 Fleet Street, the London home of John Murray I, drawn in the mid-nineteenth century, thirty or more years after Murray had moved west to Albemarle Street

Below: Newstead, Wimbledon by Hallam Murray, 1890s. The house was demolished, its foundations lying beneath the Centre Court of the All-England Tennis Club, Wimbledon

George Reid, one of the most accomplished of Scottish late nineteenth century portraitists, here evokes the sheer pressure of work that faced John Murray III in this 1881 painting

A posed dynastic photograph, probably taken at their home, Newstead, Wimbledon, showing three generations: John Murray III, IV and V, 1890

Isabella Bird on an expedition, 1890s. A virtual invalid when at home in Scotland, when travelling in distant and dangerous countries Isabella Bird wore an iron brace to support her back

David Livingstone hated his portrait by Henry Wyndham Phillips (1857) until, seeing his reflection by chance in an African lake, he realised that it was a good likeness

Charles Darwin by Julia Margaret Cameron, 1868

John Murray IV and his wife Evie, at home at 50 Albemarle Street, 1880s

John Murray IV and Hallam Murray in the Trade Department, 50a Albemarle Street in 1903. Hallam (standing), the younger brother of John Murray IV, was a distinguished artist and graphic designer whose book covers put Murrays in the forefront of book design in the early twentieth century

Book cover designs by Hallam Murray

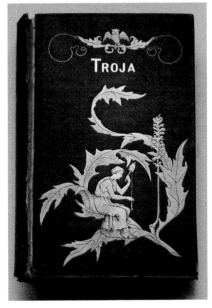

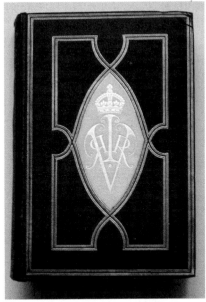

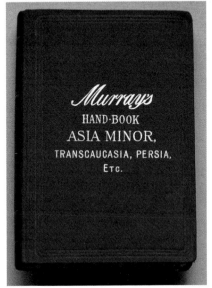

Above left: Schliemann's *Troja: Results of the Latest Researches and Discoveries on the Site of Homer's Troy* (1886)

Above right: The Letters of Queen Victoria (1907)

Right: Cover of a John Murray Hand-Book for Travellers, 1895

50 Albemarle Street exterior, 1935

The John Murray Warehouse, Clerkenwell Road, 1960s

Page spread from a John Murray list, 1935

You Remember the Quantity of times I have been at your home in Albemarle Street.[13]

Murray must have heard of Byron's death before Fletcher's letter reached London. Tom Moore was told of it by an assistant in a bookshop, on the morning of Friday 14 May 1824:

Calling at Colbourn's library ... was told by the shopman that Lord Byron was dead. Could not believe it ... Hurried to inquire. Met Lord Lansdowne, who said he feared it was but too true. Recollected then the unfinished state in which my agreement for the redemption of the Memoirs lay. Lord L said, 'You have nothing but Murray's fairness to depend upon'.... Hastened to Murray's, who was denied to me.[14]

Murray was not at home to Moore. The problem was that Moore had recently had second thoughts about selling the Byron Memoirs to Murray outright, and had managed to persuade the publisher to convert the sale into a loan of 2,000 guineas with the manuscript as security. He had already spent the money, but with Byron dead he now wanted to reclaim ownership of the Memoirs, and publish them to his own profit.

Shortly before Byron's death Moore had approached Murray's rival Longman's, who were willing to advance him the money he would need to pay Murray and retrieve the manuscript, though of course in return Longman's expected to publish the Memoirs. But the loan agreement with Murray had not yet been signed, and Moore knew that the Memoirs were in a legal limbo, and that Murray could do what he wanted with them. Like Moore, John Cam Hobhouse was keeping a journal: thus we have two exceptionally detailed narratives of what happened at Albemarle Street, and elsewhere in London, during the tempestuous days immediately following Byron's death. Moore and Hobhouse may have disagreed passionately about what should be done with Byron's Memoirs, but as diarists they concur remarkably over how the story unfolded.

After Hobhouse's first pangs of grief had subsided, his mind turned in the same direction as Moore's, to the Memoirs. 'It had so happened,' he writes in his diary for 14 May 1824,

that a few days before Thomas Moore had told me that he had made
an effort to get the Memoirs out of Mr Murray's hands by coming
to some arrangement with Messrs Longman's the booksellers, who
had promised to advance him 2,000 guineas on his insuring his life,
which soon would enable Moore to repay Murray the loan advanced
to him. I was not aware whether or not the money had actually been
paid to Murray, and consequently in whose hands the Memoirs were.
I called on Kinnaird, [who] very generously wrote a letter to Moore
offering to give him £2,000 [*sic*] at once in order to secure the MSS
in whose ever hands it was, for the family of Lord Byron – that is to
say, in order to destroy the same MSS.[15]

This is the first mention of the idea that the Memoirs should be
destroyed, on the grounds of their presumed impropriety. There is
no evidence that Hobhouse had read them. He simply seems to have
felt, as he did with *Don Juan*, that suppression was the safest course
to protect what remained of Byron's good name. Oddly, Douglas
Kinnaird *had* read them, and liked them, but he seems to have
assumed that Byron's family, chiefly his widow Annabella and his
half-sister Augusta Leigh, would want them suppressed, and would
pay for that to be achieved. Moore's journal for the same day, Friday
14 May, takes up the story: 'Found a note on my return home from
Douglas Kinnaird, anxiously inquiring in whose possession the
Memoirs were, and saying that he was ready, on the part of Lord
Byron's family, to advance the two thousand pounds for the MS in
order to give Lady Byron and the rest of the family an opportunity
of deciding whether they wished them to be published or no.'[16]

Moore went to see Kinnaird the next day, Kinnaird repeating his
suggestion that Annabella should pay Murray the £2,000, or '2000
guineas' as Moore has it this time, to get the manuscript out of
Moore's hands. 'But this I would not hear of,' writes Moore: 'it was
I alone who ought to pay the money upon it, and the money was
ready for the purpose [the loan from Longman's]. I would then
submit it (not to Lady Byron), but to a chosen number of persons,
and if they, upon examination, pronounced it altogether unfit for
publication, I would burn it.'[17] Moore was beginning to construct a
line of defence around the Memoirs. Ingeniously, he accepted that

burning was on the cards, and adopted it as one possibility, to disarm his opponents. But he did not say who his jury might consist of, or who would select it. Meanwhile his diary entry continues. There was 'No answer yet from Murray. Called upon Hobhouse.'[18] Murray was actually at Hobhouse's rooms in Albany, five minutes' walk from Albemarle Street; Hobhouse writes that he had sent for him: 'to sound him respecting the Memoirs – for I own I did him the injustice to think he might prove the obstacle to their destruction. He came. Whilst he was with me Tom Moore's card was put into my hand, and Moore was shown into the other room.'[19] Moore does not record hearing Murray's voice while he waited: the doors and walls are thick in Albany.

Hobhouse reports that Murray was 'truly affected' by Byron's death:

> He proceeded to speak of the Memoirs – told me they were still in his hands, that Moore had talked of paying the money, but had not done it. He then added that he had thought of giving up the MSS at once to Mr Wilmot Horton [a cousin of Byron and Augusta Leigh who had acted for Annabella during the separation], to be by him delivered to Lady Byron or Mrs Leigh – as for the money he had advanced to Moore, he did not care whether he got it or not.[20]

Hobhouse thought this unfair: Murray should get his money back from the Byron family. Murray 'made no difficulty about this', and when Hobhouse asked him to go through his letters from Byron and destroy anything scurrilous, 'Murray solemnly promised he would do so.' Fortunately Murray did not keep this promise.

Murray was shown out, and Moore brought in. Hobhouse was immediately struck by the difference between his behaviour and Murray's: the bookseller had been solemn, but Moore began the conversation with some small talk. Hobhouse revealed that he had just been talking to Murray, who regarded the Memoirs as his property and was considering handing them over to Byron's family. This angered Moore, who said it was shameful that Murray should not admit that in fact he, Moore, owned the Memoirs. He spurned offers of financial help, saying he could produce the money to redeem the

Memoirs himself. He had no objection to handing the manuscript over to Augusta Leigh, providing he could do so in person: he wanted to show her what a sacrifice he was making. Meanwhile, concluded Moore, he would like to walk down to Murray's, pick up the Memoirs and take them home with him.

Hobhouse thought this was all fine, 'except the latter part – I did not like his taking the MSS home', especially as Moore admitted that he had let several people see them when he was abroad. He had even allowed Lady Burghersh, in Florence, to copy much of it, though he said he had later seen her burn the copy.[21] Moore insisted that Byron had wanted people to read the Memoirs, but under pressure from Hobhouse he admitted that Byron's words were 'Show them to the elect.' Hobhouse said that Byron could not possibly have meant that Moore should show them to anyone whom he wanted to impress with this evidence of his intimacy with Byron. More than twenty people seem already to have looked at the Memoirs: these included Washington Irving, Lady Caroline Lamb and Percy and Mary Shelley. Most left no comment, though William Gifford, who read the manuscript at Murray's request, reported according to Hobhouse that it was 'fit only for a brothel, and would damn Lord Byron to certain infamy if published'.

After their conversation in Albany, Hobhouse took Moore to see Kinnaird. Moore repeated that the manuscript was essentially publishable. The first part, he said, needed the removal of one rather charming but risqué anecdote, that Byron had not waited to consummate his marriage to Annabella until they could go to bed, but had made love to her 'on the sofa before dinner on the day of their marriage'.[22] The second part contained 'all sorts of erotic adventures' and needed pruning.[23] But the more Hobhouse heard about the manuscript, the more he became convinced that the whole thing should be destroyed. Kinnaird agreed, but felt that Moore should be allowed the dignity of handing over the manuscript voluntarily. He drew up a document for Moore to present to Murray:

> Mr Moore has the right to demand from Mr Murray the restoration of the MSS on paying him (Mr Murray) £2,000 for which he holds Mr Moore's bond at this time and the MSS as the security for the

same, Mr Moore proposes to meet Mr Murray at Mrs Leigh's house and in her presence to pay over to Mr Murray the MSS [*sic*] and to hand them over to Mrs Leigh to be entirely at her own absolute disposal.[24]

Moore agreed to this, but then disgusted Hobhouse by saying that he certainly hoped that, in return for this sacrifice, he would be appointed Byron's official biographer. Hobhouse was reminded of Rousseau consoling himself for the death of a friend by reflecting that he might be left his overcoat. It was agreed that the transfer of manuscript and cash would take place at Augusta Leigh's London home on Monday 17 May, and Hobhouse set off for Albemarle Street to make the arrangements with Murray. As he was going, Moore called him back, having recalled a clause in his agreement with Murray that gave him three months to raise the money in the event of Byron's death. If he were to invoke this, it would delay the proposed burning of the Memoirs, and the manuscript might be saved. Nevertheless, after Hobhouse had gone, Moore called on Longman's and arranged to borrow a little over £2,000 from them on the following Monday morning, in the hope that this would acquire him the manuscript right away.

Finding Murray at home, Hobhouse showed him Kinnaird's letter to Moore. Murray was agreeable to its terms, but said the figure was 2,000 guineas, not pounds, and he also wanted payment of interest on the loan, and the reimbursement of his expenses – solicitor's fees, stamp duty and so on. According to Hobhouse's diary, he did not question Hobhouse's conviction that, whatever Kinnaird might have written, the Memoirs must certainly be burnt. If Hobhouse had been asked what game he was playing, he would probably have said he was trying to protect the feelings of Annabella and Augusta, to save them from the exposure of Byron's intimacies with them – specifically, his incest with Augusta and his rumoured fondness for anal intercourse with his wife. It seems unlikely that these matters were revealed in the manuscript, and Hobhouse claimed he had never read it, so his determination to protect the two women is puzzling.

The women were puzzled themselves. When Hobhouse called on Augusta Leigh that Saturday and told her of the proposed destruction of the Memoirs, 'she did not at first understand it', he writes in his diary. He claims however that she 'was much pleased afterwards'.[25] In her own account, Augusta portrays Hobhouse as incoherent in his fanaticism to burn the manuscript. She says that he 'flew into a fit of vehemence' and called her a fool for not immediately understanding him.[26] Similarly, word came to Hobhouse that Annabella was in a state of distress about Byron's death, and wanted to have detailed accounts of his last days. Clearly she was not yet interested in the Memoirs.

Hobhouse, though, was not on his own in his determination that the manuscript should burn. He was supported from the outset by Murray. It is deeply puzzling that both men should have a fanatical conviction that the flames should consume a work of literature by one of the world's great poets, which neither of them had read. Murray had taken the same vow of chastity in this respect as Hobhouse. Over *Don Juan* Murray had been judicious rather than rigid, eventually allowing almost all the poem to appear in print. He had constantly protested to Byron about bad taste, but in the event had only acted as a mild censor. So why was he now in the ranks of the witch-hunters? We do not know. With Byron dead, there was no longer an intimate and familiar correspondent to whom he could unburden himself on such matters while they were unfolding.

On Sunday 16 May, Kinnaird went off to Scotland, depriving Moore of his immediate support. Moore now enlisted a friend, a fellow Irish poet Henry Luttrell, who was among those few who had actually read the Memoirs. Moore was now saying that, if the manuscript was to be burnt, he did not want to be there, to which Hobhouse shrewdly replied that he should be in attendance, so that he could deny the validity of any spurious 'Byron Memoirs' that might be published, by stating that he had seen the real thing burnt. Moore reluctantly allowed that this made sense.

Luttrell proposed to Moore that the two of them should pay a Sunday call on Robert Wilmot-Horton, Augusta Leigh's man of business, who was to be at the Monday meeting. He was at home, and Moore endeavoured to persuade him how unjust it would be to

Byron's memory to 'condemn the work wholly, and without even opening it, as if it were a pest bag'. It ought to be looked at carefully by himself, by Colonel Frank Doyle who was to represent Lady Byron, and by anyone else whom the family might choose. 'Was glad to find that Mr. Wilmot-Horton completely agreed with these views,' writes Moore:

> It was even, he said, what he meant to propose himself. He under-took also to see Mrs. Leigh on the subject, proposing that we should meet at Murray's (instead of Mrs. Leigh's) to-morrow, at eleven o'clock, and that then, after the payment of the money by me to Murray, the MS should be placed in some banker's hands till it was decided among us what should be done with it.[27]

Moore also called on Frank Doyle, Annabella's representative, whom he knew well, and who received him neutrally: 'He gave no opinion on the subject but in order to make sure that the conditions were right repeated over what I had said.'[28]

Monday 17 May dawned, and Moore, who had sent Hobhouse a note telling him to 'meet at Murray's at eleven o'clock', set off for Longman's to collect the money. He found Murray's rivals 'much pleased' that there was a chance they might publish the Memoirs.[29] Moore does not specify what arrangement he had come to with Longman's, but presumably he told them that it was likely that Murray would not wish to publish any of the Memoirs, and that they would then be able to issue an expurgated edition. He does not seem to have revealed this plan to anyone else, though he made it sound convincing enough for Longman's to hand over £2,100 when the money arrived from the bank at half past ten.

By the time Moore had collected Luttrell it was already eleven. They ran into Hobhouse just outside Albany. Hobhouse was in a thoroughly bad temper with Moore for altering the day's arrange-ments, and for going behind his back to get Wilmot-Horton's support. Tempers began to rise as they went into Hobhouse's apart-ment, and Hobhouse summoned Murray, who soon arrived. 'On hearing that Moore proposed that the MSS should be read, and extracts made for publication,' writes Hobhouse,

Murray became angry. He sat down, and with a very determined voice and manner protested that the MSS should be burnt forthwith, according to Moore's written proposal. Moore then said that the MSS was his, and that he had now a right to redeem them, upon which Murray said as follows – 'I do not care whose the MSS are – here am I as a tradesman – I do not care a farthing about having your money, or whether I ever get it or not – but such regard have I for Lord Byron's honour and fame that I am willing and determined to destroy these MSS which have been read by Mr Gifford, who says they would render Lord Byron's name eternally infamous. It is very hard that I as a tradesman should be willing to make a sacrifice that you as a gentleman will not consent to!!' Moore replied something to this, when Murray rose and said, 'By God, then I say I will burn the papers, let come what will of it – you agreed to it – you proposed it – you have acted anything but like a man of honour!'[30]

This does not sound like the urbane Murray who had written wittily and obsequiously to Byron over so many years; but Moore's diary records that there was indeed a heated speech by the book-seller:

> A good deal of loud talking during which Murray threatened to burn the MS himself, and applied some impertinent epithet to my conduct, which induced me to say with a contemptuous smile – 'Hard words, Mr. Murray – but, if you chuse to take the privileges of a gentleman, I am ready to accord them to you.' As near as I can recall this was what I said – but whatever it was, he saw its meaning, and was more courteous.[31]

By daring to insult a gentleman, Moore was saying, Murray ran the risk of being challenged to a duel. Backing down in the light of Moore's warning, Murray told the company that Wilmot-Horton and Doyle, the two businessmen representing Annabella and Augusta, were waiting at 50 Albemarle Street 'in order to see the MSS burnt'.[32] On hearing this, Hobhouse, Moore and Luttrell followed Murray out of the Albany.

Walking along Piccadilly, heading west, they turned right, crossed the street and entered the first front door on the left. Its brass plate was already worn down by polishing: *Mr Murray*. 'My house' Murray always called it in his letters, never 'my shop', let alone 'my offices'. Inside there were the Murray children running up and down stairs, among them the sixteen-year-old John who already knew he would succeed his father in due course. Family tradition has it that young John was invited into the gilded drawing room to watch what happened next, but neither Hobhouse nor Moore mention his presence, and Murray is unlikely to have exposed his son to the vicious outbursts of temper that were to explode like pistol shots for the remainder of that May morning. If young John Murray did witness anything, as he claimed, it was surely by putting his head round the door, or eavesdropping from the middle drawing room beyond the big salon.

The weekend had been wet, but Monday brought more seasonal weather so there was no need for the fire which was now burning in the elegant grate. Thomas Phillips's portrait of Byron gazed out over the golden room. Doyle and Wilmot-Horton, like a pair of pantomime broker's men, were waiting. The arguments began all over again, with Hobhouse and Moore immediately at each other's throats. Moore claims that he explained his wishes 'with respect to the disposition of the MS as quietly as the impatient taunts and objections of Hobhouse would allow me. His whole manner, indeed, was such as made me feel it necessary to keep a strict rein over my temper – resolving, at the same time, to take note of any thing that could be fairly considered as insulting, and call him quietly to account for it afterwards.'[33]

Moore was becoming more concerned about his honour, and the need to defend it with pistols, than he seemed to be about the fate of the Byron manuscript. 'We had a good deal of squabbling,' Hobhouse writes, 'Moore still struggling against the burning.'[34] Meanwhile the manuscript in Byron's energy-charged handwriting was brought, as well as the copy that Moore had had made for safety. The shell of the copy survives in the Murray Archive. Measuring 18 by 32 centimetres, it is a plain paper notebook in stiff mottled-green covers from which about half the pages have been torn. The remaining pages are blank. The notebook was originally purchased from a stationer in Paris, and somebody, possibly John Murray III, has written on the first surviving page: 'This book contained a MS copy of part of Lord Byron Memoirs (the only copy made) the leaves on which it was written were torn out & burnt along with the original MS. in Albemarle St.' This page is numbered 289. According to Doris Langley Moore, who does not give her source, the Memoirs 'formed a substantial though uncompleted book ... consist[ing] of over four hundred pages ... written by Byron between 1818 and 1821'.[35] Other commentators are of the opinion that it was a much briefer work.

According to Hobhouse, Wilmot-Horton said that it seemed to him unnecessary to proceed to Augusta Leigh's residence, as he had her permission to burn the manuscript. This major change of tack might have been expected to stir Moore to expressions of outrage, but the little Irishman was outnumbered by English bullies. Was it true, Doyle asked him, that he left the final decision about the two manuscripts to Mrs Leigh? 'It was,' said Moore. ' "Well then," replied Doyle, as Augusta's representative, "I put them into the fire." ' So Hobhouse records it. His account continues: 'accordingly Wilmot and Doyle tore up the MSS, and the copy, and burnt them'.[36] But Doyle was Annabella's man of business, not Augusta's, and he had no right to take such action. Moreover he subsequently admitted in a letter to Wilmot-Horton that he had no idea before he came to Albemarle Street that they might burn the Memoirs, and that Annabella 'certainly gave no consent to the *destruction* of the manuscript'.[37]

This is curious enough; but far odder is Moore's failure, in his lengthy diary account of what happened, to mention the actual burning. It is simply not there. The diary continues straight on from describing the arguments with Hobhouse to mentioning that Murray was 'frequently asked to produce the Bond and agreement between him and me, prefatory to my paying the money which was all that now remained to be done. Mr W. Horton, having been for some time impatient to be gone, now took his departure, and Doyle soon followed him. The agreement was at length found.'[38] That is all he says: no description of tearing out of the pages and stuffing them into the fire. Moore was witnessing the worst possible outcome of his hopes. He would now have to pay an enormous amount of money without getting anything in return. So why is he silent about what happened in front of his eyes? Wilfred S. Dowden, who edited Moore's journal for publication, calls the omission 'interesting',[39] and goes on to imply that the Memoirs may in fact have survived. Moore's original biographer, Lord John Russell, omits Moore's entire account of the events at Albemarle Street that morning, with the excuse that the scene was 'painful'.[40] Hobhouse persuaded Russell to drop it, because it would stir up painful memories. Dowden leaves it out of the body of his edition of the Moore journal, only including it as an Addendum to his sixth and final volume, with the hasty and peculiar explanation that the pages were 'damaged', but eventually 'recovered and transcribed'.[41]

What about the other witness? 'Young Mr Murray – then sixteen; the only person of those assembled now living – was also in the room.'[42] So wrote Samuel Smiles in 1891 by which time John Murray III was eighty-three and had only a few months to live. At various times the old man jotted down scraps of reminiscence, which were never published, but survive in the Murray Archive. These give a fragmentary, and not altogether accurate, account of the contents of the Byron Memoirs. The story about Byron consummating his marriage on the sofa has been transmuted into this: 'As a proof that Lady B. did not intend to separate herself from Ld B. he mentioned that he went with her[43] an hour before she left him. This fact was mentioned in his memoirs.' John Murray III means that the Byrons made love, despite the fact that they were parting. The entry is dated 1829, only five years after the burning, when Murray III was twenty-one, but it looks like the handwriting of a much older man. There is no date on some of his later recollections of the events surrounding the burning. His only description of the actual event is this: 'Mr W. Horton & my Father burnt the MS.'[44]

Moore's failure to state that the manuscript was burnt may perhaps be put down to his obsessive belief that he was being insulted, and that he ought to be challenging Hobhouse to a duel. Meanwhile Murray was supposed to be producing the legal documents in the case. Here is another oddity: why were these not found before the burning? But when he went out to fetch them, he came back empty-handed, claiming he could not find the agreement. This, writes Hobhouse, set off a fresh argument, as to who actually owned the manuscript – rather late to have such a discussion, if the burning had already taken place. Moore had claimed that the agreement, which he had signed two years earlier, had allowed him three months after Byron's death to raise the money to buy the Memoirs back. But when Murray's solicitor eventually turned up with the documents the relevant clause proved to be very different. It decreed that, if the money had not been repaid to Murray during Byron's lifetime, 'he [Murray] shall be at full liberty to print and publish the said Memoirs or Work for his own Use and benefit within three months after the death of the said Lord Byron as he shall think proper'.[45]

Moore was utterly taken aback by this discovery that Murray had become in effect the owner of the Memoirs from the moment of Byron's death and for at least three months thereafter. In his journal, he wonders privately whether Murray and his solicitor had tampered with the original agreement. The contract did not release Moore from repayment; indeed it specified that Murray had the right to demand the money whenever he wished. Moore was therefore faced with paying 2,000 guineas and getting nothing in return – paying for the manuscript's 'destruction by Murray'.[46] This is the first time he mentions that the manuscript has actually been destroyed. Moore writes that he thought of making this point but then changed his mind, and says that with mature consideration he is glad he paid up, since it was the honourable thing to do. He records that Murray did say: 'I do not feel that I have any right to take the money.'[47] But, when Moore insisted, Murray accepted the banknotes, and these extraordinary proceedings came to an end.

Moore records that, as Murray showed them out of his house, he apologised 'in his tradesmanlike way' for any offence he might have caused. Moore, who was still furious about the slurs on his honour, responded coldly, and set off for Longman's with the news that the Memoirs had perished.[48] Longman's agreed with him that Murray's determination to destroy the manuscript had largely been caused by fear that they might get hold of it and publish it, fear of rivalry. 'So far he had triumphed,' wrote Moore.[49] *So far?* Do these words contain a hint that all was not yet lost with the Memoirs? Did Moore know of a surviving copy? Given the number of people who had read the Memoirs, it would be strange if nothing had been preserved.

By Wednesday morning, 19 May, the press had got hold of the story. An article in *The Times* alleged that Augusta Leigh had burnt the Memoirs while Moore looked on. Corrections were subsequently published, and on 27 May the paper carried a letter from Moore in which he set out the facts – and stated that the manuscript had been 'torn and burned before our eyes'.[50] But that was not the end of the rumours. Other papers printed stories such as that the Memoirs had been stolen from Moore's rooms, and that Hobhouse had forcibly held Moore down while the burning took place. In July, the first number of the new *John Bull Magazine* published what purported to be the chapter from the Memoirs in which Byron described his wedding night – more Mills & Boon than Byron: 'I . . . drew her to my arms, which now clasped her to my bosom with all the warmth of glowing, boiling passion, and all the pride of victory. I pressed my lips warmly to hers. There was no return of the pressure. I pressed them again and again – slightly at last was I answered, but still that *slightly* was sufficient.'[51]

Meanwhile acquaintances were stopping Moore in the street and congratulating him on having saved the country from moral pollution by allowing the Memoirs to be burnt. Twelve days later, Murray set out his own account in a letter to Wilmot-Horton. If he had been driven solely by commercial interest, wrote Murray,

I would have announced the Work for immediate publication and I cannot doubt that under all the circumstances the public curiosity about these Memoirs would have given me a very considerable profit beyond the large sum I originally paid for them but you yourself are I think able to do me the justice of bearing witness that I looked at the case with no such feelings and that my regard for Lord Byrons memory and my respect for his surviving Family made me most anxious that the Memoirs should be immediately destroyed since it was surmised that the publication might be injurious to the former and painful to the latter.

    As I myself scrupulously refrained from looking into the Memoirs I cannot from my own knowledge say whether such an opinion of the contents was correct or not.[52]

John Murray III gives a different picture in his fragmentary 'Reminiscences'. According to him, 'The burning of L[or]d Byrons M[emoir]s was a sacrifice on my fathers part of many 1000l [thousands of pounds]. He often regretted that he had not made [a] selection – and destroyed only the offensive parts.' To which Moore, had he read these words, would surely have said: 'I told you so.'

It would be possible to construct some colourful theories to explain why Murray had been so vociferous in his demand for the burning. In her book *The Late Lord Byron*, Doris Langley Moore calls his behaviour 'enigmatical', and describes him as 'resolute for doing away with a sensationally interesting unpublished book as . . . no publisher in history has ever been before or since'.[53] To begin with a comparatively unsensational explanation, Murray could have decided to keep the Memoirs for publication at a later date, when the fuss had died down. He therefore encouraged Hobhouse and the others to believe they were burning the real thing, rather than a dummy which he had substituted. However, the nation's moral climate grew stiffer rather than looser, and there never came a time when he felt able to publish the Memoirs. Such a theory leads to the assumption that the Murray family have secretly guarded the Memoirs over the years. John Murray VII says this is an understandable suspicion, and recalls that his father, Jock Murray (John Murray VI), was convinced that the manuscript had been stowed away somewhere in the building. 'Every time we had workmen in, doing alterations, he would be peering behind panels and under floorboards, still hoping it would turn up.'[54] This is hardly the behaviour one would expect if the manuscript had been secretly passed down through the generations.

    Alternatively, the burning was real enough, and had been ordered by Murray's influential Tory friends, who feared that Byron, though dead, might become the focus of political insurgence. There are a few fragments of evidence to support this. John Barrow, one of the inner ring of prolific Tory contributors to the *Quarterly Review*, wrote to a colleague at the Admiralty on 16 May 1824, the day before the burning: 'I have laid an injunction on Murray who, if I know him at all, will be ready to do what is right and what I advise him.'[55] The letter purports to be concerned about Lady Byron – but why should Barrow, whom Doris Langley Moore describes as 'a stranger' to the Byron circle, trouble himself about her? Barrow was Second Secretary to the Admiralty; behind him, as First Secretary, squatted the figure of another *Quarterly* Tory, who was also a Member of Parliament, John Wilson Croker. In his book *Barrow's Boys*, which chronicles the many explorations around the globe instigated by Barrow, Fergus Fleming describes Croker as 'famously unpleasant ... a talented but vituperative self-server who was loathed universally by his enemies and held in fearful respect by his right-wing political supporters. Publicly he was acknowledged as the best debater in Parliament. Privately, he was described as tasteless, shameless, malevolent and unscrupulous.'[56]

Croker, who is said to have been the first person to use the word 'Conservative' in its modern political sense, is often regarded as having hastened the death of John Keats with a vicious review in the *Quarterly* in 1818.[57] 'Who killed John Keats?' Byron asked.

> 'I', said the Quarterly,
> So savage and tartarly,
> 'It was one of my feats.'

Croker was implacably opposed to political reform. A letter he wrote to Murray about *Don Juan* during the furore over that poem raises the unlikely but fascinating spectre of Byron as a leader of political insurgents, a role in which, asserts Croker, he has been miscast by Hobhouse and Leigh Hunt. 'A man of his birth,' Croker continues in his anatomy of Byron as a potential revolutionary,

> a man of his taste, a man of his talents, a man of his habits can have nothing in common with such miserable creatures as we now call *radicals* . . . No, no, Lord Byron may be indulgent to these Jackal

followers of his ... but he never can ... continue to take a part so contrary to all his own interests and feelings & to the feelings and interests of all the respectable part of his country.[58]

And yet, Croker goes on, only yesterday at dinner somebody remarked that they had seen a letter from Byron, saying that 'if the radicals only made a little progress and showed some real force, he would hasten over [from Italy to London] and get on horseback to head them'. Croker dismisses the idea, saying that Byron cannot be serious; and if he were serious, he would not be writing about it openly.

Four years later, Byron was proving Croker wrong, by accepting the role of a popular leader in Greece. British support for the Greek campaign for independence from the Turks came mostly from such 'radicals' (that is, pro-reformists) as Hobhouse, now an MP, elected on the radical ticket, and Kinnaird. Byron's Greek venture may possibly have been seen by Croker and his friends as a rehearsal for assuming leadership of the radicals in Britain. Byron's death, of course, put a stop to all that. A true conspiracy theorist might suggest that there was something fishy about it, that he died largely because of the incompetence of the doctors, one of whom might conceivably have been planted by the British government. But no sooner was he gone than the Memoirs reared their head, threatening not to besmirch Byron's character, for virtually everyone who had read them agreed that on the whole the book portrayed him attractively. Instead, they threatened to refurbish his image, and to reinforce what Fiona MacCarthy calls 'the accretions of sanctity that follow unexpectedly early deaths'.[59]

It is not inconceivable that hardline members of the Tory government such as Croker felt that the suppression of the Memoirs would be a sensible precaution against a Byron cult with political overtones.[60] Hobhouse, of course, was also determined to suppress the Memoirs, by burning. We may assume that Hobhouse did indeed want Byron to become a posthumous focus for the reform movement, and since he himself thought the Memoirs had no saving grace, he was only fearful that they would damage Byron's reputation and make this impossible. It may be that he refused to read the Memoirs himself because he did not want to tarnish his own Byron-worship.

Up to this point, casting Croker as the villain seems quite convincing. But alas another letter in the Murray Archive from Croker to Murray undermines this theory. It was written on 23 May 1824, a week after the burning. When he has dealt with some *Quarterly* business, Croker adds a postscript:

> In what a bungling rambling way the Byron Memoirs story is told in the Literary Gazette (I think it is called). I can make neither head nor tail of it.
>
> Folks tell me that you have an excellent case & that Moore's is but so-so; but as it now stands before the public I defy any one to judge the right from the wrong.[61]

This is hardly the tone likely to be adopted by a prime mover behind the burning; and we must reluctantly clear Croker's name. The article he refers to was in the *Literary Observer*, and we will come back to it shortly.[62]

A third possibility is that Murray wanted to keep the manuscript out of the hands of Longman's at all costs. Even destruction was preferable to letting his rivals have it. But he was in no real danger of losing it to them – everyone except Moore agreed that the Memoirs were morally and legally Murray's property. Indeed, Moore himself was inclined to this view, though that probably would not have stopped him from selling the manuscript to Longman's if he thought he could get away with it. The most persuasive answer to the mystery is also the least sensational, and the most subtle. It is to be found not in the manuscripts of the Murray Archive, but in the 'public prints' – the reports of, and comments on, the burning of the Memoirs in the newspapers and magazines of the day.

The article in the *Literary Observer* mentioned by Croker was reprinted in the *Courier* on the Saturday following the burning, 22 May 1824. It does indeed read confusingly – as do all accounts of the events surrounding what somebody later called 'this celebrated bonfire'.[63] But the final lines of the *Courier* article are the essence of clarity. The conflagration, we are told, has been 'the topic of much conversation in the higher circles', and everybody has agreed in praising 'Mr Murray's conduct, as a gentleman and a man of honour . . . [I]n sacrificing his interest to his principles, he has acted as few tradesmen would have done.'[64] This was the social recognition that Murray had been seeking for years. He had finally been promoted to 'gentleman'. The size of the gulf separating tradesmen from gentlemen in the early nineteenth century can hardly be exaggerated. Did Murray, perceiving the opportunity for altruism over the Memoirs, believe that it might make it possible for him to cross the enormous divide, and acquire the same status as the gentleman scribblers who hung out in his own drawing–room? Who else had more to gain from this praise of Murray than Murray himself? That the status of gentleman should prove to have been self-conferred would be entirely typical of this ultimately tantalising and unsolvable story.

PART THREE

1825–2002
Dynasty

12

Tortoises dancing on dough

———————

SCARCELY HAD THE Byronic ashes been swept from the drawing-room grate at 50 Albemarle Street than the post brought a note from a young man who had just sent the manuscript of his novel *Aylmer Papillon* to Murray. The sooner it was put on the fire, wrote the boy, the better. 'As you have some small experience in burning MSS you will be perhaps so kind as to consign it to the flames.'[1] Nineteen-year-old Ben D'Israeli had left school, and was articled to a firm of City solicitors. He was already well known to Murray, having been introduced as a boy to the publisher's circle by his father Isaac D'Israeli. He wanted to be a writer, and so he lingered at number 50, basking in the same enthusiastic friendship with Murray that his father had once enjoyed. Somehow he and Murray came up with the extraordinary idea of starting a daily newspaper.

With Byron dead and the row about the Memoirs mainly over, Murray was lacking excitement in his life. It is hard to come up with any other explanation for this madcap scheme.[2] The *Quarterly Review* had been profitable for some while now, and its success may have given Murray reason to believe he could do well with another periodical. But his involvement with *Blackwood's* in 1818–19 had not been a success: he withdrew from co-publishing it after only a few months because he hated the personal attacks that were the magazine's hallmark.[3]

The pair's hubristic idea was to create a rival to no less a paper than *The Times*, which in those days was something of a scandal sheet with liberal sympathies. Murray's daily would be a conservative counterblast. But Murray knew no more about running a paper than did his very young partner in the venture. As Disraeli's great competitor W. E. Gladstone put it many years later in a review of Smiles's biography of Murray, 'The history of commerce or letters offers to us no more curious picture than that of the sagacious veteran of the book trade drawn into a wild and impossible undertaking by the eloquence of a youth of twenty.'[4] Murray was to put up half the money; Disraeli, to use the spelling of the name which he now adopted, would find the rest in the City. It was a cloak-and-dagger affair at first, with the project's supporters having code-names. These included Sir Walter Scott ('the Chevalier') and John Barrow at the Admiralty ('Mr Chronometer'). Disraeli rushed to Abbotsford and offered the editorship to John Gibson Lockhart, Scott's son-in-law, who knew nothing about newspapers. He assured Scott that it would be a very distinguished position, not merely the editorship of the paper, but 'the Directeur General of an immense organ'.[5] Lockhart had the sense to say no; he took over the editorship of the *Quarterly Review* instead, following the retirement from ill-health of Gifford, and the swift departure of Gifford's successor J. T. Coleridge. No one of stature could be found to head the *Representative*, Disraeli's Americanesque choice of name for the new paper. Common sense should have prevailed at this point, yet Murray assured Scott that there was no risk involved: 'The more we have thought and talked over our plans, the more certain are we of their inevitable success, and of their leading us to certain power, reputation, and fortune ... I have a family ... I would not engage in this venture with any hazard, when all that is dearest to man would be my loss.'[6]

In truth, Murray made a bad business decision. Somebody had told him that the annual profit of *The Times* was £40,000. Others warned him of the risks, but he did not listen. There was no stopping Disraeli, either. He hired his architect cousin George Basevi, who had been to Paris with Murray, to design the paper's office, a large house in Great George Street, Westminster. Then there was printing machinery to be acquired:

> Estimate for two Patent Printing Machines, for printing a Newspaper, with inking Rollers, Blankets &c complete, the Cylinders to be 22 inches diameter, provided with double feeders, capable of throwing

off from 1600 to 2000 impressions per hour with each machine – Also
for a two horse power Steam Engine ... Fixing the whole in George
St Westminster for the sum of £2680.'[7]

Murray seems to have balked at this, because in the event the paper
was printed by Clowes in the Strand.

Disraeli then signed up a team of foreign correspondents who
would be paid by the article. 'I wish to make this journal the focus
of the information of the whole world,' Murray told one of them
grandiosely.[8] There was still, however, no editor. Eventually, after
they had postponed the launch, a man named Tyndale was found;
but Smiles describes him as 'obscure and uninfluential', and he was
soon replaced, though not successfully.[9]

There was indeed a niche for the *Representative*, 'a daily paper of
sound politics', as one of Murray's Tory friends put it, 'fit to place
upon our breakfast table'. It would exclude the 'filthy details' of
divorce cases, and reports of the Bow Street appearances of prosti-
tutes and drunkards:[10] what we would now call tabloid journalism
was well established by the 1820s. The *Representative*, however, went
too far the other way. It was launched, as a four-page broadsheet
the same size as *The Times*, on Wednesday 25 January 1826. Smiles
describes it as 'a failure from the beginning ... badly organised, badly
edited'.[11] Much of the first number was taken up by an interminable
leading article by Lockhart on the present condition of Europe: 'We
have said that we contemplate no immediate interruption of the
general tranquillity.' Despite the team of correspondents, the foreign
news was largely pilfered from overseas papers, and the original articles tended to be out of date. A report from Paris was a week old,
and one from Warsaw, which appeared in a subsequent issue, had
been written a month earlier, on Christmas Eve. The paper came
briefly to life with a gossip column 'Table-Talk', which informed
readers that the Countess St Antonio had imported a pair of Italian
trumpeters from the Opera orchestra into her drawing room 'where
they surprised and pleased as distinguished a society as the present
early state of the season can produce'. This was followed by an inel-
egant catalogue of shipping news, law, stock exchange and sporting
reports: 'His Majesty's Stag-hounds meet on Friday at Iver Heath at

half-past ten.' The first issue petered out, as it had begun, in a jumble of classified advertisements. There was no sign of 'Table-Talk' in the next day's issue, and from now on gossip was scattered randomly around the paper. Even the political orientation of the *Representative* began to seem hazy; a report of a dinner in memory of Tom Paine was superficially hostile, but suspiciously lengthy and detailed: 'A person, who appeared to be a tallow-chandler, and who called himself a republican, then sang a song, which he said was made on the French Revolution, about despots, the cap of liberty, and the opening bud of reason.'

The assembled company at the dinner then toasted the *Representative*, on the grounds that 'its sentiments correspond with its title, for it prefers the representative to the monarchical system'. Curiously, the paper chose not to deny this.[12] There was a similarly lengthy and sympathetic report the next day of a meeting of the British Catholic Association, which regularly petitioned Parliament for the extension of civil rights to the nation's Roman Catholic minority. By the beginning of the paper's third week, the advertising had shrunk so drastically that the front page, which should have been full of small ads, had to be bulked out with parliamentary reports. By mid-February almost all attempts at newsgathering had ceased, and most of the paper was being lifted from Hansard. Murray meanwhile had taken to his bed with the stress. In 1824 he had bought himself a private residence in London, 14 Whitehall Place, and he was not at Albemarle Street to answer letters. Rumours of his ill-health abounded in rival newspapers. But where was Disraeli? His letters to Murray suddenly stop. It seems that he and the City financier he had drawn into the scheme failed to come up with their share of the cash, leaving Murray to bear the entire financial weight.

More than the *Representative* was now at stake. The economic boom which the country had been enjoying had suddenly ended in a crash, and the very month that Murray launched the newspaper saw the collapse of two of the Edinburgh publishers with whom he had close dealings, Constable and Ballantyne. This caused tragedy for Sir Walter Scott, whose financial affairs were disastrously entangled with both. Meanwhile several London bookseller–publishers were also in difficulties. 'These are severe shocks in the trading world of literature,' wrote Washington Irving at the end of January 1826, a few days after the *Representative* had gone on sale. 'Pray Heaven, Murray may stand unmoved!'[13] Somehow he did, despite having to shoulder the burden of the newspaper until the end of July, when it merged with the *New Times*. As often happens in such situations, by the end of its independence the paper had recovered some of its advertising, and was running quite well; but Murray had now become totally negative about it. 'I have cut the knot of evil,' he wrote to Irving, 'and am now ... returned to reason and the shop.'[14] There was a brief period of recrimination with the D'Israelis, with Isaac defending his son against what he imagined to be Murray's criticism. Murray admitted he had yielded to young Benjamin's 'unrelenting excitement', but denied that he resented the lost money: 'I solemnly declare, that I neither care nor think about it more than one does of the long-suffered agonies of a diseased tooth the day after we have summoned resolution enough to have it extracted. On the contrary, I am disposed to consider this apparent misfortune, as one of that chastening class which, if suffered wisely, may be productive of greater good.'[15]

He claimed he could make the money back in 'a very few months'. Smiles gives the sum involved as 'not less than £26,000'; in modern terms, several million.[16] The house in Whitehall Place had to be sold.

The Murray–D'Israeli friendship suffered another major blow with the publication by Henry Colburn of an anonymous roman à clef, *Vivian Grey*, in which Murray appeared as a scheming but disappointed politician, the Marquess of Carabas. He enjoyed this joke even less when he discovered that Benjamin Disraeli was the author: 'He [Carabas] was servile, and pompous, and indefatigable, and loquacious, so whispered the world: his friends hailed him as, at once, a courtier and a sage, a man of business and an orator.'[17] Yet, as Murray admitted shortly after the shutting down of the *Representative*, the fault in his relationship with young Disraeli had really been his own: 'From me [he] received nothing but the most unbounded confidence and parental attachment; my fault was in having "loved not wisely but too well".[18]

John Murray was approaching fifty. 'The heyday of my youth is passed,' he wrote to Scott.[19] With Byron and young Benjamin gone, what excitements could life and work at 50 Albemarle Street still offer? A young American, Edmund Griffin, drew a vivid picture of Murray in the year after the birth and death of his newspaper. Despite his determination to be rid of most of his hangers-on, Murray seems to have been as hospitable as ever, and Griffin joined in a dinner party at 50 Albemarle Street. Those present included Washington Irving, Lockhart and Tom Moore, who was determined to tell the funniest stories of the evening, and sang songs charmingly at the piano after supper. Griffin was disappointed by the conversation – 'no discussion of any length or interest took place' – but Murray impressed him in a quiet way: 'He is a good-looking man, with a preoccupied and anxious air. This gives way, however, to true Scottish sense and cor-diality in conversation. He has . . . a good memory . . . of all the eminent literary characters of the age. The memoirs of himself and his times would be invaluable.'[20] Griffin was told that millions of pounds had passed through Murray's hands, but that he was 'by no means exorbitantly rich'. The latter was certainly true; and as to the former, the ledgers tell a different story. When in 1831 Washington Irving found it difficult to believe that his later books were not selling as well as a distinguished author's should, Murray gave him some hard facts: 'The publication of Columbus cost me, Paper, print, advertising, Author, £5700; and it has produced but £4700. Granada cost 3073£ and its sale has produced but 1830£ making my gross loss £2250.'[21]

Distinguished men of letters like Irving expected substantial advances, so Murray tried to recoup by keeping other projects, however promising, on a tight rein. Benjamin Disraeli had recom-mended the publication of a splendid three-volume set of Irish folk and fairy tales, collected and superbly written by the antiquary Thomas Crofton Croker, possibly a distant relation of Croker of the Admiralty and, coincidentally, an Admiralty clerk. Murray managed to buy the copyright for a mere £80. *Fairy Legends and Traditions in the South of Ireland* was a success when Murray published it in 1825. Sir Walter Scott loved it, and spread the word, and Murray signed Croker for a sequel. He could not get away with £80 this time, but he kept his offer as tight as possible, and Croker accepted £300. Considering all the travelling and research the books demanded, this was far from being fairy gold.

Crofton Croker may have believed in fairies himself – some of his fellow collectors did – but his books were not regarded as primarily for children. Murray did not attempt to be a children's specialist, but he did have one spectacular hit in this field. It came from the family of one of his father's authors, the poet and inventor Edmund Cartwright. His daughter Elizabeth had married a clergyman, raised three boys and written a history of England for children. At the end of each chapter were 'Conversations' between some child readers and the author, who gave her name as 'Mrs Markham' ('mark 'em'?). Here they discuss the Normans:

> *Richard.* I shall be very glad, mamma, when you come to a good king. It is very disagreeable to hear about bad people.
> *Mrs Markham.* It is one of the great drawbacks to the pleasure of reading history, that it is such a painful record of human crimes.
> *George.* I was very sorry that Robert joined William in using his brother Henry so ill; for I feel a sort of liking for Robert.
> *Mrs M.* So do most people, I believe, when they read his history; but it is more because his misfortunes, and the ill usage he afterwards met with, excite our compassion, than for any real merits which he possessed. He was an undutiful son, and an unkind brother.[22]

This first 'Mrs Markham' book was published by Constable in 1823, and was not a success. However, when Murray took it over he had the author revise it, and put it into his school book list and sold it to teachers throughout the country. Sales grew steadily, until a large and regular circulation was reached.[23] Smiles writes: 'The book has subsequently undergone frequent revision, and down to the present date [1891] it continues to be a great favourite, especially in ladies' schools.'[24] *A History of England* and its Murray-published sequels which included a history of France, and histories of Poland

and Malta written entirely in the form of conversations, did continue to be *read*; but anyone who believes that children *enjoyed* Mrs Markham should seek out the disparaging references in the stories of E. Nesbit.

Murray did not make his business arrangements with 'Mrs Markham', but corresponded instead with her husband, the Rev. John Penrose. In contrast, another historian for children, Maria Callcott, had been exchanging letters with Murray for at least twenty years before she came up with her own bestselling history-for-children in 1835. In the 1810s she had solicited Murray's help in getting naval preferment through J. W. Croker for her first husband, Captain Thomas Graham RN. Smiles describes her clashing over politics with Croker at Albemarle Street: she 'was not only a Whig, but a high-spirited woman'.[25] First as Maria Graham, then as Maria Callcott, she became a successful author of travel books. She had a high admiration for Murray, and knew when to use it in flattery: 'All great men have to pay the penalty of their greatness and you *arch bookseller* as you are among the rest – you must now & then be entreated to do many things that you only half like to do … Every body on the continent is so convinced that you can do what you please, that they don't think a thing worth reading unless your name appears on the title page.'[26]

This letter was written to urge Murray to publish a book translated from the German by the Grahams' young friend and travelling companion the painter Charles Locke Eastlake. We shall meet Eastlake again later as the suitor and ultimately the husband of another Murray author, Elizabeth Rigby. Maria Graham, who had spent the summer of 1819 in the wild mountains east of Rome accompanied by her husband and Eastlake, wanted to introduce Eastlake to the Murray circle:

> I want him to see the sort of thing that one only sees in your house at your morning levées, the traffic of mind & literature if I may call it so. To a man who has lived most of his grown up life out of England it is both curious and instructive & I wish for this advantage for my friend. And in return … I promise you great pleasure in knowing a gentleman of as much modesty as real accomplishment, & whose

taste & talents as an artist must one day place him very high among our native genius.[27]

Maria Graham began her career as a Murray author with John Murray II, and evolved, as Maria Callcott, into a lucrative author of history books with John Murray III. Under her first married name she wrote *Three Months Passed in the Mountains East of Rome, During the Year 1819*, published in 1820, with illustrations by Eastlake. This took a new perspective on Italy, breaking away from the highbrow tone of the guides published on classical Italy for Grand Tourists, towards a clear exposition of the country's dangers and social difficulties:

> When there are so many travellers in Italy, and when so many travellers have published tours, picturesque and classical, and have exhibited that 'fair and fervid' land in all her various aspects: as 'native to famous wits'; as the cradle, if not also the grave, of the fine arts … it may appear presumptuous in one not capable of adding any thing to what is already known on any of these points, to write at all upon that country.
>
> Yet there is one subject on which modern travellers have been silent: the state of the present inhabitants of the near neighbourhood of Rome … [V]isitors to the 'eternal city' seem to have forgotten that there are still living men to till the ground, and to dress the vineyards that surround it. And it is natural that it should be so. The apparent deadness of the Campagna, during the season when most travellers cross it, the scanty population, whose habits and manners savour of an older world, the wall of ruin that surrounds every thing that is new and fresh in Rome, force the thoughts back upon the past, and veil the present, as the future, from our eyes.[28]

Graham challenged herself, and indeed her husband and Eastlake, to spend the summer of 1819 in the Apennines east of Rome, bandit country, infested with brigands who robbed, pillaged and kidnapped with impunity. Gritting her teeth, and bravely accepting the dangers, Graham found good copy out in the hills. Such was the stuff of the women whom Murray encouraged into authorship.

> Every day while we remained at Tivoli, brought some new particulars concerning the [outlaws'] marches. It was ascertained, that the

whole number amounted to about one hundred and forty, divided into companies, not exceeding twenty in each, for the sake of more easy subsistence. The head quarters appeared to be at Rio Freddo, and in the woods of Subiaco ... Every evening the episcopal church bell rang at Tivoli, to set the guards at the different bridges leading to the town, as the people were in nightly expectation that the brigands would enter it in search of provisions ... On the night of 21st or 22nd [August] seven robbers had gone into San Vetturino, armed chiefly with bludgeons, and had taken nearly all the bread in the town ... But the most enterprising gang lingered about Tivoli, where there are a number of rich proprietors, who might have furnished a considerable booty.[29]

When with Croker's help Graham was given command of a ship, Maria travelled with him to South America. Graham died at sea, and, undaunted, Maria settled down to write *Journal of a Residence in Chile*, which Murray published in 1824. Subsequently, in 1828, she married the artist Augustus Wall Callcott, and changed the direction of her writing from travel to history. Following Mrs Markham's popularity, she hit the jackpot with *Little Arthur's History of England*, which Murray published in 1835. Addressed to 'my dear Little Arthur' it was written more simply and colloquially than any rivals. *Little Arthur* ran and ran: it was reprinted constantly during the Victorian and Edwardian eras, and was even considered serviceable in 1936, when Murray's issued a centenary edition. It was updated regularly until it went out of print in the 1960s. Murray's apparent encouragement of Croker to smooth Captain Graham to the command of a naval ship was one of the rare cases where we know that the publisher exploited his Tory connections, albeit for somebody else's benefit. Murray's typical position towards Tories was to keep them at arm's length: he was furious when the historian Henry Hallam, whose *Constitutional History of England* (1827) had been rubbished in the *Quarterly Review*, complained that Murray had a mutual back-scratching arrangement with the Tories who wrote for that journal. Murray responded that he had had quite a few favours from the Whigs, but as for the Tories, far from accepting bribes, he had virtually been subsidising the government with his generous fees for

Quarterly Review articles: 'I paid to the utmost their Under Secretaries of State – Secretaries of State Bishops & even their prime Ministers for advocating their own Cause they took my money but never did they confer the slightest favor in return either upon Gifford or myself. So much for my Tory relations.'[30]

Besides editing the *Quarterly*, Lockhart had also taken over Gifford's unofficial position as Murray's chief reader, and continued to give Murray practical advice. When Wordsworth told Murray in 1826 that 'I have at last determined to go to the Press with my Poems as early as possible' and was looking for a publisher, [31] Lockhart gave a warning. Wordsworth 'is and must continue to be a classic Poet of England', but Murray should remember the money he had lost on Crabbe. It all depended, said Lockhart, on what terms would be acceptable to 'the great Laker, whose vanity, be it whispered, is nearly as remarkable as his genius'.[32] In the event, Wordsworth suggested a modest contract, with no advance, but even so Murray seems not to have wanted the Laker on his list, since he failed to reply by Wordsworth's deadline, and the collected poems went elsewhere.

Murray remained an equivocator by nature, a characteristic, though infuriating to Byron, which could sometimes be fruitful. It encouraged him to disseminate opposing points of view, for while publishing the writings of Thomas Malthus, the inventor of the theory of the population explosion, Murray also published the attack on Malthus, *The Law of Population* (1830) by the radical politician Michael Thomas Sadler. These were exciting times intellectually, and the Murray list had a generous share of important new books. *Principles of Political Economy and Taxation* (1817) by David Ricardo, son of a Dutch-Jewish London stockbroker, was a key work on the new science of economics. Murray showed no hesitation when signing up scientists. He reported to Walter Scott in November 1815: 'Sir H. Davy read his Paper to-day at the Royal Society, on his most valuable discovery of the means of preventing the fatal accidents in collieries from inflammable air.'[33] Davy's safety lamp for miners became available a few months later. Such discoveries and inventions, however, tended to be announced in scientific journals rather than books, and it was not until 1827 that Murray was at last able to capture Sir Humphry Davy between hard covers.[34] That year, he paid Davy a lavish 500 guineas for the copyright of his *Six Discourses Delivered before the Royal Society*, and recouped only £381. Davy was also a poet, and a friend of poets: he had helped to correct the proofs of the Wordsworth–Coleridge *Lyrical Ballads* in his younger days, and he persuaded Murray to publish his treatise on salmon-fishing, *Salmonia* (1828). This was a success: as Davy pointed out impatiently to Murray: 'If the accounts I have received from my friends of the reception of *Salmonia* by the Public be correct & you only printed 1000 copies, a new edition must be wanted.'[35] Swallowing the commercial failure of Davy's *Discourses*, Murray did better when he published a work by Davy's former assistant Michael Faraday, the inspiring teacher of science two hundred yards up Albemarle Street at the Royal Institution. Faraday distilled his teaching into his *Chemical Manipulation*, a textbook for chemistry students first published by Richard Phillips. Murray bought the title in 1829.

Another discovery was Mary Somerville, the Scottish-born physician's wife who had managed while bringing up a family to educate herself in advanced mathematics and physics, largely through personal contact with Davy, Faraday and the other leading scientists of the day. She translated the pioneering science treatise *The Mechanism of the Heavens* (1831) by La Place and wrote *On the Connexions of the Physical Sciences* (1834). These rapidly became standard works. Murray was her generous and supportive publisher, though he knew he was on to a good thing when in 1838 he bought an interest in the copyright to *Connexions* to ease a financial disaster faced by the Somervilles.[36]

Nevertheless, Murray felt more comfortable when he dealt with travel writers. He commissioned no portraits of scientists, but quite a gallery of explorers hung in the Albemarle Street reception rooms.[37] Still on the walls today are Captain Sir John Franklin, Sir John Barrow and David Livingstone. When not writing for the *Quarterly Review*, Barrow supplied Murray with a whole series of travel books by the 'boys' he had despatched around the globe from his desk at the Admiralty. The African interior vied with the polar regions for prominence in the Murray list. Sir Francis Head, a colourful retired soldier also known as 'Galloping Head', wrote on his experiences in the South American gold-rush, *Rough Notes Taken during Some Rapid Journeys across the Pampas and among the Andes* (1826). Murray got his travel books cheap: no one expected him to finance the journeys, and he paid Head only 100 guineas. Far from feeling cheated, Head called Murray 'honourable and liberal'.[38] He later told John Murray IV of his good health and his robust physical regime: 'For fifty two years I have never missed a day getting on horseback until this malady [shingles] attacked me, and I attribute my wonderful good health to this constant practice.'[39]

But he also spoke his mind directly to John Murray III when in the late 1840s he was refused permission to republish his *Quarterly* article 'Stokers and Pokers' because this ran against the copyright rules of the journal. 'I don't know what are the rules of the *Quarterly*,' he blasted,

> but your good father's rule was to make it a rule to do whatever I asked him to do. He would have boiled his boots and fried his trousers if I had recommended it … I never injured his boots or trousers; on the contrary, the more he trusted me, the more careful I was with him. Now my dear Sir, you must undergo the same ordeal, and rest quite satisfied that, in spite of all you say, you *will* publish my article … The first time I come to London I will call in Albemarle Street, and settle it with a yard-arm conversation.[40]

That is of course a splendid way to deal with a publisher, and indeed the book was published.[41] Head's visits to Albemarle Street were blessedly rare, and generally when there was a frost, because he hunted six days a week, coming home each night 'as covered in dirt as a Peelite party'.[42]

The twenty-six-year-old John Murray III was now being left in charge of the business from time to time. 'I do not know whether you are at home or whether your son is on guard & you at play,'

Maria Callcott wrote to Murray on 22 August 1834. The younger John had hated his schooldays at Charterhouse, which in those days was crammed into a small site in central London. Bullying was rife. By an unkind irony, he too had eye trouble. His son wrote that it was:

> an inflammatory malady of the eyes which greatly hampered his enjoyment of life and his power of taking part in games. I never knew him except as a very short-sighted man; and his was a form of short-sight which derived no aid from glasses. As we grew older, we children were accustomed to act as eyes for him in recognising friends. In spite of this, his powers of observation in regard to scenery, architecture, painting, etc., were extraordinary; and he never seemed to forget what he had once seen.[43]

Released from school, John Murray III was sent for one year to Edinburgh University. His landlord reported: 'I never saw a finer young man under my roof, so perfectly behaved was he, in every respect so agreeable – good temper, sobriety, attention to his studies, an obliging disposition, polite and pleasing manners ... these were qualities by which he uniformly distinguished himself.'[44] Despite the brevity of his period in Edinburgh – evidently his father wanted him to join the firm as soon as possible – John Murray III showed a real talent for geology and mineralogy, and this remained a lifetime hobby. He was at the celebrated dinner, in February 1827, when Sir Walter Scott finally admitted to being the author of the Waverley novels, but he was equally inspired by a trip to Ruthwell in Dumfriesshire, where some prehistoric animal tracks had been discovered in the sandstone. Having seen them, young Murray was invited to a gathering at which the eccentric palaeontologist William Buckland attempted to reproduce the phenomenon:

> 23 Jan 1828. I went on Saturday last to a party at Mr Murchison's house, assembled to behold tortoises in the act of walking upon dough. Prof. Buckland acted as master of the ceremonies. There were present many other geologists and savants ... At first the beasts took it into their heads to be refractory and to stand still. Hereupon the ingenuity of the professor was called forth in order to make them

move. This he endeavoured to do by applying sundry flips with his fingers upon their tails; deil a bit however would they stir; and no wonder, for on endeavouring to take them up it was found that they had stuck so fast to the pie-crust as only to be removed with half a pound of dough sticking to each foot. This being the case it was found necessary to employ a rolling pin, and to knead the paste afresh; nor did geological fingers disdain the culinary offices. It was really a glorious scene to behold all the philosophers, flour-besmeared, working away with tucked-up sleeves. Their exertions, I am happy to say, were at length crowned with success; a proper consistency of paste was attained, and the animals walked over the course in a very satisfactory manner; insomuch that many who came to scoff returned rather better disposed towards believing.[45]

Tortoises dancing on dough: as John Murray III would soon find, this was not a bad metaphor for the plodding nature of a publisher's job. Yet out of the drudgery something magical and timeless could emerge, and could survive indefinitely, like those mysterious footprints in the sandstone.

In 1828 John Murray III spent the summer in Scotland, researching Byron's childhood in Aberdeen for Thomas Moore, who was writing the poet's biography. The following year, however, he was more ambitious, travelling to Holland, Belgium and north Germany. 'Having from my early youth been possessed by an ardent desire to travel,' he recounted, 'my very indulgent father acceded to my requests on condition that I should prepare myself by mastering the language of the country I was to travel in. Accordingly in 1829, having brushed up my German, I first set foot on the Continent at Rotterdam.'[46]

Young Murray went without a guidebook, for there were none in existence for most of the places he intended to visit. 'The only Guides deserving the name', he recalled, 'were: Ebel, for Switzerland; Boyce, for Belgium; and Mrs Starke for Italy.'[47] Mariana Starke was a Murray author who had spent seven years in Italy, caring for a relation with tuberculosis. Her *Travels on the Continent* (1820) was full of practical advice as well as historical information, and must have helped set the standard for the project that was soon conceived by

John Murray III. Indeed, Mrs Starke wrote that the European scene had changed so much since 1800 'that new Guides for Travellers are extremely wanted'.[48] 'I set forth for the North of Europe unprovided with any guide,' Murray recorded, 'excepting a few manuscript notes about towns and inns, &c., in Holland, furnished me by my good friend Dr Somerville, husband of the learned Mrs Somerville. These were of the greatest use.'[49]

After Holland, Murray had no notes to help him. Truly a publisher's son, he seems to have perceived right away that a book might solve this need. 'I set to work to collect for myself all the facts, information, statistics, &c., which an English tourist would be likely to require or find useful. I travelled thus, note-book in hand.'[50] Working with square sheets of paper which he folded in half and wrote upon in columns, he 'noted down every fact as it occurred'. These gradually built to form the groundwork from which the first Handbook evolved, and were later bound together into two large volumes, lettered on the spines 'H. B. Northern Germany Original MS'.[51] The first volume opens with some maxims for travellers on the management of expenses: 'One of the greatest annoyances in travelling, is continual exposure to imposition; but this may by good management, be frequently avoided, either altogether or in part, as by bad management it may be greatly increased.'[52]

Meanwhile, the younger John Murray's parents and sisters were on holiday in North Wales, where they paid a call on the survivor of the Ladies of Llangollen, Britain's first openly lesbian couple. John Murray the elder took it all in his stride, but his wife was shocked:

> Miss Ponsonby; or I might rather say Mr for she has no resemblance to a woman ... wears no cap, but just a man's hat, which she hangs up in the hall when she comes into the house, and as she wears a riding habit at a little distance she has all the appearance of an old gentleman – this does not at all agree with my idea of propriety, and I cannot see what they could have gained by so doing, which they might not equally have had by appearing like women.[53]

Thus Annie Murray wrote to her son, who left for the continent while the family was in Wales. Annie expresses the usual maternal concerns when a son is facing his first foreign trip: 'I hope you have got some warm worsted Stockings; and be sure you have a great coat, and a Cloak to keep out the weather ... you must not go to places where there is danger – such as Mines ... We shall not know where to write to you ... you must let us know.' Young John seems to have paid no attention to his mother's plea: 'I ... penetrated into Carinthia and Carniola, where I visited the almost unknown cave of Adelsberg, with its subterranean lakes and fish without eyes, and I descended the quicksilver mine of Idria, in which it is death to work more than six hours in a week underground.'[54] His father was anxious also – 'I am always frightened for what might be occasioned from your defective sight'[55] – and was altogether astonished when John Murray III returned home and proposed that the firm should publish a series of continental guidebooks which he would write himself. The older man agreed in principle, examined the notes his son had made and decided that they were worth publishing. He gave the project the code-name 'Handbook'.

We have a glimpse of John Murray III in August 1830, not abroad collecting material for future Handbooks, but looking after Albemarle Street while his father is staying with Lockhart in Scotland. 'I received your packet of letters,' the older Murray writes. 'I shall be very glad to be allowed to read the MS. Life of Bp. Middleton ... Print 750 of the Novel ... Let Parker do as he suggests with regard to the Index to the *QR*.'[56] Young Murray shows due deference towards his father, and the letters he writes for the firm are in his father's name, though this is barely verifiable because of father and son having the same name. Writing to the son, the older Murray, now aged fifty-one, admits to being a demanding father–employer: 'it is my habit to be far more critical & censorious towards the merits of my own family'.[57]

It was not always clear which Murray was in charge of what. Charles Dickens, writing in April 1839 to recommend Robert Bell as a contributor to the biographical dictionary *Universal Biography*, addressed his letter to 'John Murray Junr. Esquire'. He added: 'I beg my compliments to your father. I address this letter to you under the impression that it may reach *both of you* sooner by finding you in Albemarle Street.

I hope you may one of these days have it in your power to retort an introduction upon me.'[58] From time to time it was convenient for the older Murray to negotiate at a distance. Sir Ralph Rice, representing Mariana Starke, was furious that Murray's had 'sacrificed' £800 worth of *Directions for Travellers* and 'made waste paper of them' when it turned out that they did not hold the copyright. He was kept at arm's length. 'I must mention', wrote Murray on behalf of his father and with extreme caution, 'that from what I can understand of Mr Murray's intentions, I do not think [he] would make any further concessions or accept this offer on any other terms.'[59]

George Borrow, who became a Murray author in 1840, found the elder Murray the more relaxed of the two. 'I shall be most happy to see you,' he wrote to John Junior, 'and still more your father, whose jokes do one good.'[60] A pencil-and-chalk drawing of the older Murray by William Brockedon, made in 1837, however, shows a weary and wary man, with a slight stoop and a haunted look, very different from the young publisher in the oil painting of many years earlier.

One aspect of the business that was evidently uncongenial to young John was its social life. It appeared that he simply was not making enough effort. His father wrote to him from Scotland: 'I am surprised that you do not feel, much more at least than you appear to do, the necessity and duty of going to such important parties as you are occasionally invited to. It is as much a department of your business as Advertising.' He added, 'I would advise ... dining three times a week at the Athenaeum,' and warned that otherwise 'at my death or infirmities all my valuable connections would be lost to you'.[61] In January 1836, John Murray III signed articles of co-partnership with his father. He was now twenty-seven, with an apartment of his own across Piccadilly, at 11 Ryder Street, St James's. The new arrangements gave him a quarter share of the firm's profits, excluding the *Quarterly Review*, in return for which he must 'appropriate the whole of his Time, and use all his energy and activity to promote the success of the said Business'. The document, in which the older Murray's profession is given as 'publisher', states that the Murrays are renting a warehouse, but makes no reference to the shop. There is no mention of bookselling, but the 1831–4 ledger for the Family Library series divides the number of copies sold into two categories, 'Shop' and 'Trade', so evidently the shop was still a significant part of the business. The document concludes by stating that, while the firm's imprint remains 'John Murray', all bank accounts shall be under the names 'John Murray & Son'.

Meanwhile young John Murray nearly acquired a part-time colleague, younger than himself. The firm had published a book by a woman author on her travels in, yet again, Belgium and Germany, and she asked the older Murray to use his influence and get her twenty-year-old son a job at Post Office headquarters. Murray managed this, and the boy started work. But his mother reported that he had nothing to do in the evenings – could Murray possibly give him some work as a proof-reader? Murray seems to have decided that this was taking kindness too far, and said no. The lad, whose name was Anthony Trollope, eventually learned to fill up his spare time by writing novels.[62]

There was to be no rushing the Handbooks. The older Murray was adamant that there must be exhaustive research trips, checkings and recheckings. Young John would make preliminary journeys, write them up, and then have these 'Routes' tested by friends. As the young man explained to a contributor, the books were to be confined to 'plain matter of fact and practical information … not a mere compilation from other works, but the result of *personal observation*.'[63] The descriptive passages were to be 'limited to very condensed notices of the most remarkable places and to such facts only as are essential to enable a traveller in passing thro' a county to know what he ought to see, why he ought to see it, in what manner he may see it best'.[64] Looking back from the end of the century, John Murray III marvelled that all this had been achieved with the early Handbooks not only before the age of railways, but before most roads had been properly surfaced. He recalled how the high road from Hamburg to Berlin in 1829 had been 'a mere wheel track in the deep sand of Brandenburg'.[65] The elderly Goethe was living in Weimar in 1829, and the boy called on the great man, presenting him with the manuscript of some lines addressed to him by Byron.

He remembered that Goethe had been wearing a brown dressing gown – and a clean shirt.

Not until 1836, seven years after the first exploratory trip, did the older John Murray give the Handbooks the go-ahead. The first result was a plump little volume in a red binding, with 'HANDBOOK FOR TRAVELLERS ON THE CONTINENT' lettered in gold on the front, with the title in full inside: *Hand-Book for Travellers on the Continent: Being a Guide through Holland, Belgium, Prussia and Northern Germany, and Along the Rhine, from Holland to Switzerland, Containing Descriptions of the Principal Cities, their Museums, Picture galleries, &c.; – The Great High Roads; – and the Most Interesting and Picturesque Districts; also Directions for Travellers; and Hints for Tours, with an Index Map*, John Murray [and Son on first edition] 1836. Its 462 pages of double columns are crammed with an extraordinary quantity of information, written by the young John Murray with style and maturity, strong descriptive power, and a passion for detail:

> The Dutch are not altogether absorbed in commerce, so as to be able to devote no time to literature and the arts; witness the Society called *Felix Meritis*, which is founded and supported entirely by merchants and citizens … In its nature it bears some resemblance to the Royal Institution in London. It contains a library, museum, collections of casts of ancient statues, of chemical and mathematical instruments, and a very fine concert room and observatory.'[66]

Amsterdam's red-light district, the 'Speel Houses', gets due mention: 'These vile haunts of vice … tolerated by the government … are merely alluded to as one of the curiosities of Holland; and on account of a strange practice, not yet quite extinct among the sober citizens, of taking their wives and daughters at times to see them, in order to inspire them with a horror for vice, by the sight of it in its most disgusting and odious form.'[67]

Given the length and scope of the Handbook, the young John Murray remains tantalisingly invisible: for example, when describing the grave of Goethe in Weimar, he gives no indication of his having met the great man. If the attitudes of the Handbooks are generally bourgeois, it can scarcely be a surprise. This was the age in which the bourgeoisie began to travel: until 1815 travelling for pleasure had been limited to the upper classes. The characteristic journey had been the Grand Tour, taken by young aristocrats during their education. Byron's travels had been on that model. Now the young English milords on horseback or in their own coaches were giving way to the family parties, travelling as much as possible on the new railways. John Murray III and the Handbooks could not have come on the scene at a more appropriate moment. As an indication of the success of this pioneering achievement of publishing, John Murray III inscribed his own copy: 'This copy of first edition to be preserved. The work was begun by me on my first Travels on the Continent 1829 & completed abroad & at home. Nearly 50,000 copies have been sold of it & in process of years the book has been almost re-written. John Murray Augt 1862.' This first volume received enthusiastic reviews. *The Times* wrote:

> Mr Murray has succeeded in identifying his countrymen all the world over. Into every nook which an Englishman can penetrate he carries his RED HANDBOOK. He trusts to his MURRAY as he would trust to his razor, because it is thoroughly English and reliable; and for his history, hotels, exchanges, scenery, for the clue to his route and his comfort on the way, the RED HANDBOOK is his 'guide, philosopher and friend.'[68]

This first Handbook was swiftly followed by those to *Southern Germany* (1837), *Switzerland* (1838) and *Northern Europe: Denmark, Norway, Sweden and Russia* (1839). Murray wrote the first two himself, but by the third had begun to recruit collaborators. He looked for men and women who were acknowledged experts on the country or area concerned and made the clear and direct approach to their subject characteristic of a Murray. Few people in the 1830s knew as much about Spain as Richard Ford, who had travelled in the country extensively, and whose curiosity about Spain's political and artistic history, its landscape and culture pours out from the pages of his notebooks, drawings and watercolours. By 1839 Ford was living near Exeter, contributing articles and reviews on subjects connected to Spain for the *Quarterly Review*. His pamphlet *An Historical*

Enquiry into the Unchangeable Character of a War in Spain (1837) was just one of Ford's publications that prompted Murray to write to him:

> What think you of a Handbook for Spain. If you will undertake such a work – following the plan of the Handbook for North Germany – so as to make a volume of about 400 pages, My father directs me to say that he will be happy to give you Two Hundred Guineas for the Copyright … The work in your hands wd I am sure not be a mere day itinerary but full of entertainment & information. You have doubtless correspondents in Spain who wd give you intelligence respecting recent & in many instances deplorable changes which have take place since you left the country … It is not unlikely you may think it infra dig to be known as the author of a Guide book – in that case the author's name may be suppressed, though Mr Murray wd prefer that it shd be affixed.[69]

In the event, the first edition of the *Handbook to Spain* was a disaster, because Ford had referred to Spanish customs in a manner which Murray felt would damage his interests. The edition was suppressed, only twenty-five copies being saved. Among the paragraphs which had to be deleted from the rapidly rearranged second edition was this:

> Then inhabitants [of Spain] never would amalgamate, never would, as Strabo said, put their shields together, never would sacrifice their own local private interests for the general good; on the contrary, in their hour of need, they had, as at present, a constant tendency to separate into distinct juntas, each of which only thought of its own views, utterly indifferent to the injury thereby occasioned to what ought to have been the common cause of all.[70]

The antiquary Thomas Crofton Croker, already a Murray author with his books on Irish fairy lore, was approached to write a Handbook for London. Croker combined his career as an Admiralty clerk with a life of literary and historical research and writing: he was a long-time friend of Thomas Moore, and was working on a life of Moore when he died. Murray felt Croker would be the ideal author of a guide to London. 'Our conversation last week respecting the Handbook for London Past & Present, left me with the impression that you fully enter into the spirit of the project, & will, I doubt not, do it ample justice.' Murray went on to set out the guiding principles of the exercise: 'The object being to produce a work at once practically useful to strangers in London, & preferably readable as a book of entertaining information, & anecdotes connected with the remarkable Localities & Buildings of the Metropolis.'[71]

It was not always plain sailing. To the expert on Middle East politics, Henry Parish, John Murray III described what it was that he personally wanted from a handbook:

> What I require when I go to a foreign country is what can I see here that I cannot see elsewhere, what is best worth notice & why is it worth notice. I am thankful to be told where there is a fine point of view & what are its peculiar characters & the objects which appear in it. I am equally obliged to the guide who will point out to me the interesting localities such as the spot where Mahomet passed the breach in the wall – & the square where the Janissaries were annihi-lated by Hassin Pacha – I shd be glad to be told a few interesting details or anecdotes connected with these two events, but I by no means wish to be burthened with all the details of the siege or of the Reign of Sultan Mahomed … There is no reason in the world why a Guide book shd be dull & dry – although such works commonly enjoy the reputation of being so.[72]

The *Handbook for Travellers in the East* was to have been one volume, but with Parish's enthusiasm engaged it expanded to two, embracing Greece, Turkey, Egypt and Palestine. But, within five months of beginning his work on the Handbook, Parish had brought in too many overt allusions to politics, 'quite irrelevant in a Guide Book', which echoed the troubles Murray had had with Richard Ford. Murray told Parish that these:

> would prove ruinous to the Work as a literary speculation … Aware how much your own mind was engrossed by the Eastern question, I made an express stipulation with you before you began that there was to be no politics in the book … The remarks directed against Russia would alone suffice to exclude our book from the Countries where that Power has rule, & therefore the impolicy of their intro-duction in a Guide Book must at once be obvious.[73]

As a postscript, Murray warned: 'Unless I am much mistaken, a Statement in page 3 of your MS would subject the Publisher to an action for Libel!!' Amended, the book was published in 1840.

The Handbooks were soon selling solidly, with frequent reprints. Some sixty years after they first appeared, the archaeologist Austen Henry Layard recalled: 'It was a memorable day for me when I breakfasted with you in your lodgings in Ryder Street – when you asked me to make some notes for your Handbook on Russia & Sweden during a tour that I projected, in my humble fashion, in those lands.'[74] Layard's book on his discovery of the remains of Nineveh was published by Murray in 1848, when the author was only thirty-one. Pirate editions of the Murray Handbooks began to appear, and in 1839 the German publisher Karl Baedeker entered the market with a similar series of guides, written in German, beginning with the Rhineland. Baedeker's preface to this first volume included a lavish acknowledgement to 'the most distin- guished [*ausgezeichnetste*] Guide-book ever published, "Murray's Handbook for Travellers", which has served as the foundation of Baedeker's little book'.[75] Indeed, looking back late in life Murray accuses Baedeker of lifting passages wholesale from the Handbooks. Describing a valley in Switzerland, the Handbook had stated: 'The slate rocks here are full of red garnets.' Baedeker had garbled this as 'overgrown with red pomegranates', and repeated the mistake through many editions.[76]

Murray makes the accusation of plagiarism in 1860 in a letter to Baedeker's son Ernst, observing that the early Baedeker guides were 'very nearly direct translations from mine ... although in the course of time they have diverged from my model'.[77] But if Karl Baedeker was something of a rogue, he was always amiable when he wrote in a variety of languages to Albemarle Street. In 1839, he offered mate- rial for *Northern Europe*: 'I am only too pleased to devote all my knowledge and my copious notes to your book ... Your most devoted Baedeker.'[78]

W. B. C. Lister's bibliography of the Murray Handbooks (1993) identifies many of the contributors who wrote for them over the years, and picks out the threads of the multitude of editions.

Gladstone allowed a brief travel diary to be quoted in the *Handbook to Sicily* (1864), and Ruskin was so critical of the superficiality of the comments on works of art in *Northern Italy* (1842–3, written by Francis Palgrave) that he was engaged to rewrite them for the 1847 edition. 'Your writer', Ruskin told Murray, 'is a man of good taste and judgment – or at least of *fair* average taste – but he has not had time . . . I was a fortnight on ladders.'[79]

Over the years, innumerable readers wrote to the firm, some innkeepers offering bribes for a favourable mention, or threatening legal action if their premises were criticised.[80] An emollient request came from a citizen of Morat in Switzerland in 1866, whose streets Murray had described as 'dismal': 'Could you alter a severe paragraph on our dear little town in your world-famous Handbook for Switzerland?' he asked.[81] Others made constructive suggestions for improvements – this letter came from Manchester:

> Mrs Gaskell presents her compliments to Mr Murray . . . She begs to tell him that there is now at Caen, Normandy, a new hotel which is thoroughly clean, comfortable and respectable. It is called Humby's Hotel, and is kept by an Englishman of that name . . . The other hotels in the town are so exceedingly dirty and ill-conducted that this new one supplies a great want . . . Mrs Gaskell speaks from quite recent experience.[82]

And this arrived from Leipzig:

> I travelled in Switzerland last year and while at Meyringen lived at Michel's, hotel de la Couronne. I knew Michel, who had been my guide on a former tour through that country, to be a good and honest and well educated man, and while I congratulated him to find him now in a good establishment, with a handsome wife and pretty children, he spoke to me of his further prospects in life of the wishes that were left him, & amongst the last the most prominent was that to be *named in your Guide* after the two other hotels. He told me he did not know a way to attract your attention, as he was not able to write an English letter . . . I can accordingly recommend my friend Michel with good confidence . . . Excuse the liberty, I have thus taken.
>
> Felix Mendelssohn Bartholdy[83]

Mr Humby and M. Michel duly got their mentions, while *Punch* wrote admiringly:

> Once I could scarce walk up the Strand
> What Jungfrau now could us withstand
> When we are walking hand in hand
> My Murray.

13

On the Great Game

◆

THERE IS A stark entry in one of the office letter-books, among the transcripts of letters to authors and other correspondents: 'Mr Murray died June 27th 1843 – Aged 65'. He had been unwell since the spring, but John Murray III wrote to Hobhouse that his father's death was 'totally unexpected by me'.[1] According to one of the obituaries, 'His death was occasioned by general debility and exhaustion, but he had rallied so often, that no fears were entertained by his family or his physicians till Monday morning [the day before his death], when all hope was at an end.'[2]

There had been a slow decline over a period of years. 'George Paston' (the pseudonym of Emily Morse Symonds, biographer of John Murray III) writes: 'As his health failed, John Murray [II] spent a good deal of time at watering-places, vainly seeking cures for rheumatism.'[3] He was buried in Kensal Green cemetery in north London, the date on his gravestone wrongly giving his death as 22 June. He chose the self-reproachful epitaph 'Enter not into judgement with Thy servant O Lord, for in Thy sight shall no man living be justified.' The obituaries however were full of unanimous praise. 'Albemarle Street has lost its great publishing potentate,' declared the *Court Journal*,[4] while the *Spectator* opined: 'Literature and society have sustained a great loss.'[5] The *Illustrated London News* judged Murray, rather oddly for a man who had brought the best of contemporary literature and scholarship to a wide readership, to have been 'emphatically the publisher of the Aristocracy'.[6] But it was the *Atlas* which described him in the two words he would surely have chosen himself: 'a gentleman'.[7] Indeed he was given a lengthy obituary in the *Gentleman's Magazine* of August 1843, at the head of which his name was printed: 'JOHN MURRAY, ESQ., F.S.A.' To the *Gentleman's Magazine* Murray was 'the distinguished publisher', whose career 'is one continued history of princely payments. His copyrights were secured at the most extravagant prices – for he never haggled about the sum if he wanted the work.'[8] Coincidentally, Murray's obituary is immediately preceded in the *Gentleman's Magazine* by that of James Hakewill whose expensively-procured engravings had so plagued him in 1818.

The *Athenaeum* obituary looked to the future: 'For seventy-eight years *two* John Murrays have been connected, in an eminent degree, with all that is useful and elegant in literature; we have now a *third* John Murray, to whom we wish all the success he so well merits.'[9] By the time of his father's death, John Murray III was already thirty-five, and as Paston observes had 'been kept too long in the background'.[10] The business was not in the best of health. A year before his death, Murray had reported 'nothing but loss',[11] and his son reckoned that a grand style of living, and his father's generosity to many of his authors, had taken its toll. By any reckoning, it would take months, maybe years, of hard work to get the firm back on a sound financial keel.

In this situation, it was a devastating blow for the younger John Murray to learn at the reading of the will his father had made only a week earlier that the entire estate had been left to Annie. This amounted to £57,000, not including the value of the house. Far from being the next potentate of Albemarle Street, John Murray III found himself reduced overnight from co-partner to tenant. He was required to pay interest to his mother, and to purchase old stock from his father's estate. He had planned to marry an Edinburgh banker's daughter, Marion Smith, but this would now have to wait. A month after his father's death, he wrote of 'the painful situation in wch I am placed',[12] although in the event the 'painful situation' resolved itself two years later when his mother died.

There was one bright feature in the publishing landscape. A year before the death of John Murray II, Charles Dickens sent a copy of a printed letter to 50 Albemarle Street. It began: 'You may perhaps be aware that during my stay in America, I lost no opportunity of endeavouring to awaken the public mind to a sense of the unjust and iniquitous state of the law in that country, in reference to the wholesale piracy of British works.'[13] The worldwide success of *The Pickwick Papers*, *Oliver Twist* and other early novels had made Dickens a prize victim for American literary pirates. To fight this off, he began a campaign for a new Copyright Act which would at least prevent the importing of cheap pirate editions into Britain and the colonies.

The Murrays, father and son, were among the London publishers who gave Dickens their support, and it may have been through them that the campaign got a sympathetic response from William Gladstone, then a junior minister at the Board of Trade. Gladstone was a Murray author: his *The State in its Relations with the Church* had been published in 1838, so there was an additional reason for him to respond when in August 1842 John Murray II organised a deputation to call on him. An invitation went out to Dickens, who had just left for Broadstairs and could not turn round and catch the mail coach back to London. He wrote to the Murrays 'If any conveyance *but* tonight's Mail could have brought me to town in sufficient time to join the Deputation who wait on Mr Gladstone, then I should unquestionably have been a member of it ... I would have sacrificed any consideration of convenience or personal comfort, for the lightest feather of a cause in which I have taken, and shall ever take, such an earnest interest.'[14]

The 1842 Copyright Act, drawn up in response to the campaign, made it illegal to import foreign reprints of British books into the United Kingdom home and colonial markets. The way was now open for British publishers to take over the supply of cheap books. As Gladstone put it in a letter to the elder Murray, their task was to make available 'new and popular English works at moderate prices. If it be practicable for authors and publishers to make such arrangements, I should hope to see a great extension of our book trade.'[15] A few days later, Gladstone wrote to thank Murray for a copy of *The Military Operations at Cabul*, by Lieutenant Vincent Eyre, just published by Murray, which began with an account of the murder of Sir Alexander Burnes in Afghanistan just over a year earlier. 'I have read it with great pain and shame,' Gladstone told Murray. 'May another occasion for such a narrative never arise.'[16] Burnes, three years older than John Murray III, was a Scot who had joined the Indian Army in his teens, and had shown himself adept at native languages. He was a graphic travel writer, firmly in the Murray tradition, which had already begun to form through the published writings of Henry Ellis and John Franklin. Burnes reported in 1827 from the Indus valley in north-west India:

> The Koree produces abundance of fish and some of them of a very choice kind. Fresh water fish were found in great numbers after the late inundation – porpoises are even seen above Lucput – The birds however which frequent it are beyond all description numerous, flimingoes [sic], cranes, pelicans, ducks, gulls &c with a long list of aquatic birds the names of which I have never heard and many I never before met with. The Pelican is a favourite food with the Lohanus, a tribe of Hindoos, who are a very industrious race, and make up the greatest proportion of the population of Sinde.[17]

Burnes soon became a spy, and in 1830 led a 700-mile expedition up the Indus to Lahore to take five English dray horses to the ruler of the Punjab as a gift from King George IV. The trip was cover for some clandestine surveying as part of 'the Great Game', as Kipling later called the British spying operations against Russian ambitions in India. The term had in fact been coined by the British spy Arthur Connolly, who was beheaded for espionage at Bokhara in Central Asia in 1842.

'The principal object of my journey was to trace the course of the Indus,' wrote Alexander Burnes in *Travels into Bokhara*.[18] After delivering the dray horses, he was sent to explore the countries bordering on the Oxus river and the Caspian Sea, including Afghanistan. 'I was directed to appear as . . . a Captain in the British Army returning to Europe,' he explains. Despite this he wore native dress and spoke fluent Persian, greatly adding to his appeal when he came back to England in 1833, where his book was published the following year by Murray. His picture in the Murray portrait gallery is a small canvas of a young man with a very European moustache, dressed in Afghan native costume and a large turban.

Like T. E. Lawrence a century later, 'Bokhara Burnes' became a celebrity, the darling of the Royal Geographical Society, and one of the youngest ever recipients of a knighthood, who was granted a half-hour audience with the new monarch, William IV, in Brighton Pavilion. Then Burnes went back to Asia, to Kabul, where he was given insufficient support for his schemes for preventing the Afghans forming an alliance with Russia, and was killed by a mob.

John Murray had already experimented with literature for the mass market. The Family Library series, launched in April 1829, eventually totalled nearly fifty titles at five shillings a volume. The series opened with Lockhart's condensed version of Sir Walter Scott's life of Napoleon, and encompassed a wide range of non-fiction. On the whole, however, the Family Library did not include reprinted titles, and the elder Murray tended to overpay the contributing authors. He had paid Sir John Barrow 300 guineas for his book *The Eventful History of the Mutiny and Piratical Seizure of H.M.S. Bounty: its Causes and Consequences* (1831) – a work which spawned a thousand theories and at least three films – and even Barrow thought the payment was excessive. Keeping the series in print became too expensive, and it was sold *en bloc* to Thomas Tegg & Co., a publisher who also specialised in remaindered books, before it could drain away further funds.

Under the protection of the new Copyright Act, John Murray III began his reign at Albemarle Street by issuing a set of books in dingy green and purple bindings stamped on the cover 'MURRAY'S COLONIAL & HOME LIBRARY'. He considered starting the series with Southey's life of Nelson, having rejected Lord Mahon's *Spain under Charles II* as being too specialised: 'I am obliged in the selection of books to study the taste of the middle and lower orders among whom my readers lie in a great degree and I have some doubt whether they have sufficient knowledge of Spain and its history.'[19] Some were priced as low as two shillings and sixpence. Military history predominates, but there is a sparkling exception – the book that Murray chose in the autumn of 1843 to open the series. This is how it begins:

It is very seldom that the preface of a work is read; indeed, of late years most books have been sent into the world without any. I deem it, however, advisable to write a preface, and to this I humbly call the attention of the courteous reader, as its perusal will not a little tend to the proper understanding and appreciation of these volumes.

The work now offered to the public, and which is styled *The Bible in Spain*, consists of a narrative what occurred to me during a residence in that country, to which I was sent by the Bible Society, as its agent, for the purpose of printing and circulating the Scriptures. It comprehends, however, certain journeys and adventures in Portugal, and leaves me at last in 'the land of the Corahai', to which region, after having undergone considerable buffeting in Spain, I found it expedient to retire for a season.[20]

It could almost be *Tristram Shandy*, and it continues in the same oddly comic manner, with the author describing how a sailor on the boat taking him to Spain dreams that he has fallen overboard, and immediately does exactly that. This is the world of George Borrow, a nineteenth-century Baron Munchausen, who had knocked on Murray's door two years earlier to offer, successfully, his book *The Zincali: An Account of the Gypsies in Spain*: A portrait of Borrow was eventually commissioned for the Albemarle Street drawing room, and the artist, Henry Wyndham Phillips, has tried to make him look like a latterday Byron, with Byronic open-necked shirt. In later years John Murray III's children nicknamed Borrow 'Scratchy Man', because he would pursue them with threats to scratch their faces.

Borrow was married to a wealthy widow and lived in a remote corner of Suffolk where he had 'not the least idea as to what is going on save in my immediate neighbourhood'. Despite being 'quite retired', he wrote occasionally 'for want of something better to do'.[21] His eccentric letters are written in a distinct upright hand embellished with long spiky loops. He liked to inform his publisher of his whereabouts, and always sent details of trips to visit his mother in Norwich. Every Christmas he despatched a local Suffolk turkey up to Albemarle Street. Borrow suffered from hypochondria, and the Murrays did their best to help. 'I return you my best thanks for the remedy,' he wrote, 'from which I have already derived considerable benefit. When poured into the ear, I find that, besides removing pain to a great degree, it produces delicious slumber. Don't you think that it might be administered to horses having the influenza?'[22] Sometimes Mary Borrow wrote too: 'Perhaps Mr Murray will see fit before long to write a few lines of enquiry to Mr Borrow as to health and progress with vol 4 [of *Lavengro*] …my truly excellent Husband … every now and then requires an impetus to cause the large wheel to move round at a quicker pace.'[23] Mary Borrow requested that this letter be burnt, but it never was. Her other requests were heeded, however, and John Murray III obligingly carried on a correspondence with Borrow whose book about his adventures in Spain, the work of an unreliable narrator if ever there was one, got the Colonial & Home Library off to a splendid start.[24]

Authors came and went, but the tradition of having them to stay began in the days of John Murray III with a visit by thirty-five-year-old Elizabeth Rigby. The daughter of a Norwich doctor, Rigby came to 50 Albemarle Street in February 1844 and stayed for three months. Her *Letters from the Shores of the Baltic*, describing a visit to Russia and Estonia, had been published by Murray's in 1841. On the strength of this, Lockhart invited her to write for the *Quarterly Review*: 'You are the only lady, I believe,' he told her, 'that ever wrote in it except Mrs Somerville who once gave us a short, scientific article.'[25] He added that Rigby, whom he had called his 'Queen Elizabeth',[26] was the only contributor Croker had ever praised, apart from himself. She eventually became infamous for her 1848 review of *Jane Eyre*, which she thought immoral and vulgar, and therefore undoubtedly the work of a man.[27]

In her journal, Miss Rigby describes the Albemarle Street house as welcoming – 'I feel myself in a second home' – and John Murray III as 'truly agreeable'.[28] She had earlier written enigmatically in her journal, on hearing of the death of John Murray II: '[John Murray III] is an admirable young man, and though he is not what his father was, he will be that which he is not.'[29] The published excerpts from the journal lack descriptions of family and professional life at number 50, though there are accounts of dinner parties, of which there were

many. At this date, John Murray III, newly in office, was still entertaining his father's circle: 'Mr Lockhart . . . to dinner – also Turner,
the artist, a queer little being, very knowing about all the castles he
has drawn.'[30] Elizabeth Rigby, nicknamed Lofty Lucy as she was
almost six feet tall, was inclined to describe other people as 'little',
particularly Turner, 5 feet 4 inches tall. Another night brought a newer
recruit to the Murray list, Scratchy Man himself: 'Borrow came in the
evening: a fine man, but a most disagreeable one; a kind of character
that would be dangerous in rebellious times.'[31]

Not yet married, was John Murray III considering the matrimo-
nial possibilities of the lanky Norwich doctor's daughter? Certainly
he took considerable trouble to encourage her as a writer, particularly so when she decided to write fiction: 'I like your charming
Tale so well, that I will (with your consent) print it in the Colonial
Library – though my rule has been to exclude works of fiction.' He
continued: 'It is just not quite long enough to fill one number, but
if you will throw in another small story . . . I shall be happy to give
you for the copyright Sixty Guineas.'[32]

Murray's 'no fiction' rule was one which deprived him of, among
other things, *Moby-Dick* and *Billy Budd*. Attempting to convince
himself that they were travel books he had published Herman
Melville's *Typee*, under the title *Four Months among the Natives of the
Marquesas*, and *Omoo*. Critics doubted that Melville had actually
travelled to the South Seas and experienced life there. 'How incredibly vexatious', the author responded,

> when one really feels in his very bones that he has been there, to have
> a parcel of blockheads question it. Not that Mr Murray comes into
> that category. Oh no – Mr Murray, I am ready to swear, stands fast
> by the faith, believing *Typee* from Preface to sequel. He only wants
> something to stop the mouths of the senseless sceptics – men who go
> from their cradles to their graves, and never dream of the queer things
> going on at the Antipodes.[33]

Melville, when he crossed the Atlantic in 1849, attended a Murray
dinner and wrote about it in his direct and metallic American
manner:

It was a most amusing affair. Mr Murray was there in a short vest and dress-coat, looking quizzical enough; his footman was there also, habited in small-clothes and breeches, revealing a despicable pair of sheepshanks. Lockhart was there also in a prodigious cravat. He stalked about like a half-galvanised ghost – gave me the tips of two fingers when introduced to me. Then there was a round-faced chap by the name of Cooke who seemed to be Murray's factotum. His only duty consisted in pointing out the portraits on the walls, and saying that this or that was considered a good likeness of the high and mighty ghost Lockhart.[34]

If he saw Elizabeth Rigby as the next Mrs Murray, John Murray III made a mistake in inviting the handsome, but very short, painter Charles Eastlake to dinner when, once again, Rigby was in residence in spring 1846. Despite their differences of stature, a romance blossomed, and when Elizabeth next visited Albemarle Street it was as Mrs, soon to be Lady, Eastlake, when Charles was knighted and elected to the presidency of the Royal Academy. A year later, in July 1847, John Murray III married his Edinburgh girl, Marion Smith, 'Menie'. This time, the entire literary community must have been waiting for the appearance of the heir. A daughter, named Marion after her mother, arrived in due course, and then, on 18 December 1851, the year of the Great Exhibition, John Murray IV duly came into the world.

On the night that Byron's portraits looked down on the beginning of the Rigby–Eastlake romance, Elizabeth noted in her journal that the company included 'a heavy, shy-looking, plain little man',[35] A. W. Kinglake, author of the bestselling Middle Eastern travel book *Eöthen*, published two years earlier. John Murray III had rejected *Eöthen* because he found it too flippant. He was proving to be more straitlaced than his father, and a sternness of tone becomes apparent in the Letter-books. The Rev. Charles Wordsworth, for example, is berated for wanting to take his Greek grammar to another publisher: 'You brought your Grammar to Albemarle Street at a time when it was unknown, and when Mr Murray's name was of some use to it ... The fortune of your book is now made; you will not use me as a stepping ladder, and now kick me off? – If you do, I will venture to say that author never so treated bookseller before.'[36] Hermann Melville, who had complained about sales of *Omoo* and *Typee* in the Colonial Library series, is rapped over the knuckles for supposing Murray 'to be reaping immense advantages' while the author had nothing.[37]

And when the campaigning woman journalist Harriet Martineau delivered another book about the Middle East, which Murray had commissioned, she got a slap from Albemarle Street: 'When I consented to publish your travels in the East I certainly never contemplated, nor did you give me the slightest hint to induce me to suppose that it was a work of infidel tendency, having the obvious aim of depreciating the authority & invalidating the veracity of the Bible.'[38] Among the passages that Murray objected to was one in which Martineau observed that through its expression and behaviour the camel 'feels itself a damned animal'. As a result of Murray's objections Martineau tartly removed the book, calling Murray 'a Censor of the Press', and took it off to be published by Edward Moxon where it made a tidy profit.[39] Yet Murray is the man who was shortly to publish the book which, above all others, was to deal the nineteenth century's most devastating blow to Christian belief.

14

Dr Darwin, I presume?

⌐⌐⌐

THE MISSIONARY AND explorer David Livingstone had returned triumphantly in November 1856 to Britain from his first series of epic journeys of discovery in southern Africa. By Christmas, he was facing the full blast of publicity and adulation. Murray rapidly signed him up for an account of his experiences, assuring him 'that if you will trust your work to me I shall make it a point of honour – as it will be to me a source of gratification – to secure to you the largest possible pecuniary advantage'.[1] Livingstone was to receive 2,000 guineas as an advance on two-thirds of the profits of the book, conspicuously better than the half-share in profits that was Murray's standard rate. Livingstone took rooms in Sloane Street, and devoted himself to writing an account of his African adventures, rising at 7 a.m. and working so fast that the manuscript was finished in under five months. On 22 May 1857 he wrote, in the big manic handwriting that was already becoming familiar in Albemarle Street, about the drawing illustrating the episode in *Missionary Travels and Researches in South Africa* in which Livingstone is mauled by a lion.

> Mr Clowes [the printer] has just sent me proofs of the plates or drawings – the lion encountre [*sic*] is absolutely abominable. I entreat you by all that is good to suppress it. Every one who knows what a lion is will die with laughing at it. Its the greatest bungle Wolf [the artist] ever made. I told him about it, and I told him the proportions were much too great on the side of the lion. Its like a dray horse … I dont send back the plates to Mr Clowes but to you begging mercy against being caricatured.[2]

Word came that Oxford University proposed to give Livingstone an honorary degree. 'This will look well on the title page,' he wrote shrewdly to Murray.[3] However, like most authors receiving large advances, he began to be anxious about sales: would Murray recoup what he had so generously paid out? A bookseller in Glasgow, where Livingstone had been to college, told him he was ordering as many as two hundred copies, 'so if it does not sell well', Livingstone wrote to Murray, 'a heavy sin will be at my door!'[4] Murray had supplied Livingstone with an editor, the Rev. Thomas Binney, who 'smoothed some harsh sentences which might have given offence to the sensitive'.[5] But when the proofs came Livingstone was horrified by what he called 'the process of emas-culation' to which the book had been submitted. For example Binney, or some other editor, had removed the word 'circumcision' from the description of an African ritual, thereby rendering it meaningless. Worse, Livingstone's down-to-earth style had been polished beyond recognition. Protesting furiously to Murray, Livingstone admitted that his prose was sometimes 'uncouth', but insisted that it was also 'clearer, more forcible and more popular' than anything the editor could suggest.[6] Murray let him have his way; many of the alterations were undone, and the book's great success, when it was published in November 1857, was largely due to its direct language.

Like many travel writers, Livingstone's self-sufficiency seemed to wither away when he was within reach of his publisher: would Murray recommend a house agent, so that Livingstone and his wife could move out of central London and the glare of publicity? Would he provide a copy of a book that Livingstone had left in Africa? Would he provide a set of naval almanacs? Would Mrs Murray please apologise for him to Lady Eastlake whose dinner party he had for-gotten to attend? Meanwhile he sat for his portrait, to be hung next to Byron in the Murray gallery, and was not impressed by the result: 'My friends call out against the portrait by Phillips,' he told Murray, adding that one of them 'says it will do for any one between Captain Cook & Guy Fawkes'.[7] So as not to offend him, the picture was taken down and put away. This was hardly fair: Phillips had caught exactly the irritable impatience of the man. There was always plenty for him to be irritated with: by Christmas, *Missionary Travels* was supposed to be plentifully available in the shops, but when Livingstone was passing through Manchester, a friend tried to buy a copy so that it could be autographed. He searched in vain. 'He got it at last by offering 2/6 to any boy who could procure it for him,' Livingstone reported.[8]

And then, suddenly, he was gone, back to Africa. 'We sail on Monday next,' he wrote from Birkenhead on 6 March 1858.[9] Eighteen months later came a letter with the address given as 'River Shire', reporting that 'We have just traced this river up to its source in Lake Nyassa,' and including lyrical descriptions of the scenery.[10] Another letter to Albemarle Street is taken up with Livingstone's attempt to draw the Sanjika, a fish which his party had found in the Nyasa waters. Murray family tradition has it that Livingstone reported seeing his reflection in the lake, and decided that the Phillips portrait was accurate after all. When word of this came back to Albemarle Street, the picture was taken out of store and hung, and even today Livingstone glares across the middle drawing room.[11]

In the Introduction to *Missionary Travels*, Livingstone tells this story of one of his childhood enthusiasms:

> On one of these exploring tours we entered a limestone quarry – long before geology was so popular as it is now. It is impossible to describe the delight and wonder with which I began to collect the shells found in the carboniferous limestone which crops out in High Blantyre and Cambuslang. A quarry-man, seeing a little boy so engaged, looked with that pitying eye which the benevolent assume when viewing the insane. Addressing him with, 'How ever did these shells come into these rocks?' 'When God made the rocks, he made the shells in them,' was the damping reply. What a deal of trouble geologists might have saved themselves by adopting the Turk-like philosophy of this Scotchman!

Livingstone's playful tone indicates that he had long abandoned allegiance to a fundamentalist solution to the problem of squaring the evidence of geology with the claims of the Bible.

In this debate, the most significant intellectual battle of the nineteenth century, no publishing house played a more crucial role than

John Murray. One of Byron's last works deserves to be treated as a contribution to the argument. In his verse-play *Cain* (1821), Lucifer seems to stand in for post-Darwinian man, sneering at God:

> If he made us – he cannot unmake:
> We are immortal![12]

By contrast, in 1827 the young John Murray III had watched William Buckland taking a reactionary position with his dough-dancing tortoises. Buckland, an Anglican clergyman who lectured eccentrically in geology at Oxford, took his eccentricities to the extreme: he kept reptiles under his sofa, and claimed to have eaten every known animal. Summoned to judge whether the blood of a saint, which appeared miraculously each year on the altar steps of an Italian basilica, was genuine, he horrified pious onlookers by licking it up and pronouncing it to be bat's urine. Buckland not only believed that Noah's Flood had been a historical event, but further argued that it was the sole cause of fossils and other geological relics. In 1830, however, a Murray book banished this theory to the dustbin of intellectual history.

Principles of Geology, by Charles Lyell, involved neither tortoises nor Byronic challenges to the deity. It was a cool-headed exposition, backed up by painstaking research, of something that everyone but religious fundamentalists takes for granted today: that geological change, whether due to erosion or more dramatic causes such as earthquakes, is part of the ordinary life of the planet, and always will be. No Flood or other form of divine intervention is necessary to explain the processes by which mountains have been formed and fossils deposited. The implication for Lyell's readers in 1830 was giddy. They found themselves contemplating the blasphemous hypothesis that the Earth was incalculably older than the Bible supposed. Moreover, Lyell's worldview opened up the possibility that the same kind of slow but constant change might be going on in the animal kingdom. In her biography of Charles Darwin, Janet Browne writes bluntly: 'Without Lyell there would have been no Darwin.'[13]

Charles Lyell was no Byronic iconoclast, but a gentleman dilettante who had taken to geology when he should have been stu·'ying the law. Socially, he proved to be the perfect Murray author: he became a reviewer for the *Quarterly*, and joined the Athenaeum. Although young John Murray was a keen geologist and would later write his own book on the subject, his position was closer to Buckland than to Lyell. Thus it was broad-minded and businesslike of the Murrays to issue *Principles of Geology* in a form that would make it affordable to all classes. During 1830 to 1833 it was published in four parts, at six shillings each.

The reviewer in the *Quarterly,* G. P. Scrope, was on Lyell's side, judging the Buckland approach to be 'injurious to both science and religion'. He continued: 'we hail with the greatest satisfaction the appearance of Mr Lyell's work, which henceforward, we can hardly doubt, will mark the beginning of a new era in geology'.[14] Charles Darwin was turning thirty when he read the first instalment of Lyell's book on board the *Beagle*, bound for South America. He was immediately electrified by its ideas.[15] Yet fifteen years were to pass before he, too, became a Murray author, and almost thirty years before the manuscript of his masterwork arrived at Albemarle Street.

During that period, Lyell extracted the maximum publicity from his book. He has been described as the first popular science writer, and his lectures have been compared to pop concerts. By 1848 he had been knighted, and later he was elevated to the baronetcy. Murray did well out of him financially, though there was nothing very original in his later books. Meanwhile Darwin published his journal of the *Beagle* voyage, not with Murray but with Henry Colburn, and went to ground to mull over his startling theories of evolution. He emerged briefly in 1845, in a commercial frame of mind. Darwin was convinced he had been cheated by his publisher: Colburn admitted that the *Journal of the Beagle Voyage* was a bestseller, but had not paid a penny to the author. Would Murray make Darwin an offer for a thoroughly revised second edition, if he could first untangle himself from Colburn? Murray suggested a flat £100 for the copyright, which Darwin at first thought was generous: he evidently knew nothing of the advances that had been paid out in Albemarle Street over the years. He then asked Murray for a further

£50, to which Murray agreed. Darwin was evolving into a professional author.

He was certainly worldly and adept when it came to dealing with the printer, Clowes, and the proofs. Like Lyell with *Principles*, Darwin had opted for initial publication in parts, with the entire book eventually being issued cheaply as a Colonial & Home volume. But the Murray–Darwin relationship, though always courteous, was businesslike rather than revealing or intimate: Darwin showed none of the flamboyant theatricality of many of the authors who would form legendary relationships with Murray's over the generations. It is clear that Darwin always preferred to confide in his family and close-knit circle of friends rather than to anyone outside. It is his books and their dramatic impact on Victorian society rather than Darwin himself that feature so strongly in the Murray Archive. He and Murray probably saw no necessity to meet, and it is likely that Darwin never went to 50 Albemarle Street. Certainly there was no chance for Lady Eastlake to encounter 'little' Mr Darwin at the Albemarle Street dinner table.

Charles Lyell wrote plaintively to Murray on 13 November 1859: 'Can you not send me Darwin's book. I was to have one of the first copies.'[16] Considering the amount of encouragement that Lyell had lavished on Darwin, who was finally bringing out his *chef d'oeuvre* fourteen years after the *Beagle* journal had been transferred to Murray, it was remiss of Darwin not to ensure that Lyell was one of the first people to receive the finished book. The opening chapters of a new manuscript had arrived at Albemarle Street early in April 1859. They were brought, according to legend, by Darwin's butler,[17] yet Darwin told Murray that he was posting the MS. Accompanying them was a letter in which Darwin demonstrated his worldly wisdom about publishers. He knew very well that Murray would be unlikely to read the whole book, so he told him what he could skip.

If Murray had the patience to read the entire opening chapter, Darwin said, 'I honestly think you will have a fair notion of the interest of [the] whole book.' If he cared to go on, he would find 'a dull & rather abstruse Ch[apter]' followed by a far more interesting one, entitled 'Struggle for Existence', which expounded the idea of natural selection. 'It may be conceit,' continued Darwin, 'but I believe the subject will interest the public, & I am sure that the views are original. If you think otherwise, I must repeat my request that you will freely reject my work; & though I shall be a little disappointed I shall be in no way injured.'[18] The book had not arrived out of the blue. At Darwin's request, Lyell had discussed it with Murray, assuring him that it was not blasphemous: 'not more *un*orthodox than the subject makes inevitable', was how Darwin put it, emphasising that there was no discussion of such theological issues as the origin of man or the book of Genesis.[19] Lyell reported back to Darwin that Murray's response was encouraging, his only objection being to Darwin's unwieldy title, which at this stage was *An Abstract of an Essay on the Origin of Species and Varieties through Natural Selection*. Murray did not like 'Abstract', but Darwin explained that this meant the book was a summary of a much larger work, which he had not yet written.

Encouraged by Lyell's report of his conversation with the publisher, Darwin sent Murray a list of chapter titles on the strength of which Murray made an offer for the book, two-thirds of the profits, which Darwin thought 'handsome'.[20] Murray would happily have gone ahead, without any further information about the book, but Darwin wanted Murray to know what he was publishing, and so posted him a copyist's MS of the early chapters. He did not need an intellectual response from Murray, but seems to have regarded him as a sort of everyman, or intelligent common reader, whose professional opinion would determine whether such a book should be published and whether the public could cope with what was coming: 'Murray ought to be the best judge, and if he chooses to publish it, I think I may wash my hands of all responsibility – And he made a very good bargain for my Journal.'[21]

There are distinct echoes here of John Murray II having the responsibility for *Don Juan* laid on his shoulders by Byron. For all the differences between the generations, there is, particularly during the nineteenth century, the continuous personality called 'John Murray': John Murray II dissolves, in the cinematic sense, almost unnoticed into John Murray III, both of them being made of the same mixture of the cautious and the adventurous, the same canniness and naivety, decisiveness and procrastination; both of them conservative and innovative at the same time.[22] On this occasion, John Murray III was decisive: he obeyed instructions and read the first three chapters, and told Darwin that they were fine and that the offer stood. So, by mid-June 1859, Darwin was battling gloomily with the proofs, wondering, in a letter to Murray, how he could have written so badly. He eventually took to his bed with the stress of it all. When he saw the corrections, Murray remarked that Darwin had virtually rewritten the book. He ordered 1,250 copies from the printer, which showed he was optimistic.

On the other hand, he must have also been aware that there was trouble coming. Though he may only have given Darwin's manuscript a cursory glance, he did show it to two readers. The first, the lawyer George Pollock, reported cautiously that he thought the book was 'beyond the apprehension of any living scientist', but added that Darwin had 'brilliantly surmounted the formidable obstacles which he was honest enough to put in his own path'.[23] Murray himself remarked that, in his own opinion, Darwin's theory of natural selection was as absurd as contemplating a poker and a rabbit breeding together. Murray also continued the tradition of consulting the editor of the *Quarterly Review* about anything controversial. That position was now held by a Norfolk clergyman, the Rev. Whitwell Elwin. He reported unfavourably, criticising Darwin for printing his theory without supporting evidence: this was why Darwin had wanted to call the book an Abstract, he saw it as a summary rather than a full argument. But of course this was just a smokescreen: Elwin was privately horrified by the whole venture, which he later described as 'wild and foolish'.[24] History blames Elwin and others of his conservative frame of mind for their short-sightedness. Yet arguably they were only putting up their own heroic struggle for life, while privately aware that this time round they were no longer to be the favoured race; natural selection had passed them by.

Darwinian debate raged, and by publication day, 24 November 1859, Murray had sold his entire first print-run of the book which its author had eventually titled *On the Origin of Species by Means of Natural Selection, or the Preservation of Favoured Races in the Struggle for Life*. T. H. Huxley, Darwin's lieutenant, gave the book stunning reviews in *The Times*, the *Westminster Review* and *Macmillan's Magazine*. The backlash reached a climax the following summer when 'Soapy Sam' Wilberforce, the Bishop of Oxford, made his damning attack. 'How could anyone seriously believe that mankind had developed from turnips,' he boomed in the *Quarterly*. The clash between science and religion was in full swing, symbolised by the famous British Association meeting in Oxford in June 1860 when Huxley and the Bishop debated face to face.

By the time of Darwin's death the book had sold a further 16,750 copies, considerably fewer that the 40,000 copies sold by John Churchill of the most celebrated earlier attempt to express evolutionary theory, Robert Chambers's *Vestiges of the Natural History of Creation* (1844).[25] Darwin would continue to be a stellar author on the Murray list with *The Descent of Man* (1871, in two volumes) selling like a Dickens novel, and finally his monograph on earthworms, *The Formation of Vegetable Mould, through the Action of Worms: with Observations on their Habits* (1881). This title, with evidence taken from observations on the activity of worms in the Darwin garden, went through six editions in one year.

If John Murray had been in the modern habit of lunching authors to mark their publication dates, there would have been two guests at his table on 24 November 1859: the heavily bearded, anxious Charles Darwin, and a ruddy-cheeked, genial individual whose name has already featured much in this book. Samuel Smiles was on to his fourth or fifth career by the time he came up with a bestseller that, in its different way, had almost as much influence on the Victorian outlook as *The Origin of Species*. Born and bred near Edinburgh, Smiles had trained and worked as a doctor, before becoming a journalist. This career he in turn abandoned for railway building: Cannon Street station in the City of London was one of the fruits of his management of the South Eastern Railway. Railways took him into authorship, and in 1857 Murray published his biography of the locomotive engineer George Stephenson. This was such a success, going through five editions in its first year, that Smiles embarked on a set of *Lives of the Engineers* (1861–2) which became a standard item in every gentleman's library.[26]

Meanwhile Smiles had persuaded Murray to publish a work of popular philosophy, *Self-help*, described by the critic Walter Houghton as 'a popular handbook for Victorian Dick Whittingtons'.[27] The script had already been rejected by the publishers Routledge and was languishing in a drawer at home, although Aileen Smiles in her biography of her grandfather assures readers that 'there was no difficulty about the publisher. It had to be Mr. Murray, then at the top of the publishing business.'[28] Smiles, in his plain prose, gave what turned out to be a rallying cry for thousands of young men to work hard, save hard and to improve themselves. The book sold 20,000 copies in its first year and an astonishing 130,000 more over the next thirty years,[29] as well as being translated into seventeen languages. 'The spirit of self-help is the root of all genuine growth in the individual,' preached Smiles, 'it constitutes the true source of national vigour and strength … where men are subjected to over-guidance and over-government, the inevitable tendency is to render them comparatively helpless.'[30]

In his next bestseller, *Thrift* (1875), the subject is inextricably bound up with the morality of the times: 'It is only when men become wise and thoughtful that they become frugal … The savage is the greatest of spendthrifts for he has no forethought, no to-morrow. The pre-historic man saves nothing.' The bestselling *Duty* followed in 1887. The financial arrangements over publication were that Murray and Smiles split the profits for the first year and after that Smiles would take two-thirds, Murray one-third. Smiles was evidently popular at Albemarle Street, because eventually they invited him to write the life of John Murray II.

Samuel Smiles did once have lunch with Darwin, although their publisher was not present. Smiles called on Darwin to collect his signature for a petition that the naturalist Thomas Edward should be granted a civil pension. He found Darwin 'delightful … full of talk, and he, as well as myself, could scarcely eat for *speaking*'.[31] Perhaps they discussed the possibility of there coming a point at which conscious self-help is not enough, a point when instinct takes over; perhaps they explored the morality of evolutionary theory. It is also possible that they compared notes on their publisher and how much he was paying them.

On 10 November 1871, the American journalist Henry Morton Stanley stepped into an African village and gave his legendary greeting to a white man whose whiskers were now as grey as Darwin's beard. David Livingstone had been traced, and of course there was a book in it. But when he was offered *How I Found Livingstone* Murray was suspicious. Were the letters quoted in it really by Livingstone? Robert Cooke, a Murray cousin who was now working at Albemarle Street, noted: 'In some quarters it is openly talked of as a *hoax*, or if not, that poor Livingstone is off his head, and these letters have been concocted for him.'[32] Livingstone himself soon wrote to Murray to confirm Stanley's credentials, but by that time Stanley's book had gone to another bidder. However, after Livingstone's death in 1873, Murray published his *Last Journals*.

That book shows how Darwin's thesis had already become absorbed into the Victorian mind. The extent to which Darwin had won the battle against Wilberforcian orthodoxy is shown by the honorary doctorate that was conferred on him in 1877 by the University of Cambridge. And Livingstone's *Last Journals* allude to Darwinism in a casual, even knowing, manner. 'Darwin's observation shows a great deal of what looks like instinct in these climbers,' Livingstone writes in his description of a jungle climbing plant. When discussing the landscape he refers approvingly to the Lyell–Darwin school of geology: 'Mr Darwin saw reason to believe that very great alterations of altitude, and of course of climbing, had taken place in South America and the islands of the Pacific ... A very great alteration has also taken place in Africa.'[33] Perhaps the biggest alteration of all was in the minds of such people as Livingstone, who managed to assimilate the theory of evolution into their Christian outlook.

John Murray made a personal contribution to the scientific revolution of the nineteenth century by publishing, in 1877, his own book *Scepticism in Geology and the Reasons for It*, under the pseudonym 'Verifier'. The scepticism of the title is directed openly at Lyell, and only slightly less directly at Darwin, with Murray arguing that earth-quakes cannot have changed the face of the planet: 'they are power-less to effect even a fracture in solid rock'. 'Verifier' – let us call him Murray from now on – adds that common sense also shows that the erosion of weather could not possibly have 'carved out mountains, dug valleys'.[34] His central platform concerns time, and he exploits the profound disagreements among geologists about the age of the earth:

> It is necessary to protest against the insatiable demands of geologists for time, or rather against the substitution of time for proof of what they assert. They see in their visions results which do not follow their premises, but which they assure us will happen, or might happen, provided we put off the fulfilment for 'an incalculable period of time' . . . In truth, the geologists draw bills at very long dates, which are never paid because they never arrive at maturity.[35]

Murray argues that Darwin's theory of evolution cannot be right because it suggests that the world has been created 'unfinished and imperfect . . . capable of improvement',[36] and uses the discovery, by Livingstone, of the Zambesi Falls as fresh evidence:

> The discovery of the Zambesi Falls would seem to have been reserved until the present time in order to refute a leading tenet of geology, and to prove the utter impotence of water to cut through hard rock. The conclusion seems irresistible that the fissure was made for the river to pass through, possibly by some shrinkage of the basaltic rock, when cooling down from an incandescent state, perhaps on the sudden contact of water and ice.[37]

Murray concludes by reflecting on the parallels between the cir-culation of water in the atmosphere and on the earth by trying to hold the line proclaimed by Church and state that man was at the centre: 'Such is one of the complicated arrangements analogous to the circulation of the blood in the human body, by which the earth was made habitable for man. What undeniable proof of well-concerted design! how worthy of the most sublime intelligence!'[38]

Scepticism was highly praised by an anonymous professor of physics nearly forty years after it had been published, who had no idea who the author was, feeling sure he 'must be a scholar of some standing, for he is certainly a shrewd reasoner, and is a master of a pleasing style, to say nothing of having complete command of the geological literature of his time'.[39] The book was successful enough to go into a second edition.

Not only did Murray have complete command of the geological literature of his time, he had also published most of it. What did John Murray mean by making this fundamentalist contribution to the great debate?[40] He had attacked two Murray authors, Lyell and Darwin, and drew on a discovery of a third, Livingstone, to show that Lyell and others were wrong. Was he stoking up interest to increase sales of Lyell, Darwin and Livingstone? Perhaps, but if sales did increase it was unlikely to have been as a consequence. Why did he leave it so long, over forty years after Lyell had published, and twenty after Darwin and Livingstone? An answer to this may be that Murray had other things to do, ruminated slow and thought long, and did not see himself as part of the vanguard of research and opinion: hence the title, *Scepticism*, and his pseudonym, 'Verifier'. While being by profession a publisher, Murray was also, by inclination, a geologist, and though they emerged in their own gradual geological time, these were his personal interpretations of the facts as he saw them.

The geological processes that Murray tried to explain moved even more slowly than the relations the firm had with the Crown. During the first decade of the twentieth century John Murray – by then it was John Murray IV – worked tactfully and painfully with the royal family over the editing and publishing of Queen Victoria's letters. Murray was considered then to be the obvious choice of publisher, but this was only inevitable because John Murray III had explored the landscape before: he had dealt with courtiers and officials over the sensitive subject for a mourning monarch of the creation of a permanent memorial to Prince Albert. Murray's had not been the obvious choice of publisher for other great royal involvements; they were not, for example, connected formally with the Great Exhibition,

Prince Albert's extraordinary achievement in steel, glass and innumerable objects in Hyde Park in 1851. That event produced books and guides, catalogues and companions; but Murray's were not there.

The firm published Prince Albert's speeches in 1864, and a further opportunity to work for the royal family arose when, together with the architect Sir George Gilbert Scott, and with engineers, sculptors, mosaicists, engravers, printers and lithographers, Murray's produced the elephant-sized, green-leather-bound, gold-embossed volume *The National Monument to his Royal Highness the Prince Consort* (1873). The Albert Memorial, as it rapidly became known, had been designed in 1872, and the Murray-produced volume published the following year comprised an explanatory text, and engravings of sections and elevations of the Memorial, and of statuary, reliefs and mosaics, in black and white and full colour. The engraving and printing was done in England, but the chromolithography was so specialised, and demanding of such a high quality, that the Berlin chromolithographer W. Loeillot was engaged for the work. Despite the extreme care given in the checking and completing of this grand production to be presented to the Queen herself, one infelicity slipped through unnoticed and uncorrectable: the citation of the publishers within the margins of the chromolithographs is expressed in the German manner, running the words 'Albemarle' and 'Street' together – 'London, John Murray, Albemarlestreet. 1872'. The Memorial was unveiled by Queen Victoria in 1876.

John Murray III was a man of great integrity and physical stamina to whom work was both a delight and a recreation, as well as a way of making a living and carrying on the duties placed upon him as the head of the Murray dynasty. When Elizabeth Rigby described him as 'not what his father was, he will be that which he is not', she was being more prescient than she knew. As the initiator and in some cases the author of the Murray Travellers' Handbooks, John Murray III had travelled thousands of miles in all conditions of weather and highway, understanding through personal experiences something of the hardships that the authors of the Murray travel books had to endure. If his own experiences barely registered in the scale of those of Alexander Burnes and John Franklin, he had felt the wind in his hair and had known the uncertainty of where he would sleep the next night.

15

Kind Mr Murray, the King of Publishers

—◆—

THE PORTRAIT OF John Murray III by Sir George Reid shows him at his enormous roll-top desk with its multitude of pigeon-holes, slots and drawers, attempting to write on top of an unruly pile of papers. Bundles silt up beside him tied with tape, and the brass studs of the writing slope catch the light. He sits, not at all at ease, on the edge of his chair looking out at us, his frock coat neat, but his bow tie rotating and his hair looking as if the wind is blowing through it from behind. Anxiety and responsibility crowd upon him like a pair of invisible furies. As his son John Murray IV wrote, 'he preferred to work – and he worked almost every evening – in the midst of a family-party, working, talking, playing games, which however never seemed to disturb him . . . He would walk every day, the youthful tours to gather Handbook material having taught him the value of exercise.'[1] Whatever the weather, he insisted on walking the mile and a half between the station and his Wimbledon home daily.

On one of his journeys home, in 1882, John Murray III was spotted on the train by Rowland Prothero, later the editor of the *Quarterly Review*, and his friend Francis Compton MP: 'Opposite to me in the railway-carriage sat an elderly man, wearing no glasses, but, with the most strained, tired-looking eyes that I have ever seen, absorbed in correcting double-column proof-sheets in smallish print. I recognised the proofs as part of *Murray's Handbook for France* . . . "That man," I whispered to Compton, "is correcting Murray's Guide to France." "It's old Murray himself . . . I'll introduce you."'[2]

Apart from proofs, John Murray III read little that was new: Horace's *Odes*, Scott's novels, Crabbe's poetry and Boswell's life of

Johnson were the favourites not only of his youth but of his age. He was, as Prothero, later Lord Ernle, put it, 'a strong but moderate Conservative and Churchman, he knew the needs of men and women of his generation and type ... He could not, I think, have been at ease with the effervescence of the 'nineties. His father might have published *The Yellow Book* or *The Savoy*. Not John Murray III.'[3] The butler at the Murrays' Wimbledon home, James Mills, had a firmer grasp of recent literature than did Murray. Paston tells the story of how, one evening after dinner when the butler was handing round coffee, discussion turned to Dickens. In which novel did such-and-such a character appear? Mills handed the coffee to Murray, and whispered, 'Nicholas Nickleby.' Aloud, Murray responded 'I have reason to believe that the character to which you refer is in Nicholas Nickleby!'[4]

Following his father's example, John Murray III had chosen Wimbledon as his retreat from publishing life. He bought four acres of open ground on the brow of a hill, with a lake, and built there, on Somerset Road, a modest mansion which he considered naming Murrayville.[5] He settled on Newstead – Byron would have loved that – but to many people who knew him well it was 'Handbook Hall'.[6] To expand in London he bought in 1855 the house next door, 49 Albemarle Street, and changed its number to 50a. The new premises housed the offices and the warehouse, and number 50 continued as a family home. The maiden aunts, John Murray III's sisters Christine, Hester and Maria, were 'very well and happy', living upstairs.[7] Two hundred yards up the street, in his apartment at the Royal Institution, Michael Faraday enjoyed a similar domestic ménage, as members of his and his wife's extended family ebbed and flowed around him.[8] However grand and famous the House of Murray was and would become, 50 Albemarle Street was always home.

Robert Cooke, a first cousin, had joined the firm in 1837, after an apprenticeship with Longman's, and became second in command. Murray and Cooke worked well together, and Cooke was clearly at the hub of the business, left in charge when Murray was away. His letters to his boss are full of details of everyday life in the publishing

world of the mid-nineteenth century. There are reports of problems
with the warehouse and in one instance a flood: 'the legs of the
shelves holding the Q.R. [*Quarterly Review*] are gone through the
floor and they are now prop'ed up by ladder and poles'.[9] There are
familiar hiccups with distribution, although all are reassuringly
small-scale: 'I have found the long lost parcel . . . It waited a long
time and was then put into the cupboard out of the way and of
course forgotten.'[10] Cooke loved to gossip about authors and the
publishing world. 'Lord Lindsay was married on Wednesday. I have
followed his directions and ordered 750 and the a/c for printing
immediately.'[11] There is news of 'Mr Shaw going into partnership
with Spottiswood. The firm will now be called Spottiswood and
Shaw.'[12] On the back of an envelope are costings for printing a run
of two thousand copies for the seventh edition of Lyell's *Principles* at
prices of twenty-one shillings and at eighteen shillings, and a hurried
and energetic note to Murray advising a further printing of
Markham's *England*: 'We must reprint . . . at once because the schools
are re-opening. We only have 900 left. The additions will do another
time I suppose.'[13] Among the useful advice and news are the quirky
domestic details of a family-run firm – 'Your shoes will be ready at
12 tomorrow and I will send them off direct to M. Bank' – and a
message for Menie that Frances, the housekeeper, has made '2lbs of
Pine apple, 2lbs of apricot and is going to make 2lbs of greengages,
in all 6lbs of Preserves. Is this enough?'[14]

One entry in the ledger for this time might well have been
queried by the accountant. This was note of the sum of £25 10s on
30 June 1861, for the stuffing of a gorilla skin. In 1861 few would
have known what a gorilla was, let alone what its hide was doing in a
publishing house. Until now the animal had been virtually unknown
outside the African jungle, but the young explorer Paul du Chaillu
changed all this. His tales of the discovery of the animal, in
Explorations and Adventures in Equatorial Africa, were published that
same year by Murray and his collection of gorilla skins was sold to
the British Museum. He did not stop at the skins, writing in 1864
from West Africa: 'I send by this vessel two enormous male Gorillas,
the biggest of which I present to the British Museum. I send also a

collection of skulls and what I think a new and very interesting species of Anteater besides two or three thousands insects and about 500 butterflies ... I have received Speke's book through the kindness of my friend Mr Murray.'[15]

Unable to find interest in his work in his adopted homeland of America, du Chaillu had written to the great naturalist and opponent of Darwin, Richard Owen, in whom he found powerful support. Despite his animosity towards Darwinism, Owen put du Chaillu in touch with Darwin's publisher, John Murray, and helped vastly with publicising the young explorer's work. Owen arranged for du Chaillu to lecture at fashionable scientific venues, central among which was the Royal Geographical Society. The arrival of du Chaillu and his adventures at the Murray offices at the moment when man's place in nature and his relationship to the ape were being hotly debated, was bizarre and the comedy of the situation did not go unnoticed at the time. As an obituarist wrote:

> He was lecturing at the old Ethnological, and in the audience was a scientific man of some distinction, a member, if I remember rightly, of the British Museum staff, who was one of his most bitter opponents. At the conclusion of the lecture this man rose and practically declared du Chaillu to be an imposter! This passed all bounds, and while the startled audience was wondering what would happen du Chaillu leapt from the platform and mounting a chair close to the speaker, shook his fist in his detractor's face, denouncing his conduct in no measured terms. The meeting broke up in confusion and du Chaillu chuckled as he told how his big opponent refused to leave the room until assured by his friends that the enraged explorer was not waiting for him with a revolver![16]

Du Chaillu was 'to the end ... a child at heart, full of southern vivacity, the life and soul of any company'. 'Old John Murray', he declared, 'is not a publisher, he's a gentleman.'

Exploration, discovery and travel, particularly in Central Asia, were now a speciality of the Murray list. The author of one such title, *Travels in Central Asia* (1864), the erudite and politically astute Hungarian Arminius Vambéry, wrote to Murray: 'In every case is the Russian Aggression in Central Asia favourable for the sale of our book; and as for England, I hope she will awake from her dangerous slumber, and stand prepared for every eventuality.'[17] Vambéry must have been a perfect player of the 'Great Game': he travelled in Central Asia dressed as a native, and could write in twelve languages, speak sixteen and understand twenty. Retiring into academe, he became Professor of Oriental Languages at the University of Budapest in 1865.

More typical of the John Murray travel author was the unique group of brave, indomitable women, each of whom packed her bags, put on a good thick skirt and set off into the unknown. One was Maria Graham, whose travels took her to India, Italy, Chile and Brazil. Others in the nineteenth century included Isabella Bird, and in the twentieth Freya Stark and Dervla Murphy. Isabella Bird had had no linguistic training for her forays into foreign parts. At home she was an invalid who rose late and wore an iron brace to support her diseased spine. On her travels to the Far East and Central Asia and around the world to China, Hawaii and the Rocky Mountains, her vigour revived to the extent that she could live a life of hardship and endure extreme physical conditions. Her *Journeys in Persia and Kurdistan*, published by Murray in 1891, was composed of her letters home, shocking Layard the Nineveh archaeologist: 'I have only read a few chapters of Mrs Bishop's book,' he wrote to Hallam Murray, John Murray III's second son, pointedly using her married name.

> I must say that I think a woman must be devoid of all delicacy and modesty who could travel as she did, without a female attendant, among a crowd of dirty Persian muleteers and others. Had there been an imperative act of duty or some precise end in view it might have been different, but as far as I can gather she had no object but to satisfy her curiosity and love of travel.[18]

Isabella Bird, the daughter of a clergyman, was, like her husband, who died young, a medical missionary in the Livingstone tradition. Travelling in Korea and China, she founded several hospitals along her route, and at home was involved with Murray himself in the establishment of a missionary training college in Livingstone's memory. But, as Layard pointed out, she also travelled for the sheer fun, or hell, of it. Leaving Baghdad in midwinter with snow thick on the ground and winds screaming, she spent much of the journey frozen to the saddle. She was brave and determined, describing herself on one night cowering with four hundred mules in a lofty stable, in pouring rain and freezing temperatures. 'The odour is overpowering,' she wrote. She reached Teheran in February 1890, 'after a most awful journey of 46 days from Baghdad, 30 of which were over ranges of mountains in snow from 1–3 feet deep'. Then she went to Isfahan, 'where the fanatics ... pursued me with howls and curses through the bazaars for two miles, an ordeal which I would not willingly encounter again'.

In her letters home, Miss Bird wrote frankly about what she saw. At times this was all too frank for her publisher's wary and commercial eye. But she knew her own mind and while she was grateful for Murray's editorial comments, she stood firmly by her judgement. 'I will consider the subject and see what may be omitted with due regard to the truthfulness of the picture.'[19] Responding to Murray's anxiety about overly 'realistic' description of the Japanese peasantry in *Unbeaten Tracks in Japan* (1893), she warned the publisher that he would find a description of the Canton prison in her new manuscript worse. But Miss Bird was adamant that such facts had to be recorded.[20]

Although a fearless traveller and feisty writer, quite able to look after herself in unknown lands, Isabella Bird seemed to have needed Murray to be her nursemaid when at home. Her chatty letters are full of requests for help. Quite reasonably she asks for advice 'regarding a literary matter':[21] she seems to have had an offer from another publisher. But some of her instructions are eccentric: 'I must ask you to help me by finding out through the Colonial Office whether Mr Bloomfield Douglas, the Resident, has resigned'; and, while Murray is about it, there are a few other things she needs from the Colonial Office, such as figures for the population of the town of Molacca. Murray went to enormous trouble to locate the right sort of tricycle for her,[22] and the story goes that he not only found an appropriate machine, but taught her how to ride it up and down Albemarle

Street.[23] Murray took all of this in his stride, but then he was 'always so willing to help' wrote Miss Bird, with genuine affection.[24]

Layard may have been reactionary in his outlook but in practical terms he had a point. Then, as now, there were places in the Muslim world where any woman going unveiled ran a considerable risk. Even male travellers were in danger: the Emir of Kashgar, on the western edge of China, punished offences with flogging, mutilation, hanging, and sometimes strangulation with his own hands. The Murray Archive contains a letter that in 1869 was smuggled between two Britons, Robert Shaw and George Hayward. In Bokhara they had been imprisoned by the Emir in separate quarters, and Hayward prophesied that Shaw would return to England 'to be feasted and feted', while he himself would continue to wander around Central Asia, 'still possessed with an insane desire to try the effects of cool steel across my throat'.[25] He was right on both counts. Shaw was awarded a gold medal by the Royal Geographical Society, and Hayward, remaining in Central Asia, was captured and had his head cut off on the orders of another local ruler. This tragedy is com-memorated by Sir Henry Newbolt's poem 'He Fell among Thieves' (later published by Murray), in which the brave Englishman, know-ing he is to die in the morning, spends the night recollecting his Oxbridge college and his public school:

> He saw the School Close, sunny and green,
> The runner beside him, the stand by the parapet wall,
> The distant tape, and the crowd roaring between,
> His own name over all.[26]

It may be churlish to point out that the real Hayward went to a modest school in east London, and almost certainly did not go to Oxbridge. Yet there is no evidence that he faced death with anything other than bravery.

The same stiff upper lip characterises Francis Younghusband, one of the last of those to report from Central Asia to Albemarle Street during the nineteenth century. Younghusband attended Clifton College, Bristol, and was the nephew of Robert Shaw, Hayward's fellow traveller. He made his first Himalayan journey when he had just turned twenty-one, and crossed the Gobi desert. By 1896 he had written *The Heart of a Continent: Travels in Manchuria, across the Gobi Desert, through the Himalayas, the Pamirs and Chitral 1884–1894*. Murray accepted the MS, and in the end had to write a preface to the book himself:

> The appearance of this volume has been delayed by a variety of unseen causes. Before the manuscript was completed, the author was suddenly called upon to go to Chitral, during the campaign which was being carried out in that country in 1895. Again, last December, when but a few pages were in print, he was unexpectedly summoned to a distant part of the world at a few hours' notice.
>
> Before leaving, he requested me to see the work through the press. This task has been an unusually interesting and agreeable one, but has been attended by some little difficulty, for some of the places named are not to be found on any existing maps, while, in as much as many of the incidents described are known to the author alone, the process of verification, when any uncertainty arose, was in some instances impossible.

A letter from Younghusband to John Murray IV, written during an expedition to Lhasa in May 1904, catches the spirit of these extraordinary traveller–authors, whose minds would turn to Albemarle Street in the most unlikely circumstances:

> Your letter of April 15th and the proofs of *The Heart of a Continent* reached me safely a few days ago. Though we have been bombarded all day long ... I ... am sending you the first instalment of corrected proofs ... We had a narrow shave here the other day when the Tibetans attacked the Mission. Somehow or other they got right up under our wall and I was awakened at dawn by wild shouts & firing & looking out of my tent saw shots being fired through our loop holes in at us – only ten yards away. However as soon as we had turned out, they were soon wiped out. With kind regards to Mrs Murray.[27]

★

Du Chaillu remained in touch with the Murray family for the rest of his life. His later works created technical problems after the gorilla furore had died down, and sales slumped. 'The work is full 2/3rd too long & wearisome & must be confined to one Volume,' complained

Robert Cooke to John Murray III in 1876. 'If Milton undertakes it, he might do it well but it will be a toughish job.'[28] Du Chaillu, in the nicest possible way, was always asking for money. A letter of 5 August 1863 finds an exhausted Cooke describing one of du Chaillu's visits to Albemarle Street: 'He has been again today, to say he wants £55-0-0 more and I have let him have it!!! He goes off to day, with about 50/- in his pocket and I have to pay his lodgings!!! £5.0.0.' Du Chaillu's letters to Murray, in his ornate and curly French hand-writing, are effusive and fond. Their author clearly needed and valued his friendship with the inhabitants of 50 Albemarle Street, asking always to be remembered to all the members of the family in the most courteous way, and referring to John Murray III as 'kind Mr Murray, the king of Publishers'.[29] Addressing a booksellers' trade dinner in 1890 he expressed his fondness for the profession that supported him and his work. This is how he was reported: 'Birds of zum feather should fly togedder. Ash for me, I say to mineself, Poul, I am vond ov my publishers, an as for dose dear booksellers, vy, I do lurve dem. Iv dey vere ladies I should say "Vot darlings dey ar." '[30]

If ever there was an author requiring the firm, brusque hand of the third-generation John Murray, it was Henrich Schliemann, the virtuoso self-taught archaeologist and linguist, author of five best-selling titles in the 1870s and 1880s, and a consummate crook. Schliemann discovered the ancient sites of Troy and Mycenae, and his accounts of these astonishing excavations were published by Murray in lavish productions, illustrated with black and white engravings and fold-out maps. The covers were designed by Hallam Murray with beautiful gold-embossing design. *Troja* (1884) is especially fine.

Murray had difficulties with Schliemann not least over his duplicitous attempts to mastermind the publication of the French (Hachette) and German (Brockhaus) editions of his books before the Murray edition had appeared, and quite without Murray's permission. 'I must entreat you not to interfere with my maturely considered business arrangements,' Murray wrote, understandably annoyed.[31] 'I am not any more your friend because you degrade me before Mr Brockhaus and you degrade me before the English public,' shrieked Schliemann to Murray.[32] However, Murray the publisher remained calm in the face of these bullying and irrational letters and replied immediately in a firm, reassuring tone: 'You are an exception to the rule of authors in interfering in these things. Please confide in me. I alone am responsible for the proper production of this important publication.'[33] Schliemann claimed hysterically that he would have to travel to London incognito to read the proofs of his second book, *Mycenae* (1878), as the press were waiting to pounce on him the minute he arrived. Murray assured him that all would be well for 'The streets are empty and you may walk through without meeting friend or foe ... You need not put yourself into a fever.' The books made money for both author and publisher, and Murray was happy to 'take on myself all the risque and Expenses of the Illustrations ... I for my part glory in your Discoveries and am proud to be associated with you.' The two clearly became quite close: on 13 October 1879 Schliemann wrote to his publisher: 'A letter from the old Grand Duchess of Mecklenburg has made me laugh very much for she writes as if she were deeply in love with me. You must read the letter.'

Schliemann really could have appeared in an old one-reeler – the baddie who ties the heroine to the railway line. He smuggled thousands of gold articles out of Turkish territory and, when he was caught, was able to retain the booty after paying modest compensation to Turkey. His brilliance was dazzling. It is said that once, on the island of Ithaca, he was reading *The Odyssey* when a crowd of local men from the fields became curious about what he was doing and, to amuse them, Schliemann read out loud from his book, translating from the ancient Greek into modern as he went along. The men carried him in triumph and admiration into the town. Schliemann retained his respectability during his lifetime. 'I am the most popular man in Greece,' he wrote to Murray in January 1877, 'and if the King has been angry at me for having, much against his will, demolished the Venetian Tower in the acropolis, at all event my telegram to him from Mycenae has made him my friend.'[34]

Schliemann made full use of his publisher's establishment connections by asking Murray to persuade none other than Gladstone to write a preface for *Mycenae*: 'We brought yesterday the ancient discoveries to Mr Gladstone; he did not quite promise to me to write the preface ... but you are all powerful with him, and he will at once give you the firm promise if you explain to him that Alexander von Humboldt always joyfully wrote the prefaces to works on those countries which were of peculiar interest to him.'[35] Gladstone shared Schliemann's passion for Homer and did indeed write the preface: very long and dull it is, too. Schliemann had wondered about dedicating the book to 'the Emperor of Brazil, the King of Greece, Gladstone or maybe all three', but in the event Gladstone was the sole dedicatee.[36]

It also seems to have been Gladstone who sowed the seed of one of the last memorable books to have been published by John Murray III. During 1879, Gladstone remarked: 'I am reading with great interest Curwen's History of Booksellers – or rather Publishers. I always maintained that an *extremely* interesting work might be produced upon the activities of the Book-trade.'[37] George Paston believed that this may have prompted Murray to write to Samuel Smiles in July 1879, reminding him that he had once said he would like to write the life of John Murray II: 'My Father, I venture to think, deserves a Biographer. I do not know where he would find so good and appreciative an one as you.'[38]

Smiles's granddaughter Aileen Smiles says that by this time in his career he had become 'a factory for biographies'.[39] His usual payment was £500 in advance, followed by a hefty share of the profits. The Murrays doubled the advance, even though Smiles did not expect to spend more than a year on the job. In fact he seems to have retreated in alarm almost as soon as he saw the size of the archive, leaving young John Murray IV to do the spadework for him. 'For over ten years I was engaged in collecting and arranging the correspondence before handing it over to Dr Smiles ... this had to be done in leisure hours.'[40] Smiles gives John Murray IV all due credit, and admits that he himself found the research dispiritingly heavy-going. Aileen Smiles confirms that 'It was a long and tedious business and poor Grandpa caught a bad cold searching through those germy archives.'[41]

Consequently it was 1891 before the public could buy *Memoir and Correspondence of the late John Murray, with an Account of the Origin and Progress of the House, 1768–1843*, in two volumes, later abridged into one. Among the reviewers was Gladstone, who wrote rather forlornly that he was 'the only man now living' who had had John Murray II for his publisher.[42] Gladstone's review, an assessment of John Murray II himself rather than a review of the book, was published in the recently inaugurated monthly *Murray's Magazine*. Founded in 1887, this had a more popular style than the *Quarterly Review*. *Murray's* was the brainchild of Edward Arnold, nephew of Matthew Arnold, who was beginning a career in publishing, and felt there was room for a new magazine miscellany of fiction and non-fiction, presented in a cosy middlebrow fashion. It lost money from the outset, but Murray himself was delighted by Arnold's editorial skills, and rewarded him with a set of sterling silver dinner cutlery. However, Arnold's judgement was not faultless. He rejected a plan to serialise Thomas Hardy's *Tess of the D'Urbervilles* on the grounds that it dealt with 'immoral situations', and 'the less publicity they have the better'.[43] *Murray's Magazine* lasted just long enough for Gladstone's article to appear, then expired at the end of 1891. John Murray himself did not last much longer. 'I am 82 years old, & nearly blind,' he wrote to Sir George Grey at the beginning of 1891,[44] but he was hale enough to give a newspaper interview to promote Smiles's book.

This lengthy interview with a nineteenth-century Murray survives in a press cutting in the Archive. 'At last we are to have an authoritative history of the house of Murray – the most famous and most interesting publishing concern extant,' wrote a reporter of the *Pall Mall Gazette*, under the heading 'A CHAT WITH MR JOHN MURRAY'. The interviewer and Murray are examining twenty or so large brown paper parcels containing letters:

> 'And whom are all these letters from?' I asked Mr Murray.
> 'From all my father's friends,' he replied. 'One of these friends was Lord Byron. When Byron left England for the last time in 1816, my father made it his duty to write to him once a week, or at least very constantly, so as to keep the exiled poet *au courant* with everything that was going on in England generally and in the metropolis in

particular. He told him what was being said and done in society . . .
My good friend, Lady Dorchester, while going through some of
Byron's papers bequeathed to her by her father, John Cam Hobhouse,
Byron's executor, came upon sixty or eighty letters written by my
father to the poet. Having read through them with great interest, she
forwarded them to me, with permission to publish them if I thought
fit.'

For the remainder of the interview, Murray reminisced about
Gifford and the *Quarterly Review*. Then, as the reporter was leaving,
John Murray IV made an appearance:

Mr John Murray, junior, produced a parcel of unpublished letters by
Sir Walter Scott. 'While Dr Smiles's book was going through the
press,' said he, as he untied the precious parcel, 'we found these forty-
two unpublished letters in a safe. They are from Sir Walter Scott to
my grandfather, and each letter contains upon the fly-leaf a note of
my grandfather's reply. Practically all of these will be incorporated in
the two large octavo volumes of which Dr Smiles's book will
consist.'[45]

The Murrays were beginning to appreciate the literary value of
their archive. Meanwhile, having lived to see the publication of
Smiles's two volumes, John Murray III died at Albemarle Street on
2 April 1892, aged eighty-three, of 'Senility, Degeneration of
Kidneys'.[46] He had written to his sisters, 'I am growing blinder and
blinder, and am losing memory sadly. Not that I complain with so
many blessings around me.'[47]

Once again it was a case of 'John Murray is dead, long live John
Murray!'

16

A *very* busy day

⌒

JOHN MURRAY IV was educated at Eton and at Magdalen College, Oxford after which he was packed off to America to learn about the book trade there before taking up his apprenticeship in the family firm. While his father and his cousin Robert Cooke had a good working relationship, this was not the case between father and son. John Murray IV was miserable at Albemarle Street. 'Ever since I came to work here,' he wrote unhappily to his father,

> but more especially since I have been engaged to be married the conversations you have had with me regarding my prospects, have been of so gloomy and discouraging a nature as to make me quite dispirited … I can only come to the conclusion that you and Cousin Robert are of opinion that I am incompetent to fill my present and prospective position … A business of this nature is not to be thoroughly learnt in five years, I suppose, but the constant insinuations that I have hitherto done nothing … pain me more that I care to confess.[1]

John Murray IV's own regime at Albemarle Street began in 1892, and its difference to his father's era was immediately apparent. Though John Murray III died in the 1890s, the material in the Murray Archive begins suddenly to have a twentieth-century look about it. There are armfuls of newspaper cuttings, many of them pasted into big volumes, and John Murray IV's extensive and neatly written diaries, a fanatically detailed record of a stupendously ordinary life. Each day, the fourth John Murray records which train he took from Wimbledon to Waterloo, and which train he took back again. Saturday mornings were spent at the office in those days, at least by senior staff, who went in to open the post. Murray tells us again and again that he had 'a *very* busy day', but there is nothing about the books he was reading or editing, nor meetings with authors: no gossip to enjoy. However he never fails to record the weather, and there are usually details of his wife's and his children's health. On 12 June 1884 'John Murray V made his appearance: a very fine boy', and the next day at the office: 'Such greetings at Alb. St!! busy day … EM [Katherine Evelyn Murray, John Murray's wife, who was always called 'Evie'] going on nicely – boy charming – EM pains bad all day.' Also meticulously listed are the contents of the shooting 'bag', and Murray's scores at golf, his favourite occupation for a Saturday afternoon. Although the diary is formal and written without emotion, his constant mentions of a sick child seem all the more distressing, hopelessly juxtaposed as they are with the weather report and the day's Bible reading: 'cold, dull, raw: (Amy good night) Pr[overbs]: 8.35'.[2] We have a clue to what was wrong with John and Evie Murray's eldest child when Isabella Bird enquires of John Murray III's 'anxiety regarding the spine of your grandchild'.[3] The diary records Amy's death at just five years old in May 1884, a month before the birth of John Murray V.

In the summer of 1892, Murray and his family moved from Wimbledon to Albemarle Street, leaving Newstead to be occupied by his brother Hallam,[4] with whom he came to have a bitter quarrel. This was never made up, and split the Murrays tragically. The roots of the quarrel are unknown, although John Murray IV did write to his children a few months before his death admitting that 'one of the greatest trials of my life has been the breach with my brother Hallam due entirely to the policy of secrecy & want of personal discussion when he [Hallam] left the business'. Murray revealed little more, except to add: '[Hallam] pleaded for this politely and I weakly gave way. All would have been cleared up in a friendly way by free discussion.'[5]

The diary hides more than it discloses about serious personal concerns in its keeper's life. In any case, the volume for the period of the breach is missing. John Murray IV never wrote about his feelings for his brother, nor indeed for any other member of the family, and at a glance there appear, in this watershed year for the Murrays, to be only two things of real interest recorded: a brief description of electric lights being fitted and turned on for the first time at Albemarle Street, and a few curt references to cocaine, which Evie is evidently taking for depression. How best then to describe this era of the Murray publishing house?

Pasted into one of the albums of press cuttings in the archive is a review of Samuel Smiles's biography of John Murray II written with a little less sympathy for the dynasty than we might expect. The review in itself takes us no further. Bur it reminds that one should ask what knowledgeable but less sympathetic outsiders now thought about the firm and the dynasty. What follows is a device for doing that, and it may also help bring to life John Murray IV, given the comparative stiffness and formality of his records in the archive. The speaker is an invented character, an imagined version of a member of another real publishing family, but everything factual he says about John Murray IV is based on documentation in the archive.

★

Longman is the name, Charles James Longman. You won't have heard of me, but you'll probably have spotted my family flitting in and out of this narrative at odd moments, such as the occasion when we were hovering in the wings over Byron's memoirs. Do you remember how we lent Tom Moore 2,000 guineas, so he could settle up with Murray? It was some time before we saw it back again, I can tell you. And of course we never got to publish the Memoirs. That's the up-and-down luck of the book business. A lousy way to make money. But not a bad way to have some fun.

I've just popped up to correct a few misapprehensions, while giving the Murrays our heartiest congratulations on all the attention that's being paid to them. They sent me because I'm the Longman family historian, the same generation as John Murray IV, Sir John Murray, as he eventually became. I was born the year after him, in 1852. Yes, I'm a congratulation-bearer. But dare I admit there is just the tiniest corner of me that wonders how the House of Murray goes on attracting the limelight, decade after decade, century after century.

And dare I point out that Longman's, having started in 1724, were at this publishing business almost a half-century before any Murray?

We've now chalked up something like 270 years, quite a bit more than the Royal Family of Albemarle Street. And for most of that time you could still find us in our original home, 39 Paternoster Row, in the spot where British bookselling really started, the churchyard of St Paul's Cathedral.

We don't go in for the personality cult in my family – none of this papal or Dalai Lama stuff about the successor waiting in the wings, named with the same name as the rest of the holy dynasty. And John begat John, who begat John, who begat John. What has that got to do with publishing, for goodness sake? And it's what brought the whole enterprise to an end, eventually, because suddenly the successor didn't want to be a successor. But I mustn't reveal the denouement.

Over at Longman's, we don't care if you're called John or William or Thomas or Edward. We don't even particularly care whether you're called Longman; quite a few non-relatives have been involved over the years. And we certainly don't waste money and energy on proving that we're gentlemen. We're not: we're in trade, and you won't find us sending our sons to Eton, where John Murray IV went, and where you can wager they didn't teach him how to become a publisher. Publishers shouldn't try to be scholars. If they're really brainy, they see through their authors in a trice. And seeing through authors isn't a publisher's job. That's for the critics to do. A publisher has to believe in the book he's publishing; no one else will.

All right, I've been rumbled, and I admit it: I went to Harrow. But that doesn't negate what I have been saying. The best place to train to be a publisher is behind a stall in a street market, selling things to people who don't really want them or need them. That'll teach you how to flatter your way into their pockets, and how to peg your price to what they can just afford. Whereas John Murray IV got his ideas about life on the playing fields of Eton, and among the fritillary-groves of Magdalen College, Oxford, where he spent a mere two years, not taking his degree. After this he was sent to America. Quite mind-expanding, one would have thought. Yet not so many years later, when he became an influential founding member of the Publishers' Association, he played a crucial part in the invention of that dreadful straitjacket, the Net Book Agreement, with its fixed prices and almost complete ban on the competitive element in bookselling.

But then Murray's, I suspect, needed the Agreement to sell any books at all. It never ceases to amaze me how such an uncommercial publishing house should have such a vast reputation. I mean, compare the backlist on which Longman's rests securely with the equivalent titles at Murray's. Longman's was partly founded on *Robinson Crusoe*, plus Johnson's *Dictionary*. Actually, if you go back to our beginnings, we made our original money selling soap.

I accept that Murray sold a lot of Byron. We made a bad mistake with Byron: he had been rude about several of our authors in *English Bards and Scotch Reviewers*, and what a money-spinner *Childe Harold* and its successors became! But then John Murray II – who always puzzles me, compared to his predecessor and his successors – started to play the censor. And there are enough censors, both official and unofficial, without a publisher trying it too.

But you have to take your hat off to John Murray II for signing up Byron, especially as I'm sure he had never read more than a few lines of *Childe Harold* – he left all that to Gifford. John Murray IV turned out to be more neurotic in this respect. He tried to read each manuscript that was submitted to the house, line by line. Someone else could have been doing that for him, and probably was: the publishing house, which in Byron's time had employed perhaps five people, by 1900 had a staff of about fifty. But John Murray IV had an eye for detail. It was he who as a young man had organised the thousands of letters in the archive so that Sam Smiles could write his book on the house of Murray, and what a solemn book it is!

Yes, John Murray IV had an eye for detail. His own reign at Albemarle Street was largely characterised by big projects of editing rather than publishing: the big Byron letters edition, and the letters of Queen Victoria. He did a good job reorganising the firm, I will allow him that. The moment his father was dead, in 1892, he got things on to a firmer keel financially. The Murray Handbooks to all those faraway places had been fun but costly, and John Murray IV passed them on to the shoulders of a specialist guidebook publisher,

Stanford. He lifted the ban on poetry and fiction. All right, it's a gamble, but where is the fun in publishing if you can't have a flutter on some poems or a novel? And among the new Murray poets, Henry Newbolt ('Play up! Play up! And play the game!') was a brisk seller, though I will have you know that *we* discovered him first in *Longman's Magazine*. As for fiction, the fledgeling Edith Wharton nested in Albemarle Street for a while, though she disliked the way that Murray editors – was it John Murray IV himself? – 'improved' her American style in her first long novel, *The Valley of Decision*, which came out in 1902. I remember John mentioning that she had been rather fierce about upping her royalty arrangement.

Yes, there were some changes made, and on the whole they were the right ones. But there was one fly in the ointment. John Murray III had done a Lear and split the kingdom between his two sons, the heir and the spare. John the elder (John Murray IV) got the Winter Palace in Albemarle Street, plus the business itself, while his younger brother Hallam had to make do with second place in the publishing house, plus the Summer Palace – the family's Wimbledon mansion, Newstead, which by now was enormous: nearly twenty bedrooms, stabling for half a dozen horses, a tennis court, and even a lake. But Hallam Murray didn't want a lake. He was an accomplished painter and designer, who illustrated other people's books, and was happy looking after the design side of the publishing business until he and his brother fell out.

Over what they quarrelled, nobody knows. Every scrap of paper relating to the conflict has been destroyed – with the exception of that letter, in which John Murray IV regrets it all on his deathbed. A bit late by then. And don't ask me what happened to Hallam. All I know is that he got rid of Newstead not long after the First World War. It was soon demolished, to make way for the tennis club. So next time you're watching a nailbiting Wimbledon final, don't forget that the secrets of the Murrays lie buried beneath the Centre Court.

Not that I think the trouble between the brothers was anything murky. Probably just an argument about whose offspring would succeed to what; and property of course, chattels, stuff. Heavens, they were dynasty-conscious. Whenever John Murray IV mentioned his son, the fifth John, in correspondence, he abbreviated the boy's name thus: 'JM[V]'. And you should have seen the lad's coming-of-age dinner in 1905 in a West End restaurant – a vast gathering, with speeches, all reported in the trade papers. The Crown Prince was toasted by the current editor of the *Quarterly Review*, a fellow named Prothero, who declared that the name of Murray 'was bound up with a noble chapter in the history of human thought', and it would be the duty of John Murray V 'to adapt himself to modern needs without swerving a hair's breadth from the ancient standard of honour'.[6]

Blow me down, why didn't they pack up the publishing, and go off and rule some tidy little middle European kingdom? And you know, the Byron Room at 50 Albemarle Street always seemed to me more like a salon in Paris or Vienna than a British drawing room. We too gave literary dinners at Longman's, but somehow we couldn't get the atmosphere quite right. Certainly our hospitality never got written up in the same way by visiting Americans. And nobody ever burnt a manuscript in our grate.

Don't get me wrong. There was no hostility between London's two most senior publishing houses. We used to cement our friendship each summer before the First World War with a game of cricket, Murray *v.* Longman. As far as I recall, the spoils of victory were fairly evenly shared. Oddly, I don't think old 'Play-up' Newbolt ever took part in those matches, though he was virtually on the staff of Murray's, and had a little office where he edited something called the *Monthly Review.*

I have one score-card left from those matches, and I'm sorry to say it records that John Murray IV was out for a duck. But he usually did better than that – a very decent all-round sportsman, who rarely missed his golf on Saturday afternoon. But I didn't get the impression that his home life was abundantly happy. In choosing a wife, John Murray IV had followed family tradition and headed north of the border, it being considered desirable to get a top-up of Scots blood in each generation of Murray's. But he got more than that this time. His bride, Evelyn Leslie (known as 'Evie'), daughter of an Aberdeenshire

Justice of the Peace and Member of Parliament, produced a nursery-full of children in due time, but she also brought, metaphorically, a black dog into the family. She suffered from depression, and we will see this passing down the generations.

I would guess that poor old John Murray IV had quite a tough time of it, with Evie under her cloud of gloom in one corner of number 50, and he working away at his desk in the evenings, there being nothing else to do. Only one of his surviving letters makes any reference to the predicament – it was written to the mother of A. C. Benson, of whom more later. She had perhaps been recommending a medical man, for he wrote: 'I know Dr Crouch well, as my dear wife was under his care for a long time – till the shock of the war caused her a permanent injury to the vessels of the brain and for 3 years now she has been a helpless invalid – her memory gone & no hope of recovery.'[7] The poor lady was on medication – cocaine, I believe. But remember that she had a son in battledress, against whose survival the odds were quite heavily piled. Worries at home; worries at the office. In the early 1900s, worries *about* the office, fears that the building itself, the precious sanctuary, number 50, might succumb to the developers. Men would suddenly be found in the basement, poking at the subsoil, and by way of passports they brandished papers with the heading PICCADILLY UNDERGROUND RAILWAY. 'Albemarle Street Station?' It was several years before this fear was banished, and the developers were seen off the premises. But even then victory was partial: John Murray IV had to relinquish his building in Dover Street which backed on to 50 Albemarle Street, and which he had been using as a warehouse. It became part of Dover Street station, now replaced by Green Park station.

Of course, the railway battle generated yet more publicity for our dynastic friends, and a gratifyingly broad stream of would-be Murray authors queued up outside Palazzo Albemarle. Those who were unsuccessful included George Bernard Shaw, and that tiresome Mr Rolfe, who called himself 'Baron Corvo'. Shaw, who had yet to achieve a wide reputation, airily dismissed the rejection by Murray of *Man and Superman*: if Murray would care to read it again in ten years, suggested Shaw, he would understand what it was all about.

As for 'Corvo', he protested not that his curious novel *Hadrian the Seventh* had been turned down, but that someone had scribbled in the margin of the manuscript.

This was in 1903–4. About a dozen years later, when the Great War was at its height, you could still, metaphorically, see a string of most distinguished authors queuing outside number 50. However, this time they were mostly dead: Charlotte Brontë, Thackeray, Browning, Ruskin and Thomas Hardy. Only the last-named was still alive, and he wrote the nicest little note to thank Mr Murray for informing him that Smith, Elder, who had published some of his work, were now a part of John Murray. No doubt Miss Brontë, Mr Thackeray, Mr Browning and Mr Ruskin would have written in the same manner had they not been stone-dead. Need I explain that they were all Smith, Elder authors? It was scarcely a takeover, more of a benevolent rescue of a financially stretched bunch of friends: George Smith, the firm's late co-founder, had originally learned the trade as an employee of Murray's. Still we've seen a lot of that sort of thing recently – Hutchinson with Hurst & Blackett, Routledge and Kegan Paul. Even George Allen have teamed up with some new house. Macmillan's started it all when they took over Bentley's.

I know, you're wondering how I came to see that letter from Hardy. Quite simple: Sir John – John Murray IV – showed it to me. As the years passed, and he was at the helm for a long time, 1892 to 1928, his heart seemed to lie more and more with the archive, or at least with the memorabilia that were spread out on view in the drawing room. He wasn't a great one for literary dinners or for encouraging authors to treat the place as their club as some of his ancestors had done. Indeed he said he had made it a rule not to lunch out, as it broke up the day too much.[8] But he loved to show off the relics. Tall, with sad eyes and a walrus moustache, increasingly cadaverous as the years passed, Sir John Murray, KCVO, was something of a relic himself. Well, I must go.

★

Besides tending the archive, John Murray IV busied himself both with grand and immense literary projects, and with difficult, inconsistent authors. The pioneer gardener William Robinson wrote the bestselling *The English Flower Garden* (1883), a book that became a landmark in the design and understanding of the nature of its subject. This was the era in which the domestic garden developed its informal, cottagey aspect, in contrast to the articulation of rolling acres as favoured by such Picturesque gardeners of the previous century as Capability Brown and Humphry Repton.[9] Robinson, a down-to-earth gardener with a down-to-earth name, brought the hum of the bees and the sweet smell of stocks back into fashion, and into the newly expanding suburbs. But Robinson also had a down-to-earth uncompromising manner. He was direct, and spoke his mind, but also changed his mind in what appear to be a series of voltes-face which the ever-tactful and diplomatic John Murray IV was at pains to handle. Robinson had grown rich on the profits of his books, his publishing company and his horticultural sales, but at times even he was overcome by the complexity of it all. He wrote to Murray in 1903: 'Sometimes I think is it high time for me to get out of business, and I should not mind transferring the copyright of these books to you or anybody who could make good use of it. Perhaps you would kindly consider this matter. Of course the author's work I should always have to do but perhaps it would be better if I had nothing to do with their production.'[10]

Only eight years later, however, he is complaining to Murray about the commission he is paying on sales – Robinson handled the printing of his books, Murray the sales. Murray wrote back wearily:

> A ten per cent commission on both sides of the account barely pays the true proportion of our permanent establishment charges, viz rent, rates, salaries, taxes etc. When the commission is only levied on sales it does not pay those charges. I think I may say that in publishing your books for these many years we have made practically nothing out of it except the credit. We have, moreover, on very many occasions given you advice as to printing, binding etc., and you now ask us to do so again.[11]

'I have always printed my own books,' Robinson responded vigorously, 'as I have decided views about printing and engraving and so I must go on doing to the end. There seems therefore to be no other way out of the difficulty than that of my ceasing to publish with you, to my deep regret.'[12] Murray smoothed a way out of this impasse for Robinson, and they were soon back in business together. But Robinson was a wasp not a bee, and ten years later he stung again:

> I regret to say I do object to the jacket. No advertisement of mine or or [*sic*] any other books on the cover please! Use a 'quiet' wrapper as before: a drawing of your brother's was used on wrapper & may be again – otherwise nothing but the name of the book & author all 'run on' in old faced type – no 'display'! … PS I do not trouble you with my reasons for the course I take, & it only applies to my book.[13]

Grand and immense projects brought with them other kinds of problems. One grand project was intended to be the definitive edition of Byron's Letters and Journals, which Murray worked on with Prothero. The editor-in-chief of Byron's letters and journals was initially Byron's grandson, Ralph Milbanke, as he called himself, taking his grandmother's maiden name. His real surname was King, and through his father he inherited the title Earl of Lovelace. His mother, now generally known as the mathematician Ada Lovelace, was correctly Ada King, Countess of Lovelace. Milbanke also inherited the copyright of certain Byron papers, and soon began to demonstrate the megalomania common among literary executors. His particular obsession, nobody knows quite why, was to prove his grandmother totally innocent of any blame for the break-up of her marriage to Byron. To this end he determined to prove that Byron did indeed have an incestuous relationship with his half-sister Augusta.

It quickly became impossible for the Byron letters project to continue with Lovelace involved. To his credit, he realised this and resigned, and published a bizarre book of his own. This was named after the incestuous sister in Byron's *Manfred*, its full title being *Astarte: A Fragment of Truth Concerning George Gordon Byron, sixth Lord Byron*. It begins with an extraordinary statement: 'Lord Byron's life contained nothing of any interest except what ought not to have been told.' But half-mad Lovelace could be perceptive. At one moment he remarked: 'Byron's character was a labyrinth of irreconcilables. Every conclusion requires qualification.'[14]

But for much of the time Lovelace simply rages, and he repeats a double insult coined long before by William Hazlitt, 'Lame Gifford, and one-eyed Murray'.[15] Lovelace repeats this in such a manner that one knows he is thinking of the modern Murray and his sidekick Prothero. Despite this, John Murray IV and Prothero accommodated Lovelace. They agreed not to include any letters that would offend him, although they had the right to publish them without his permission. They got their own back in a privately printed book *Lord Byron and his Detractors*, in 1906. Sir John wrote the bulk of it, and in the preface said he wondered why Lovelace 'should have felt called upon to elaborate the blackest charges [incest] against his Grandfather, in order to absolve his Grandmother from certain minor criticisms'.[16] On one level, he seemed to find *Astarte* amusing but, of course, the Murray name had been besmirched and that needed seeing to. [17]

In fact Lovelace died before the book could be circulated, but there was no abatement of the hoo-ha over Byron. For example there was a long-running campaign, co-ordinated year after year from Albemarle Street, to get some sort of Byron Memorial into Poets' Corner at Westminster Abbey. Ada Lovelace was among the campaigners: 'Do the clergy', she wrote, 'feel their Church so tottering that they think themselves obliged to affect an extra-Morality, to prop it up for yet a little longer?'[18] The great and good supported various petitions, and the campaign was still being waged in 1924, the centenary of Byron's death, when a letter to *The Times* was signed by Lloyd George, G. M. Trevelyan, Thomas Hardy and Rudyard Kipling. The answer from the Abbey was still 'no'. According to the Dean, Herbert Ryle, Byron had 'earned a world-wide reputation for immorality'.[19] And that was that.

In view of the Byron connection, it might have been thought that Murray's were not the most appropriate house to publish the letters of Queen Victoria, but no other company stood the slightest chance. The project originated with the sinister courtier Lord Esher, who cast around for someone who would co-edit the letters with him,

John Murray V with Lord Gorell, a partner in the firm, at 50 Albemarle Street, 1930s. Lord Gorell was a poet and sometime Chairman of the Society of Authors

John Murray V at 50 Albemarle Street, by Mark Gerson, 1960s. Thomas Phillips' 'cloak' portrait of Lord Byron hangs above the fireplace

Jock Murray (John Murray VI), in his trademark red braces and bow tie, in the Drawing Room at 50 Albemarle Street, standing where his uncle took a more formal pose twenty years earlier

The energetic and debonair war hero Patrick Leigh Fermor, whose books, in particular those describing his epic pre-war walk across Europe, opened up new modes of expression in travel writing, in Greek costume c.1930

Leigh Fermor discovered Byron's slippers in the home of a descendent of Byron's boatman. They had been kept in the family since Byron's death in 1824

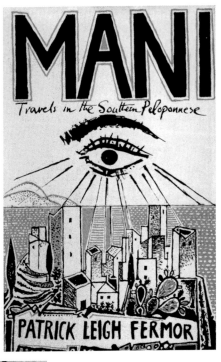

Cover design by John Craxton of *Mani* by Patrick Leigh Fermor, 1958

Staircase, 50 Albemarle Street, 1943. The bust at the turn of the stairs is of David Smith, an Edinburgh relation of Marion, Mrs John Murray III, by Jonathan Steel, 1865

Jock Murray (left) and the caretaker's dog with Axel Munthe, the author of *The Story of San Michele* at 50 Albemarle Street in 1936

Osbert Lancaster, Freya Stark, Cecil Beaton and John Betjeman at a Murray party in 50 Albemarle Street, Dec 1970

Right: Jock and Diana Murray at 50 Albemarle Street, 1970s

Below: Jock Murray (centre left) with Kenneth Clark (right) and Stephen Hearst, Head of Arts Features, BBC TV (left of Jock) at the launch of *Civilisation*, BBC Television Centre, 1969. On Jock's initiative, Clark's *Civilisation* became a pioneer 'tie-in' publication between the BBC and a commercial publisher

Ruth Prawer Jhabvala at 50 Albemarle Steet, a photograph taken when *Heat and Dust* won the Booker Prize in October 1975

Dervla Murphy, author of many travel books, including *Full Tilt* (1965) and *In Ethiopia with a Mule* (1968)

Don Mackean, author of *Introduction to Biology*, with Kenneth Pinnock, Director of Murray's Educational division at 50 Albemarle Street, 1976. Jock Murray far left

John Murray VII at 50 Albemarle Street, 1980s. The young publisher waiting in the wings

The John Murray Archive departing 50 Albemarle Street for Scotland, March 2006

Card to mark the departure of the John Murray Archive to Edinburgh, by David Eccles, 2006

Humphrey Carpenter arriving at 50 Albemarle Street in 2002

someone who would do the real editorial work. His eyes fell upon the novelist A. C. (Arthur) Benson, son of a former Archbishop of Canterbury and brother of E. F. Benson, the author of the 'Mapp and Lucia' stories. Arthur Benson, who had written the words to 'Land of Hope and Glory', was an Eton housemaster, looking for a change of career. He was already a John Murray author, his book *The Schoolmaster: A Commentary upon the Aims and Methods of an Assistant Master in a Public School* (1902) having done very well. Esher was quite content that Benson and Murray should work together on what was said to be the first-ever collection of letters by a sovereign to be published. Benson's diary records a visit to Murray's, soon after his schoolmaster book had been finished:

I found the great man [John Murray IV] sitting by a window looking into Albemarle St, at a desk covered with letters and documents; writing hard by a warm fire so that his face was flushed. He smiled very warmly, his great mouth full of crooked teeth. He is a fine manly fellow – not much of a taste in literature I expect, and with plenty of wholesome priggishness – a kind of decoction of Caledonianism – which stiffens this worthy English merchant. He talked rather pleasantly about the book – and then he said he would like me to see his Byron. He led me through the counting house below and said, 'We live next door.' Took me through a sort of back serving room and into his dining-room – a dark room with *many* interesting pictures in florid gold frames – the house of Murray – and all the literary men of the beginning of [the nineteenth] century – but we passed so quickly through that I have forgotten all of them – they struck me very much – old Mr. Murray [presumably John Murray III] must have been a hideous man.

Then we went up to the drawing room where he introduced me to Mrs Murray – very pleasant – and to his delightful son and daughter – and showed me some more beautiful pictures. I remember the Byron and the Gray best. The room was richly furnished; but I like his living next his shop, in the same old fashioned house – it is unlike Macmillan with his many palaces, grinding the noses of authors.'[20]

Benson was very struck by the young John Murray V and found him 'delightful', noting: 'I ought to see more of him.' Macmillan had published Benson's life of his father, and clearly the experience had not been altogether pleasant for him.

The project was hush-hush to begin with, and was referred to in writing as a 'proposed work of a very exceptional character'.[21] It was to be kept confidential until King Edward's announcement in *The Times*. This Benson clearly found irritating. 'I feared it would get into the papers before the announcement,' he complained. 'It was becoming rather trying to be obliged to nod and wink in reply to questions. But when I got back here I found that practically everyone knew.'[22] As soon as the news was official there was a general flurry of interest, including letters from printers queuing up for the honour of working with Murray on the Queen's letters.

John Murray IV took a keen interest in the editing of the volumes: eight in all were proposed. He tactfully complained of a 'certain want of variety', and 'perhaps a little tendency to dwell on trifles'. He would prefer more on the China war or the Afghan war, he explained.[23] But editorial decisions were complicated by the number of parties involved and by the fact that this book was 'unlike others'.[24] There was consternation that the King was going to refuse to allow all the more interesting personal letters to be included. 'I hope this is not the case,' wrote Benson to Murray. 'Of course the most private could not go in – but "private" as distinguished from public official has a wide connotation.'[25] Murray particularly hoped that the correspondence with the Duchess of Kent was not going to be left out: 'I am much struck by some of those [letters] from the Queen to her mother. Her position was a most delicate one in regard to the Duchess of Kent both shortly before, and after the coronation, and these letters display much firmness of character and sense of character.'[26] Murray also picked out some paragraphs about 'the attendance of ministers at the birth of a royal infant' which he found 'curious' and bound to 'interest many readers'.[27] Neither these passages, from the Queen's memoranda to George Anson, private secretary to Prince Albert, nor the Queen's letters to her mother, appear in the published volumes.

The book was far from plain sailing from John Murray IV's point of view. There were endless delays, often for utterly Byzantine reasons, such as the need to draw up an authoritative royal genealogy. Amazingly one did not already exist except for an incomplete one started under George II. Eventually Garter King of Arms agreed to do the work for nothing since it was for the royal family.[28] Further hiatuses occurred whenever King Edward VII's approval was needed for some editorial decision. Policy questions would be passed obsequiously to him, together with relevant portions of the text. But since his Majesty never read anything except the newspaper and an occasional novel, no reply would be forthcoming. Murray felt that the volumes should be illustrated by portraits of the leading figures featuring in the letters. Huge amounts of work and effort went into choosing a picture and photographing it, and then a message would eventually come from Esher, 'The King does not care much about the portrait',[29] and the picture would have to be dropped. 'It would be as well', wrote Benson to Murray, 'for you to put your view about the public expectations ... before Esher sometime, or to send me a letter which I can send on to him, and which he can submit if he thinks fit. But it will not Do to say that the public will expect a thing and that their expectation is justified ...We must remember, that in dealing with our august friend we are dealing with a ... naturally touchy person.'[30] Murray also had to be patient with Lord Esher, whose instructions were supercilious and perfunctory to the point of rudeness. Quite often he replied to the publishers via Benson. Meanwhile Murray had to pay for vast amounts of type to be kept standing and waiting.

When publication day was finally in sight there was a further fuss about a very sombre and tasteful advertisement published by Murray's for the book. According to Esher there would be the most ghastly scene if the King actually saw the advertisement but he was fairly confident that he probably would not. 'H.M.'s objection is to anything in the nature of a "puff",' to which Murray replied, 'No one dislikes a puff advertisement ... more than I do,' and that this was the last thing it was meant to be or indeed was. Then, finally, when it was all done, Murray found himself locked in a legal battle.

In the early 1900s, *The Times* ran a so-called Book Club, sidestepping the Net Book Agreement by offering nearly new books at a reduced price on the grounds that they had been used by subscribers to *The Times* Library. Things came to a head when the first edition of Queen Victoria's letters appeared in 1907. The paper complained that, at three guineas for the three volumes, it was grossly overpriced: ten shillings was suggested as closer to the actual costs. Murray was accused of having 'exploited the great personality of Queen Victoria for his own ends, and coined the national interest in her doings for his own enrichment'.[31] *The Times* rashly printed a letter in which Murray was compared to Judas Iscariot demanding his pieces of silver. Murray sued for libel. Joseph Dent, the publisher of the Everyman Library, sent him a rallying letter: 'We all regard your fight as being in the interest of the trade … there is no craft hardly that leaves one with less remuneration. But it is a great craft and I rejoice to be ever so humble a member in work that is, I believe, most valuable to the public weal.'[32] Murray won the case, was awarded £7,500 damages, and then did a deal by which Murray's and *The Times* quickly made up their differences and jointly published a cheap one-volume edition of the book.

After publication of the first volume of letters, Esher changed his tune towards John Murray IV. In July 1909 we find him writing to 'My dear Murray', thanking him profusely for all his trouble, and taking a particular and marked interest in Jack, the young John Murray V. There is suddenly talk of the Viscount popping in to Albemarle Street, and a very chatty little notes for 'My dear Jack'.[33] It was John Murray V who would help Esher with the editing of an abridged version of the girlhood diaries of Queen Victoria, *The Training of a Sovereign* (1914). The house of Murray was now firmly established as publisher to the royals, *par excellence*.

By the end of his working life, Murray was spending at least half his time on committees of such institutions as Great Ormond Street Children's Hospital. It was for this, just as much as for the Victoria letters, that he was knighted, two years before he died in December 1928. His obituaries paid most of their attention to his work as a publisher: 'The death of Sir John Murray removes nearly the last of the old-fashioned publishers. Publishing used to be a profession; it is degenerating into a form of exploitation demanding … the qualities of the impresario and the advertising agent rather than the combina-tion of . . . the family solicitor and the connoisseur.'[34] Another read: 'Religious without display, gladly helpful, devotedly loyal and patri-otic, he was a gentleman, beyond which nothing more estimable could be said.'[35] That was one of the trade journals: he would have been pleased by the reference to a 'gentleman'. Interestingly, his will said that he regarded the Archive and other historic items at number 50 as 'a public trust', and urged his executors to 'get the collection exempted from death duties'.[36] Another press report stated that if the contents of the Murray Archive went on sale the price would 'put them utterly beyond the reach of the home collector, or of the public institutions in this country'.[37]

But the dynasty was running into trouble. At the age of thirty-two, in 1916, John Murray V had made a dynastic marriage to Lady Helen de Vere, daughter of a wealthy old fellow called Lord Brassey, whose fortune had come from his father's railway building. But, as time passed, there were no children from this union. So where was John Murray VI going to come from?

17

Robin

—◆—

THE BRASSEY—MURRAY wedding, at St Paul's Knightsbridge in August 1916, received extensive coverage in the social columns. One newspaper speculated that the bridegroom was descended from 'the ducal Murrays of Blair Atholl'.[1] His name was given as 'Major John Murray, Scottish Horse', and he was married in uniform. 'It was quite quiet,' reported another paper, 'there were no bridesmaids or pages.'[2] However, the *Evening Standard* noted the presence of one small boy: 'Master Robin Grey, in a white man-o'-war suit, [who] distributed the wedding leaflets so liberally that the supply gave out'.[3]

Six years later, in the autumn of 1922, this child was settling in at Eton. 'My darling Grumpa,' he wrote to John Murray IV, his grandfather on his mother's side,

> I like all the Masters so much . . . I simply love carpentry and am making Evelyn [his sister] a cupboard and a standard lamp . . . Please give my best love to all.
>
> Your
> adoring
> Jock[4]

The boy's full name was John Arnaud Robin Grey. Had he changed from calling himself, or being called, 'Robin' at the age of six to 'Jock' at the age of thirteen as a step towards becoming the sixth John Murray? Or was it just other schoolboys teasing him with a nickname that referred to his Scottish ancestry? We do not know; but it is clear that his grandfather was happy to go along with the change. 'My dear Jock,' he wrote from Albemarle Street,

You seem to have made a capital start [at Eton] and I hope you will go on liking the dear old place more and more. When I first went there 59 years ago I knew no one, and had never been to school before so I was very miserable for a bit ... As Uncle Jack and Aunt Helen are going to be away on the 8th October, I might come down that afternoon if you are free.

Your loving Grandfather

John Murray[5]

It may already have become clear to John Murray IV, at least, that 'Uncle Jack and Aunt Helen' were unable to produce the heir, and that the succession would have to pass to their nephew.[6] Did he say something to Jock, on his visits to Eton, along the lines of the panegyric that Prothero had delivered in 1905 at the dinner to celebrate John Murray V's coming-of-age? 'Publishing', Prothero had declared 'is a laborious and arduous work ... [But] to publish only what is good, honest and pure, and what really represents the highest thought, the highest knowledge, and the highest aspirations of the nation – that, I say, is a very great and noble task.'[7] Probably he did not. The Murrays have never talked like that, and though John Arnaud Robin Grey is mentioned in his grandfather's will, he is not singled out for special treatment. It looks as if John Murray IV had no special plans for Jock while he was still a schoolboy. Things would work out.

Jock's mother was John Murray IV's daughter Dorothy. The Murrays had not had much success down the generations in marrying off their daughters: John Murray II had three daughters who all died unmarried; John Murray III had two. Dorothy might have felt that her chances of matrimony were reduced by the fact that she had a cleft lip and palate. Her brother, John Murray V, wrote her a poem when she was about to have an operation for it: the handwriting suggests he was about twelve:

> Oh! my dearest Dorothea!
> Never! never! never! fear,
> Though the surgeon's knife being near.
> But mind you feel sure

That your *lip* he will cure;
To that *you* are quite secure.[8]

The operation was indeed a success, and in due time Dorothy found a husband, Thomas Robinson Grey, known as Robin, an alumnus of Eton and Magdalen. He was called to the bar, but following his marriage to Dorothy was made a partner in Murray's and worked at Albemarle Street in the accounts department. At Wargrave, near Henley-on-Thames, where he and Dorothy lived, he started the village Boy Scout troop, and was its first scoutmaster. An obituary describes him as 'cheery and kindly'.[9] Dorothy seems to have played a similar role in the WI, judging by two lines of McGonnagallish verse in one of her Christmas cards:

And may the Women's Institute at Wargrave well fulfil
Its aim, inspired by Industry and mutual Goodwill.[10]

Dorothy's first child, their daughter Evelyn, was born in 1905, and Jock followed on 22 September 1909. The Murrays had not improved their looks as the generations passed: the anxiety and tension which are evident in the features of John Murrays II and III had given way to the stolid, military bearing of John Murrays IV and V. Thomas Grey's genes changed that, giving the good-looking Jock a long thin mobile face in which sensitivity and good humour were clearly visible. He was on the shy side, and went through a bad spell of stammering. 'It was a terrible handicap,' he recalled, 'but I went to see a man called Lionel Logue who subsequently helped King George VI. He taught me something which I often tell young stammerers: beat time with your hand in your pocket, with one finger, in the rhythm of what you are saying, and this will help you get over the blockages.'[11]

From the beginning he made friends easily. Barnes, the butler at Albemarle Street, became an early friend. Jock often stayed at Albemarle Street in the school holidays from Sunningdale where he was a boarder from the age of eight, and though the day might begin badly with his grandfather losing his temper over the post and flinging the paper knife and the package it refused to open across the gilded drawing room, there was fun to be had when luncheon loomed and Barnes arrived to discuss seating arrangements with Sir John. Since 1812 certain authors believed they were always welcome at the Murray table, with or without an invitation, so it was Barnes's job to be the bouncer, and correct such misunderstandings that might arise. 'Barnes kept a blacklist in his wasp-coloured waistcoat,' recalled Jock. 'I used to wonder what it was that made some [authors] unwelcome ... Occasionally, I found out.'[12] Jock and Barnes became bosom friends, with the butler teaching the boy the correct way of helping guests on with their coats. This, years later, used to surprise some American visitors.

Even though during the First World War there were anti-Zeppelin guns pounding away in Hyde Park, and shrapnel raining down on the roof of number 50, other children could be found for company. 'There were lots of families in Berkeley Square and Bruton Street,' Jock recalled, 'so we had children to play with. I remember it being very noisy with horses and hansom cabs on the cobbles but not many people about . . . You could count the people in the road from Albemarle Street to Piccadilly Circus.'[13] Living as he was at number 50, Jock saw little business going on. This all happened next door, at 50a. But there was one occasion on which his attention was caught from that direction: 'During one of my holidays from school, when my grandfather was ill, Conan Doyle called in with new stories, which we published as *The Case-Book of Sherlock Holmes* in 1927. He treated me with such courtesy as though I was a grown-up, asking me to let him know if anything more was needed, that I fell under his spell.'[14] Jock had been thinking a little about becoming an architect. But now his views were changing: 'if this is an author, I said to myself, what fun to be a publisher!'

Conan Doyle had become a Smith, Elder author in 1891, with *The White Company*. His letters to the Smiths confirm his unwillingness to rescue Sherlock Holmes from an early grave: 'It is *impossible*', he complained in 1903, when more Holmes stories were in prospect, 'to prevent a certain sameness and want of freshness.'[15] It took a little time for Murray's, once they had become his publisher by taking over Smith, Elder, to realise what a goldmine they had acquired in

Conan Doyle. But from the late 1920s they were issuing such cheap reprints as the Conan Doyle Uniform Edition, at the knockdown price of three shillings and sixpence, as well as omnibus editions, 'Six Volumes in One', of Sherlock Holmes and the historical romances.

Beside Conan Doyle there was little on the Murray list to catch the eye of a schoolboy. John Murray IV had tried to make a reputation for publishing successful popular fiction in cheap editions, but there was nobody on the staff with the knack of finding up-and-coming novelists of distinction, and the output in this department proved to be mostly ephemeral. Two exceptions were the Foreign Legion adventure books by P. C. (Percival Christopher) Wren, beginning with *Beau Geste* (1924). Jock would presumably have been encouraged to read this,[16] but as for the second exception, a sentimental novel about the love of Harrow schoolboys for each other, he probably would not. *The Hill* by H. A. Vachell was first published in 1905 and was still in print fifty years later. It is hard to imagine the young Jock tucking into nightly instalments of John Verney's blossoming feelings for a sixth-former: 'You – you like me better than any other fellow in the school?'[17]

As a boy Jock showed a strong sense of design, and it was decided that he should study typesetting. He came away, however, with experience of more than the printer's craft. Instruction in typesetting was to be given by the illustrator, engraver and writer Robert Gibbings, a big bearded man whose Golden Cockerel Press put into practice the precepts of Eric Gill. Jock was sent to see Gibbings at his Thames-side home at Waltham St Lawrence, not far from Eton, and the instruction began. Jock was distracted from technicalities, for Gibbings was looking even more like Old Father Thames than usual. 'He was in his nudist phase,' Jock recalled, 'and as I was only fifteen years old I found this embarrassing.' Gibbings insisted that Jock undress too. 'It was all right for him,' says Jock wryly, explaining that Gibbings was so hairy that he seemed to be wearing a fur coat.[18] 'My main claim to fame is that I am the only publisher who has typeset in the nude.' But he told John Betjeman's biographer, Bevis Hillier, that his instructor was not Gibbings but Eric Gill.[19] In 1924, the year that Jock was fifteen, the sexually rapacious Gill had just begun to indulge himself at the Golden Cockerel with Gibbings's wife Moira, and indeed with Gibbings himself. Fiona MacCarthy's biography of Gill records bisexual orgies providing an exotic accompaniment to typographical experiments,[20] and it seems unlikely that Gill, whose sexual victims included at various times his own daughters and even the family dog, would have hesitated to attempt to involve an Eton schoolboy, should the opportunity have arisen. What is more, the features of the naked boy in Gill's famous 'Prospero and Ariel' statue, carved for Broadcasting House six years later, seem to bear a certain resemblance to the young Murray. Jock was soon keeping Gibbings at arm's length. 'I saw you once in a car near Reading station,' Gibbings wrote to him plaintively late in 1931, 'and waved violently but your beautiful companion thought I was being fresh with her & merely frowned. You always seem to be attended by beauteous damsels; can't you bring a few over here. I'll promise to behave with the utmost decorum.'[21]

'My rooms are in the cloisters and rather dark but with bright shades and cushions it will look quite bright.' This is Jock reporting to his grandfather on his arrival at Oxford in the autumn of 1927. His college, of course, was Magdalen. 'I feel I am going to enjoy my time here thoroughly. There are many Etonians here.' This solved the problem of his social life. He went on to tell his grandfather, who had just a few months left to live: 'I shall indeed try to uphold the great family traditions here.'[22] There was no great family tradition of scholarship at Magdalen. John Murray IV had got a Third in Classical Moderations, before leaving the college prematurely, and though John Murray V managed a Second in Modern History, Jock himself eventually only got a Third in the same subject. 'I don't know that my Oxford experiences will be particularly enlivening,' Jock reported to 50 Albemarle Street, 'I have not as yet been chased down the High by "Progs" nor yet have I been caught scaling the walls of Magdalen.'[23]

As for his sexual education, 'Magdalen was still celibate. Although I thought of women all the time, and was fascinated by them, I was frightened to get too deeply involved.'[24] He could easily have been drawn into the company of the 'rugger buggers' and rowing men who dominated much of Magdalen life. 'I am sorry to hear that you have fears of my turning into a "hearty" however I can relieve your anxiety,' he assured his grandfather at the end of his first term.[25] He tried to give the impression that he was working academically: 'Plato calls and Voltaire is chirping in the corner how can I turn deaf ears to such a summons.'[26]

Jock had come up to Magdalen as John Grey. Lightly armed with his Third, he went down in 1930 as John Grey Murray, his last name being added by deed poll. He began work at Albemarle Street, and in 1933 became a partner. By this time a handful of women were employed: Jock remembered his grandfather and uncle anxiously discussing the first Murray lady employee during the First World War: what should she wear and what about the lavatory arrangements? These anxieties are recalled in brief memoirs of two women who joined Murray's at that time, as shorthand typists. Maude Haywood arrived in 1917, finding an establishment that was still largely Victorian in manner, with a liveried footman and morning prayers conducted by the irascible John Murray IV. She recalls him breaking off the Collect for the day to bark at a latecomer: 'Come in, blast you!' Yet, when Maude Haywood's mother had a stroke in 1927, Murray 'sent a message to say that he would pay all expenses if I would put her in a nursing home'.

Both Maude Haywood and Nancy Littlejohn, who arrived in 1916, recalled the anxiety over dress for the female staff. This was solved by issuing them with dull brown overalls. As to the lavatory, there was only one in the general office area, so a timetable had to be worked out for its use: 'What happened in emergencies, I just don't remember,' writes Nancy Littlejohn. For many years there was also a single telephone, fixed to a pillar slightly too high for Nancy to reach in comfort. Standing on tiptoe, she would take the calls from printers and binders waiting for their instructions, and would occasionally pass the earpiece to Murray. The old man was too deaf to manage the instrument: 'Will someone come and speak to this fool, he won't speak up!' he would roar within inches of the mouthpiece.

The death of John Murray IV in 1928 caused a major upheaval. Number 50 Albemarle Street, which had been his residence since he handed over Newstead to Hallam, now reverted to being the business premises. Number 50a was sold. Some members of staff jointly wrote a comic poem celebrating the change, which reveals the height and complexity of the building, and that some employees were obliged to climb multitudes of stairs to get to their offices:

> Now the Advert. Dept. is up sky-high, up sky-high, up sky-high,
> They climb right up and they never say die
> Right up in the sky at '50'.[27]

John Murray IV's death left the childless John Murray V, Uncle Jack, as 'senior partner'. He had been a distinguished soldier during the First World War, serving with the Scottish Horse, and commanding a battalion of the Scots Guards. Rising to the rank of lieutenant colonel, he was twice awarded the DSO, following service in Gallipoli, Egypt and France. In 1932 he was knighted, like his father, principally in recognition of his publishing Queen Victoria's letters. The final volume, of seven, had just come out. Nonetheless, John Murray V was temperamentally ill-suited to being a publisher.

The other partners were Jock's father, Robin Grey the elder, Lord Gorell, a literary man with an inherited title, who was also Chairman of the Society of Authors, and William Farquharson, the production manager. It was not a happy team. Gorell and Farquharson were at each other's throats, the former complaining that the latter bad-mouthed the other partners behind their backs, and that he did his best to delay or scupper the publication of books that did not take his fancy. Since Farquharson never read any books, said Gorell, his likes and dislikes were unpredictable and irrational. Gorell became obsessed with the absurd idea that he would be the next Viceroy of India. His office was stacked high with books about that country, and he suffered a crushing disappointment when the job was given to a relative by marriage of the Murrays. As to Farquharson, a member of staff once described him as a little Hitler; so he might have been in favour of Murray's publishing of *B.U.F: Oswald Mosley*

and British Fascism (1934) by James Drennan, a book which praised
the British Union of Fascists.

Gorell's complaints about Farquharson come in a letter to Uncle
Jack in November 1930, just after Jock had arrived. Gorell went on
to observe that the quality of the Murray dust jackets has become
deplorable: 'At present these are arranged for by a man without
artistic appreciation & without the least knowledge of the contents
of the book ... I propose ... that Jock should take these over subject
to you, that he should make it his business to study our rivals'
methods & devices & bring up ideas for consideration. We have at
present no thinking dept. at all.'[28] Gorell's suggestion was accepted,
and Jock began to explore ways to improve the look of Murray
books. But still the list was in the doldrums. In January 1930 the new
and forthcoming titles led on *King Edward VII and his Court* by Sir
Lionel Cust, KCVO, the former Surveyor of the King's Pictures, and
this sets the tone for a string of military, diplomatic and aristocratic
reminiscences. The blurb for *All the Days of my Life* by Lady
MacDonald of the Isles suggests that the company had become
official publisher to the aristocracy:

> This little book forms a link between the spacious days of Queen
> Victoria and the more crowded environment of today ... The writer
> ... pauses for a moment, like a bee, to suck honey from the exotic
> flowers of Mayfair, she floats away to the Highlands and Islands of the
> West Coast, and then returns to her Yorkshire wolds. Wherever she
> goes she finds beauty and interest ... There is no jazz in this book,
> there are no drunken scenes, and no divorce courts, but there is a
> great deal of pleasant human nature.

The fiction section shows that Murray's was indeed determined
to stand aloof from fashionable novels about jazz, drink and divorce,
which had reached a consummation in 1930 in Evelyn Waugh's *Vile
Bodies*. What could they offer in response? A 'thrilling mystery
story', *The Mammon of Righteousness* by P. C. Wren; a thriller by R.
J. Fletcher in which the heroine – 'young, lovely, immensely rich'
– is menaced by 'a villainous Chinaman' and his English partner,
'victim of opium and bound by her craving'; and *The Lady of the*

Cromlech by Hugh de Blacan: 'This is a tale for lovers of the open road, of wine, laughter and song, of sport and adventure, and especially for those who know, or mean to know, the hills, moors and rivers of Ireland, a land wherein these good things abound.'

Nevertheless, there were signs that Murray's was beginning to come to life again, to publish books that had an edge, or at least to refuse to publish stodge. One title that John Murray V turned down because it was 'an old-fashioned, solid – even stodgy – bit of work' was A. J. Finberg's biography of J. M. W. Turner, offered by the author towards the end of 1933. In a letter written after he had been rejected, Finberg was nonplussed. He had taken great pains, he told Jock, to ensure that what he had written was old-fashioned, solid, even stodgy, 'and that it had no allurements whatsoever for the general reader', but was to be considered purely as a work of history, 'ie, as to whether the work was thorough and the new information considerable and reliable'.[29] As he had made this quite clear to Jock's uncle when he delivered it, Finberg found it 'rather absurd to be told that the work is exactly what I represented it to be, [and] that the general public want something shorter and snappier'. When in 1939 the work was eventually published by the Oxford University Press it revealed itself to be precisely the kind of book that would have been a natural title for John Murray perhaps twenty years earlier. Solid it may be, but it is also thorough, and seventy years on it has probably not been fully superseded.

The Murrays were still interested in themselves as a subject for biography, commissioning the controversial feminist novelist, playwright and biographer Emily Morse Symonds, whose pseudonym was George Paston, to write *At John Murray's: Records of a Literary Circle 1843–1892* (1932). With the encouragement of John Murray V, she began where Smiles had left off.[30] Noting that times had changed, Rowland Prothero, by now Lord Ernle, wrote in the Preface: 'The three-volume novel is dead. The biographies which were a feature of last century are sharing the fate of great London houses. They are being converted, so to speak, into labour-saving flats, and M. [André] Maurois has shown a special genius in adapting collections of letters or biographical facts into literary kitchenettes.'[31]

Over the sixty years between 1870 and 1930 a quiet revolution had taken place in publishing. Ernle notes that in 1870 more books on theology were being published than on any other subject, while in 1930 fiction outnumbered theology by four to one.

Much of Jock's work in these early years at Albemarle Street was menial: he recalled that he had been 'taken on as slave and bottle-washer'.[32] He helped to assemble each issue of the *Quarterly Review*, which had somehow survived into the Jazz Age with signed articles on world affairs, and he also assisted with the *Cornhill Magazine*, a publication which had been acquired by Murray's with the takeover of Smith, Elder. This gave a prominent place to fiction: Thackeray had been its first editor, and had suggested its title: 'It has a sound of jollity and abundance about it,' he had written.[33] The magazine had in its early days serialised Trollope, George Eliot and Hardy,[34] and Jock's brief was to revitalise the dust jackets. No one, however, had told Jock not to revitalise the book lists, and so from the very beginning of his time at Albemarle Street he was able to make his mark in the choice of books that the house took on. Jock Murray, aged twenty, played a key part in editorial decisions which helped to change the direction of Murray's, and to enrich its future.

Jock also played a key role in organising an exhibition which brought 'The House of John Murray' as it termed itself in the exhibition's catalogue out of Albemarle Street and into the public eye. The exhibition *Manuscripts, Autograph Letters, Portraits, and other Objects of Literary Interest Illustrative of the House of John Murray . . . from 1768 to the Present Day* was held at the booksellers J. & E. Bumpus of Oxford Street in July 1931. This spread John Murray and its inheritance out before the public to an extent that had never happened before. The firm, 'which claims to be the oldest publishing house in the world that has never changed its name in any way nor become a company',[35] now revealed the full extent of its literary riches. Byron, of course, led the way: the first sixty exhibits were devoted to his relationship with the firm, with original MSS of *Childe Harold*, the letter that Caroline Lamb forged to obtain Byron's portrait from John Murray II, and a note written by Thomas Moore to John Murray III (October 1830) in which he remarks of Byron's letters to John Murray II, 'How

strange that a nobleman should write such letters to his bookseller.'
Closing with the Deed of Separation between Byron and his wife,
the section makes plain, and indeed trades on, the extent of this
writer–publisher relationship that has become a yardstick for all
others. Further exhibits included Darwin's response to John Murray's
acceptance of *Origin of Species*, the copy of *Jane Eyre* that Edward
Wilson had taken with him of Scott's expedition to the North Pole
in 1904, and Queen Mary's corrections to *The Girlhood of Queen
Victoria* (1912).

Back in 1887, the firm had published a powerfully written account
of working with cholera victims in Naples, *Letters from a Mourning
City* by a thirty-year-old Swede, Axel Munthe. Having trained as a
doctor, Munthe was now a dashing young psychiatrist who was
widely believed to be the illegitimate son of a member of the
Swedish royal family. Other books by him followed at long intervals,
and just as Jock had started work at Albemarle Street there arrived a
parcel containing his latest, *The Story of San Michele*. Munthe was
now in his seventies and was losing his sight. *The Story of San Michele*,
the first book he had written in English, takes its title from the
ancient villa on Capri which Munthe resolved to make his home
from the time when, as a student, he first saw it. Most of the book,
however, is an account of his adventures as a doctor, working among
the beau monde of Paris and Rome; and one of the publisher's
readers was worried by its apparent lack of veracity: 'Unfortunately
Dr Munthe embroiders the facts with a good deal of deliberate
fantasy, & one is never sure as to how much he is inventing in his
descriptions. The best pages are very good indeed; & the book is
very lively, full of human interest.[36]

It is believed to have been Jock Murray who swung the balance
of opinion in favour of *The Story of San Michele*. Murray's had published it by the end of 1930, and its enormous success undoubtedly
encouraged the firm to look for further books which blended travel
with wry observations on human nature. *The Story of San Michele* was
never to go out of print during the remainder of the twentieth
century. They had now found the road which led them to the discovery of some of their best and most characteristic authors. An early

example is Walter Starkie, the violin-playing Irish professor of Spanish who, according to the blurb about his George Borrowesque first book, *Raggle-Taggle*, (1933), 'fiddled his way' through the gypsy camps of Hungary and Romania. Unfortunately Starkie's work was uneven and, in the diary he had begun to keep intermittently since joining Murray's, Jock records the difficulty of telling him so:

> Walter Starkie called in, smarter than usual but wearing the same coat with moth-eaten ash-strewn fur collar. Had difficult job of telling him that the 1st part of his Italian book is too long & not at all up to standard. Very touchy & very angry. Took him up to see [C. E.] Lawrence [literary adviser to Murray's] which made matters worse, for C.E.L. said that sales of his last books were going down. He swore he'd never write more & certainly not for us.[37]

However, it was agreed that Murray's should make cuts for Starkie's approval, and Jock saw him off in a taxi, 'less angry & saying that he is going to get drunk tonight'. Jock comments: 'Like all Irish he likes to say what he thinks others will like to hear but expects in return to be told what he likes hearing. As a friend, good company for a limited time, an engaging entertaining companion, but in anything to do with himself a complete lack of sense of humour.' Jock was becoming an excellent judge of character, which is perhaps a more important asset to any would-be publisher than an extensive literary knowledge.

Axel Munthe was the first and by no means the last of Jock's authors to need a factotum as much as a publisher when he visited London. 'He would often herald his arrival,' recalled Jock in a broadcast at the time of Munthe's death,

> with a request that I should find for him rooms in London from which he could hear the birds sing, and asking me to get him a new suit of clothes and a few bottles of wine . . . One autumn, shortly before an operation on his eyes, I took him back to Capri. He had moved from San Michele because tourists left him no privacy there, and I stayed with him at his solitary tower of Materita further up the hill . . . We lived a Spartan existence, for spaghetti and figs were his customary diet. During the day a friend would come . . . to read to

him in several languages and at night he would play the piano when insomnia prevented him from sleeping.'[38]

Spaghetti and figs, and the sound of the piano on the night air: sometimes it was very pleasant to be a publisher. C. E. Lawrence wrote inside a copy of his book *Dead Water* (1932) which he gave to Jock, the verse:

> John Grey Murray
> How well it is in such a day,
> With all its selfish noise and worry,
> That somebody who's really 'Grey'
> Can brighten all who come his way
> With added charms that are true 'Murray'.[39]

18

A *German?*

B Y THE TIME Jock began to assist with the *Cornhill*, its days of glory were over. The magazine that had serialised the fiction of George Eliot, Thomas Hardy and Mrs Gaskell, and had given the world its first sight of poems by Tennyson, Browning and Swinburne, was now offering its readers short stories by unknown scribblers, and non-fiction as dull as that which bulked out the *Quarterly Review*. Nevertheless Jock reckoned he had learnt something by working on the *Cornhill*. When he arrived at Albemarle Street, the editor of *Cornhill Magazine* was Leonard Huxley, son of T. H. Huxley and father of Aldous, who was said to be such a good letter-writer that to receive a rejection from the *Cornhill* was better than to be accepted elsewhere. Jock recalled that Huxley taught him how to deal with authors, how to soothe them, how to edit them. 'Like a diamond,' he used to say to the more verbose authors, 'your work will sparkle if cut.'[1] Meanwhile, Jock pursued the task he had been set, of putting an equivalent sparkle on the exterior of Murray publications.

It took a while, but the end result was startling. *John Murray's Summer List 1934*, subtitled *For the Trade*, shows the new look taking root As a result of Jock's taste in design, this previously stodgy pamphlet suddenly seems to be *en fête*. Even the comparatively decorous opening section, which features such typical Murray books of the period as *My Pilgrimage to Mecca* by Lady Evelyn Cobbold and *Nature's Quest* by Frances, Countess of Warwick, has acquired Eric Gill's sans-serif typeface, the very modern Gill Sans. A full page of dancing Pilgrim Fathers (and Mothers) leads from this into books recommended for Christmas, many of which are for children. Samples of their illustrations abound: line-drawings from *The Polar*

Piggy, *The Lost Princess* and *Katie the Caterpillar*, none of them destined to become a classic, all breathe the comfy middle-class air of the period. A few pages back, and not specifically for children, are two of Arthur Rackham's illustrations to Walter Starkie's excursion among the gypsies of Spain, *Raggle-Taggle*. Albemarle Street is altogether decked out in a New Look, and there is no doubt as to who initiated it.

Indeed there is proof: a bundle of letters written in the mid-1930s by Eric Ravilious and Edward Bawden, the outstanding young artists whom Jock had commissioned to design book jackets, reveals the depth of Jock's involvement with the process of design. The attitude that the garden writer William Robinson was still clinging to in 1921 would survive at Murray's no longer. Ravilious created what we would nowadays call a house logo for the *Cornhill*, featuring (of course) a luxuriant sheaf of corn. The letters show that Jock took a close interest in the process of engraving and then reproducing the block, that he paid generously, and that he ensured that the designers of jackets had been given an opportunity to read the books. Bawden was disappointed when his jacket design for *The Lady of Bleeding Heart Yard*, a biography of Lady Elizabeth Hatton by Laura Norsworthy (1935), was abandoned. 'I am aggrieved that the wrapper design is not being used; it is seldom one has a chance of being able to do an imaginative portrait for a biography ... When will writers cease to be consulted by publishers on the question of the wrapper design! Shall I live to see that happy day!'[2]

Ravilious dominates *John Murray's Spring List 1937*, for the cover reproduces another of his designs, a dramatic portrayal of what, had this been winter, might well be a partridge in a pear tree. The next list, summer 1937, represents a turning point of another sort for Murray's, and again the credit goes to Jock. Freya Stark has already arrived, for *The Valleys of the Assassins* was first published in summer 1934:

Alone with her guides – the sullen Hajji; the gay Marmud; Keram Khan with his pipe of opium; Shah Riza quilt maker and philosopher, and the one-eyed Alidad – Freya Stark, travelling and filling in the outlines of the map in unknown parts of Persia, has achieved something of very real importance. In this book there is something more than a recounting of adventure, for there is humour, a keen understanding of the people, and a literary style that is unusual and compelling. The author is already well known as an explorer; this book should earn for her a writer's laurels.

This publicity paragraph was probably written by Lord Gorell, whose own poems, *Unheard Melodies*, had preceded Stark's book in the list, and who had allowed himself to be described as 'the kin of Keats'. Gorell's writings have not lasted, but the poet whom Jock announced to the world in the 1937 summer list eventually became Murray's biggest success in poetry since Byron.

'The verse is nostalgic,' the anonymous blurb reads in that Summer list, 'and designed for those who appreciate Sunday in a provincial town, the subtleties of high, low and broad churchmanship, gaslit London, bottle parties in the suburbs, civil servants on the hike, and half-timbered houses on the Southern Electric.' Jock always used to claim that he and John Betjeman had been friends at Magdalen, where they had overlapped for one year. It seems unlikely that the Etonian freshman would have become close to the Old Marlburian buffoon who was already in his third year, and who was abruptly sent down, at the end of it, for doing no work. Yet it is clear from Betjeman's letters to Murray that they were firm friends at least by March 1931, a year after Betjeman left Oxford, when Betjeman wrote to thank Jock for sending him a book at the *Architectural Review*, where he was then working. He also presented Jock with a copy of his first collection of poems, *Mount Zion*, printed by the dilettante Edward James in 1931. Betjeman was soon asking Jock: 'Would you care to reprint Mount Zion with considerable additions?'[3] Thus *Continual Dew* was born; and Jock was not shy of claiming credit for it:

> If the publisher has the stamina to follow his enthusiasm right the way down he'll make a success of it. I don't want to be conceited but I remember well that my grandfather had not published any poetry for a long time, and since I knew Betjeman at Oxford I came back with

a sheaf of his poems. My grandfather said, 'My dear young fellow, we can't start publishing this sort of thing.' I told him I thought they were good and would catch on. I felt so strongly that I offered to guarantee them with 100 shares of Bovril that he had given me for my 18th birthday. He agreed and I never had to sell the Bovril shares.[4]

But the dates don't fit: Jock's grandfather, John Murray IV, died in 1928, so perhaps it was John Murray V, Uncle Jack, who took this negative stance towards Betjeman. As to the Bovril shares, we shall see that Jock's memory of the success of *Continual Dew* was somewhat rosy.

Besides containing a generous selection of Betjeman's early poems, ranging from 'Death in Leamington' to his notorious prayer for bombs to eliminate Slough, the book is a *jeu d'esprit* in which Jock played a crucial though uncredited role. Not content merely to print the poems, he allowed Betjeman to assemble a team who devised a series of hilarious jokes: gold leaf on the paper's edge, and a section printed on Bible paper, as if the whole thing were some Strict Baptist prayer book. The dripping tap on the title page, irreverently mocks the title's allusion to the Book of Common Prayer ('pour upon them the continual dew of Thy blessing'), and the typeface is evocative of a Sunday school handbook. Osbert Lancaster, whom Betjeman had known since Oxford, was among those who contributed drawings and decorations. When it had all been done, Betjeman wrote a note of thanks: 'My dear Jock, I feel it unlikely that you will sell more than a dozen copies & I do appreciate the charity, for I can only call it that, which has made you publish the verse in so exquisite a style. You & Lord Gorell will get your reward in heaven.'[5] Unfortunately, Betjeman was right about sales. Two thousand copies were printed, but in the first year, despite some excellent reviews, *Continual Dew* sold only seven hundred. The accounts show that Jock was obliged to contribute £53 out of his own pocket, a considerable sum for a young publisher to find, even if it was less than the value of his Bovril shares.

If Freya Stark has left an enduring image in the popular mind, it is of a stylish elderly lady with a panama hat jammed down on her head. She sits astride either a camel whose haughty features reflect her own or a long-suffering pony, several sizes too small. But this is Freya in her sixties, well after the Second World War. The Freya that Jock Murray knew in the 1930s was in her early middle age, forty to his twenty-four, and still attractive. Jock discovered Freya at the back of a drawer. Huxley, the *Cornhill* editor, died in 1933, and when Jock was clearing out the old man's desk he came across articles by Freya on travels in the Middle East and Canada. These had been published pseudonymously in the magazine a few years earlier. Impressed, he invited Freya to Albemarle Street and proposed a book.

Continual Dew had been a simple editorial task: all that was needed was to restrain Betjeman's sillier ideas, such as his suggestion of calling the book *Left Wing Lyrics*. Freya required more careful handling. She was excited to find herself 'drinking a glass of sherry under the eyes of Lord Byron',[6] and when *The Valleys of the Assassins and Other Persian Travels* was published in May 1934, Jock charmingly sent a telegram of congratulation to Freya's home in Italy, along with a cheque. Describing herself as 'chronically bankrupt', Freya sketched the financing, or the lack of it, of her next expedition: 'the real crisis will only develop after I get to Arabia and begin to have to buy camels'.[7] It is surprising that she did not send Jock on ahead to buy them. Her dependence on him, like Isabella Bird's on John Murray III, soon became a byword in publishing circles. 'Freya's descents on 50 Albemarle Street,' writes her biographer Molly Izzard, 'which she treated as an amalgam of travel agency, parcel office, shop window, telephone exchange, appointments diary and social club, were a test of stamina for her host.'[8]

It took time for the pair to get the measure of each other. During the preparations for her first book, Jock was still 'Mr Murray'. By the time she was writing *The Southern Gates of Arabia* (1936), the book that made her name, she was calling him 'John': 'John likes my first chapter and he and I agree on having lots of good pictures.'[9] But eventually she got it right: 'Jock came down was as pleasant as ever, and took me for a day out right across Wales to the western coast.'[10] At Christmas 1935, when she was staying in the West Country, she wrote:

My dear Jock,

I feel rather homesick for Sidmouth. It was all so pleasant that now it scarcely seems as if it had *been* except in a particular world of its own. I must say thank you, though it doesn't really say as much as I mean.

Yours ever, Freya[11]

A letter to her mother records that Freya and Jock spent Christmas in a Sidmouth hotel. They were in separate rooms, but on Christmas morning Freya 'woke up and found a stocking full of all sorts of excitement at the foot of my bed – all tied up in blue and tinsel: Jock had spent the evening before my arrival preparing it. He is such a dear.'[12]

On 31 March 1939, *The Times* announced the engagement of John Grey Murray and Diana Mary James, 'third daughter of the Hon. Mrs Bernard James and the late Colonel Bernard James, of Fingest Grove, near High Wycombe'. Sixty-four years later, in June 2003, Diana Murray, well into her nineties and having been Jock's widow for a decade, sat opposite the writer of this book in the middle drawing room at Albemarle Street, her vigour and enthusiasm for life scarcely dimmed by her age.

HC: When did you first set foot in this building?

DM: I suppose when I was about sixteen. I was born in 1911, so if you do the sums that would be 1927, something like that.

HC: And what brought you here first of all?

DM: Well, family friends, and both my grandfathers were published by Murray's. One was a chemist called Lord Shuttleworth, who was taught by Faraday, and the other was Sir Woodbine Parish, a diplomat who wrote about the Argentine. And I'd known Jock since I was about eighteen.

HC: Where did you first meet him?

DM: At a rat hunt! One of our neighbours, in the country, with a big cornfield, once a year used to have a party, and chase rats with tennis rackets and things – a very period thing. Jock always said the rat got away but I didn't. But we didn't marry for quite a long time.

HC: Tell me more about your own family.

DM: The educationalist Sir James Kay-Shuttleworth was another relative, and my mother was a great educational pioneer – she was a school governor at the age of seventeen, up in Lancashire, in the days when the children in the mills worked part-time at eight years old.

HC: I know music has always been a very important part of your life.

DM: I started off playing the cello when I was just four, and I went on till I was about eighteen. Then I switched to singing. I don't think I was much good at the cello, but it did help with singing.

HC: I've been told that you are passionate about twentieth-century music – Berg, modern composers.

DM: That's the only music I can listen to since Jock died – nothing except post-Berg. It's a tragedy of my life. I thought music would be my great comfort and joy.

HC: Another big thing in your early life was flying?

DM: Yes, I had a pilot's licence. I was always mad about aeroplanes. I even used to make model ones.

HC: You don't sound to me like somebody who would have been thinking about marriage.

DM: Well, Jock was always in the background. Always. And he got a pilot's licence too – but he hated flying. I always did a lot of reading for him, before we were married. And bits of editing, and I was in and out of this building. An important point to make about Murray's is the part the wives have played nearly all the way through. In some cases they had so much to do they nearly fell by the wayside. John Murray III had a wonderful wife, from Edinburgh, and she coped with all sorts of things. The wives had a *huge* amount of entertaining to do. Some of them were very good at it, and others found it exhausting.

HC: By the time you came along it was very much a dynasty.

DM: I think it was a dynasty all along, from the start. No family could ever have been closer. Our children were in and out [of Albemarle Street] all the time. And their friends – they used to use the waiting room to change in.

HC: But were you conscious of the need to produce the next John Murray?

DM: Not in the least!

HC: It didn't worry you?

DM: Not in the least!

HC: Because John [VII] is your second child. You started off with one of the girls, Joanna, born in 1940.

DM: Well, they all took part in it. The family involvement with Murray's was so great, you can't imagine. It came first. You learn that if you're a Murray wife. You have to accept that you come second.

HC: But until Jock came along it really was a dull period in the firm's history.

DM: Yes, they didn't do very much. But Uncle Jack was a very good historian. And there was always quite a lot going on, authors who did well. It's very difficult to explain how much the publishing took over Jock's life. He really loved it, with all his different qualities – he was very interested in production; he worked in a printers for six months before he came in. At Oxford, of course, he made a lot of friends, including Betj[eman]. You know the story, of course, of our getting Betjeman's poems? Jock was very keen to publish them, and went to Uncle Jack, and told him so, and Uncle Jack said: 'A *German?*' Jock had an enormous talent [as an editor] for making people realise that alterations which he himself had suggested were necessary. When he thought cutting was needed, he could get authors to think that the idea had come from themselves. He did this all the time, even with people like Kenneth Clark and Freya Stark – he got them to alter typescripts very happily, thinking it had all been their own idea. I think that was one of his secrets. He always said, 'If you cut that, the echo will remain.'

HC: So he was a natural editor?

DM: Absolutely. They trusted him at once, even people like K. [Clark].

HC: I wonder where he got that from, because he'd not had an especially literary upbringing?

DM: No. I don't think he was especially widely read, though he could talk about books very, very well.

HC: He wasn't a voracious reader?

DM: No – well, he was a voracious reader of typescripts.

HC: But not of new books from other publishers?

DM: Well, certain amounts, but not . . .

HC: Who were his favourite authors? I don't mean living authors, his own authors. Did he read Trollope or Jane Austen, for example?

DM: He was keen on Jane Austen, but he was much more interested in the present. He was such fun; you can't imagine what fun he was. He was so amusing; though underneath it all was this melancholy. He always had that, like many funny men.

HC: Now, Uncle Jack, what sort of character was he?

DM: Very, very conventional. *Amazingly* conventional. But a darling, very, very kind and sweet. Upright. Totally upright. He even kept his stamps separate, the ones for his office letters and his private letters. He was a charming person, but had a ferocious temper, and he did let it fly occasionally.

HC: He was married, but they had no children.

DM: Helen was a complete invalid. They didn't know about it in those days, but she was anorexic. I don't think she was when they married, but she became anorexic very soon after. She was a Brassey, old parents, immensely rich. He was devoted to her, but she wasn't any help to him at all.

HC: Besides Betjeman, Jock's other great discovery in the Thirties was Freya Stark.

DM: I'm afraid she didn't care for me at all. But I had to kow-tow, because of her being Jock's author. She was very cruel to me, really. She'd say in quite a loud voice, at a party here, 'It's such a pity that one's most interesting men-friends choose such boring wives.' She even tried to stop my marrying Jock. She had her eye on him, I think. She sent a letter, a short time before we were married. It was very unloyal of Jock to show it to me. It said that she didn't think it was a suitable marriage, etc etc, and that he didn't love me, that sort of thing. I'm sure he destroyed it.

He never did. It is dated 19 March 1939:

My dearest Jock,

Your letter [announcing his engagement] has come this moment & leaves me electrified, & if I had time & were not leaving tomorrow morning for Aleppo I would wait a little before writing – But my dearest Jock as it is I will write bang off & stick to the truth which is always the best way.

I expect you know, or did you not, that I would have loved you to marry me? Not that I am not ridiculously old for you, but I know that it would have been happy. It is happy anyway, so it does not matter. But Jock dear you will be a very lonely creature if you do not find someone who can make you *not lonely* – Do, also be *sure*. Would you like come to Aleppo for a weekend & get away from it to think? Do not jump just from Monotony into Matrimony. Do forgive this Jock, it is not of anybody but of yourself that I am thinking. When you *really* love, you are *sure*: you have no doubts. Lots of people can do with less than that, but I don't believe you can, not happily. And my dear Jock you are not in love: not unless you have become so in the last 4 weeks, which is of course possible to the creature Man. If that is so, I send you most loving blessings: there is no other real happiness in this world – I hope that you may have it – Do send a telegram to Aleppo, forgive & destroy this terribly frank letter, & *fly out* if you have *any* lingering doubt. Yours *very* lovingly

Freya

19

It's ours!

'IT LOOKS AS if we are losing the war,' John Betjeman wrote cheer-ily to Jock on 25 November 1939, signing the letter: 'Love & kisses, George Gordon (Lord Byron)'.[1] Jock and Diana had been married by special licence in Eton College Chapel in March, and for the time being Freya had accepted defeat. As Diana recalls, Jock had wasted no time getting into uniform:

DM: He was first of all down on the south coast, in the Battle of Britain. He joined up in the ranks, in the artillery.

HC: In the ranks?

DM: Yes, of course. He wouldn't think of doing anything else. I've still got the four two-florin notes that were the King's Shilling in those days.[2] He was Gunner Murray, 772331, and I got my Wife's Allowance. When Joanna was born I sent her to America with my sister when she was three months old so that I could be with Jock – much more important. I know it was awful, but my sister was going, and she had had a baby at the same time as me. We were at Brighton. I saw the pier being taken down, and you weren't allowed out on the seafront. I had a special pass for where I was staying – I was in an empty hotel, the only person there. Jock was moved to Larkhill [army training camp on Salisbury Plain], and I went with him. By that time I was expecting John, I suppose. At Larkhill, Jock worked in the cookhouse – cracking open a thousand eggs without breaking a single yolk, that was his record. They wanted to commission him, and he agreed rather reluctantly, because he had been so happy not to have to make any decisions. It had been quite a difficult time here [at Albemarle Street], but he had good people to take his place while he was away. Noel Carrington came in, but there wasn't much going on, really.

Noel Carrington, an experienced publisher who took Jock's place at Murray's during the war, was the brother of the Bloomsbury painter Dora Carrington. He wrote long letters to Jock which throw light on how Murray's functioned during the war, and how the firm survived the vicissitudes of the time. Among the shortages they had to endure was paper rationing. 'I wish I felt that I had managed to do what I should have liked for Murray's this last year,' he wrote at Christmas 1942.

> Nearly all the good things in the list, Stark, Scott, Ingrams,[3] Lancaster are your left-overs. And the fiction is the worst ever. Did you write to V. S. Prichett as you said? I haven't heard more of it. But I hope to see him over Christmas in the country. Short of a few really good books it would be so much better to drop fiction for the time being and use the paper keeping the good stuff in print. I should like to see a sort of Priority List of authors who have some unique quality to build up the Murray prestige, Munthe, Stark, Lancaster and keep them going *unrationed*.[4]

The poor-quality fiction that Murray's were publishing was driving Carrington mad:

> As to the other books here – I do not see the chance of a real improvement unless you come to an understanding with your uncle for a kind of New Deal. The Memoirs he will naturally expect to accept as always ... But this fiction stuff. Could you not put the case for not accepting any more novels whatsoever for duration, excep-tions being Kathleen Norris (awful woman) and anything in the category of *literature*, should such a rare bird fly in at the window? I have read most of what we have issued this year and they vary from harmless to contemptible. I don't think your uncle can be set on continuing such stuff. It is really only the tradition of producing a list for the travellers.[5]

Another wartime substitute was Olive Farquharson, the daughter-in-law of the former production manager William Farquharson, who had died suddenly in 1936.[6] Farquharson's son, William Lawrence Farqharson, had joined the firm in the 1930s, and Olive was elevated from her secretarial job to take her husband's place while he served in the navy. Diana Murray recalls Olive, later a national figure in the

Women's Institute, as being bossy and self-important. After he returned to civilian life, Farquharson had an affair with one of the secretaries at Murray's, and when this was exposed he shot himself.[7]

Jock noted in his diary that he found it odd going to Albemarle Street in 1940 when he was not supposed to be working there: 'The sight through the drawing rooms of Carrington in my chair in the little room at the end gave me a shudder; but even so the kindness & welcome gave me a feeling of sliding into a nitch that was still my size & was still being reserved for me.'[8] Uncle Jack, who was in the Home Guard, took every opportunity to wear his uniform and First World War medals. Jock describes walking with him through St James's to the Admiralty Arch: 'We must have made a sweet picture ... JM [Uncle Jack] saw a uniform through the corner of his eye & swinging around performed the first motions of a magnificent salute. I with greater experience in such things spotted that it was only an NCO.'[9]

Meanwhile Diana had begun war work:

I was doing a lot of singing for the troops – Gilbert & Sullivan, Solveig's Song [from *Peer Gynt*], well-known things. I don't expect I was any good, but it went down well. This was when Jock was doing his OCTU [Officer Cadet Training Unit], at Alton Towers in the Midlands.[10] Well, then we had a sad embarkation leave, because we feared he was going for ever – but he turned up with his regiment in Ireland, so I decided to go there to join him.

But first Diana prepared for the birth of their second child. 'I wonder', Jock wrote in his diary, 'whether it will be a son.'[11] As with her first child, Diana chose to give birth in Oxford, near her family home at Fingest, near Marlow. On 24 June 1941 she wrote to Second Lieutenant John Grey Murray from the maternity department of the Radcliffe Infirmary:

My bones tell me that it won't be many hours now until our Chipmunk puts in an appearance. Darling and dear Jock, I am glad to be in familiar surroundings but O how I wish the show were on the ground again and that I could hope for a glimpse round the corner of a familiar figure on an absurdly lovely funny little bicycle.

My courage for the instant is a bit in the boots but I pray it will rise again to meet new demands.[12]

John Murray VII was born the next day. As soon as she could, Diana handed him over to her mother, and went to join Jock in Northern Ireland. 'It's obvious where the priorities lay,' says John Murray VII: 'My mother gave first place to my father, while his top priority was Albemarle Street. We children didn't play much part in the picture. But it was fun growing up at my grandmother's house at Fingest. She already had an incredible number of people living there, evacuees and so forth, and yet somehow there was plenty of room for small children.'

Diana takes up the story of her Irish adventures:

> We were in Armagh, and then Ballymena, and I worked in an arms factory, a horrible, horrible job. But it was interesting. Very rough people. Of course they were all Protestant – a Catholic wouldn't have been allowed near the munitions. When all the bells rang for El Alamein or whatever it was, no Catholic church rang a bell. But the girls and the men, they were wonderful – after they accepted me, which was difficult, they taught me all sorts of things. How to cut the electricity so my lathe wouldn't work, how to damage it so that the whole works had to close. Then they used to dance and sing anti-English ballads, all night – they taught me lots – I'll sing one to you one day, not now!
>
> HC: How much were you doing this for the experience? You presumably didn't need the cash?
>
> DM: Well, I wasn't going to sit twiddling my thumbs. I didn't need the money. We were all paid three weeks late. And there was hardly any money in the pay packet.
>
> HC: But it was part of the war effort?
>
> DM: Of course! Jock, on exercises, was firing six-pounder shells, and I was making them. Quite romantic! Then in 1943 he came back to the War Office, where eventually he helped to plan the Arnhem drop, so in he moved here to number 50, where there was a bedroom for us, and then I suppose I had Freydis.

Jock and Diana's third child, a girl, was named after a cousin of Diana. Freydis comes from Scandinavian mythology, but does one also hear an echo of 'Freya'? Jock's backroom work on the Battle of Arnhem is abundantly chronicled in his diary.[13] His particular responsibility was for the gliders which were to land Allied troops behind enemy lines. Since he was in London, he managed to combine this top-secret War Office work with attention to the needs of Murray's.

> *7 September [1944]:* 52 Div op is on again. This time to a Rhine area, so our work may not be wasted.
>
> *11 September: Cornhill* lunch with Peter [Quennell, who was now editing the magazine]. John Piper's Devizes article arrived. A good story from Noel Blakiston has made it possible to relieve Osbert [Lancaster] from completing his contribution. To Hampstead in evening – collected my first windfall pears & gave to Mrs Tapp [the housekeeper at 50 Albemarle Street].

For a year or two until his marriage, Jock had lived in an elegant little Georgian house adjacent to the old royal palace at Richmond. John Murray VII had been christened John Richmond Murray in memory of happy days there. Now, Jock had bought Cannon Lodge, a substantial mansion just a few hundred yards from Hampstead Heath. Diana Murray recalls the acquisition of the house:

> It was in Cannon Place, just off the main road that runs along the Heath, and Jock bought it as a bombed wreck – there'd been a bomb in the garden, which hadn't exploded, but the impact had shattered windows and brought ceilings down (we never had any spare money, and it took us twelve years to make every room habitable again). I think Jock paid £5,000 for it, and I didn't actually know he'd bought it; it was a secret. And then, in the toe of my stocking at Christmas, I found a photograph of it, on which he had written 'It's ours!' But you know it was never, in his mind, more than an annexe of number 50. There is not the slightest doubt that Albemarle Street remained Jock's real home. It took me quite a while to accept that.

Certainly in the autumn of 1944, while Diana was at her mother's at Fingest, Jock was enjoying himself at Albemarle Street, living a bachelor life out of the pages of Evelyn Waugh:

> *11 September:* Supper at Pratts [Club in St James's Place]. Cyril Connolly, Roy Campbell & Osbert there. Cyril very kind about

Cornhill. Very large supply by air being carried out on scale of 700 or so C47s per day largely with petrol.

15 September. Last-minute urgent requirements for 52 Div.

16 September. Dutch op will now come off unless weather is very bad.

19 September. Bar lunch with PQ for *Cornhill* which are now urgent for new number. Airborne op yesterday ... 312 out of 332 gliders effective.

Jock has pasted into the diary a newspaper photograph, taken from the the air, showing dozens of the gliders lying scattered across the Dutch fields after their crews had made successful landings. However, the tide of good news then turned.

25 September. 2nd Army advanced elements cannot get over to relieve 1st Airborne in Arnhem. Casualties are mounting & early this morning enemy started infiltrating into their very restricted position ... Attempt made to cross river to them but enemy firing on fixed lines & casualties prohibitive ... Worked late No. 50.

Another newspaper cutting that Jock has pasted into the diary, dated 29 September, reports that vast numbers of troops were missing: the Germans claimed they had wiped out or wounded six thousand men. Two days later, Jock's only comment in the diary is laconic: 'Papers very full of the Arnhem effort.' With this he turns his attention back to publishing: 'Lunch with Jock Gibb who has been having a tussle with Methuen.' Jock Murray was awarded the MBE the following month for his contribution to the Arnhem operation, though his son John says he continued to feel deeply guilty at having played a part in sending thousands of men to their deaths.

Jock's diary shows that, in the weeks following Arnhem, he began to put his mind to building a new exciting Murray list to mark the start of the post-war era. Heading it was Osbert Lancaster, the cartoonist, illustrator and friend of John Betjeman who had scored a big success for Murray's in 1939 with *Homes Sweet Homes*, a tongue-in-cheek survey of British domestic architecture, which coined such terms as 'Stockbroker Tudor'. During the autumn of 1944, Jock often spent the evening with Osbert and Karen Lancaster at their London flat, taking with him a bottle from the Albemarle Street cellar to counteract the austerity of the heavily rationed food. They discussed possible sequels to *Homes Sweet Homes*: maybe a history of caricature? Lancaster sometimes had to put last-minute touches, late at night, to one of his cartoons for the *Daily Express* or *Sunday Express*; but one evening he took out his flute and played Mozart to Jock, who was greatly amused at Lancaster's 'cheeks blown out & moustache waving like antennae'.[14]

Freya Stark now came regularly to London, not merely discussing plans for her new book but carrying on a close friendship with Jock. Jock rarely declined her invitations to dine, and he noted in his diary, without comment, that John Betjeman 'said he thought I was in love with Freya'.[15] Despite the commercial failure of *Continual Dew*, Betjeman was preparing a new book of poems, and meanwhile Jock had spotted authorial potential in Peter Scott, son of Robert Falcon Scott, 'Scott of the Antarctic'. Peter Scott had been commanding a small gunboat and had written about the role of such vessels in the war. 'First part is admirable,' wrote Jock when the typescript arrived at Albemarle Street. 'We *must* publish even if it were only to get him as a JM author for the future.'[16]

Scott's *Battle of the Narrow Seas* was published in 1945, but by *Country Life* rather than Murray's. This may have been a conse-quence of the paper shortage which bedevilled all British publishers during and immediately after the war. Further, Uncle Jack tended to put a brake on Jock's enthusiasm: Jock remarked that his uncle was 'hankering after elderly people's autobiographies', whereas Jock's own view was that 'with so little paper we must aim at a new young authors and bread-and-butter titles'.[17] Uncle Jack also insisted on reading the proofs of every single new book, complaining that if he did not he would find words like 'shit' and 'farting' when the book came out.

Even after VE Day, Tuesday 8 May 1945, Jock himself was still a part-timer at Albemarle Street: the army had posted him to the Sarum School of Air Support near Salisbury. But he declared cheerfully in his dairy: 'County Pictorial Guides going ahead. John Betjeman, John Piper general editors ... J.P. doing wrapper.'[18] This project, a series of lavishly illustrated guides to the architecture of British counties, seems curious in view of the fact that Betjeman had already edited, and Piper had contributed to, the celebrated Shell Guides which had begun to appear during the 1930s. Behind it, as Jock's diary confesses, lay a sentimental desire to repeat the success of the Murray Handbooks. But nostalgia was not enough: although the Betjeman–Piper *Murray's Buckinghamshire Guide* emerged in 1948 with a distinctively Piper dust jacket, the volume on *Berkshire*, published the following year, failed and the series fizzled out with *Lancashire* six years later in 1955. It was, however, John Piper who put Jock in touch with just the sort of new author he was looking for. He wrote in his diary on 31 July 1945:

> Drove to Hampstead to call on Kenneth Clark. John Piper had told me he was retiring from National Gallery & wanted to write ... He spoke of his plans & wanting to write 4 books. He had made no publishing arrangements & asked if JM would be interested. I said yes & said how advisable it was to keep a continuous arrangement between author & publisher ... True he has eye very much on main chance ... [But there is] no doubt that K. can write.[19]

Meanwhile Jock was also concerning himself with an author who had been dead for 120 years. Byron was back again.

It all began straightforwardly enough, with a plan to publish an abridgement of the 1904 edition of Byron's letters, complete with Prothero's notes. Harold Nicolson, an experienced Byronist, told Jock that he thought Prothero had been a brilliant editor. But then they started to discover the truth. 'Byron evening with PQ,' Jock wrote in his diary on 29 October 1945. He and Peter Quennell, whose *Byron in Italy* had been published by Collins in 1941, met for an early supper at Pratt's, then settled down at number 50 with candles, a decanter of vintage port and a stack of Byron's letters.

> Went through Prothero edition comparing the letters selected for new edition with originals. Several surprises. Discovered passages which Prothero had left out without marking with asterisks. This said PQ

shook his trust in [Prothero] as an unprejudiced editor. Turned up the 3 unprintable stanzas of the Familiar Verses to JM 'Your [sic] in a damned hurry' [20] . . . Examined Byron's letters to Hanson, Hobhouse, Lady Melbourne. Those to Augusta touching delicate ground. Postponed them till a future evening. Must try & look at them quietly first. Stopped worked [sic] & finished the port at 3:30 a.m.

A week later, Jock ran into Harold Nicolson at the Beefsteak Club. He was a great joiner of clubs – 'He believed in going out and meeting people,' recalled John Murray VII. 'We of course talked again of Byron,' wrote Jock, '& of the copy of Moore's Life [of Byron] annotated by Hobhouse. At passage where B[yron] & H[obhouse] part Moore becomes dramatic & poetic. Hob comments that he parted from B because B was engaged in practices that no Englishman would wish to witness.' [21] None of this was news to Nicolson, who was himself secretly bisexual. While working on his own Byron book in 1923, he had written to John Murray IV pointing out that the Murray Archive revealed that Byron's last love-poem had been addressed to a boy. Nicolson said that he had hoped to avoid 'the half-truths and dissimulations of ordinary biography', but clearly he must keep quiet, and be careful not even to allow the expert Byronists to become aware of 'this side to Byron's character'. [22] Sir John entirely agreed, adding: 'Next time you come we must talk the matter over.' [23] A later note from the old man praises Nicolson for being so discreet.

Peter Quennell, Jock's other confidant in this matter, had written two biographical studies of Byron. He was the first writer to drop hints about the poet's homosexuality, and presumably hoped to get another book out of these discoveries. A writer who lived by his pen, Quennell was perennially short of money and would scribble plaintive notes to Jock: 'Back from Brighton without a sou . . . Mr Quennell's compts to Mr Grey Murray: & maybe have his tiny reading fee before luncheon today?' And when he got it: 'Darling Jock, Thank you so much. You're as kind as you're intelligent and good-looking.' [24] In his diary for 21 March 1946, Jock noted: 'PQ brought in his new girl for me to see this evening. None other than Catherine Macmillan, daughter of Harold Macmillan . . . I hear that some of [her] relatives are much disturbed.'

The 'Byron nights', which continued at intervals, were 'men only' affairs. Harold Nicolson now joined 'PQ' and Jock, and one evening while they were reading a letter in which Byron described 'a little Greek boy friend', as Jock put it, Nicolson came up with an unusually candid remark: 'When one is "queer" one is reluctant to claim great men as being "queer" also.' Jock does not comment on this revelation, but continues: 'I bound both of them to secrecy on these matters & suggested we kept an open mind till we had completed in our researches. Harold eyed the fireplace & said "another bonfire perhaps" with a smile.'[25]

Going downstairs that evening, Nicolson patted the Byron bust, and a few days later remarked that he was sure the poet would approve of their prying into his sex life. Quennell's two-volume edition of Byron's letters and journals was advertised in the autumn of 1946, but in the event was not ready until almost four years later. Although new material was included, much was still held back. Meanwhile in August 1947 Jock recorded the arrival at Albemarle Street of a scholar who had ambitious plans: 'Mr Marchand at 6 o/c re his biography of Byron. An American – earnest & dull. PQ with us till 7 o/c.'[26] Leslie Marchand was already forty-seven when he arrived at Albemarle Street. Compared to the frothy Quennell and the Bloomsbury-minded Nicolson he must indeed have seemed dull. But it was his exhaustive, painstaking scholarship which broke through the protective cordon and, so to speak, allowed the lipstick to stain the statue.

Previous editions of Byron's correspondence had not only made excisions but had also tidied up the punctuation. Byron had himself appealed to John Murray II for help with punctuation: 'Do you know anybody who can *stop* – I mean point – commas and so forth, for I am I fear a sad hand at your punctuation.'[27] Tidying up Byron's non-existent punctuation detracted, according to Marchand, 'from the impression of Byronic spontaneity and the inrush of ideas in his letters, without a compensating gain in clarity'. Marchand added: 'I feel there is less danger of distortion if the reader may see exactly how he punctuated and then determine whether a phrase between commas or dashes belongs to one sentence or another.' Thus the twelve volumes were a monument to perseverance and also made much more evident, by the precision of their editing, the lightning and the effervescence that passed through Byron's mind.

Things were now going well enough for Jock to consider improvements at number 50. 'One day,' he wrote in his dairy, 'it would be good to make the old dining room[28] into a big worthy waiting room with book lined walls . . . But where to put present Exchequer Department? . . . Ideally the Advertisement Dept should come down lower. My idle moments are filled with architectural thoughts.'[29] The same diary entry records finding an American publisher for John Betjeman's poems, which were now selling much better at home. Betjeman's first post-war collection, *New Bats in Old Belfries* (1945), had to be reprinted after only a few months; and the *Cornhill* was doing well again. Since its rebirth, Quennell had managed to rake in articles and fiction from a broad spectrum of writers including Max Beerbohm, Elizabeth Bowen, Clive Bell, Louis Aragon and Arthur Waley. And there was a new name being mentioned at Albemarle Street. 'Last night,' wrote Jock on 22 August 1947, 'I read a rough incomplete TS [typescript] on Greece by Patrick (Paddy) Leigh Fermor. Very struck by his ability to write. PQ had told him I'd be interested in the idea of a book. Talked with PQ re a possible article or two for *Cornhill*. Am arranging to see him next week . . . The difficulty will be the form or shape of the book.'

From the outset, Jock perceived that the man who had walked across Europe as a teenager, and had kidnapped a German general in Nazi-occupied Crete, would not be an easy author. Jock met the man himself at Albemarle Street a few days later:

> Told him we liked his scrap of TS on Greece but that it lacked shape & contained some purple passages; with this he agreed. He showed the areas of Greece he intended to include & of which he has personal knowledge. He agreed to work out a Table of Contents & Synopsis & Introduction for me to consider. Says that he and Joan Eyres Monsell [Leigh Fermor's future wife] & Costa (photographer) are going to Central America to do 2 books for Lindsay Drummond [a small publishing house]. We plan to meet round Sep: when I get back.[30]

Jock was off to stay with Freya Stark in Italy; Diana was going too.

A mutual friend, Stewart Perowne, had called on Jock, and reported his concern about Freya's extravagances: she had recently added two bathrooms to her house in Asolo. Jock, whom Freya treated as her banker-cum-patron, was not surprised: there had been an occasion in Paris when she had demanded that he finance the purchase of a mink coat by buying all her copyrights outright. He had of course refused, and there had been a two-week breach in the friendship. When the Murrays reached Asolo they found that the building of the bathrooms had necessitated demolishing much of the house. Osbert Lancaster had designed the bathroom that Freya herself would use, fixing the shower over a giant scallop shell, so that by the use of a mirror Freya could see herself as Botticelli's *Birth of Venus*.

There was another surprise in store for Jock and Diana. At tea one day, Freya opened a letter from Stewart Perowne and found that it contained a proposal of marriage, on a 'Persephone basis'.[31] Perowne was homosexual, and seems to have meant that he wished to be free for half the year to pursue his own way of life. Jock wondered whether Freya, who after consulting Jock had accepted the proposal by telegram, really understood this. When Perowne next saw Jock in London, he said rather nervously: 'I hope she is not expecting too much.'[32] The Murrays took this to mean there would be no sex.

Freya decided that at her wedding, which would be in London, Jock would give her away. Diana was not at the service, although Freya was staying with them at Cannon Lodge. The wedding reception, at Albemarle Street with Diana as hostess, was enormous: Jock counted 210 heads, including the Regent of Iraq, who seemed to want to be shown round the premises. A few days later, Freya sent a postcard of thanks from Italy. It was also signed by Stewart; but his Persephone absences soon began. Freya wrote to Jock that she had no idea where he was.

Jock still hoped that Stewart would take some of the financial responsibility for Freya off him. Meanwhile at Albemarle Street, Osbert Lancaster's new book, *Classical Landscape with Figures*, was doing well, as was a new book by the former Director of the National Gallery, Kenneth Clark. Discussing the publication of his Slade Lectures on the history of landscape painting, Jock asked Clark not to use the word 'lectures' in his title. After several changes they settled on *Landscape into Art*. Publication in 1949 gave Clark his first taste of being a popular author, a condition he was to enjoy for the rest of his life. He recalled in his autobiography *The Other Half* how the successful reception of the book drew him into 'signing copies, attending literary luncheons, and giving little talks. Genuinely successful authors are said to hate these accompaniments of their popularity, but I was not successful enough for that.'[33]

The children's list was also waking up after the war, with Kathleen Hale's superbly drawn series of Orlando the Marmalade Cat picture books. Another popular series of Murray picture books featured the adventures of a tiny elephant called Mumfie. These were the work of Katharine Tozer, who to Jock's great sorrow had died in childbirth, leaving her husband to publish the Mumfie stories that were found among her papers. The photographer Lisa Sheridan had found a bestselling formula with her books of informal portraits of Princess Elizabeth and Princess Margaret Rose, which Murray's were publishing. Jock surveyed the prospects in his diary, and on the whole found them good:

> Publishing delays increase & costs are rising quickly ... My days seem filled with callers & telephones & dictating. No time for thinking, learning & reading. One cannot scheme without thinking nor can one plan without reading & increasing knowledge. I am absolutely ignorant & rely dangerously on instinct. Nor can one plan publishing without meeting people & that takes a very great deal of time. But I do make time in which to count my blessings.[34]

20

Gentleman of the Road

━━━

ISAAC D'ISRAELI, WHO supplied John Murray II with books about the comic side of authorship in the early decades of the nineteenth century, would have found plenty of material at Albemarle Street in the late 1940s and 1950s. One of the most interesting specimens was Adrian Conan Doyle, son of Sir Arthur and the author of Sherlock Holmes sequels. Adrian so disliked Hesketh Pearson's biography of his father that he went around the country removing copies from public libraries and destroying them. He would also challenge hostile critics of his father to a duel: Harold Nicolson received such a challenge in 1949 for sneering at the late Sir Arthur in a review. Although no actual duels seem to have taken place, the *Daily Mirror* reported Adrian 'jousting' in the New Forest. Jock remembered him turning up at Albemarle Street dressed in chainmail, demanding the pistols owned by Sir John Moore, the hero of the Battle of Corunna, which had come into the possession of John Murray II.

In this period of post-war austerity, it could be desperately hard to survive on a literary income. Jock was shaken when he visited the widow of the Egyptologist Sir Flinders Petrie, whom he found dressed in her husband's old clothes. Yet Freya Stark continued to live like a princess. Osbert Lancaster drew a cartoon, which Jock found hilarious, of Freya in the desert, discoursing to a group of Bedouin and a camel with the caption 'Freya Stark explaining to a relatively unsophisticated audience the genius of Mr Norman Hartnell'. Jock noticed that Osbert had put her in the awful hat in which she was married.

Freya was soon back in London, where she stayed in the spare bedroom at Cannon Lodge as usual. After she had breakfasted in bed, she and Jock would incarcerate themselves and revise her latest book, a collection of essays called *Perseus in the Wind*. Jock contributed to it as well as editing it, pepping up her prose with *bons mots* from the commonplace book which he had started keeping in a series of tiny notebooks carried around in his pocket. A selection from it was published after Jock's death, as *A Gentleman Publisher's Commonplace Book*, designed and edited by his son.

As John Murray VII approached his tenth birthday, which fell in 1951, the year of the Festival of Britain, he began to be inculcated into the mysteries of Murray's. This included occasional visits to Clerkenwell, the Murray warehouse which had been acquired with the takeover of Smith, Elder. Nothing much had changed there since the First World War, and it was rumoured that if you searched hard enough among the miles of wooden shelving, you could still find unopened packets of first editions of Thackeray's novels.

Here worked the 'looking-out men', who searched the warren of shelves for the small orders sent in by country, provincial and foreign booksellers; the stockmen, who handled incoming books from the printer; and the packers, who dealt with the bulky requirements of the London shops. The telephones were of the Victorian 'daffodil' type, and there was one very small lift. Michael Holman, who worked there during the 1950s, recalls that John Murray V ('Uncle Jack' to Jock, 'Sir John' to the rest of the staff) paid an official visit to Clerkenwell about once a week. Jock, whom Holman describes as 'the Crown Prince of the firm',[1] made far more of an impression than his uncle. He would always introduce even the humblest members of staff to authors, should their paths cross at Albemarle Street.

As Holman realised, it was Jock, rather than his uncle, who was responsible for the growing number of bestsellers in the Murray list. Jock was the opportunist of the firm. Having read a magazine article by him, Jock approached Sir Arthur Grimble, a former colonial governor in the Pacific, to write *A Pattern of Islands* (1952), based on his experiences. This became a set book for schools all over the Commonwealth and sold in enormous numbers. Uncle Jack's chief preoccupation now was the circulation of the *Quarterly Review*, which he himself was editing, but he was also the guardian of the royal connection. Within weeks of King George VI's death in February 1952, he persuaded the Palace to allow Murray's to publish a selection of the late monarch's speeches and broadcasts in time for Christmas.

Jock notes in his diary that Uncle Jack was giving him a generous share of the firm's profits; in 1948 he received £1,500 after tax. This was about twice the salary of an Oxford don. Jock also records the founding of a new Murray imprint, Gryphon Books, named after the mythical beast in the Murray colophon. This published cheap editions of, among others, P. C. Wren and Osbert Lancaster from an address in Lincoln's Inn Fields, but its more cunning purpose was to increase the Murray ration of paper.

Food rationing was continuing too. Patrick Leigh Fermor and Freya Stark wisely lived abroad, but when Leigh Fermor returned to England he found that his publisher Lindsay Drummond had gone into liquidation. Jock immediately acquired one of his planned books, and together with Leigh Fermor expanded it from the extended captions for photographs (by Costa) of the journey they had made through the Caribbean into an entirely different kind of book, *The Traveller's Tree*. Despite Jock's delight in it, Leigh Fermor virtually rewrote the book in proof. He was also a difficult author to deal with because he tended to be on the move from one friend's house to another. An undated note to Jock from a farm in Kent gives instructions on how to find him: 'I will be here till Friday morning, when I lunch with a Greek in London, and go to Gloucestershire (c/o Monsell, Dumbleton Hall, Glos) till Tuesday. Then Travellers, or c/o Barbara Rothschild in the telephone book. I could easily look in on Friday if you would like me to.'

Parts of *The Traveller's Tree* were written in a hotel in Devon, others in Paris, and yet others in a Benedictine abbey in Normandy, in friends' houses in Andalusia and Tuscany, and at perhaps a dozen more addresses. With so much hospitality, it is not surprising that the book was a long time coming. *The Traveller's Tree* finally emerged in late 1952, to a chorus of praise from reviewers. Harold Nicolson wrote in the *Observer* that Leigh Fermor was a 'natural romantic' with a deep sympathy for the underdog. There were excellent sales:

it was reprinted several times during the next year, and Jock began to encourage Leigh Fermor to write an account of his marathon walk across Europe as a teenager.

Freya Stark, meanwhile, continued to distract Jock with her unexpected arrivals in London, further news of her collapsing marriage, and her narrowly timed departures for Italy. Shortly before his diary stops, Jock describes her nearly missing the Golden Arrow boat-train at Victoria. London was less hectic without Freya, but there was always John Betjeman to make Jock laugh. He describes Betjeman getting on a crowded train at Paddington and shouting: 'It's all right, Mervyn, all these shits will be getting out at Maidenhead.'[2] Betjeman's written communications with Jock tended to be cryptic: he sent semi-legible lists of friends to whom complimentary copies should be given. These were written on the backs of picture post-cards of his favourite Cornish church, St Enodoc, or of pederastic paintings of shepherd boys. One typewritten note claimed: 'This is written in Crystal Palace low level refreshment room.'[3]

Jock regarded Byron studies as a man's world, and he had been very embarrassed when dictating to his female secretary what he described as an 'improper passage' from the Byron archive.[4] He had now, after his initial dislike, taken to the American scholar Leslie Marchand, whose visits to Albemarle Street for Byron research were eagerly awaited. In one of his final diary entries, Jock notes that few of the staff at number 50 bothered to come into work on the day of George VI's funeral, to see the cortège pass along Piccadilly. But nearly a year and a half later, there was fierce competition for places on the Albemarle Street balconies to get a glimpse of the Coronation procession. And a new recruit joined Murray's.

On 9 August 1953 a young man, Kenneth Pinnock, answered a job advertisement in *The Times Educational Supplement*, which gave only a box number (no mention of John Murray). 'I should like to be considered for the post of Educational Manager,' he wrote. 'I have "lived" educational publishing . . . I have a great many friends who are teachers.' Indeed he had been one himself. He was called to Albemarle Street for an interview, where the candidates assembled in the Byron Room, and were ushered in one by one to meet Jock: 'Young, bespectacled, with a manner as soft and easy as one keyed-up could desire, Jock broke the ice by talking about the house. The caretaker was away, he said; and after office hours Byron fans would ring the bell and ask to be shown Byron's portrait, his boot and other relics: so he would oblige himself. "The nicest of them give me a tip," he said.' Pinnock was offered the job, but nobody mentioned money until Uncle Jack let slip, in the course of a telephone conversation, that the salary would be £800 plus a share of the profits. In fact Pinnock was earning nearly as much from his present employer; what really appealed to him about Murray's was that he would have virtually a free hand controlling his own department, of two female clerical staff and two full-time travellers.

His office was high up in number 50, and there was no lift. 'How lucky for me,' he wrote to a friend,

> that I am a featherweight; but what an extraordinary firm of cliff-dwellers this is, with layer upon layer, each quite different from t'other . . . First floor, the last of the Murrays in the direct male line [Uncle Jack], preserved in the mellow amber light of the Byron Room which is more home to him than the London flat he lives in. Second floor, the business and production manager, whose education finished – and also began – at 16, when he left Pitman's commercial college to join Murray's. Fourth floor, the Educational Department's general office; and on the fifth floor there are the servants' bedrooms tucked behind the pigeon-infested parapet of the house.

Outside Pinnock's own office was shelved the *Quarterly Review*, going back to 1809. 'The Murrays had been in the house since 1812,' Pinnock ruminated; 'how long will these old stairs bear the constant traffic?' Pinnock's room was dominated by 'an enormous and hideous portrait of one of my predecessors, Sir William Smith', whose Victorian classical dictionaries were still on the Murray educational list, along with the *Eton Latin Grammar*. Clearly it was time for change.

Ken Pinnock commuted daily from Canterbury, a lengthy journey which he sometimes had to make six days a week. Number 50

Albemarle Street was still open on Saturday mornings, and heads of departments were expected to put in an appearance now and then, though a grumpy notice on the front door (presumably the work of Uncle Jack) warned potential visitors that Saturday was a 'very inconvenient' time to call. The idea that members of the public might arrive without appointments, and expect to be seen, now seems antiquated; yet there are legends of bestsellers coming Murray's way because callers with unsolicited manuscripts were always received courteously, which was not by any means the case with all London publishers. One wonders why Uncle Jack did not simply leave number 50 locked up for the weekend; but of course the old man, who turned seventy in Coronation Year, did not lightly abandon Murray traditions. Who knows what private torments he went through, not long before Ken Pinnock's arrival at Albemarle Street, when Jock insisted that something must be done about death duties? The Attlee Labour government had raised these to an appalling level, and unless Murray's took legal steps pretty quickly, the entire publishing house was likely to go under with the demise of one of the partners.

Jock went the rounds of other publishing houses who were, or had been, in a similar situation. Armed with their advice, he hired a specialist lawyer to convert the partnership into a limited-liability company under the style of John Murray (Publishers) Ltd.[5] The shareholders were to be Jock and Uncle Jack, who could invite others to join the board, and it was emphasised that there would be 'no change' in the Murray style of business.

Nor was there; at least, not yet. Indeed throughout the 1950s continuity rather than progress was the theme at Albemarle Street. There were still employees who had joined the firm when the century was young, and could remember clerks in frock coats and a footman attending to visitors in the hall. Certainly there were more women working at number 50 than ever before. One was an earthy Welsh girl who was remembered as a bit of a troublemaker; another, in contrast, was the tactful Jane Boulenger, who began as Jock's secretary and graduated to editorial and rights responsibilities.

Most of the staff, however, were men, and were totally deferential to Jock (always 'Mr Murray') and Uncle Jack ('Sir John'). Uncle Jack had one curious foible: somewhere in number 50, a lavatory was set aside for his use only. He hated the feeling that other people were queuing outside when he was relieving himself. The excessively modest and unassuming Leslie Miller, who presided over a roomful of accounts clerks where (unless Robert Browning's 1886 report was right) the dining room had once stood, had one afternoon to go upstairs no fewer than four times in fairly quick succession to the Byron Room to consult Sir John over some small financial matter. The elderly knight, who appeared to be reading a book at his desk beneath Byron's portrait, was in fact fast asleep, and Miller did not want to rouse him. When Sir John finally did wake up, as Miller was approaching for the fourth time, he delivered a mild rebuke when he realised what had happened: 'You could have made your presence known, Miller.'

There was less deference at Clerkenwell, and less still on the road, among the reps. Like most other publishers at this period, Murray's employed a full-time team of travelling sales representatives to get the books into the shops. In the eyes of those confined to the publishing office and the warehouse, these individuals led invariably glamorous lives, and there were always would-be reps waiting in the wings. One of these, Bill Day, has left an account of his experiences representing John Murray (Publishers) Ltd the length and breadth of the United Kingdom. It is quite literally an account, for it is written on blank pages of the ledger in which he recorded income and expenditure, and is curiously reminiscent of the book business in the days of John Murray I and II.

Bill Day had joined Murray's in 1926, and by 1948 was in charge of the country booksellers' orders at Clerkenwell. Frankly, he was bored: 'We had two publishing seasons, Spring and Autumn, and there were several weeks in between when we were very slack at Clerkenwell. I therefore put forward a suggestion that perhaps I could travel.' He was given a slice of the Home Counties, had a couple of days with one of the established reps to learn the ropes, and was then on his own, 'raw', as he puts it, not even with a motor-car. 'I had to make my way by train and bus.' John Murray VII, who did a little repping when he was learning the business, recalls that a frequent snag was early closing day, on which the shops would shut at lunchtime and not reopen. It was a different day of the week from one town to another, adding a further level of complexity to the difficult task of organising an itinerary.

Day did well on this trial trip, and the next year, 1949, was appointed to the job full time. 'So I became a Gentleman of the Road.' It was a good time for selling books: W. H. Smith was expanding its Home Counties coverage, and Bill was in demand to help stock airport bookstalls at Croydon, Northolt and the fledgling Heathrow, then known simply as 'London Airport'. Paper rationing was coming to an end, and it was the heyday of the lending libraries, both public and commercial, and these provided a certain amount of business for the reps. The commercial libraries, such as Boots the Chemist, mostly stocked popular fiction. Murray's leading authors in this category were Conan Doyle and P. C. Wren, though Bill's wares also included a couple of living novelists, Dorothy Whipple and Kathleen Norris, who turned out romantic and family novels for Murray's by the sackful. During the war, Lawrence Farquharson had jokingly complained that Whipple was using up most of the firm's paper allowance. Bill also found it easy to get big orders for the paper-covered edition of *The Story of San Michele*.

Then the 1950s bestsellers started to trickle through, starting with *A Pattern of Islands*. 'Newspapers had Books of the Month then,' writes Bill, 'and it became *Daily Mail* and *Evening Standard* choices, and also Book Society Recommendation.' This made it easy to sell; nevertheless when Bill got back to London he was congratulated for his sales figures by Uncle Jack, and rewarded with the use of one of the firm's somewhat elderly motorcars.

Bill was now repping the length and breadth of Britain, but it is striking how very few Murray bestsellers and significant titles from the 1950s percolate through to his journal. There is no sign of Patrick Leigh Fermor's one and only novel, set on a mythical Caribbean island in the early 1900s, *The Violins of Saint Jacques* (1953),[6] nor of Charles Lindbergh's autobiography, *The Spirit of St Louis* (1953), which brought the great aviator, paranoid about press attention, to stay with Jock and Diana. The debut of a new Murray author, Lesley Blanch, *Vogue* journalist and first wife of French novelist Romain Gary, with a study of the sexual and romantic experiences of four nineteenth-century women adventurers, *The Wilder Shores of Love* (1954), goes unremarked by Bill, though Jock remembered Blanch behaving almost as colourfully as her subjects – she could work on her texts only when wearing a certain pair of Turkish slippers. Her later Murray books included *Round the World in Eighty Dishes* (1956), and *The Sabres of Paradise* (1960), about the nineteenth-century Caucasian tribes' resistance to imperial Russia.

The 1950s at Albemarle Street were teeming with exciting new names and book projects. Jock went off to meet the teenage Françoise Sagan at Victoria Station when she arrived to publicise the Murray translation of *Bonjour Tristesse* (1954). Kenneth Clark delivered Jock a bestseller, *The Nude* (1956). The Benedictine nuns of Stanbrook compiled *In a Great Tradition* (1956), their tribute to the abbess Dame Laurentia McLachlan, friend and correspondent of George Bernard Shaw, who lay dying in hospital. Jock claimed he was the only man to have seen the eighty-seven-year-old nun in bed. Patrick Leigh Fermor wrote his account of the monastic life in *A Time to Keep Silence* (1957).

Jock was managing more than the publishing side of things. With Leigh Fermor he advised on the French translation, for the magazine *Réalités*, of *The Violins of Saint Jacques*. Writing to Jock from West House, Aldwick, 'Boggers' (that is, Bognor Regis, West Sussex), Leigh Fermor showed his natural anxiety about the dangers of hurried and misapplied translation:

> There is absolutely nothing to indicate that [the translator] would be able to catch the feel, texture, faint poetical rhythm (as it were) of the violins, without which there is very little point. Also if it is to be serialised in Réalités I bet it will be simplified, chopped up & buggered about for the general public. I wouldn't so much mind this happening *after* a careful translation had been done by somebody I knew all about for publication as a book (which I very much hope for) but the book obviously won't be translated twice – once for a mag, once for a book – and this seems to me the wrong way round.[7]

The rhythm of the violins of Saint Jacques had also touched the theatre world, and in 1956 Leigh Fermor appealed once more to Jock. He had just had an enquiry about musical rights for *The Violins of Saint Jacques*, which led ultimately to the opera composed by Malcolm Williamson (first performance December 1966). Then there had been an approach from two mysterious film directors wanting to make a stirring war film about Leigh Fermor's SOE exploits in Crete in 1944, based on the book *Ill Met by Moonlight* by Billy Moss. Patrick Leigh Fermor was to be played by Dirk Bogarde:

> That curious Burand & Pecuchet couple of the film world called Michael Powell and Emmerich Pressburger, suddenly turned up here 2 days ago to confer about the German General film in Crete (also for Rank) which they are going to do this summer, in Crete if possible (I doubt it), otherwise, Sicily, Corsica, Sardinia or Andalusia. Xan [Fielding] is going to be the local agent and adviser, which I'm glad about. It really is an awful world – the film one – and its inhabitants consist almost entirely of anthropoid apes.[8]

Leigh Fermor also caught the Byron bug, being determined to seek out the pair of slippers the poet had worn about the house he occupied in Missolonghi:

> I asked all over [Missolonghi]. . . for an old man who had a pair of Byron's shoes. They all said they'd never heard of him, and he must be an imposter. But I tracked him down in the end, a very decent wall eyed old man called Charalamhi Baïyórgas or Kotsákaris, descendant of a family that played a considerable part in the siege. Along with a lot of scimitars, yataghans, pistols, powder horns etc, he produced a parcel, already addressed, on the strength of my letters last year, to 'the Baroness Wentworth, Crabbet Park, Sussex'. Since then, though, he seems to have fallen in love with them . . . Byron, when he was in Missolonghi, often went out duck shooting in the lagoon in the boat of a fisherman called Yanni Kazis . . . . Byron died . . . his slippers were left in the fisherman's house, eventually left to the fisherman's daughter. When she died she left them to Baïyórgas in whose house she lived for the last few years of her life. He treasured them.[9]

Leigh Fermor photographed them, and made an outline drawing of each slipper.

Leslie Marchand at last completed his magisterial three-volume life of Byron, *Byron: A Biography* (1957), having patiently toiled in the Murray Archive since the end of the war. In the pipeline from Osbert Lancaster was an omnibus edition, *Here, of All Places*, of all his witty books on architecture in Britain and America, and Patrick Leigh Fermor's *Mani* (1958). This evocative and pioneering account of the Mani, a remote area of the Peloponnese, has a compelling cover, designed by John Craxton, showing the sun (which is also an eye) hanging over a many-towered town in the Mani.

Bill Day now had plenty to occupy his mind:

> I was given Mr Severn's [his predecessor's] notebook of names of buyers and addresses of booksellers, a pity he had not kept it up to date, and had relied on his memory. Not a very good start and most disconcerting to call and find a gentleman you wanted to see had either died or moved to another firm or the address given was incorrect. Took me some time to live this down and have correct records. I was not too pleased therefore when I got to Oxford and Sir Basil Blackwell asked to meet me on my first visit to tell me that my predecessor was irreplaceable. What a welcome.

By 1958 Bill had indeed lived this down, and was present if not at the birth of a bestseller, *Parkinson's Law*, then in its infancy:

> I had been given a 'proof' of the American Edition [of *Parkinson's Law*] in Albemarle Street, also extracts were appearing in the *Economist*. Having read it and seen its potential (and Mr Murray managed to get Osbert Lancaster to illustrate it) I knew we had a bestseller. Later Prof. Parkinson came with Mr Murray to Manchester. He had been invited to be Guest of Honour at the Annual Dinner of Booksellers for the Manchester–Liverpool Area. Parkinson was holding forth beforehand about how inefficient and lacking in push and drive the English were compared with the Americans so I decided next morning to show him the English push and drive ... We got a taxi and rushed him round the city. It worked like a dream.

Back at Clerkenwell, Michael Holman did not expect *Parkinson's Law* to be the runaway success it became. 'The book had already been turned down by several publishers,' he writes, 'and, on the face of it, it was not a John Murray book, but someone took the decision to publish.' No prizes for guessing who.

21

Such fun

—

JOCK HAD NOT merely accepted Parkinson's Law, he had asked for several readers' reports, on the strength of which he asked for structural changes. Parkinson obliged, and as Bill Day had foreseen, the Osbert Lancaster illustrations greatly increased the book's appeal. But the star of 1958 at Albemarle Street was, beyond argument, John Betjeman. His *Collected Poems*, a modest-looking book the size of an Anglican hymnal, was published just before Christmas. Everyone at number 50 expected it to do well, but not as well as it did: the soaring sales figures were soon inviting comparisons with Byron. The telephone at Clerkenwell was red-hot with repeat orders: this was the start of the Betjeman era.

The day after publication, Tuesday 2 December, the Byron Room rang with laughter as Betjeman shared his publication party with *Mani* by Patrick Leigh Fermor, who had contributed a deft parody of Betjeman to the 1,000th edition of the *Cornhill*. Deft as it was, the parody did not take account of the fact that you cannot really mock Betjeman, because he perpetually mocks himself. The publication party guests included Frederick Ashton, A. J. Ayer, Cyril Connolly and Ian Fleming. It was one of many parties that glittered at Murray's in the 1950s; some even got reported in the *Tatler*. 'We had more parties than most publishers,' says John Murray VII. 'After all, they didn't have a Byron Room, and if you've got a room like that, you have to use it, don't you? Also it was my father's way of widening his contacts. Quite a few books rolled into Murray's as a result of conversations at those parties.'

Ken Pinnock usually tiptoed past parties, on his way downstairs from his Education eyrie: 'I didn't like them very much, because the hubbub was so great. I could attend if I wanted to, but nobody minded if I didn't. The atmosphere in this respect was, to me, amazingly free and easy; a kind of family. And the house provided us with a properly human environment.' Pinnock was now finding, and creating, his own bestsellers. These were less obviously glamorous than Parkinson and Betjeman, but were crucial to the finances of the firm. One of the technical artists he employed told him of a biology teacher in Hertfordshire who was working on a book that looked promising. The teacher, D. G. (Don) Mackean, showed Pinnock 'an untidy wad of drawings on thin typing paper'. Realising that school satchels were being replaced by briefcases, Pinnock decided to use a much larger format than normal, as pupils could carry the book home comfortably. For almost the first time in a biology book all the diagrams were on the same page as the text relating to them. Don Mackean's diagrams were heralded as being in a class of their own. *Introduction to Biology* scored an immediate hit with schools on its emergence in 1962. It soon reached the half-million mark, easily dwarfing sales of Betjeman's verse autobiography *Summoned by Bells*, which was published at roughly the same time. Betjeman's *Collected Poems* have sold two million copies, but to date *Introduction to Biology* has totalled some eight million copies around the world, in numerous translations.

D. G. Mackean is one of two educational authors to have their portraits hanging on the stairs at 50 Albemarle Street. The other is Tom Duncan, author of several Murray bestsellers on school physics. Ken notes that these are on 'Nuffield lines': Murray's was one of two firms to be appointed the official publishers to the Nuffield Foundation project for disseminating the New Maths, another much needed money-earner to subsidise the Murray general books.

Although many mediocre general books were getting into the Murray list, Jock was still keeping up a high rate of new discoveries. In 1959 a curious novel *My Caravaggio Style*, in which a young bookseller forges the Byron Memoirs, was published. The forgery met the same apparent fate as the real Memoirs. This was the Byron debut of Doris Langley Moore, who had been in love with the poet since arriving from South Africa forty years earlier. She was a poor novelist, but proved to be a superb Byron scholar, writing three key books about him, beginning with *The Late Lord Byron* (1961). Jock saw the quality in these books, and published all of them.[1] He praised all three as 'marvellous',[2] but had the sense to let *My Caravaggio Style* go to Cassell.

Jock was making little effort to build a fiction list, but he did accept Ruth Prawer Jhabvala. Her earlier novels had been published by Allen & Unwin, where their promotion lacked energy. Prawer Jhabvala's new book, *The Householder*, was read by a part-timer at Albemarle Street, Osyth Leeston. 'The author,' she wrote in August 1959, 'is apparently known as "the Jane Austen of India" . . . a Polish lady of British nationality married to a Parsee architect. She is about 30 and her two previous novels are very highly thought of . . . She is very reserved.' Prawer Jhabvala's typescripts would arrive with long gaps in them, because her Hindu typist could not, for religious reasons, type anything to do with sex. Yet when *The Householder* was published in 1960, the film rights were immediately sold to Ismael Merchant and James Ivory, beginning an association which continued into the twenty-first century.

Another important discovery was made for Murray's by John Betjeman's wife Penelope Chetwode, who was obsessed by George Borrow and Richard Ford's writings on horses in Spain. She came regularly to Albemarle Street where Jock would closet her with their books and her preferred refreshment, chocolate cake and ginger beer. The result was *Two Middle-Aged Ladies in Andalusia* (1963), one middle-aged lady being the author, the other one of the Duke of Wellington's mares on which she rode.[3]

A few months later, the typescript of a single chapter turned up at Albemarle Street at Penelope Chetwode's recommendation. Jock passed it to his secretary, Jane Boulenger, who reported:

MS by Miss Murphy.
This is a natural in the same way as Mrs Betjeman's book was – an entertaining mixture of gusto, intelligence, instant reactions and an idiomatic gift of vivid description, combined with an utterly unself-conscious indifference to personal hazard and discomfort. A careful eye on it would steer it away from the occasional lapse into the trivial.

Sitting in the middle drawing room at 50 Albemarle Street, smoking a cheroot and drinking stout, Dervla Murphy recalls why she chose Murray's. She first came to Albemarle Street 'to worship from the pavement. Brought up as I was in County Waterford by a librarian father, and a mother devoted to eighteenth- and nine-teenth-century literature, I had always been aware of Murray's.' When her mother died, Dervla Murphy bicycled from Dublin to Delhi carrying a revolver, which she used three times. The journey took nine months and cost £61. In Old Delhi she met Penelope Betjeman: 'We were both cycling through the bazaar. There weren't too many Europeans doing that in those days! Penelope asked me how I had got there from Ireland, and when I said "By bicycle", she asked if I kept a diary. I said I didn't, but I wrote at great length to my friends, who passed the letters around.'

HC: You hadn't planned that there would be a book in it?

Dervla: Well, I had always wanted to write, and to travel.

HC: How much were you conscious of the tradition of women travel writers?

Dervla: Oh, very much. Through Freya, mainly. And Isabella Bird.

HC: You overlapped with Freya here for quite a time. And what about the Murrays themselves?

Dervla: Uncle Jack was still here when I first came. I was terrified of him. He used to emerge through that door, and he hated smoking. Jock and I would be puffing away in his office – furtively putting out our cigarettes.

HC: What did Uncle Jack look like?

Dervla: Tall and formidable. I don't think I ever actually had a conversation with him – I was much too much in awe. But the wonderful thing about this house is, it became a sort of home to authors (you might see some of them, revising their typescripts). It wasn't just their publisher's office.

HC: So anyway, Penelope said, 'There's a book in it,' and suggested you show it to Jock?

Dervla: Yes, and I was absolutely scandalised, the idea of sending a typescript of mine to Murray's! But the news got around that I'd cycled to India, and I got a letter from another publisher, to whom

I showed the letters, written in diary form. And they suggested that perhaps there could be a bit more about attempted rapes and things, to spice it up. Then I had a letter from Penelope, saying: 'Have you sent your typescript to Jock Murray yet?' So I took a deep breath, and sent off the third carbon copy – barely decipherable! – and got a telegram back accepting it.

HC: You had no agent – people generally didn't in those days – and you were given what was called the standard contract for *Full Tilt* (as the book was to be called), and an advance of £300, which sounds mean by present-day standards, but which was actually twice what most Murray authors received at the time.[4]

Dervla: It was a lot of money in those days.

HC: Give me a description of Jock when you first met him.

Dervla: One of the first things I noticed about him was an essential shyness and diffidence – it was part of his charm. And then his wonderful bow ties.

HC: And his hair slightly longer than was fashionable?

Dervla: Yes, faintly poetically long. Never went grey.

HC: Tell me how *Full Tilt* got edited – I gather it was something of a family affair?

Dervla: Yes, Jock and Diana and I used to work together on the typescript at Cannon Lodge. And go over it all. And they had quite different roles, because Jock concentrated on the tiny details, while Diana took more the overview of it all. The house had an incredibly friendly feel. Eventually the top floor, which had been the nursery floor, became what was known as the 'murky corner', where I stored all my things between journeys. It really did become my second home.

HC: Did the small advances always finance the trips adequately?

Dervla: I took advances only when the book was finished and accepted. I couldn't bear to sign a contract before the trip. I would feel in debt to my publisher, and perhaps the book wouldn't be worthy. Two of my books Jock very rightly turned down. One on Turkey, which would have been the fifth book, and the other one some years later on Mexico. No doubt they would have sold a certain number of copies, had they been published, but Jock thought they weren't up to standard, and he was absolutely right.

HC: And when the books were going well, you didn't mind being
edited?

Dervla: Not at all – we were always at one on it; there wasn't any
conflict. With the earliest books, Jane Boulenger was my editor.
She taught me a huge amount, such as the length of sentences. I
had an awful lot to learn. I think you have an awful lot to learn
the whole time.

HC: You must have had other publishers trying to poach you over
the years?

Dervla: Yes. But I think they realised at once there was no hope! If
they'd offered me five times the advance, it wouldn't have worked.

HC: What is so special about being a Murray author?

Dervla: The sheer friendliness, the lack of any sort of friction. And
obviously one feels honoured to be published by Murray's.

HC: What about the social side here – you've presumably been to a
good many parties in these rooms?

Dervla: No. Don't like parties. I was at the party for the 200th birthday, in 1968, a few weeks before my daughter Rachel was born.
But otherwise I keep well away from social occasions.

HC: You mention Rachel's birth in December 1968. You didn't
disclose at that time who her father was. I'm sure you know that
some people said it might be Jock.

Dervla: Really? Jock! Now there's a revelation! What an extraordinary idea! I must tell Rachel.[5]

Full Tilt: Ireland to India with a Bicycle was one of the publishing suc-
cesses of the mid-1960s, with serialisation in the press and on radio.
Jane Boulenger, who had edited it, was duly praised in Dervla
Murphy's autobiography: 'In eight years of working together [Jane
Boulenger] taught me an immense amount about the art and craft
of writing.'[6]

Jane Boulenger had come to Murray's about twelve years earlier,
after being employed by the government of the Bahamas to research
an official history of the islands. 'I was sent to Albemarle Street,' she
recalls,

by two good friends, both writers, William Plomer and Richard
Church. They recommended me to Jock, though I was not a good

secretary – my shorthand was hopeless, and my typing was almost worse. And I didn't really want to be a secretary. But I was his secretary for quite a long time, and then sort of worked my way up. Jock very kindly put me in charge of Subsidiary Rights, which meant that I met foreign publishers, and went to New York and Boston. But my real aim was to edit books.

I worked at the very top of the building. Jock's office was on the first floor (next to the middle drawing room, where tea and dried-up cherry cake was served at mid-afternoon), so I had to rush up and down those stairs. On the ground floor, Miss Douglas was the receptionist, and she ruled everybody. Sir John had his desk in the corner of the Byron Room, and some people – including Mabel, his secretary – were frightened of him; but he was very sweet really, though a great stickler for doing the correct thing. Eventually I used to be invited to lunch with them. His wife had such a white face, and never ate anything properly. She used to nibble charcoal biscuits at meals.

I worked a lot on the Betjeman books – he used to call me 'Mademoiselle' because of my French surname, and I responded by calling him 'Mr Betjehomme'. I used to work rather late in the evening with Jock, because he was always doing things at the last minute, and Betjeman used to come in almost every night at drinks time – six o'clock or after – and Osbert Lancaster would turn up too. And Jock would sort of hustle us girls out – we weren't to be seen or heard. Nobody ever told me I was an editor. I was just asked to get on with a particular book. And I was still P.A. to Jock. I did the editing mostly in my own time, and I wasn't paid for it. Well, Jock did once give me ten pounds, and another time he presented me with a very old portable typewriter.

We had an editorial meeting every single morning, which I found rather boring, though after it we would go up the road for coffee. Nobody would have time for that these days. I left Murray's around 1972–3. I needed more money, because I had my mother to look after, but they wouldn't make me a director because I was a woman. At the Frankfurt book fair I met some people from Sotheby's, who offered me much more money and a directorship to start a publishing arm. I was dreadfully torn, and though I accepted I used to go back to Murray's on Saturdays, to work with Jock (unpaid) on putting letters into the archive.

When he was in London, Patrick Leigh Fermor would join Betjeman and Lancaster for the evening drinks at number 50, a gathering that of course echoed John Murray II's salon in the Byron days. 'Upstairs,' Leigh Fermor writes,

> behind a desk with its orderly maelstrom of papers, Jock would be sitting in scarlet braces, lopsided bow tie, and undone cuffs flying loose like fins ... Drinks would appear – Chambéry for Jock – and Osbert Lancaster might wander in after his daily cartoon, full of wonderful gossip; or Kenneth Clark with an armful of illustrations; or Betjeman, with news of a huge Early English church in the Fens, where an aged vicar preached a long sermon studded with Latin and Greek to a congregation of one reed-gatherer. Could they talk about it with John Piper?
>
> Inevitably, Byron pervaded the premises ... One evening ... sitting round the famous fireplace, Jock was carefully unfolding the poet's letters and reading them aloud to Peter Quennell and Harold Nicolson: a book was being planned and they knew the poet's life backwards – or almost. But after an hour, at the mention of a date, Nicolson's lowered eyelids suddenly sprang open. 'Ah!' he exclaimed, 'so that's what he was up to that Thursday night.'[7]

Diana was sometimes drawn into the masculine after-hours salon at Albemarle Street:

> Osbert was very much the centre. He would come in, on his way back home, with his *Express* cartoon – Jock kept them all. And then other people would wander in, just traipse in and out. If Paddy Leigh Fermor was in London, the party would go on even later. I would sometimes be there: in the end, maybe around eight or nine o'clock, I'd put the dinner in the oven, come down from Hampstead and join them, in the hope that I could eventually take Jock home. He had no sense of time at all.

Jock would come home to Cannon Lodge, 'poised above all London, between the Heath and a kestrel-haunted steeple', writes Leigh Fermor, and would unpack a manuscript or a set of proofs from his postman's satchel. Like Dervla Murphy, Paddy relished the joint editorial skills of Jock and Diana, 'a perfect duet', demonstrated at

Cannon Lodge. In Leigh Fermor's case the book would already have had months of revision. His manuscript of *A Time for Gifts* (1977) has clouds of alterations and second thoughts, neatly boxed, arrowed and directed, on every page. When he was writing *Mani* he asked Jock to clear up his typing bills in London, adding, as he sent another fifty or sixty thousand words to be typed:

> The book will involve so much cutting, polishing, reshuffling etc, that I will have to have the whole thing re-done in the end. But it's a good idea to see bits of it in a different shape from my own beastly tangle of erasures and blots and balloons ... There's great excitement here over the plowing – swearing, cracking of whips, jangling bells and plodding often on every available strip of soil on this arid island. Since the rain, grass has been coming up in all sorts of unexpected places: bright green, like mustard and cress on preparatory school flannels.[8]

'Paddy was perhaps the most difficult person to edit,' recalls Diana, 'because everything had to be gone over a hundred times, with one word being changed.' One of Leigh Fermor's concerns in *Roumeli: Travels in Northern Greece*, published in 1966 after many delays, was that the map should not actually give away the precise location of the remote places he had described, lest they be overrun by tourists. Leigh Fermor also needed fairly frequent injections of cash. 'HAVE MADE BANK MANAGER HAPPY,' Jock telegraphed him a month before the publication of *Roumeli*, after depositing several hundred pounds, not all of it earned yet, in his account at Hambros.

Jock was by now a familiar figure in Hampstead. Ian Norrie, who sold books in the High Street, describes him paying regular Saturday visits to the shop, the postman's satchel bulging with the latest Murray titles. 'How are you off for Dervla?' (or Betj, or Osbert, or Paddy), he would ask, and if necessary would supply copies on the spot. 'If I asked for something he hadn't got,' recalls Norrie, 'he might say, "I think there's one at home," and return with it later.'[9]

Besides working as unofficial Murray rep for the area, Jock was always alert to the arrival of local celebrities in the shop. 'I don't know that he ever commissioned a book on my shop floor, but he was a publisher who was on duty, as is a policeman, twenty-four hours a day.' Norrie went to Sunday lunch at Cannon Lodge, and noted that 'Diana remained at her place between courses while her husband removed plates. "Jock allows me to prepare the meal," she told me, "but I am not allowed to get up once it has been served."' Diana admits that she was often stretched to the limit: 'We did entertain in a *huge* way. Not on the scale of the John Murray II or III era, but I would get a telephone call which said that all sorts of people were turning up that evening for supper – could I produce something?' Diana knew that Jock was equally under stress, especially when writing rejection letters: 'He'd spend a sleepless night turning down a book, and he'd write a wonderful letter, perhaps suggesting it should go into a library of manuscripts, a research place. He'd find some way of softening the blow.' And there were other stresses. 'We never had money,' says Diana.

> We always had second-hand cars, we never had a house in the country, we never had exciting holidays. Any money over went straight into books. Uncle Jack gave £12 a quarter towards John's Eton fees, which weren't big at all. I think we'd all been brought up with a sort of Lutheran approach to money. The Scottish side of the Murrays meant that we weren't at all extravagant. Jock got good wine, and I remember he once said: 'We can't afford to have a cook *and* wine – which shall we choose?' So I became the cook. From then on, I did all the cooking.

But family life at Cannon Lodge was on the whole merry. 'Jock was such fun', says Diana. 'Sometimes he used to dress up. He could have been a wonderful actor. We had an imaginary Great-Aunt Ida, the children always believed in her, and she used to visit us once a year. And of course "she" was Jock dressed up, and talking in a little mincing voice, and he'd give them sixpence each, and hobble around the garden. Oh, we had such fun!'

★

Diana's memories include Freya Stark's seventieth-birthday party, held in January 1964, by which time she was probably seventy-one.

Jock said: 'Good heavens, she's going to be in London for her birth-day, what shall we do?' I said: 'I know exactly. Take a room some-where, and have a dinner party of twenty men, and she would be the only woman.' And that's exactly what he did. She was staying with us, but I didn't go, I didn't want to. And the men were nearly all field marshals, politicians – she liked important men. And then between the courses they moved her around. She said afterwards to Jock: 'I think we got the proportions of the sexes exactly right last night.'

The guest list entirely confirms the story: seventeen distinguished guests, not another woman among them. They included Jock's son John, who was just emerging from Oxford and joining the firm. 'Freya was my godmother,' he explains,

> which is why I was there. When I was at Eton, she used to take me out to tea – once it was to Cliveden, where I met the Astors, who were about to be engulfed by the Profumo affair. I had an open invi-tation to visit her in Asolo, where I used to go if things got very difficult. I used to help her drive the little Topolino Fiat she used in Italy; she could manage the clutch and the accelerator, but I had to work the brake. When I was with her on the Bosphorus, about to swim from Europe to Asia, she decided the moment had come to tell me the facts of life, on the assumption that my father hadn't – which was true. Freya's version of the facts of life was somewhat unusual. But she was life-affirming, and I was devoted to her.

By the time of Freya's party, 50 Albemarle Street was undergoing a long-overdue structural renovation, made necessary by wartime damage as well as age. Murray's troubles included 'loose slates on the roof, dry rot in the beams, and beetle in the woodwork, not to mention a certain instability about the balcony'.[10] Uncle Jack, like Jock, hoped the workmen might uncover the hiding place of a copy of Byron's memoirs, but there was no such luck, and the work had to be partly funded by Jack selling some of his own collection of early printed books at Sotheby's. In March 1967, after the repairs were finished, Jock received a confidential approach from the University of Texas, offering to buy the Murray Archive. The letter bears a note in his hand which simply says: 'Answered by tele-phone', with, of course, a firm refusal. Six months later, Uncle Jack – Sir John Murray, KCVO, DSO and Bar – was dead. Jock was in charge at last.

22

Harvest

—◦—

B UT THE RELIEF came almost too late. Uncle Jack had been at
work at Albemarle Street to the end, dying on 6 October 1967
after only one day's illness. John Murray VII recalled that despite all
the work that had been put into the firm to avoid death duties, Jack
had done nothing about this with regard to his own capital. He
believed a deceased's estate should pay the government what it
claimed, so death duties on his estate were high. Despite having
looked ill for most of her married life, Helen survived Uncle Jack by
four years.

By the time John Murray V was in his grave, Jock was only a
couple of years from his sixtieth birthday. Nevertheless he was as
active as ever, gaining a new freedom on his uncle's death. Jock's
charisma filled the building, his charm in voice and smile infecting
everyone. But when the genes for depression revealed themselves
the manic energy which kept him up to 3.30 a.m. on Byron nights
or with Osbert Lancaster began to give way to bouts of despair.
Jane Boulenger remembered that he used to go, as he put it, 'sheep-
shearing', escaping to stay with relations who had a sheep-farm
outside Sedbergh in Westmorland. Diana Murray was uncertain
when her husband began to succumb to the 'black dog'. 'He was
so amusing,' she says, 'but underneath it all was this melancholy,
as appears in Derek Hill's perceptive portrait. He always had that,
like many funny men.' John Murray VII shared this depression,
and it seems not inappropriate that John Betjeman's publishers,
father and son, should suffer from the mental ailment that plagued
Betj himself. But while he could transmute it into melancholic
poetry, they had the more mundane burden of sustaining a business

across one of the most difficult periods in the history of the firm when small publishers were going bust or being taken over one by one.

The Murray bicentenary was celebrated in the autumn of 1968 with appropriate festivities. There was a special feature in the *Daily Telegraph*, a television programme on 50 Albemarle Street presented by John Betjeman, and several hundred guests were entertained on a series of evenings in the Byron Room. Murray's autumn list was prefaced with a brief history emphasising continuity. The firm was now led by the founder's great-great-great-grandson, and the *piano nobile* of 50 Albemarle Street remained virtually as it had been when Byron and Scott met there for the first time in 1815. Indeed the autumn 1968 list, like the one for the following spring, suggested that little change was contemplated editorially either. Many of the authors listed had been habitués of Murray catalogues for years: C. Northcote Parkinson, Françoise Sagan, Ruth Prawer Jhabvala, Magnus Pyke, who had been writing popular science for Murray's since the 1950s, Kathleen Hale, who was now sending Orlando the Marmalade Cat to the moon, and of course Freya Stark, Dervla Murphy, Osbert Lancaster and John Betjeman. Even some of the romantic fiction of Kathleen Norris, who had died in 1966 after years of supplying Murray's with middlebrow novels, was reissued. And when Murray's launched a new bestseller a year after the bicentenary, it was by a familiar author whom Jock had been nurturing since 1945.

Kenneth Clark, who had become known for his television performances as well as his books of art history, was invited to lunch by David Attenborough who wanted the BBC to make a series of fifteen films which he thought might be called *Civilisation*. 'I don't think he really intended to use that word,' writes Clark,

> but it slipped out. I was munching my smoked salmon rather apathetically when I heard it, and suddenly there flashed across my mind a way in which the history of European civilisation from the dark ages to 1914 could be made dramatic and visually interesting . . . When we came to the coffee I said 'I will do the programmes. I will write and narrate them. I do not need any outside help.'[1]

When Jock heard of the project, he was determined to co-publish what is now called a tie-in. Clark, as part of his contract for the programmes, had already agreed that the BBC should publish the book, but wanted Jock involved. As John Murray VII recalled: 'My father gently pointed out to K that he was contracted to give us an option on his next book, and the BBC were only offering a low royalty. So my father suggested we should do it jointly with the BBC. This was arranged, and my father negotiated a higher royalty for K which made a considerable difference to the amount he earned from the book.'

Civilisation was a spectacular success at Christmas 1969. Jock arranged for a royalty cheque of many thousands of pounds to be tucked into the toe of Clark's Christmas stocking. The *Bookseller* recorded that Jock had been helping with packing and deliveries himself, the report noting that he was now Chairman of Murray's. John Murray VII by contrast had no official rank: 'I was simply my father's son, which was difficult, and as such could do no wrong. I was doing a bit of everything – editing, selling, processing orders etc – but nobody would criticise me, or say what they really thought about me, because he was my father.' John emerged from Oxford in 1963, and decided to go to Ashridge Management College, where, as he says, 'I was taught to run a steel mill. I was the only person in my year who came from a company of less than five hundred employees. When I tried to apply time and motion to our warehouse with a staff of about thirty-five people, it was disastrous!'

Osbert Lancaster was the core of Jock's evening salon, but John found that Lancaster 'wasn't nearly as amusing as his cartoons – very gruff and rather terrifying. He would come through the front door around six o'clock, on his way back from the *Express*, and say, "Is your dad at home?" I would take him up, and hand him over. I did not take part in those evenings with Betjeman and Co. From the start, I realised that I had to do my own thing.'

So John Murray VII began to build up his own small group of authors. This was harder than it had been for his father, for literary agents were now beginning to dominate the scene, demanding high advances for authors which Murray's could not afford to pay. This was becoming a serious problem for small to middle-sized publishers. Dervla Murphy was one of many who remained loyal, and among the new authors whom John found and nurtured were the architectural historian Joseph Mordaunt Crook, and Peter Hopkirk, whose *The Great Game* has become a modern classic. 'And earlier than that, I did rather well with craft books that sold in large numbers.' But his creativity and energy were channelled into marketing the general books.

In more fundamental ways too, John Murray VII showed that his time at management college had not been wasted. Though he observes that his attempt to make a time-and-motion study of the Murray warehouse at Clerkenwell failed, he learnt the inner workings of the firm and scrutinised outdated procedures including those for invoicing. The invoices were drawn up by hand, at Clerkenwell, with the aid of a ready reckoner – initially there were no adding machines. Whenever prices changed they and bookshops' discounts had to be manually recorded. Under-copies of the invoices were sent daily to Albemarle Street to be looked through, and when errors were spotted they were sent back to be corrected. These methods were not unique to Murray's: in the 1960s most modest-sized publishers had such office practices.

Slowly and steadily, procedures were modified and brought up to date. Sometimes this required tough decisions, and not only on the operational side of the business. The *Quarterly Review* had been allowed to die with Uncle Jack, but Jock wanted to keep the *Cornhill* going, on the grounds that it brought new authors to Murray's. It had a late flowering in 1968, a double number to mark Murray's bicentenary, publishing new writing by Penelope Gilliatt, Bevis Hillier, Brendan Lehane and others. But John realised that it tended to feature writing from new books published by other firms, defeating the magazine's object of attracting new talent. There were also only a few hundred subscriptions in all. Jock was now editing it with Osyth Leeston, and John saw the magazine as a waste of Murray's limited resources. At the end of 1974, Jock allowed John to announce its temporary suspension, on account of the poor national economic situation, and it was never resurrected.

At this time the firm had no effective budgeting controls, and it was not possible to discover accurately whether Murray's were in the black or the red until the year's end accounts. By the late 1970s the overall financial position was serious, the firm being £1,200,000 overdrawn at Coutts. 'My father thought we were going bust, and with reason.' John had to produce a plan for Coutts for reducing this overdraft. After he had presented it to the Coutts directors the managing director asked if he had any questions. 'Yes,' he said. 'As you are asking us to reduce our overheads what are you doing about yours? I saw twenty-five secretaries in the office as I came through. How do you justify these? Is the high interest you are charging us paying for your overstaffing? All the managing director said was "You are the first person ever to have asked us that question." Shortly after this we negotiated a much lower percentage interest above bank rate.'

At this time the future for a medium-sized publisher, even one less in need of reconstruction than John Murray, was far from rosy. Serious consideration was given to a plan to link up with the recently formed publishing group of Chatto, Bodley Head and Cape. Together they had not only made themselves a force to be reckoned with but had achieved enough critical mass to set up their own warehouse and an effective paperback list, which they saw as increasingly necessary when most books, as today, were bought in that format. It is interesting to reflect that, had this link gone ahead, Murray's would have lost their independence much earlier and would now be, like those imprints, part of the Random House Group. The idea was eventually rejected because Murray's cherished their independence and had the freehold of 50 Albemarle Street as a safety net which the bank accepted as security.

As John took on greater power at Albemarle Street, Jock spent less time on the business side. He immersed himself in Byron and all his other authors. He told the press that he wished to atone for the burning of the memoirs by publishing Marchand's edition of Byron's *Letters and Journals* in twelve volumes. Diana allowed Jock to talk about Byron at only one meal a day, 'either lunch or dinner, but not both. Nevertheless I always said ours was a *mariage à trois*. Sometimes we'd have a plan to go somewhere and do something – and then Jock would hear that a Byron letter had turned up and plans were immediately altered.'

Leslie Marchand's ground-breaking edition of *Byron's Letters and Journals* began to appear in 1973, and took twenty-one years to complete. Jock kept the press fed regularly with appetisers. 'Eight new [Byron] letters have been found,' he told the *Radio Times* in October 1974. 'Two in Leningrad, two in Johannesburg, three in Chicago, one in Sussex.'[2] There was, however, nearly a major loss when a number of important manuscripts and letters were stolen from 50 Albemarle Street. Two small safes were built into the cupboards in the Byron Room where researchers' work in progress could be held overnight, so that letters did not have to be taken down to the strongroom every time. Since the safes were normally invisible, it never crossed anyone's mind that they might themselves have been removed. The missing items, valued at £30,000, included Dickens, Darwin and Queen Victoria letters, as well as Byron items. The police decided to operate a sting, and Jock and John were asked to fill a suitcase with what looked like £1,000 in cash as a ransom. A policeman posed as John at a rendezvous in a north London cemetery, and the thieves were duly arrested, and the stolen papers retrieved.

In October 1975 Ruth Prawer Jhabvala won the Booker Prize for her novel *Heat and Dust*. Only this and Thomas Keneally's *Gossip from the Front* were on the 1975 shortlist, and the judges made their decision on the £5,000 prize a month before it was announced. 'I am afraid that our wonderful secret must be kept until November 19th when the Award is actually made,' Jock wrote to Mrs Jhabvala. Nevertheless the prize was prestigious for Murray's. Among other things, it brought Ismael Merchant to London to set up a film of *Heat and Dust*. 'Ismael asked for a single desk,' recalled John, 'as a perch in number 50 for casting *Heat and Dust*. He had such charisma that no sooner had he arrived than most of the general secretaries in the building seemed to be working for him. Whenever I asked anybody to do something the answer would be "In a minute, I'm just doing this for Ismael." The arrival of Julie Christie caused a great stir.'

The same Murray list that reported the acclaim for *Heat and Dust* announced a new book by a core Murray author: 'Freya Stark, now in her eighty-second year, still indomitable, still "setting forth", heralds her new collection of essays [*A Peak in Darien*] as only she can. "Now that I find actual journeys not so easy, they still feed me with their Ariel voices and make my world feel wider than it is." '³ A year later, many of Freya's friends, this time of both sexes, gathered in the Byron Room to celebrate 'the brief visit to London by Dame Freya Stark prior to her latest expedition, down the Euphrates by raft, and across the caravan routes of the Syrian desert, which will be filmed by a BBC TV *World About Us* team'.⁴ Despite the party, Freya was in the midst of a major row with Jock, on account of his refusal to publish a multi-volume edition of her letters as the best extracts were already freely available in her travel books and volumes of auto-biography. Diana Murray recalled that this row caused the worm to turn:

> She said: 'But you publish Byron's letters!' Jock refused, and she was absolutely furious. She came to me and said what a hopeless publisher Jock had been, how he'd been her undoing, and so on. And I said: 'Freya, you've no idea what Jock has done for you – choosing your clothes, refusing to allow you to buy that mink coat to be paid for with all your copyrights.' I had a stand-up battle, but after that she was much nicer. I ought to have stood up to her years earlier.

★

By 1978 Murray's were once again scoring plenty of hits. Don Mackean's *Introduction to Biology* had long passed the two million mark, and there were big sales for a book of paintings by a former proprietress of a Plymouth boarding house, Beryl Cook. Patrick Leigh Fermor had begun to publish his masterpiece, a trilogy describing his teenage wanderings across Europe: *A Time of Gifts* appeared in autumn 1977 to great plaudits. Jock wrote to Paddy early the next year: 'May 1978 be very good to you . . . – and may it be very good for Volume II, of which I long to hear news!'⁵ Nonetheless to the outside observer the Murray list had not, perhaps, changed very much over the years. Often it was the rather odd and quirky books that became the real successes. An example is the series of volumes begun in the late 1970s when Jock and Diana Murray were staying in Yorkshire with fellow publisher Rupert Hart-Davis. Diana started reading the letters between Hart-Davis and his old Eton schoolmaster, George Lyttelton, and her enthusiasm for this sparkling and highly civilised correspondence led to the publication by Murray's of no fewer than six volumes (1978–84) of *The Lyttelton Hart-Davis Letters*. A few reviewers naturally considered the letters to be insufferably complacent and shallow,[6] but they became very popular with Murray's traditional market.

Then depression struck Jock once more – the worst and longest bout of it that he had yet experienced. 'He had one year of deep depression,' recalls Diana.

> I have no idea why. He couldn't read or write for about a year. And I said to the doctor (the GP, not the specialists, who were hopeless): 'You must be honest with me: is he going to come out of this?' And he said, 'I can't promise you anything, but I can tell you that it might happen quite suddenly.' Well, one day I went out on the Heath with Jock, and he said, 'It's gone!' And it had. He was right back to normal.'

Dervla Murphy, who dates this episode to 1978–9, when he was turning seventy, praises Diana's handling of a catatonic Jock: 'She was absolutely heroic; when he was beyond reach of anybody else, she was there, day and night.'

By now, it was becoming clear that the firm could not simply continue as it was. 'Perhaps we've gone on long enough now,' said Jock to *Publishing News* in September 1982. 'One shouldn't go on publishing after 215 years,' he suggested playfully, 'but there are my sons who are keen to do so, and a grandson who is so keen he's already tearing his rag books to bits.'[7] Jock's younger son Hallam was by now looking after Clerkenwell, having worked as a bookseller in Cambridge and as a publisher with Scolar Press, and he had bicycled alone down the West Coast of North and South America. The grandson was John Octavius Murray, born in 1976, first child of John (VII) and his wife Virginia Lascelles. Besides providing an heir, whose first name identified him as the future John Murray VIII, Virginia brought to Albemarle Street the skills of a professional archivist able to care properly for Murray's priceless collection. Predicting the future, Jock mused: 'It will be the same thing. Fascinating authors with the ability and talent to write. What else could there be?'[8] The year before this interview, *Private Eye*, in a series surveying publishers, predictably picked on John Murray's as an easy target for their satire, giving the impression that nothing had changed in Albemarle Street since the 1950s:

> Take, for example, the precious collection of vintage British fuddy-duddies that queue up nightly at six o'clock on the Murray doorstep for their permitted glass of sherry (Palo Cortado, I guess) with Jock the boss: the Poet Laureate [Betjeman], Sir Osbert Lancaster, John Piper, Lord (Nude) Clark, Paddy Leigh Fermor and that lot. Listen to their jolly talk about the glorious twenties at Oxford, Maurice Bowra, Sligger, Sparrow and all they; and watch them reel out arm - in arm to sup together round the corner at Pratt's cosy little kitchen-range club underground.[9]

The *Eye* piece went on to satirise the interior of number 50 dominated by 'boring old Byron', guessing that the building was now worth about two million. The *Eye* alleged that Murray's were still heavily dependent on Don Mackean's *Introduction to Biology*, which had now sold 'a cool 3 million'. But the article was ironically upbeat about the future of Murray's, reporting that 'the next generation too is already standing in the wings: a John Murray VIII and his younger brother [Charlie], both of them under five'. Number 50, the article concluded, would probably still be standing after a nuclear holocaust. 'Calculate for yourself whether it'll be John Murray IX or X who is dispensing the sherry in the drawing room at the time.'

In fact the Jock era was moving to a close. Clark died in 1983, Betjeman in 1984, Lancaster in 1986. The poet Gavin Ewart wrote to Jock the Christmas after Betjeman died: 'I once went to a party given by Alan Ross for poets who wrote for *London Magazine* ... There were about 8 of us there. Betjeman said to us "Of course, you're the *real* poets. I'm only a pretender!" – a subtle form of attack, with the subliminal thought that we were all pretentious highbrows.'[10] Jock's

eightieth birthday in September 1989 was marked by a flurry of interviews, from which the reader could learn that he now possessed about
eighty bow ties. He still went into the office twice a week, by Tube
from Hampstead. Diana told reporters how he had pacified a drunk,
who was making a nuisance of himself on the train, by taking
Betjeman's *Collected Poems* out of his pocket and reading them with
him. He was invited in 1988 as a guest of honour to the launch of the
Florence Trust, a studio and haven for artists in St Saviour's, Highbury,
and spent most of the reception helping with the washing up.[11]
Privately, Jock was suffering once again from depression, and could
find it impossible to work when he arrived at number 50. He maintained heavy pressure on himself, as he told Dervla Murphy in a long
and convoluted letter of November 1991:

> I am ashamed of this scatty letter but then, after 3 weeks of promoting
> Paddy L – Fermor all over the country & getting him in the Best Seller
> lists, starting a new Betjeman Society & trying to get him into Poet's
> Corner in the Abbey, & hunting for Byron's letters to Solomos who
> composed the Greek Nat. anth[em], battling with a handsome
> American female psychologist who is trying to prove that Byron was a
> manic-depressive and arranging an exhibition on Isabella Bird Bishop
> (for whom my grandfather bought a tricycle) in Japan and a Shelley
> Byron exhibition for the British Library and being beaten by two beau-
> tiful girl/lady physiotherapists to clear my bronchils, I am scatty.[12]

Less than two years later, on 22 July 1993, he died. In his address
at Jock's memorial service, Patrick Leigh Fermor, who had taken
twelve years to write the second book in his pre-war Odyssey,
Between the Woods and the Water (1986), emphasised that 'the line of
the Murrays, thank heavens, is flourishing; so are the traditions that
Jock inherited and fostered and made his own'. Three years before
his father's death, John had given *Publishing News* as optimistic a
picture of the future as had *Private Eye*: 'John Murrays in 50 Albemarle
Street for at least another 200 years'.[13] But by the mid-1990s such
bold optimism was giving way to a more complicated outlook.

In fact during the 1970s and 1980s the firm had already been
forging ahead with the necessary reforms. John says: 'I was told
by our auditors: "You've got to get a running mate or you won't

survive."' A young man called Nicholas Perren had come to Murray's straight from university in 1970. He had started postgraduate work at Sussex University, but was feeling uncomfortable about what seemed to be an inexorable drift towards an academic career. He decided to opt out of university for a year, and found a temporary job at the Clerkenwell warehouse, sending out inspection copies of educational books to teachers. Ken Pinnock spotted his ability, and moved him to permanent employment at Albemarle Street. Perren says:

> Some people had done the same job for fifty years. There had just been the huge success of *Civilisation*, but Sir John had only just died, and his spirit still hung over the general books side. Much less so on the educational side, which was run with genius by Ken Pinnock. He was the person who far and away most influenced me. He taught me so many things and two enormous lessons: one was that the most important decision in publishing is what *not* to publish; and the other was the importance of blurb writing, which he identified clearly as one of the great skills, now largely forgotten. Overall Ken taught me to pay close attention to detail, vital in small business.

Perren made no secret of his ambition. John Murray VII recalls him saying: 'I'd like to stay, but only if I'm made a director.' 'I knew', said John, 'that Nick Perren saw things very clearly.' Perren became the director responsible for education marketing in 1978.

John, by then managing director, told Nick Perren: 'In six months' time you'll become joint MD.' He said, 'We can't run it jointly,' to which John replied: 'We can for six months, and then I'll hand it over to you.' John continued: 'When Nick took over as sole MD in 1987, he cut out the dead wood and stopped uneconomic things happening. My father was now just a director, and I became chairman, and also marketing director of general books. And everybody said to me: "How on earth do you run a company where the managing director is responsible to you as chairman, and yet you're responsible to him as marketing director?" But it worked extremely well, and helped to get things into shape during the 1990s, so that we were doing fine when the takeover came along.'

When Nick Perren joined the Murray board, Jock, about to turn seventy, was still in overall command, at least of the general books, which Perren says were 'not very impressive'. There was a lack of individual responsibility for failure. In the 1970s Murray's had published two early books by Milan Kundera, *The Farewell Party* (1977) and *Laughable Loves* (1978), without realising his significance, and then let him go to Faber. The finances were tangled up with history, and when Perren became joint and then sole managing director, one of his first achievements was to wind up such antiquarian oddities as a bundle of debentures held by the Murray family, which no longer served any purpose. Perren later arranged for warehousing and distribution to be taken over by Grantham Book Services, owned by Random House, and the antiquated warehouse in Clerkenwell was closed down and sold.

Nick Perren's whirlwind leadership enabled the company not only to prosper in an uncertain publishing world but also to remain independent. His knack of recognising and encouraging talent attracted authors and publishers who had the abilities to work together to take the ancient firm into the vanguard of modern publishing without compromising its traditions. Under Perren's guidance the firm evolved into two distinct divisions which recognised that John Murray was two publishing companies in one, general books and educational publications, controlled by two separate boards. Only Perren and the head of finance operated in both camps.

Across the period of Perren's managing directorship the general books business of the firm never much exceeded 30 per cent of the whole, sensible in the light of what might realistically be achieved in the two fields. Following the appointment of Keith Nettle as educational editorial director, in 1986 Perren brought Judith Reinhold to Albemarle Street from Ward Lock Educational, where she had risen from editor to managing director. With Reinhold co-directing, there began a hugely successful flowering of Murray's humanities publishing, now led by Jim Belben, and under Katie Mackenzie Stuart a strong resurgence of the firm's science publishing begun by Kenneth Pinnock. With the later appointment of Gill Clack as editorial manager, the team was complete. From this point, the educational business began to fire on all cylinders, widening its reach in terms of subjects covered, and publishing textbooks which endured for years in school bibliographies at GCSE and A level. Books teaching science, history, geography and religion flowed out from Albemarle Street in the late 1980s and 1990s with an energy and attack that echoed the style, invention and substance of John Murray II and III. Murray was back, and making money; John Murray I might have had another six-bottle night to celebrate. This team effort was publicly recognised: in the decade from 1987 more of Murray's educational books won the prestigious *Times Educational Supplement* Secondary Schoolbook Award than any of its competitors – an unprecedented three times.

The education side could usually extract the full value from its productions, but the general side, which could not, found it virtually impossible to make profits, whatever plaudits it might later attract. Though in fact some small publishers were beginning to issue paperbacks of their own titles, singly or in small groups, the view was taken that the firm should not publish in paperback unless it could set up a substantial freestanding paperback list of its own. That it could not afford. The entire cost and commercial risk of each general book had therefore to be borne by Murray's own hardback printing, made more expensive by the fact that a small firm could not extract bulk discounts from printers. The rest of each book's potential would be effectively donated to another publisher which could put it out in paperback. Murray's share of any success achieved would be a fraction of the author's paperback royalty, too small to make an impact on sales figures but large enough to be regretted by authors and their agents. Well aware of that, the paperback publisher would often make an attempt to steal the author.

To achieve a change of direction in general publishing, Perren brought Grant McIntyre to Albemarle Street as editorial director. McIntyre had run his own academic publishing company and had recently sold it to Blackwells. Earlier in his career he had made his mark by publishing books by leading academics which reached a more general readership. The series 'Essential Psychology' and 'The Developing Child' earned him the first Tony Godwin Award for an exceptional publisher under the age of thirty-five. Grant McIntyre brought gravitas and intellect to the list, re-establishing the balance of the mid-nineteenth-century Murray imprint. He recalls:

> Chance played a big part in bringing me to Murray's. I was looking for a change in my life and wanted to go into general publishing, which is infinitely more difficult than academic publishing, being infinitely more uncertain. Nick approached my wife, Helen Fraser, who was established in that field. But she saw her future elsewhere so, though I had no track record, I set about trying to persuade him to give me a go instead – and luckily for me I succeeded.

To the post of managing editor, responsible for the progress of books from manuscript to finished copies, Perren brought Gail Pirkis, previously with Oxford University Press in Hong Kong. She not only provided the necessary structural underpinning for the department but played a commissioning role as well. Pirkis and editors like Ariane Bankes and Caroline Knox, with John Murray VII as well occasionally wearing an editorial hat, brought in a string of remarkable books, many of which were prize winners.

'We faced quite a task,' McIntyre recalls.

> For many years no one had had the time to give general editorial the lead or attention it needed and the list was pretty moribund. The forward programme amounted to perhaps a dozen books, few of which seemed likely to succeed. I was aware there were a few potential treasures in the offing but it was not clear when if ever those would be delivered. We were not at the head of any agent's list of desirable publishers and authors approaching me directly would sometimes say they felt sure I would want to publish their work because Murray's were so obviously not interested in making money like other, by implication coarser, firms. We decided to concentrate on producing a relatively small number of books, and set excellence above breadth of appeal. We sought books whose readers would be prepared to pay hardback prices and where a paperback edition, even if important, was not crucial. We decided to concentrate our resources on non-fiction, publishing only novelists or poets already established on our list, or those established on other lists who for some reason decided they would like to join us. To these we were ready to add quirky oddities which might seize the imagination.

Even so there were difficult times ahead.

> Naturally no one was going to entrust to us the best they had to offer. We had to live by our wits and we had to ratchet ourselves up over several years. Actually I think our inability to pay large advances or a full paperback royalty worked in some ways in our favour; it made us use our imaginations and bonded us as a team. It would be absurd to say that there were never painful disagreements or unhappiness but nonetheless this was a time of enormous commitment and loyalty. And as we raised our heads above the parapet we had once more as our ally the firm's extraordinarily distinguished history, given visible form by the venerable beauty of its building, which could be surprisingly seductive.

The general side was determined to achieve if not a new golden age for Murray's then at least a new silver age, and it succeeded. Despite the firm's general fiction embargo George Mackay Brown's *Beside the Ocean of Time* was shortlisted for the Booker Prize, in 1994, the Booker's heyday. Brown had been brought to the list by Hugo Brunner, along with Isaiah Berlin and other luminaries. In 2002 Margaret MacMillan's *Peacemakers* added to a hatful of prizes the Samuel Johnson Award, the richest and most prestigious non-fiction prize, and went on to be a major seller. Others authors too contributed to the richness of the list in the last years of the firm's independence: David Gilmour, Fiona MacCarthy, Philip Mansel, James Buchan and Tim Mackintosh-Smith among many. In the last independent decade of Murray's existence the Thomas Cook and Duff Cooper Prizes were each awarded twice to the firm's authors, while the Westminster Medal for military history was won by Murray authors more times than all other publishers' authors combined. Despite the firm's financial disadvantage it is probable that in this period Murray books won more prizes per published author than any other firm in London. Meanwhile at the quirkier end of the list Jock Murray's *Gentleman Publisher's Commonplace Book*, the fruit of pencilled notes nurtured over decades, and edited and designed by John Murray VII, became an unexpected bestseller, rapidly selling tens of thousands. Christopher Matthew's *Now We Are Sixty*, a brilliant A. A. Milne pastiche illustrated by David Eccles, sold hundreds of thousands of copies and was in the *Sunday Times* bestseller list for more than a year.

In Murray's last decade as the oldest independent publisher on earth, there is no question that the education side was the financial engine of the firm, the reason they could stay in business. Nevertheless the general side became a contender once again: the public was now more conscious of Murray's general books because those were the ones in newspaper reviews, and discussed on radio and television. Few people would have guessed from that coverage that the firm was competing against rivals ten times its size.

After ten years of dual control by Nick Perren as managing director and John Murray VII as chairman, the firm's financial position was secure. Nick makes clear: 'We had paid back the debts; we had money in the bank, and we were consistently making a profit. We didn't have to carry over vast piles of unearned advances from one year to the next.' Nonetheless, the fact had to be faced that the future would get harder rather than easier. On the general side, the major bookselling chains wanted to simplify their operations and deal through whole-salers with the giant publishing groups. On the educational side, the cost of a new textbook with all its necessary ancillary material was growing too large in relation to the firm's resources to be wagered on a single project. One failure might well prove catastrophic.

It was a terrible decision to have to take, but it seemed best to secure the firm's future while it was in good shape, rather than have to scramble for rescue in perhaps tougher times. After 235 years, Murray's sought a buyer.

Tim Hely-Hutchinson, at the time of the takeover chief executive of Hodder Headline and now also Chairman of Hachette Livre UK, admits that the educational side of the Murray business was what Hodder Headline was really after. He would certainly have considered buying that part of the business alone. The Murray educational list was renowned for its GCSE and A level textbooks in the UK, and the international variants, and was a perfect fit with the more specifically UK curriculum-based list at Hodder. Indeed, on the sale of Murray's to Hodder, the Hodder educational list shot up from fourth to second place in the league table before anything new had even been published. In the event, Hely-Hutchinson saw a commercial opportunity for the Murray high-profile general list within the Hodder empire as well, and was delighted to buy the whole of the company.[14] So the old company was sold and the imprint moved to the high-rise office block, 338 Euston Road, the home of Hodder Headline. Its history remained at 50 Albemarle Street, and the brass plate saying *Mr. Murray No. 50* stayed on the door. Friendships also remained: it is unlikely that there has ever been a publishing takeover of this kind, with such a strong sense of continuity and goodwill. Number 50 Albemarle Street is still used for parties where authors, publishers and now agents meet, as they have for generations.

For Diana Murray, Jock's widow, there seems to have been no warning at all:

> John was not able to tell me. On May the tenth 2002 he asked me to dinner, and he opened the door with tears streaming down his face. He said, 'I signed Murray's away at half-past seven this morning.' So I had tears streaming down *my* face – but what could I do but hug him? It was a terrible blow to me, but I think I knew it was coming. I longed for younger people to be involved, but John was determined that his sons should have nothing to do with it. He could foresee nothing but struggle, and he wanted them to be able to lead their own lives.

Epilogue

O<small>N THE NIGHT</small> of 18 March 2006, a juggernaut containing sixty crates packed with the first consignment of manuscripts and letters from the John Murray Archive set off from Albemarle Street up the A1. The letters, ledgers, miscellaneous papers, proofs, contracts and cuttings that made up the Murray Archive from the 1760s to the 1920s were catalogued, labelled and placed in heat-sealed packages, and were, for the first time in their existence, insured. Everything had to be signed for, by all parties. The operation continued over five night-time journeys and in each load was conveyed a little of this and a little of that, so that even if disaster struck something of everything would survive.

The archive, valued by Quaritch, the rare-book and manuscript dealers, at about £45 million, was sold to the National Library of Scotland in Edinburgh in March 2004 for £31.2 million, subject to their obtaining a grant of £17.7 million from the Heritage Lottery Fund. The sale was not without its critics, notably Owen Dudley Edwards who felt that the asking price 'lacked "public spirit"'.[1] John Murray VII, who had offered the archive to the National Library, felt that the price was fair, significantly below the commercial value. He decided that the money should not benefit any member of the Murray family personally but would go into a charitable trust, which then gave an immediate endowment of £2 million for looking after the archive in Scotland, with a further sum as guaranteed future funding. The trust would also secure the building at 50 Albemarle Street and its historic contents as the original home of the archive, as well as protecting other related causes.[2]

In Edinburgh, the archive is being professionally catalogued, cared for and preserved in formal and eminently more suitable but less intimate surroundings. A new permanent exhibition, with advanced and entertaining display technology, has been established at the National Library of Scotland. The archive's expert curators are winningly enthusiastic about their new treasures, now immaculately stored and available in the public domain. The agreement between Tommy Moore and John Murray II for Moore's life of Byron is no longer in a John Murray box that was a little too small for it; and is no longer in the house where it was written and signed. Likewise the letters to the John Murrays can no longer be read in the very room where they were first opened but, thanks to John Murray VII's stubbornness on these points, the Murray Archive has remained together and on the same island. Readers and researchers who visited the archive before it was moved will always remember that extraordinary extra dimension of the Mayfair house and, later, the unique and knowledgeable charm of Virginia Murray.

The library has remained at Albemarle Street, as have the paintings and the artefacts, and as have John and Virginia Murray, although they have never actually lived there. And also remaining at number 50 is all the intangible evidence that binds together the history of the publishing dynasty and its house.

Appendix

THE HOUSE OF MURRAY, 1860–1892

Scenes from a Silent Movie together with a further imaginary scene
by Humphrey Carpenter

Fade in on Piccadilly in spring sunshine. Just a few horse-drawn vehicles going up and down. Cut to the front door of 50 Albemarle Street where the butler is welcoming John Murray III, and helping him off with his coat. Murray takes his Gladstone bag, and begins to ascend the stairs – where another man, Robert Cooke, is coming down. The two men chat briefly, then Murray continues his upward journey; Cooke comes downstairs and goes out of the front door – and into the house next door.

Cut to Murray going into his room, in which the main piece of furniture is a roll-top desk, its pigeonholes and recesses stuffed to overflowing with papers, and the main desktop piled high with manuscripts. He takes off his hat and coat, and removes several manuscripts from his bag. An office boy appears and hands him the morning's post. He opens the letters with a paper-knife, and throws several into a box labelled *Complaints about Darwin*.

Close-up of one letter: 'Dear Mr Murray, We at the Philological Society are planning a new Dictionary of the English Language – the first one on strict philological principles. We seek a publisher. Might it be you?' Murray looks pensive for a moment, then drops the letter into a wire tray labelled 'Good Ideas But Too Expensive'.

The camera pulls in tight on this label, and DISSOLVE to FLASH FORWARD. Under an arch bearing the words 'Philological

Society', the members are drinking a celebratory toast to the completion of their project. Camera pulls in, and we see the title page: *Oxford English Dictionary.*

DISSOLVE to Murray, still looking pensive. Caption: IT WOULD HAVE MADE A FORTUNE FOR THE HOUSE OF MURRAY – BUT WE ALL MAKE MISTAKES.[1]

Close-up of a hairy hand knocking on a door. But it isn't Frankenstein's monster. We are in Murray's office. Murray turns and opens the door. A giant ape is standing in the passage. It dances up and down, beats its chest, then barges into the room and starts throwing the manuscripts and papers from Murray's desk all over the floor. Murray calls for help, and the butler comes running. Caption: 'DO YOU THINK IT'S ESCAPED FROM THE ZOO, SIR?' 'POSSIBLY, MILLS, BUT WE MUST BE GENTLE – IT MIGHT BE ONE OF MR DARWIN'S ANCESTORS.'

The ape removes its head, revealing a human head underneath. It shakes hands with Murray. Caption: 'GOOD MORNING, MR MURRAY. CAN I INTEREST YOU IN MY BOOK ON GORILLAS?' He reaches into the depths of the ape costume, and pulls out a manuscript. Murray sighs and adds it to the pile. Caption: 'MY NAME IS PAUL DU CHAILLU AND I HAVE DISCOVERED THE GORILLA.'

DISSOLVE to a lecture hall. On the platform, du Chaillu is holding forth about his book, to an eager audience. A large picture of the gorilla is pinned to the blackboard, and he is pointing at it with a stick. Caption: 'SOME OF THE AUDIENCE DIDN'T BELIEVE IN GORILLAS.' Close-up of audience members shaking their heads sceptically. Caption: 'WELL THEN, I'LL PROVE IT!' Two workmen carry a huge cage, covered with a black cloth, on to the stage. Du Chaillu removes the cloth, to reveal a fine specimen of a gorilla – a real one this time. The audience applauds.[2]

Cut to the exterior of the hall. A poster advertises *Explorations and Adventures in Equatorial Africa*, and says: 'Lecture by the author on 1 December 1861, with book signing.' Cut back to interior of hall. The signing is in progress, and the camera follows the queue until it reaches the table. Du Chaillu and Murray are looking on benevolently, while the books are signed by the gorilla.

The hallkeeper pins up another poster: 'Next lecture, 4.15 p.m. – Mr Charles Babbage'. 'ANOTHER OF MY AUTHORS,' Murray is saying to du Chaillu. The camera pans down the poster: 'Inventor of the flashing lighthouse, the speedometer, the black-box recorder,[3] and the computer.' 'HIS TABLE OF THE LOGARITHMS HAS BEEN SELLING WELL FOR THIRTY YEARS,' Murray is saying. 'BUT I HAVE HAD TO REJECT HIS AUTOBIOGRAPHY. IT IS FULL OF IMPROPER JOKES.'

Du Chaillu tut-tuts, and says: 'AND WHAT IS A COMPUTER, MR MURRAY?' The publisher shakes his head. 'I AM NOT SURE. AND I DON'T THINK MR BABBAGE IS QUITE CERTAIN YET.'

The curtains of the hall stage open to reveal a wild-eyed Babbage, and a large box from which cogwheels and levers protrude. Babbage is lying on the floor, trying to mend some part of the machinery with a screwdriver. On the other side of the box sits a lady, who is feeding punched cards into one slot and removing them from another. Babbage snaps at her crossly: 'DO STOP FOR A MOMENT, ADA – WHAT ARE YOU TRYING TO DO?' Comes the answer: 'I'M CHECKING DADDY'S ROYALTY STATEMENTS. I'M SURE THAT SCOUNDREL MURRAY HAS BEEN UNDERPAYING THE ESTATE.'

Murray turns on his heel, and stumps out of the hall. Du Chaillu follows him. 'WHO WAS THAT LADY?' he asks. Murray answers: 'I'M SURPRISED YOU DIDN'T SPOT THE FAMILY RESEMBLANCE. THAT WAS BYRON'S DAUGHTER ADA – SHE'S A CHUM OF BABBAGE.'[4] He sighs wearily. 'IT'S FORTY YEARS SINCE BYRON DIED, AND HIS GHOST STILL HAUNTS US.'

DISSOLVE to the interior of 50 Albemarle Street, at dusk. John Murray II is ascending the staircase. He passes a shadowy figure who is coming down. It is Byron. Murray's hair stands on end. Byron disappears through a wall. Murray goes into the drawing room. Byron's ghost is waiting for him, seated at the table with a bottle of wine. Caption: 'YOU'LL NEVER GET AWAY FROM ME, MURRAY, NEITHER YOU NOR YOUR DESCENDANTS. AND YOU'RE STILL JUST A BUNCH OF TRADESMEN. WHY DID YOU BURN MY MEMOIRS?'

Close-up of the fireplace: the Memoirs are burning once again, and with a cry, Murray dashes forward to rescue them. But the fire fades away – and so does Byron's ghost.

Murray wanders to a shelf, and takes down a book: *Thomas Medwin's Conversations of Lord Byron*. Caption: 'AFTER BYRON'S DEATH, ALL MANNER OF RUBBISH WAS PUBLISHED ABOUT HIM – AND ABOUT MY FATHER, JOHN MURRAY THE SECOND.' Camera pans to a newspaper lying on the table, folded to show this headline: 'MEDWIN SAYS BYRON ACCUSED MURRAY OF POCKETING POET'S PROFITS: MURRAY TO SUE?'

Murray shakes his head, and tosses the newspaper aside. The drawing-room door opens, and Byron's friend John Cam Hobhouse strides in. Caption: 'THE LITERARY EXECUTOR.'

Hobhouse points at Medwin's book, and shakes his head. Caption: 'PERHAPS IT'S TIME WE COMMISSIONED THE OFFICIAL BIOGRAPHY.' Murray nods enthusiastically. 'NOW WHO WOULD WANT TO WRITE IT?'

Exterior of Albemarle Street, day. An enormous queue of would-be Byron biographers stretches around the block. Murray and Hobhouse walk along it, examining the competitors' credentials, and rejecting every one of them – until they come across a tiny, impish Irishman. They both shake his hand enthusiastically. Caption: 'WHY, IF IT ISN'T TOMMY MOORE. WE HAVEN'T SEEN YOU SINCE EVERYTHING WENT UP IN SMOKE. DID ANYONE REIMBURSE YOU THOSE 2,000 GUINEAS?' Moore shakes his head forlornly.

Cut to newspaper, folded to show this headline: 'TOMMY MOORE SIGNED FOR BYRON LIFE – MURRAY TO PAY RECORD ADVANCE OF 4,000 GUINEAS'.

DISSOLVE to Moore shaking hands with Murray, and waving a big cheque. Murray looks wry.

END OF SCENARIO 1

SCENARIO 2

We join John Murray III, Sam Smiles and Charles Darwin at lunch at the Athenaeum.

Darwin: What is your book called, Mr Smiles?

Smiles: Self-Help. *(Darwin fails to catch this.)*

Murray (whose mouth is not full): S–E–L–F H–E–L–P. *(He sighs to himself. Lunching authors is not his favourite occupation, and he can see already that trying to kill two birds with one stone wasn't such a good idea.)*

Darwin: I see. *(He doesn't.)*

Smiles (loading up more bread): Let me explain, Mr Darling.

Murray: Darwin.

Smiles: 'Heaven helps those who help themselves' is a well-tried maxim, embodying in a small compass the results of vast human experience. The spirit of self-help is the root of all genuine growth in the individual; and, exhibited in the lives of many, it constitutes the true source of national vigour and strength. Help from without is often enfeebling in its effects, but help from within invariably invigorates. Whatever is done FOR men or classes to a certain extent takes away the stimulus and necessity of doing for themselves; and where men are subjected to over-guidance and over-government, the inevitable tendency is to render them comparatively helpless.

Murray: That's very good. You ought to put it in the book.

Smiles: I have. It's the opening of Chapter One.

Murray: Of course it is. How silly of me. *(He hasn't read a word of it.)*

Darwin: How remarkable. It sounds just like many passages in *my* book. Yet there comes a point, does there not, when self-help is not enough. *(He pulls a copy out of his coat pocket, and reads.)* 'One of the strongest instances of an animal apparently performing an action for the sole good of another with which I am acquainted is that of aphids voluntarily yielding their sweet excretion to ants ... I removed all the ants from a group of about a dozen aphids on a dock plant ... I felt sure that the aphids would want to excrete. I watched them for some time through a lens, but not one of them excreted. I then tickled and stroked them with a hair in the same manner, as well as I could, as the ants do with their antennae, but not one excreted. Afterwards I allowed an ant to visit them ... It began to play with its antennae on the abdomen first of one aphid and then of another, and each aphid, as soon as it felt the antennae, immediately lifted up its abdomen and excreted a limpid drop of sweet juice, which was eagerly devoured by the ant. Even the quite young aphids behaved in this manner, showing that the action was instinctive, and not the result of experience.'

Smiles: What a disgusting story. *(But the man at the next table notes it down carefully, for this is the Athenaeum, he is 'Soapy Sam' Wilberforce, the Bishop of Oxford, and he is to review Darwin's book in the* Quarterly.*)*

Murray (whose soup is beginning to look unpleasantly like the excretion of aphids): Gentlemen, I toast your success. Mr Darwin, your first printing has already sold out, and I immediately require a list of corrections for the second edition.

Darwin: In that case, I must go home at once. I expect trouble from the orthodox, you know. *(Indeed, the Bishop of Oxford already looks menacing.)*

Smiles: Let me accompany you, Mr Dawkins – I will use my influence at Charing Cross to obtain for you a first-class seat. *(They leave, but are not out of earshot when they begin to compare notes as to how much Murray is paying them.)*

Murray (sighing heavily): Authors!

Dramatis Personae

Chronology of the Murrays

John Murray I, formerly John McMurray   1737–93
Married 1. Ann (Nancy) Weemss, 1763; died 1776
          2. Hester Weemss, Nancy's sister, 1778;
             died 1814

John Murray II (John Samuel Murray)   1778–1843
Son of the above
Married Anne Elliot, 1807; died 1845

John Murray III   1808–92
Son of the above
Married Marión Smith, 1847; died 1894

John Murray IV   1851–1928
Son of the above
Married Katherine Evelyn Leslie, 1878; died 1938
Knighted 1926

Alexander Henry Hallam Murray   1854–1934
Brother of the above
Married Alicia Maria Du Cane, 1885; died 1947
Resigned from the firm, 1908

John Murray V, DSO, Croix de Guerre   1884–1967
Son of John Murray IV
Married Lady Helen de Vere, 1916, no issue; died 1972
Knighted 1932

John 'Jock' Murray VI   1909–93
Nephew of the above
Born John Arnaud Robin Grey, son of
    Thomas Robinson Grey and Dorothy Evelyn Grey,
    née Murray, daughter of the above. Added Murray
    to his surname by deed poll, 1930
Married Diana James, 1939

John Richmond Grey Murray VII   born 1941
Son of the above
Married Virginia Lascelles, 1970
Their sons are John Octavius Grey Murray
    (John Murray VIII), born 1976; and
    Charles John Grey Murray, born 1979

Notes

PROLOGUE

1. From 2004 Hodder Headline was owned by Hachette. The actual price paid was less than the *Telegraph* implied

CHAPTER 1: BLOCKHEADS MAKING FORTUNES

1. S i, 1
2. ibid.
3. Z
4. Smiles (S i, 2) erroneously gives the year of his birth as 1745
5. Family tree: Z, pp. xvi–xvii
6. Z, 7
7. Z, 8; to Captain William Fraser, 28 Aug 1779, LB, JMA MS 41903
8. First entry dated 11 Oct 1765, LB, JMA MS 41896
9. 6 Dec 1765, ibid.
10. 17 Dec 1765, ibid.
11. 15 Oct 1765, ibid.
12. 18 Oct 1765, ibid.
13. 19 May 1767, ibid.
14. Z, 14f.
15. 16 Sep 1769, LB, JMA MS 41897
16. 23 Jun 1768, LB, JMA MS 41896
17. 2 Jul 1768, ibid.
18. 18 Mar 1771, LB, JMA MS 41898
19. Z, 163; to Jacob Duché, 10 Aug 1769, LB, JMA MS 41897
20. The property also included a small house to the rear of the main building, which Murray let to a tenant. It overlooked Falcon Court,

mentioned by Boswell as a place where he turned aside with Johnson while walking in Fleet Street. Z, 19

21. William Kerr was a post office official. He looked after Murray's Edinburgh financial affairs and lent him money to start the business
22. 9 Oct 1768, LB, JMA MS 41896
23. 16 Oct 1768, ibid.

CHAPTER 2: BEER TO BENGAL

1. Z, 77
2. Colonel Robert Gordon to JM, 21 Oct 1769, JMA Acc 12604/1464
3. William St Clair, *The Godwins and the Shelleys*, Faber & Faber, 1989, 18
4. ibid., 18f. See also William St Clair, *The Reading Nation in the Romantic Period*, Cambridge, 2004
5. Benjamin Disraeli, preface to Isaac D'Israeli, *Curiosities of Literature*, Frederick Warne edn, 1881, vol. i, p. xvii
6. Murray's album of newspaper clippings; JMA MS Acc 12604/0387
7. 11 Aug 1770, LB, JMA MS 41897
8. Constable i, 41
9. 7 Mar 1769, LB, JMA MS 41897
10. 18 March 1769, ibid.
11. Z, 198
12. 'A Letter to W. Mason, A.M., Precentor of York, concerning his edition of Mr. Gray's Poems, and the Practices of Booksellers', 1778
13. 15 Apr 1778. James Boswell, *Life of Samuel Johnson*, ed. R. W. Chapman, Oxford Unversity Press, new edn 1970, p. 949
14. William Mason to Horace Walpole, 26 May 1777, *Correspondence of Horace Walpole*, ed. W. S. Lewis, xxviii Yale University Press and Oxford University Press, 1955, 310
15. 10 Aug 1769, LB, JMA MS 41897
16. 23 Apr 1788, LB, JMA MS 41905
17. To the Rev. John Whitaker about his MS on Roman Britain, 6 Mar 1783, LB, JMA MS 41904
18. ibid.
19. 10 Aug 1781, LB, JMA MS 41903
20. 5 Oct 1769, LB, JMA MS 41897
21. 10 Oct 1769, ibid.
22. 13 Apr 1769, ibid.

23. 22 Jun 1772, LB, JMA MS 41898
24. 24 Jul 1772, ibid.
25. Z, 46f.
26. John Millar, *The Origin of the Distinction of Ranks*, 3rd edn, John Murray, 1781, 285–7
27. Thomas Somerville, *My Own Life and Times, 1741–1814*, reprint edn, Thoemmes Press, 1996, 149

CHAPTER 3: LEWD WOMEN AND ANATOMICAL VIEWS

1. Archy Paxton to JM I, 13 Dec 1771, JMA MS 41898
2. To Rev. Dr Enfield, 14 Sept 1775, LB, JMA MS 41900
3. Bill dated 11 Sept 1775
4. S i, 31
5. JML
6. Z, 139
7. Capt. Weemss to JM I, 20 July 1770, JMA MS 43014
8. 25 Sept 1775, LB, JMA MS 41898
9. Z, 77
10. Auction catalogue, 22 Apr 1763, JMA MS 43009
11. Jane Collier, *An Essay on the Art of Ingeniously Tormenting; with Proper Rules for the Exercise of that Amusing Study. Humbly Addressed, Part I to the Master, Husband, &c. Part II. To the Wife, Friend, &c. With Some General Instructions for Plaguing all your Acquaintance* was first published anonymously by Andrew Millar in 1753. It was later reprinted by William Miller in 1804. Byron had a copy
12. John Murray III was offered the chance of publishing the *New English Dictionary*, which was being planned by the Philological Society. This eventually became the *Oxford English Dictionary*. Murray turned it down because he foresaw uncontrollable and probably enormous costs. On 12 May 1858 he wrote to Frederick Furnivall: 'To bind myself absolutely to publish a work w[hi]ch I have not seen & regarding the contents of w[hi]ch I am to have no control is contrary to any thing of previous occurrence in my literary experience.' (This letter is in the Bodleian Library's collection of the papers of the dictionary's eventual editor, the unrelated James Murray.) In 1862 John Murray was invited to publish an initial 'concise' version of the dictionary and this time he agreed, with a contract for delivery of the text in January

1866. The text didn't appear and the project ended in acrimony. One cannot help speculating that, if he had taken on the new dictionary, it would have given Murray's a massive financial rock for the foreseeable future, up to and including the present time

13. Roy Porter, *Doctor of Society*, Routledge, 1992, 58
14. 10 Dec 1774, LB, JMA MS 41900
15. Z/ *Stuart*, p. xi
16. ibid., 46
17. ibid., 55
18. 6 Dec 1770, LB, JMA MS 41897
19. 7 Sept 1779, LB, JMA MS 41903
20. 8 Apr 1775, LB, JMA MS 41900
21. JM I Diary, 30 Apr 1775, JMA MS 43018
22. ibid., 1 May 1775
23. ibid., 2 May 1775
24. ibid., May 1775
25. ibid.
26. ibid., 8 May 1775
27. ibid., 9 May 1775
28. ibid., 25 May 1775
29. ibid., 27 May 1775
30. ibid., 24 Jun 1775
31. Nancy to JM I, 26 Aug 1775, JMA MS 43015
32. 14 Sept 1775, LB, JMA MS 41900
33. Though Blake was paid £39 19s 6d to make four engravings (G. E. Bentley Jr, *Blake Records*, Clarendon Press, 2nd edn, (2003, 758), only three have been identified, including a male head after Rubens
34. 22 Sept 1776, LB, JMA MS 41901

CHAPTER 4: A SAD ACCIDENT

1. S i, 21
2. Samuel Bagster, *Samuel Bagster of London 1772–1851*, Bagster, 1972
3. 14 May 1778, LB, JMA MS 41902
4. 27 May 1782, LB, JMA MS 41903
5. 2 Jun 1783, LB, JMA MS 41904
6. Capt. Abraham Crawford, *Reminiscences of a Naval Officer during the Late War*, 2 vols, Henry Colburn, 1851, ii, 185–8

7. JM I to Archy Murray, 10 May and 23 Jul 1791, JMA MS 43017

8. William Richardson to JM I, 25 Nov 1773, JMA MS 43014

9. S i, 24

10. Gilbert Stuart to JM I, 23 Aug 1769, Bodleian, dep. Hughenden 245/7, fols 1–2

11. *Medical and Philosophical Commentaries*, vol. i, 1773, 98

12. Stuart to JM I, 27 May 1774, Bodleian, dep. Hughenden 245/7, fol. 36

13. Preface, vol. i, 1783

14. ibid., 7

15. ibid., 49

16. *English Review*, Jul 1783, 93

17. John Trusler, *Modern Times, or, the Adventures of Gabriel Outcast*, 4th edn, Literary Press, 1789, iii, 59

18. ibid., 56f.

19. 30 Nov 1786, LB, JMA MS 41905

20. Such as the repeal of the law that printers who dared to publish accounts of parliamentary debates could be thrown into jail

21. JM I to William Richardson, 15 Oct 1779, LB, JMA MS 41903

22. To Dr James Ogilvie, 17 Nov 1791, LB, JMA MS 41906

23. To John Richardson, 17 Mar 1791, ibid.

24. S i, 21

25. Z, 239

26. S i, 22–3

27. JM II to Archy Murray, 19–23 Mar 1793, LB, JMA MS 43017

28. 9 May 1793 LB, JMA MS 41906

29. To Cadell & Co., 25 Sept 1793, ibid.

30. Z, 242; letter to John Elder, 12 Aug 1793, LB, JMA MS 41906

31. Z, 242

32. 8 Mar 1794, LB, JMA MS 41906

33. JM II to Archy Murray, 21 Apr 1795, JMA MS 43017

34. Z, 246

35. JM II to Archy Murray, 30 Jul 1800, JMA MS 43017

CHAPTER 5: SERIOUS PLANS AS A PUBLISHER: JOHN MURRAY II

1. Soon after 7 Mar 1803, LB, JMA MS 41908

2. 7 Mar 1803, ibid.

3. JM I to Dr Ring, quoted S i, 37

4. S i, 32

5. 29 Mar 1803, LB, JMA MS 41908

6. 5 Aug 1803, ibid.

7. S i, 35

8. ibid., 32

9. 23 Aug 1803, LB, JMA MS 41908

10. 11 May 1803, ibid.

11. 6 Jan 1804, ibid.

12. — Stewarton, *The Revolutionary Plutarch*, Murray, 'new edition', 1804, ii, 194

13. Isaac D'Israeli to JM II, 14 Dec 1803, JMA MS 42160

14. D'Israeli, *Curiosities of Literature*, i, 9 (page references are to 1881 Frederick Warne edn)

15. ibid., 12

16. ibid., 71

17. ibid., 104

18. *ODNB*, entry on Isaac D'Israeli

19. Isaac D'Israeli, *Calamities of Authors*, John Murray, 1812, vol. i, pp. vi–vii

20. ibid., 202

21. ibid., ii, 51

22. ibid., 59

23. ibid., 73

24. S i, 42

25. ibid., 50

26. The pages of a book are printed on the front and back of large sheets of paper, which are then folded and bound. In the eighteenth and nineteenth centuries, unbound sheets were issued to authors and other people for proof-reading. Payment for magazine articles was calculated as so much per sheet

27. Isaac D'Israeli to JM II, October 1803, JMA MS 42160

28. S i, 51

29. ibid., 53

30. ibid., 45

31. ibid., 46

32. Introduction to 1881 Frederick Warne edn of D'Israeli, *Curiosities of Literature*. i, xiv

33. Isaac D'Israeli, *Vaurien: or, Sketches of the Times*, Cadell & Davies and Murray & Highley, 1797, ii, 219, 222–4

34. S i, 18
35. Anne Elliot to JM II, 15 Oct 1806, JMA MS 43022
36. JM II to Archibald Constable, 25 Apr 1803, JMA MS 41908
37. The only British publishing dynasty to rival Murray's in antiquity and longevity was founded by Thomas Longman I (1699–1755), a Bristol-born bookseller who had a share in publishing Johnson's *Dictionary*. He was succeeded by his nephew, also called Thomas, who made the firm a lot of money out of the Chambers *Cyclopaedia*. His son Thomas III (1771–1842) helped to lead the firm into a period of major prosperity
38. S i, 76
39. ibid., 70f.
40. 21 Aug 1806; Constable i, 80
41. Constable i, 81
42. S i, 72
43. 7 Dec 1805, LB, JMA MS 40908
44. Anne to JM II, 14 Jan 1807, JMA MS 43022
45. Mrs Rundell to JM II, 17 Sept 1808, JMA MS Acc 12604/85
46. Rundell (1811), 'Advertisement'
47. S i, 90
48. Maria Rundell, *A New System of Domestic Cookery*, John Murray, 1805, 239–40
49. ibid., 123
50. ibid., 195
51. ibid., 251

CHAPTER 6: QUARTERLY

1. Mrs Rundell to JM II, 28 Mar 1807, JMA MS Acc 12604/85
2. Mrs Rundell to JM II, 17 Sept 1808, ibid.
3. S i, 73
4. JM II to Constable, 7 Mar 1807, LB, JMA MS 41908
5. JM II to Constable, 27 Mar 1807, ibid.
6. JM II to Anne Murray, 29 Apr 1807, JMA MS 43023
7. JM II to Anne Murray, 26 Jul 1809, ibid.
8. JM II to Constable, 27 Mar 1807, JMA MS 41908
9. Constable iii, 8
10. A. N. Wilson, *The Laird of Abbotsford*, Oxford University Press, 1979, 24
11. S i, 94

12. *Edinburgh Review*, Apr 1808, 226
13. S i, 96
14. ibid., 82f.
15. *Scott Letters* ii, 103
16. Scott to JM II, 30 Oct 1808, ibid., 114
17. Scott to George Ellis, 2 Nov 1808, ibid., 120
18. ibid., 101n.
19. Scott to JM II, 15 Nov 1808, ibid., 125
20. ibid., 105
21. S ii, 104
22. *Scott Letters* ii, 124
23. ibid., 104
24. 25 Sept 1807, LB, JMA MS 41908
25. Clark, 1
26. *Life, Letters, and Journal of George Ticknor*, 2 vols, Sampson Low, 1876, i, 58
27. Clark, 4
28. ibid., 23
29. ibid., 29f.
30. 15 Nov 1808, LB, JMA MS 41908
31. ibid.
32. Scott to JM II, 25 Feb 1809, *Scott Letters*, ii 167
33. *QR*, Feb 1809, 19
34. ibid., 153
35. ibid., 172
36. 28 Aug 1810, LB, JMA MA 41908
37. Scott to JM II, 2 Feb 1809 in *Scott Letters* ii, 161
38. James Ballantyne to JM II, 3 Mar 1809, JMA MS 12604
39. William Gifford to JM II, 26 Feb 1809, JMA MS 42244
40. S i, 145
41. ibid.
42. ibid., 149. The critique is lost
43. 28 Feb 1809, LB, JMA MS 41908
44. 12 Mar 1809, ibid.
45. S i, 153f.
46. Gifford to JM II, May [?] 1809 [?], inscr '?QR2', JMA MS 42244
47. 11 May 1809, LB, JMA MS 41908
48. Gifford to JM II, 18 Jun 1809, JMA MS 42244
49. ibid.

50. S i, 159
51. ibid., 164
52. 25 Sept 1810, LB, JMA MS 41908
53. *QR*, Feb 1810, 221
54. 28 Oct 1811, LB, JMA MS 41909
55. *QR*, May 1810, 493
56. ibid., 517
57. Ballantyne to JM II, 20 Jan 1810, JMA MS Acc 12604/1043
58. *QR*, Nov 1810, 281

CHAPTER 7: LORD AND MASTER

1. To Dr Strachan, Enfield, 2 Aug 1811, LB, JMA MS 41908
2. To the Rev. Samuel Marsden, Senior Chaplain at New South Wales, 3 Oct 1811, ibid.
3. To C. P. Archer, Dublin, 16 Nov 1811, ibid.
4. 8 Jul 1812, Country Accounts to Midsummer 1812, ibid.
5. Bodleian, Vet. A6 d.755(2)
6. For further details, see 'How Murray Became Byron's Publisher', Nicholson, Appendix A, 471–5
7. Lines 171–4
8. 4 Sept 1811, Nicholson, 1
9. *BLJ* ii, 91
10. Lines 432ff.
11. Line 716
12. JMA MS 42724, 97
13. Robert Charles Dallas, *Recollections of the Life of Lord Byron*, Charles Knight, 1824, 230
14. Dallas to JM II, 1 Nov 1811, JMA MS Acc 12604/1307. See also Nicholson, 64
15. 7 May 1812, JMA MS Acc 12604/07879
16. Nicholson, 1, 14 and 23
17. ibid., 15
18. ibid., 27
19. Virginia Murray, for many years the archivist at John Murray's, recalls that Jock Murray, her father-in-law, never wanted anyone to see the letters from JM II to Byron, and they were never shown to researchers. He thought them too obsequious

20. *BLJ* ii, 197
21. To Sir Robert Wilson, 11 Dec 1812, BL Add. MS 30106 f. 366v
22. Letter to Hobhouse, dated merely 'Friday' (postmarked 17 May 1816), BL Add. MS 3456 f. 343. James Ridgway had occupied various premises in Piccadilly since 1784, and had served four years in prison for publishing the works of Thomas Paine
23. 22 Oct 1812, Nicholson, 5
24. From 1814 he was the publisher of the *Navy List*, a miracle of tiny typesetting by the printer William Clowes, who updated it every month (later, every quarter)
25. JM II to Archy Murray, 6 Aug 1813, JMA MS 43025

CHAPTER 8: THE HIGHEST HONOUR AND EMOLUMENT

1. B. H. Johnson, *Berkeley Square to Bond Street*, John Murray, 1952, 149ff.
2. Letter and schedule drawn up by David Reid, 25 Apr 1812, JMA
3. ibid.
4. Robert Browning to Mrs FitzGerald, 10 Apr 1886, quoted by Dr McAleer writing to JM V, 5 July 1961, JML
5. JM II to Archibald Murray, 6 Aug 1813, LB, JMA MS 43025
6. S i, 315
7. ibid., 314
8. MacCarthy, 301
9. Caroline Lamb to Byron, n.d. [1814?], JMA MS, Acc 12604/0355
10. Caroline Lamb forgery, n.d. [Jan 1813], ibid.
11. *BLJ* iii, 10
12. Caroline Lamb to JM II, JMA MS Acc 12604/0355
13. ibid.
14. ibid.
15. JML
16. *Life, Letters, and Journal of George Ticknor* i, 48
17. Washington Irving to James K. Paulding, 27 May 1820, in Pierre Munroe Irving, *The Life and Letters of Washington Irving*, Putnam, 1863, 455
18. Leopold Wagner, *London Inns and Taverns*, Allen Unwin, 1924, 68; Bryant Lillywhite, *London Coffee Houses*, 1963, 548

19. S i, 267
20. ibid., 267f.
21. JMA MS 43051/18
22. Scott to JM II, 11 Nov 1815, JMA MS 42535
23. S i, 268
24. James Hogg, *Anecdotes of Scott*, Edinburgh University Press, 1999, 24

CHAPTER 9: A CIVIL ROGUE

1. S i, 283
2. n.d., JMA MS 42247
3. 29 Sept 1815, JMA MS 42248
4. Modert, 50
5. Le Faye, 291
6. JM II to Annie, 18 Aug 1814, JMA MS 43023/16
7. On the other hand, Murray had begun to change this by instituting the salon in his drawing room. Frank Mumby, in his 1956 history of publishing and bookselling, points out that in Samuel Johnson's day a literary lion would be surrounded by a crowd of booksellers, eager to snap up his writings. Murray reversed this, and made the publisher the centre of a crowd of authors, who were eager that he should take them on
8. Le Faye, 297–8. Walter Scott's description of Paris comes in his book *Paul's Letters to his Kinsfolk*, published by Murray in 1815. Murray had also just co-published Scott's poem *The Field of Waterloo.*
9. Modert, 370
10. 29 Aug 1813, Nicholson, 13
11. *QR*, Oct 1815, 189
12. ibid., 193
13. Le Faye, 313
14. n.d. [1818], JMA MS 41908
15. n.d., endorsed '1812', JMA MS 42062
16. Richard Holmes, *Coleridge: Darker Reflections*, Flamingo, 1999, 438
17. 31 Aug 1814, JMA MS 42062
18. Lines 255–6
19. 4 Nov 1815(?), Nicholson, 74
20. 18 Mar 1817, ibid., 97
21. Holmes, *Coleridge*, 438

22. James Hamilton, *London Lights*, John Murray, 2007, 73

23. 12 Aug 1815, LB, JMA MS 41908

24. 19 Jul 1816, ibid.

25. 12 Aug 1813, ibid.

26. 3 Jan 1817, ibid.

27. 9 Sept 1817, ibid.

28. To an unknown correspondent, n.d. [1817], typed transcript in JMA MS 42066

29. Blackburne, 181

30. 9 Mar 1819, JMA MA 42066

31. Blackburne, 181

32. ibid., 183

33. Jane Austen, on the other hand, knew her Byron. *The Giaour* is discussed in *Persuasion*

34. 27–28 and 29 Dec 1815, Nicholson, 76

35. 5 Sept 1814, ibid., 57

36. JM II to Annie, 14 Sept 1814, JMA MS 43023/26

37. The book Mrs Rundell accused Murray of neglecting may not have been *Domestic Cookery*, but a new one, *Letters to Two Absent Daughters*, 1814, which was published by Richard Rees of Pall Mall, after Murray had been given the chance of undertaking it

38. 1 Feb 1814, Nicholson, 39

39. 8 Feb 1814, ibid., 32

40. 13 Apr 1816, ibid., 86

41. 29 Aug 1813, ibid., 13

42. 20 and 21 Sept 1813, ibid., 14

43. 22 Jun 1813, *BLJ* iii, 66

44. 22 Jun or 1 Jul 1813, Nicholson, 11

45. 12 Oct 1813, *BLJ* iii, 141

46. 17 Nov 1813, ibid., 212

47. 30 Dec 1813, Nicholson, 27

48. 20 Jan 1814, ibid., 29

49. 22 Jan 1814, *BLJ* iv, 38

50. This at least is what seems to have happened, but the whole thing is a bibliographical nightmare

51. 8 Feb 1814, Nicholson, 32

52. 12 Feb 1814, *BLJ* iv, 57

53. 2 Mar 1814, Nicholson, 34

54. 30 Apr 1814, ibid., 43

55. 9 Apr 1814, ibid., 38
56. 11 Apr 1814, ibid., 40
57. 12 Apr 1814, ibid., 41
58. JM II to Annie, 8 Sept 1814, JMA MS 43023/24
59. ibid., 5 Oct 1814, JMA MS 43023/34
60. ibid., 20 Aug 1814, JMA MS 43023/17
61. ibid.
62. ibid., 29 Aug 1814, JMA MS 43023/20
63. ibid., 5 Sept 1814, JMA MS 43023/23
64. ibid., 8 Sept 1814, JMA MS 43023/24
65. ibid., 14 Sept 1814, JMA MS 43023/26
66. ibid., 16 Sept 1814, JMA MS 43023/27
67. ibid., 21 Sept 1814, JMA MS 43023/28
68. ibid.
69. ibid., 24 Sept 1814, JMA MS 43023/29
70. ibid.
71. Lady Caroline Lamb to JM II, 18 Nov 1814, JMA MS Acc 12604/0355
72. 2 Jan 1816, Nicholson, 77
73. 22 Jan 1816, ibid., 80
74. 3 Feb 1816?, ibid., 81
75. 20 Feb 1816, *BLJ* v, 29
76. Discussed in MacCarthy, 267–8
77. Caroline Lamb to JM II, 12 Dec 1816, JMA MS ACC 12604/0355

CHAPTER 10: A CERTAIN POEM

1. JM II to Annie, 'Saturday Nt', 15 Jul 1815, JM MS 43024/37
2. ibid., 19 Jul 1815, JMA MS 43024/38
3. ibid., 21 Jul 1815, JMA MS 43024/39
4. ibid., 24 Jul 1815, JMA MS 43024/40
5. ibid., 3 Aug 1815, JMA MS 43024/43. Murray did visit Paris again, though not for twenty years
6. 27 Jun 1816, *BLJ* v, 82
7. Made by Mary Shelley's stepsister Claire Clairmont, who had become Byron's mistress
8. 27 Jun 1816, *BLJ* v, 82
9. JMA MS Acc 12604/0399
10. 20 Sept 1816, Nicholson, 90

11. 12 Sept 1816, ibid., 89
12. 6 Mar 1817, ibid., 95
13. 12 Sept 1816, ibid., 89
14. 13 Dec 1816, ibid., 91
15. ibid.
16. ibid.
17. 22 Jan 1817, Nicholson, 92
18. ibid.
19. 6 Mar 1817, ibid., 95
20. Nicholson, 105, n. 6
21. 22 Jan 1817, ibid., 92
22. *Manuscript Transmitted from St Helena by an Unknown Channel*, John Murray, 2nd edn, 1817, 146
23. 22 Jan 1817, Nicholson, 92
24. Published by Henry Colburn, 1816
25. Caroline Lamb, *Glenarvon*, Everyman, 1995, 142
26. *BLJ* v, 199
27. ibid., 255
28. ibid., 219
29. 12 Apr 1817, Nicholson, 102
30. *BLJ* v, 194
31. Dowden i, 187 and 225
32. *BLJ* v, 263
33. 29 Aug 1817, Nicholson, 107
34. ibid.
35. 9 Sept 1817, ibid., 108
36. *BLJ* vi, 58f.
37. ibid.
38. Nicholson, 109, n. 8
39. 7 Jul 1818, ibid., 110
40. 22 Sept 1818, ibid., 111
41. ibid.
42. *BLJ* vi, 71
43. ibid., 76
44. ibid., 99
45. ibid., 95
46. John Hookham Frere, *Whistlecraft 1818*, Woodstock Books, 1992, vol. iii, p. i
47. BLJ vi, 77

48. ibid., 92
49. ibid., 94
50. Quoted by Peter Cochran in typescript 'The Domestic Reception of *Don Juan*'
51. 19 Mar 1819, Nicholson, 113
52. *BLJ* vi, 105
53. ibid., 104, 105
54. 27 Apr 1819, Nicholson, 114
55. 3 May 1819, ibid., 116
56. *BLJ* vi, 125
57. 28 May 1819, Nicholson, 117
58. *BLJ* vi, 131
59. ibid., 168
60. JM II to Blackwood, 22 May 1819, JMA MS 41908
61. n.d., c.1820. Not in Murray Archive; quoted in unidentified sale catalogue, photocopy in JMA
62. 16 Jul 1819, Nicholson, 118
63. *BLJ* vi, 205
64. 16 Jul 1819, Nicholson, 118
65. Cohen changed his surname to Palgrave a few years later, and became the father of Francis Turner Palgrave, anthologist of *The Golden Treasury*
66. n.d. (16 Jul 1819), JMA MS Acc 12604/169
67. 16 Jul 1819, Nicholson, 118
68. n.d. (16 Jul 1819), JMA MS Acc 12604/169
69. 29 May 1821, Nicholson, 156
70. I, 129–31 and II, 81
71. I, 205–6
72. 23 Jul 1819, Nicholson, 119
73. ibid.
74. *BLJ* vi, 207
75. ibid., 215
76. 3 Sept 1819, Nicholson, 121
77. 14 Sept 1819, ibid., 122
78. 3 Sept 1819, ibid., 121
79. *BLJ* vi, 205
80. 14 Sept 1819, Nicholson, 122
81. ibid.
82. 9 Nov 1819, ibid., 124

83. *BW*, 579

84. ibid., 581

85. 24 Jan 1820, Nicholson, 127

86. *BW*, 579

87. 14 Nov 1819, Nicholson, 125

88. 7 Mar 1820, ibid., 128

89. *BLJ* vii, 61

90. Dowden i, 139f.

91. 24 Jan 1820, Nicholson, 127

92. ibid., n. 14

93. Nicholson, 128, n. 13

94. 9 Nov 1819, ibid., 124

95. 16 Nov 1819, ibid., 126

96. *BLJ* vii, 35

97. 13 Jun 1820, Nicholson, 130

98. *BLJ* vii, 121

99. ibid., 124

100. 14 Jul 1820, Nicholson, 132

101. 15 Aug 1820, ibid., 134

102. 14 Jul 1820, ibid., 132

103. 8 Sept 1820, ibid., 136

104. *BLJ* vii, 113

105. ibid., 158

106. 8 Sept 1820, Nicholson, 136

107. Dismantle the type and replace it in the cases

108. 12 Aug 1820, Nicholson, 133

109. 29 Dec 1820, ibid., 144

110. 21 Jul 1818, JMA MS 41908

111. 24 Dec 1818, ibid.

112. A full account of the Turner–Hakewill project is Cecilia Powell, 'Topography, Imagination and Travel: Turner's Relationship with James Hakewill', *Art History*, vol. 5, no. 4 (Dec 1982), 408ff.

113. Advertisement to Henry Ellis, *Journal of the Proceedings of the Late Embassy to China . . . Interspersed with Observations upon the Face of the Country, the Polity, Moral Character and Manners of the Chinese Nation*, John Murray, 1817

114. ibid., 94

115. John Murray [IV], 'Some Authors I have Known', *Good Words*, Feb 1895, 93

116. *Monthly Literary Advertiser*, Jan 1821, 6
117. JM II to Washington Irving, c. 1815, JMA MS 42308
118. Preface to the revised edn of *The Sketch Book of Geoffrey Crayon, Gent.*

CHAPTER 11: TORN AND BURNED BEFORE OUR EYES

1. 23 Jan 1821, Nicholson, 147
2. ibid., n. 9
3. *BLJ* vii, 125
4. 6 Sept 1821, Nicholson, 162
5. 28 Sept 1821, ibid., 163
6. *BLJ* viii, 185
7. 25 Sept 1822, Nicholson, 167
8. 11 Oct 1822, ibid., 168
9. ibid.
10. 29 Oct 1822, ibid., 169
11. *BLJ* ix, 204
12. ibid., 123
13. W. Fletcher to JM II, 21 Apr 1824, JMA MS Acc 12604/0384
14. Dowden ii, 731
15. I am very grateful to Dr Peter Cochran for transcribing and editing that part of Hobhouse's diary (what he calls the 'Narrative') that describes the fate of the Byron memoirs: BL Add. MS 56548, ff.73v–87v
16. Dowden ii, 731
17. ibid., 732
18. ibid.
19. Hobhouse 'Narrative'
20. ibid.
21. Dowden i, 261
22. Hobhouse 'Narrative'
23. ibid.
24. It is tucked into Hobhouse's handwritten 'Narrative'
25. ibid.
26. LLB, 25
27. Dowden ii, 733f.

28. ibid. vi, 2441
29. ibid.
30. Cochran
31. Dowden vi, 2442
32. Cochran
33. Dowden vi, 2442
34. Cochran
35. *LLB*, 46
36. Cochran
37. *LLB*, 27
38. Dowden vi, 2443
39. ibid., 2440
40. ibid. ii, 735
41. ibid. vi, 2440
42. S i, 443
43. Murray has written 'went to' and 'with her', and has crossed them both out
44. In fact Wilmot-Horton wrote to Lady Byron, on the day of the burning, that the Memoirs were burnt 'in my presence'; but he implies that he took no part in the burning, which seems to leave us with Murray himself – if his son is to be trusted – feeding the flames
45. Agreement dated 6 May 1822, JMA MS 42490
46. Dowden vi, 2443
47. ibid.
48. ibid., 2444
49. ibid.
50. *The Times*, 27 May 1824
51. *John Bull Magazine*, Jul 1824, 19
52. JM II to Wilmot-Horton, 29 May 1817, clerk's copy, JMA MS Acc 12604/4192
53. According to the Hobhouse 'Narrative' he himself was willing, at the last minute, to save the manuscript and let it be locked up in the bank for the time being; but the proposal was 'overruled', presumably by Murray. *LLB*, 17–35
54. Conversation with the author, 5 Jan 2004
55. *LLB*, 22
56. Fergus Fleming, *Barrow's Boys*, Granta Books, 2001, 9f.
57. Use of 'Conservative': *QR*, Jan 1830. Damaging review of Keats's *Endymion*: *QR*, Aug 1818

58. J.W. Croker to JM II, 26 Mar 1820, JMA MS 42129
59. MacCarthy, 522
60. That his memory could inspire political activism is shown by Fiona MacCarthy at the conclusion of her life of Byron: 'His richly energetic life opened up the possibility for writers and artists to play a more significant role in politics.' MacCarthy, 546
61. 23 May 1824, JM MS 42129
62. After reading these paragraphs, the historian William Thomas, who has written extensively on Croker and the politics of this period, comments: 'I cannot take seriously the threat that Byron could have led the radical movement in England. Even allowing that he had the capacity, he was surely too aristocratic and Whiggish in outlook.' Letter to the author, 22 Jan 2004
63. Sotheby's catalogue, 2 Dec 1910
64. *Courier*, 22 May 1824

CHAPTER 12: TORTOISES DANCING ON DOUGH

1. Jun 1824, JMA MS 42625
2. Except maybe the Paris-based English-language bookseller Galignani's four-page daily newspaper, *Galignani's Messenger*, published since 1814. It had contained some of *Don Juan*
3. Most famously (in 1817) on the 'Cockney School of Poetry', which included Keats
4. Review of Smiles by Gladstone; *Murray's Magazine*, May 1891
5. Benjamin Disraeli to Walter Scott, 21 Sept 1825, JMA MS 42625
6. 13 Oct 1825, LB, JMA MS 41910
7. John Lloyd to JM II, 19 Jan 1826, JMA MS Acc 12604/1705
8. Oct 1825, LB, JMA MS 41910
9. S ii, 209
10. Professor W. T. Brande to JM II, 2 Jan 1826, LB, JMA MS Acc 12604/1142
11. S ii, 208f.
12. *Representative*, 31 Jan 1826
13. Irving to A. H. Everett, 31 Jan 1826, Munroe Irving, *Washington Irving*, 201
14. LB JMA MS 41910. In *The English Book Trade*, Allen & Unwin, 1965, Marjorie Plant records that the functions of bookseller and publisher

continued to be combined by many firms until well into the nine-teenth century, though there were plenty of booksellers who did not publish

15. JM II to Sharon Turner, 16 Oct 1826, LB, JMA MS 41910

16. S ii, 215. The account book for the *Representative* gives the total expenditure 'Paid in Albemarle Street' as £13,951. Receipts are not recorded. Murray had apparently also lost money through share speculation instigated by Disraeli

17. *Vivian Gray*, Book II, Chapter 1

18. JM II to Sharon Turner, 16 Oct 1826, LB, JMA MS 41910. When Murray published Disraeli's novel *Contarini Fleming* in 1832, it was on ungenerous financial terms, offered in a strictly businesslike letter; Murray also pressed Disraeli, unsuccessfully, for the repayment of £1,500 which he claimed was owed him from the *Representative* fiasco

19. S ii, 199

20. ibid., 236

21. JM II to Washington Irving, 25 Oct 1831, LB, JMA MS 41910

22. *A History of England . . . by Mrs Markham*, John Murray, 1829, I, 93–5

23. This implies that Murray employed travelling sales representatives. Certainly members of the firm's staff sometimes made promotional journeys; one of them, Edward Dundas, visited major English cities during the autumn of 1843, just after the death of John Murray II, to push Murray books and negotiate terms with regional booksellers

24. S ii, 152

25. ibid. i, 320

26. Maria Graham to JM II, 24 Feb 1821, JMA MS Acc 12604/1185

27. ibid.

28. Maria Graham, *Three Months Passed in the Mountains East of Rome, during the Year 1819*, 1820, preface, pp. iii–iv

29. ibid., 188ff.

30. JM II to Henry Hallam, 27 Jun 1828, LB, JMA MS 41910. Another instance of the *Quarterly Review* attacking a Murray book is Croker's review of the Journal of Fanny Kemble (1835) which Croker said was in 'exceeding bad taste'. *QR*, 107 (1836)

31. 4 Dec 1826, JMA MS 42588

32. 9 Jul 1826, JMA MS 42445

33. 8 Nov 1815, LB, JMA MS 41909

34. Davy's lectures at the Royal Institution, 21 Albemarle Street, between

1802 and 1812, had proved so popular that the street became the first in London to be designated 'one way', since there was scant room for crowds of carriages to travel in both directions, dropping off and picking up Davy's audience

35. 'Sep 28' (28 Sept 1828?), JMA MS Acc 12604/1320
36. Mortgage deed between JM II and Mary Somerville, 26 Oct 1838, JMA MS Acc 12604/184. On the Somervilles' financial difficulties, Elizabeth C. Patterson, *Mary Somerville and the Cultivation of Science 1815–1840*, Martinus Nijhoff, 1983, 170ff.
37. S i, 241
38. ibid., 253
39. John Murray [IV], 'Some Authors I have Known', Good Words, Feb 1895, 91
40. P, 84
41. *Stokers and Pokers; or, The London and North-Western Railway, the Electric Telegraph, and the Railway Clearing-House*, 1849
42. P, 84
43. *JM III*, 2
44. P, 26.
45. *JM III*, 7f.
46. ibid., 40
47. ibid., 41
48. Mariana Starke, *Travels on the Continent*, John Murray, 1820, v
49. *JM III*, 41
50. ibid.
51. JML
52. This is taken from 'Walker's Original', one of a number of quotations JM III makes from past writers, including Lord Bacon, Samuel Rogers and Laurence Sterne
53. Anne Murray to JM III, 24 Aug 1829, JMA MS 43074
54. *JM III*, 44f.
55. JM II to JM III, n.d., JMA MS 43027
56. JM II to JM III, 16 Aug 1830, JMA MS 43026
57. JM II to JM III, n.d., Nov 1835, JMA MS 43027
58. 12 Apr 1839, JMA MS 42155
59. LB JMA MS 41910
60. 1 Dec 1842, JMA MS 42041
61. JM II to JM III, n.d., Aug 1830, JMA MS 43026. JM VII recalls his father Jock Murray saying much the same thing about 140 years later:

'He often told me, "You must get to more parties – it's the way to meet authors." And as to clubs, he belonged to all of them.' Conversation with the author, 30 Jan 2004

62. In 1841, Trollope's uncle Henry Milton became Murray's first regular paid reader of manuscripts, in his spare time from his job at the War Office. Other Miltons read manuscripts for the firm over the next four decades

63. JM III to William Brockedon, 12 Mar 1833, LB, JMA MS 41910

64. ibid., 3 Apr 1834, ibid.

65. *JM III*, 42

66. *A Handbook for Travellers on the Continent*, John Murray, 1836, 47

67. ibid.

68. Quoted in John R. Gretton, intro. to W. B. C. Lister, *A Bibliography . . . of Murray's Handbooks for Travellers*, 1993, p. i

69. 12 Jun 1839, LB, JMA MS 41911

70. *Handbook for Travellers to Spain*, John Murray, 1st edn, 1845, 2

71. 8 Jul 1839, LB, JMA MS 41911

72. 22 Jul 1839, ibid.

73. 22 Dec 1839, ibid.

74. A. H. Layard to JM III, 27 Mar 1891, JMA MS 42341–2

75. *JM III*, 46

76. ibid., 48

77. JM III to Baedeker, 8 Dec 1860, JMA MS 41913

78. 10 Dec 1839, JMA MS Acc 12604/1035. However, John R. Gretton has pointed out in his introduction to Lister's bibliography of the Handbook that Baedeker based most of his Rhineland guide on a German book of which he had acquired the copyright following the author's death

79. Ruskin to JM III, n.d., Jun 1845, JMA MS 42534. Murray turned down Ruskin's *Modern Painters* in 1834 without seeing the manuscript. Tim Hilton, *John Ruskin*, i: *The Early Years*, Yale University Press, 1985, 72

80. P, 50

81. Gretton, intro. to Lister bibliography, p. ii

82. Mrs Gaskell to JM III, 'Oct 23rd', JMA MS Acc 12604/1441

83. Mendelssohn to JM III, 17 Jan 1843, JMA MS Acc 12604/1803

CHAPTER 13: ON THE GREAT GAME

1. 6 Jul 1843, LB, JMA MS 41911
2. *Athenaeum*, 1 Jul 1843
3. P, 25
4. Undated clipping from the *Court Journal*, JMA MS 43054
5. *Spectator*, 2 Jul 1843
6. 8 Jul 1843. Yet the legal documents relating to his estate described him as 'bookseller'. The shop was still in existence at Albemarle Street; in 1844–5 its running expenses for the year, including 'Paper, String, Lights, Postage Stamps', came to £150
7. 2 Jul 1843
8. *Gentleman's Magazine*, 20 (Aug 1843), 210–12
9. *Athenaeum*, 1 Jul 1843
10. P, 25
11. To Horace Twiss, 11 May 1842 LB, JMA MS 41911
12. To 'Mr Robb, Glasgow, 22 Jul 1843, ibid.
13. JMA MS 42155
14. 2 Aug 1842, *JMA* ibid.
15. 6 Feb 1843, JMA MS 42259
16. 11 Feb 1843, ibid.
17. 'A memoir of a Map of the Eastern Branch of the Indus giving an account of the alterations produced in it by an earthquake of 1819 & the bursting of the dams in 1826; also a theory of the Runns formation & some surmises on the route of Alexander the Great' by Lieut. A. Burnes, ms [lithog] 1827–8, Royal Geographical Society, LMS B.63, p. 42
18. Alexander Burnes, *Travels into Bokhara*, John Murray, 1834, vol. i, p.ix
19. To Viscount Mahon, 8 Dec 1843, LB, JMA MS 41911
20. George Borrow, *The Bible in Spain*, John Murray, 1861 Colonial & Home edition, preface
21. 28 Aug 1841, JMA MS 42041
22. n.d., (Nov 1840), ibid.
23. 30 Oct 1852, ibid.
24. By mid-century, Murray's were also publishing a *Library of Railway Readings*, but nothing was as successful as the Handbooks
25. Quoted in Marion Lochhead, *Elizabeth Rigby, Lady Eastlake*, John Murray, 1961

26. *QR*, Sept 1840
27. *QR*
28. Eastlake i, 115, 119
29. 4 Jul 1843, ibid., 75
30. ibid., 119
31. ibid., 124
32. 20 Mar 1846, LB, JMA MS 41912
33. P, 52
34. Herman Melville *Journals*, North West University Press, 1989, 23 Nov 1849, 25–6
35. Eastlake i, 188
36. JMA MS 41911
37. JMA MS 42477
38. 29 Feb 1848, LB, JMA MS 41912
39. P, 76

CHAPTER 14: DR DARWIN, I PRESUME?

1. 5 Jan 1857, LB JMA MS 41912
2. 22 May 1857, JMA MS 42420–1
3. n.d., [1857], ibid.
4. 29 Apr 1857, ibid.
5. 29 Apr 1857, ibid.
6. 30 May 1857, ibid.
7. 12 Nov 1857, ibid.
8. 25 Dec 1857, ibid.
9. 6 March 1858, ibid.
10. 1 Nov 1859, ibid.
11. This story seems to be negated by the fact that an engraving of the portrait is used at the front of the first edition of *Missionary Travels*, which was published before Livingstone returned to Africa
12. Byron, *Cain*, I, 1
13. Janet Browne, *Charles Darwin: Voyaging*, Jonathan Cape, 1995, 186
14. *QR*, 43, no. 86, 1830, 414, 417
15. Darwin was also particularly influenced by another Murray author, Thomas Malthus, and his thinking on the struggle for existence in *Essay on the Principle of Population,* 1830
16. 13 Nov 1859, JMA MS Acc 12604/0064

17. Janet Browne, *Charles Darwin: Voyaging*, Jonathan Cape, 1995, perpetuates the story.

18. 5 Apr 1859, JMA MS 42152–3

19. Darwin to Lyell, 28 Mar [1859], *The Correspondence of Charles Darwin*, ed. Frederick Burkhardt and Syndey Smith, 15 vols, Cambridge University Press, 1985–,vii, 269

20. Darwin to J. D. Hooker, 2 Apr [1859], ibid., 275

21. ibid.

22. 'George Paston' writes of the year 1869: 'Though it was now twenty-five years since the death of John [Murray] II, there were still people in existence who imagined that John III was Byron's publisher, which would have made him out almost a centenarian.' P, 219

23. ibid., 170

24. Janet Browne, *Charles Darwin: The Power of Place*, Jonathan Cape, 2002, 75

25. Michael Freeman, *Victorians and the Prehistoric: Tracks to a Lost World*, Yale University Press, 2004, 80

26. I remember finding it on the shelves of an Anglo-Irish castle in the late 1970s, and astonishing the titled owner by actually *reading* it

27. W. E. Houghton, *The Victorian Frame of Mind, 1830–1870*, Yale University Press 1959, p. xvi

28. Aileen Smiles, *Samuel Smiles and his Surroundings,* Robert Hale, 1956

29. ibid., 191

30. *Self-help*, John Murray, 1859

31. Smiles, *Samuel Smiles and his Surroundings*, 135

32. Jul 1871, quoted P, 233, JMAMS Acc 12604/1269–70

33. *The Last Journals of David Livingstone*, Harper & Brothers, New York, 1875, 31, 270

34. 'Verifier', *Scepticism in Geology*, John Murray, 2nd ed, 1878, 112, 114

35. ibid., 4–5

36. ibid., 116, 118

37. ibid., 67–8

38. ibid., 116

39. *JM III*, 25

40. He was pleased when Gladstone read and liked the book, but he did not reveal to him that he was its author. P, 247

CHAPTER 15: KIND MR MURRAY, THE KING OF PUBLISHERS

1. *JM III*, 26–7
2. Preface by Lord Ernle (Rowland Prothero), to P, p. xiii
3. ibid., p. xvi
4. ibid., 307
5. ibid., 108
6. Gretton, intro. to Lister bibliography, p. xxiv
7. 16 Jul 1847, JMA MS Acc 12604/1269–70
8. James Hamilton, *Faraday – The Life*, Harpercollins, 2002, 174f.
9. 24 Jul 1846, JMA MS Acc 12604/1269–70
10. 5 Sept 1848, ibid.
11. 19 Oct 1846, ibid.
12. 9 Jan 1847, ibid.
13. 6 Aug 1858, ibid.
14. 1 Sept 1848, 15 Aug 1850, ibid.
15. P. du Chaillu to Capt. George, Royal Geographical Society, 20 Aug 1864, RGS CB/5/1861–70
16. 'Paul du Chaillu, by One who Knew Him' [signed at end 'T.L.G.'] ts, 1903, RGS/JMS/21/75
17. 31 Dec 1864, JMA MS Acc 12604/0192
18. 4 Jan 1891, JMA MS 42341–2
19. 15 Jan 1880, JMA MS 42025
20. Letter to JM III, 17 Oct 1882, ibid.
21. 14 Sept 1880, ibid.
22. 23 Sept 1882, ibid.
23. JM VII conversation with the editor, 2006
24. 16 Nov 1882, JMA MS 42025
25. Hayward to Shaw, 10 Mar 1869, JMA MS Acc 12604/180
26. A. Quiller Couch (ed.), *The Oxford Book of English Verse*, Clarendon Press, 1923 edn, 1037
27. 16 May 1904, JMA MS Acc 12604/0199
28. 24 Sept 1876, JMA MS Acc 12604/1269–70
29. 8 Feb 1862, JMA MS Acc 12604/1206
30. Unsourced cutting, 10 Mar 1890, cuttings book, JML
31. 31 Aug 1877, LB JMA MS 41914
32. ibid. 31(?) Aug 1877, JMA MS Acc 12604/0291

33. 1 Sept 1877, LB JMA MS 41914
34. 18 Jan 1877, JMA MS Acc 12604/0291
35. 7 Jun 1877, ibid.
36. 18 Jan 1877, ibid.
37. P, 255
38. ibid.
39. Smiles, *Samuel Smiles and his Surroundings*, 133
40. *JM III*, preface
41. Smiles, *Samuel Smiles and his Surroundings*, 152
42. *Murray's Magazine*, May 1891
43. Bryan Bennett and Anthony Hamilton, *Edward Arnold Lunn: 100 Years of Publishing*, Edward Arnold, 1990, 5f. Another short-lived Murray magazine, the *Academy*, ran in 1869–70. Unlike the *Quarterly*, its reviews were signed
44. 30 Jan 1891, Acc JMA MS 12064/1487
45. *Pall Mall Gazette*, 11 Mar 1891
46. JM III death certificate
47. P, 247

CHAPTER 16: A *VERY* BUSY DAY

1. 8 Jan 1878, JMA MS 43083
2. Entry for 2 Nov 1883, JML
3. Entry for 21 Jan 1884, JML
4. JM II had published the historian Henry Hallam from 1818; but the name had become fashionable since Tennyson immortalised the historian's son, Arthur Henry Hallam, in his long poem *In Memoriam* (1850)
5. JM IV to his children, 3 Jun 1928, JML
6. Press cutting, JML
7. 29 Nov 1917, JML
8. 7 June 1904, JML
9. See also Judith B. Tankard, 'A Perennial Favourite – The English Flower Garden', *Hortus*, 17, Spring 1991, 74–85
10. 14 Nov 1903, JML
11. 19 Dec 1911, JML
12. 29 Dec 1911, JML
13. 4 Feb 1921, JML
14. *Astarte*, p. xi

15. ibid., 26
16. John Murray and Rowland E. Prothero, *Lord Byron and his Detractors*, privately printed, 1906, p. vii
17. 'I have read Astarte. So far as I am personally concerned it has caused me so much amusement that I could well afford to let it pass, but I must stand up for my Grandfather and father and write an answer.' JM IV to Lady Dorchester, 15 Jan 1906, JML
18. Ada Lovelace to J. C. Hobhouse, 10 Oct [?] 1844
19. *The Times*, 19 Jul 1924
20. A. C. Benson Diary, 28 Feb 1902, Magdalene College, Cambridge. By permission of the Master and Fellows of Magdalene College.
21. JM IV to Benson, 4 Aug 1903, JMA MS 41939
22. Undated letter Benson to JM IV, JMA MS Acc 12604/1086
23. JM IV to Benson, 3 Aug 1904, JMA MS 41942
24. Esher to JM IV, 29 Aug 1906, JMA MS
25. 11 Nov 1903, JMA MS Acc 12604/1086
26. 22 Mar 1904, JMA MS 41941
27. 4 Oct 1905, JMA MS 41947
28. Yvonne M. Ward, 'Editing Queen Victoria: How Men of Letters Constructed the Young Queen', unpublished PhD thesis, La Trobe University, Australia, 2004, 162
29. Esher to Hallam Murray, 13 Jan 1906, JMA MS
30. 29 Aug 1906, JMA MS Acc 12604/1086
31. *Western Morning News*, 9 May 1908
32. 2 Jun 1908, JMA MS Acc 12604/1603
33. Esher to JM V, 24 Sept 1910, JMA MS
34. *Britannia*, 7 Dec 1928
35. *Publishers' Circular*, 8 Dec 1928
36. *Sunday Graphic*, 10 Mar 1929
37. Nottingham Guardian, 1 Dec 1928

CHAPTER 17: ROBIN

1. *Sketch*, 12 Jul 1916
2. *Belfast News Letter*, 21 Aug 1916
3. *Evening Standard,* 17 Aug 1916
4. n.d., 1922, JML
5. 29 Sept 1922, JML

NOTES

6. JM VII said in conversation with the author: 'It was always rumoured that Helen had known she could not have children before she married Jack, but nobody could bring themselves to tell him. And he was so upright that he would never have gone back on the engagement'

7. *The Coming of Age of Mr John Murray V, Report of Speeches,* privately printed, 1905, 7

8. JML

9. JML

10. JML

11. Attallah

12. *Financial Times,* 22 Dec 1990

13. *Evening Standard,* 2 Oct 1989

14. ibid.

15. 14 May 1903, photostat, JMA MS

16. Wren's books were advertised by Murray's with a series of lurid, richly coloured posters, based on the dust jackets. Wren (1875–1941) rewrote his own past, claiming to have served in the French Foreign Legion. In reality he had worked in the Indian education service, before retiring in 1917 and making a new career as a writer

17. Humphrey Carpenter and Mari Prichard, *Oxford Companion to Children's Literature,* Oxford University Press, 1984, 249

18. Attallah

19. Bevis Hillier, *John Betjeman: New Fame, New Love,* John Murray, 2002, 110

20. Fiona MacCarthy, *Eric Gill,* Faber & Faber, 1989, 155–6, 190–1, 239

21. 23 Dec 1931, JML

22. 14 Oct [1927], JML

23. 5 Dec [1927], JML

24. At Eton, he had got into trouble for the possession of what he calls in his diary 'certain French magazines'. Diary, 12 Mar 1926, JML

25. 5 Dec [1927], JML

26. 24 Nov [1927], JML

27. 'A Ditty of "No. 50"', JML

28. 3 Nov 1930, JML

29. 7 Jul 1934, JML

30. 23 Jul 1930, JML

31. P, pp. xi–xii

32. *Financial Times,* 22 Dec 1990

33. *Manuscripts, Autograph Letters, Portraits, and other Objects of Literary*

Interest Illustrative of the House of John Murray . . . from 1768 to the Present Day, exh. cat. 1931, 24–5

34. Letters from Trollope, Eliot and Hardy, and from many other nineteenth-century writers, including Charlotte Brontë, enrich the Smith, Elder archive, which was absorbed into the Murray Archive

35. Exh. cat. 1931, preface

36. Believed to be Edward Garnett, advising an American publisher. Photostat, JML

37. Diary, 3 Dec 1937, JML

38. BBC European Service, 15 Feb 1949, script, JML

39. Quoted in the preface 'Jock Murray', by Nicholas Barker, in James Fergusson, *From the Bookshelves of Jock Murray*, Heywood Hill, 1997

CHAPTER 18: A *GERMAN?*

1. Entry for Leonard Huxley, *ODNB*

2. 10 Sept 1935, JML

3. Hillier ii, 111

4. Attallah

5. 23 Oct 1937, JML

6. *Stark Letters* ii, 174

7. ibid., 188f.

8. Molly Izzard, *Freya Stark: A Biography*, Hodder & Stoughton, 1993, 21

9. *Stark Letters* iii, 5

10. ibid., 11

11. ibid., 16

12. ibid., 16f.

CHAPTER 19: IT'S OURS!

1. 25 Nov 1939, JML

2. The traditional bounty for joining the army

3. W. H. Ingrams, author of books about the Middle East. Scott is the naturalist Peter Scott

4. 23 Dec 1942, JML

5. ibid., 25 Aug n.y. [1942?], JML

6. Letters of commiseration from members of the book trade appear in the Murray files in mid-February 1936

7. See Olive's obituary in the *Daily Telegraph*, 6 Apr 1998. However, the *Bookseller*, 29 Jan 1955, and other book-trade journals at the same time record the death 'as the result of an accident' of forty-eight-year-old William Lawrence Farquharson, described as 'director and manager of John Murray's'

8. Diary, undated entry, 1940, JML

9. ibid., 1941

10. Philip Wake, who was in the same OCTU intake as Jock, says he 'never gave one the impression of being the warrior type', and claims that Jock handed him a rifle so clumsily that it shot him in the foot. Letter to JM VII, 11 Feb 1997, JML

11. Diary, undated entry, 1940, JML

12. JML. Diana does not recall why they referred to the baby as the Chipmunk, nor what she meant by the show being on the ground again. But she does remember that the 'funny little bicycle' was a folding Corgi motorbike which Jock had ridden

13. His department, Air 1(c), which he had joined in the summer of 1943, dealt with 'plans, figures and estimates' for transporting military personnel and equipment by such means as air ambulances, helicopters and gliders. Jock observed in his diary that it was 'a far cry from ... the cookhouse at Larkhill', where he had fried one thousand eggs Diary, 1 Jul 1943, JML

14. Diary, 12 Nov 1944, JML

15. Diary, 31 Oct 1945, JML

16. Diary, 10 Nov 1944, JML

17. Diary, 20 Mar 1945, JML

18. Diary, 25 Jul 1945, JML

19. Diary, 31 Jul 1945, JML

20. Prothero, and Thomas Moore before him, had omitted stanzas 12 to 14 when printing the 'Epistle to Mr Murray' ('My dear Mr Murray, / You're in a damn'd hurry / To set up this ultimate Canto'). These stanzas boast that a (female) prostitute ('Cunt') is waiting to oblige Byron as soon as he has finished writing to his publisher

21. Diary, 6 Nov 1945, JML

22. 21 Jun 1923, JML

23. 22 Jun 1923, JML

24. Quennell to Jock, n.d., JML

25. Diary, 15 Nov 1945, JML
26. Diary, 11 Aug 1947, JML
27. *BLJ* i, 28, editorial note by Leslie A. Marchand; complete letter at *BLJ* iii, 100
28. Jock is presumably recalling the use of the ground-floor front room as the dining room in his grandfather's time
29. Diary, 18 Oct 1946, JML
30. Diary, 25 Aug 1947, JML
31. Diary, 29 Aug to 15 Sept 1947, JML
32. Diary, 18 Sept 1947, JML
33. Kenneth Clark, *The Other Half*, John Murray, 1977, 82
34. Diary, 10–16 Nov 1946, JML

CHAPTER 20: GENTLEMAN OF THE ROAD

1. *Bookseller*, 25 Jul 1997
2. Diary, 31 Oct 1948, JML. 'Mervyn' was the Rev. Mervyn Stockwood, later Bishop of Southwork
3. 19 Feb 1960, JML
4. Diary, 2 Sept 1948, JML
5. *Bookseller*, 21 Apr 1951
6. Jock gave this account of the book in a talk to the Wordsworth Trust in 1992: 'Paddy was commissioned by another publisher to write an article for a book to be called (rather oddly) *Great Balls of History* – he was to write on the ball before the Battle of Waterloo. When he finally came with the typescript, it turned out to be a 45,000-word novel about an imaginary ball in the Caribbean, which we published, and which was later turned into an opera with music by Malcolm Williamson.'
7. N.d. [1954], JML
8. 20 Feb 1956, JML
9. 30 Jul 1953, JML

CHAPTER 21: SUCH FUN

1. The other two are: *Lord Byron – Accounts Rendered*, John Murray, 1974 and *Ada, Countess of Lovelace, Byron's Illegitimate Daughter*, John Murray, 1977

2. To Chloe Sayer, 22 Aug 1989, JML

3. She later wrote *Kulu,* John Murray, 1972, about a journey to the Himalayas

4. Penelope Betjeman had been given £100 for her Spanish travel book, and Ruth Prawer Jhabvala received £150 for *The Householder.* The royalty scale was usually generous, often rising from 10 per cent to 12½ per cent (and then to 15 per cent) after the sale of no more than 2,000 or 2,500 copies

5. Rachel's father is the Irish writer Terence de Vere White. Jock became Rachel's godfather

6. *Wheels within Wheels*, Flamingo, 2002, 247

7. Patrick Leigh Fermor address, JML

8. 7 Nov [1955], JML

9. Norrie

10. *Sunday Times*, 4 Nov 1962

CHAPTER 22: HARVEST

1. Kenneth Clark, *The Other Half*, 210.

2. *Radio Times*, 31 Oct 1974

3. John Murray Spring List, 1976

4. Freya Stark had been made a dame in 1972

5. 12 Jan 1978, JML

6. This editor, however, discovering the *Letters* on a bookshelf in Florence, found them to be sparkling and melancholy, evocative and infuriating, but nevertheless compulsive reading that kept him awake into the small hours. JH

7. *Publishing News*, 10 Sept 1982

8. ibid.

9. *Private Eye*, 4 Jun 1981

10. 20 Dec 1984, JML

11. A recollection of James Hamilton, whose father, Patrick Hamilton, founded the Florence Trust

12. 16 Nov 1991, JML

13. *Publishing News*, 23 Mar 1990

14. The house in Albemarle Street was not for sale, although it did belong to Hodder for a short while during the transactions, for 'technical' reasons

EPILOGUE

1. *Scotsman*, 20 Dec 2004
2. The housing of the Archive at the National Library of Scotland was aided by an initial endowment of £2 million from the Murray Charitable Trust, and £200,000 a year thereafter. The Trust has also given £280,000 for the cataloguing of the Bartholomew Archive at the NLS

APPENDIX: THE HOUSE OF MURRAY, 1860–1892

1. Murray turned down the new dictionary in 1858 and later dealings with the philological society also failed. See note 12 to Chapter 3 above
2. The expenses for du Chaillu's book include £53 15s paid to a Mr Wilson for 'Stuffing Gorilla', so we may assume that Murray's didn't stint on the gimmicky marketing
3. For trains, but it would have worked on planes, if there had been any
4. An understatement. Ada Byron, who became Countess of Lovelace, was obsessed with Babbage, and taught herself mathematics so that she could work with him.

Bibliography

MANUSCRIPTS AND TYPESCRIPTS

BL   British Library, London

Diary   Diary of John Grey ('Jock') Murray

'Experience'   'An Experience of Authors': transcript of a talk given by John Grey ('Jock') Murray at Dove Cottage, Cumbria (Wordsworth Trust), March 1992

JMA MS   Manuscript, followed by number, in the John Murray Archive, National Library of Scotland, Edinburgh

JML   John Murray Library, 50 Albemarle Street, London

LB   Letter-books (notes on letters sent, and to some extent personal diaries) of John Murray I; the same of John Murray II, kept more sporadically, and consisting solely of transcript of letters sent

NLS   National Library of Scotland, Edinburgh

Norrie   'Notes by Ian Norrie, Bookseller in Hampstead 1956–83' (typescript, 1999)

Pinnock   Ken Pinnock, 'My Time at Murray's' (typescript, c.1987)

PLF address   Address given by Patrick Leigh Fermor at Jock Murray's Thanksgiving Service, 26 October 1993

S/A   Copy of Samuel Smiles's biography of John Murray II (see below) annotated by John Murray III and others

BOOKS AND ARTICLES

Astarte   *Astarte: a fragment of truth concerning George Gordon Byron, sixth Lord Byron, recorded by his grandson Ralph Milbanke, Earl of Lovelace*, Chiswick Press, 1905

Atallah	Interview with Jock Murray by Naim Atallah, *Oldie*, 17 April 1992
Blackburne	Neville Blackburne, *The Restless Ocean: The Story of George Crabbe*, Terence Dalton, 1972
BLJ	*Byron's Letters and Journals*, ed. Leslie A. Marchand, 13 vols, John Murray, 1973–94
Bodleian	Bodleian Library, University of Oxford
BW	*The Poetical Works of Lord Byron*, John Murray, 1844
Clark	Roy Benjamin Clark, *William Gifford: Tory Satirist, Critic, and Editor*, Columbia University Press, 1930
Cochran	Peter Cochran (ed.), 'The Burning of Byron's Memoirs' (edited from BL Add Mss 56548 73v–87v)
Constable	Thomas Constable, *Archibald Constable and his Literary Correspondents*, 3 vols, Edmonston & Douglas, 1873
Dowden	Wilfred S. Dowden (ed.), *The Journal of Thomas Moore*, 6 vols, University of Delaware Press, 1983–91
Eastlake	*Journals and Correspondence of Lady Eastlake*, 2 vols, John Murray, 1895
Hillier ii	Bevis Hillier, *John Betjeman: New Fame, New Love*, John Murray, paperback edn, 2003
JM III	*John Murray III 1808–1892: A Brief Memoir by John Murray IV*, John Murray, 1919
Le Faye	Deirdre Le Faye (ed.), *Jane Austen's Letters*, Oxford University Press, 3rd edn, 1995
LLB	Doris Langley Moore, *The Late Lord Byron*, John Murray, 1961
MacCarthy	Fiona MacCarthy, *Byron: Life and Legend*, Faber & Faber, 2002
Modert	Jo Modert (ed.), *Jane Austen's Manuscript Letters in Facsimile*, Southern Illinois University Press, 1990
Nicholson	Andrew Nicholson (ed.), *The Letters of John Murray to Lord Byron*, Liverpool University Press, 2007
ODNB	*Oxford Dictionary of National Biography*
P	George Paston, *At John Murray's: Records of a Literary Circle 1843–1892*, John Murray, 1932
QR	*Quarterly Review*
Rundell (1807)	[Maria Elizabeth Rundell], *A New System of Domestic Cookery; formed upon Principles of Economy, and adapted to*

	the use of Private Families. By a Lady. Second edition . . . John Murray . . . 1807. Price Seven Shillings and Six-pence
Rundell (1811)	[The same], *A new edition, corrected* . . . 1811
S	Samuel Smiles, *A Publisher and His Friends: Memoir and Correspondence of the Late John Murray, with an account of the origin and progress of the house, 1768–1843 . . . in two volumes*, John Murray, 1891
Scott Letters ii	*The Letters of Sir Walter Scott 1808–1811*, ed. H. J. C. Grierson, Constable, 1932
Stark Letters	*Freya Stark, Letters*, ed. Lucy Moorehead, Compton Russell, ii, 1975; iii, 1976
Z	William Zachs, *The First John Murray and the Late Eighteenth-Century London Book Trade*, British Academy/ Oxford University Press, 1998
Z/SP	*John Murray: Selected Publications 1768–1792*, catalogue by William Zachs of an exhibition at the Antiquarian Booksellers Association Book Fair, Edinburgh, 1997
Z/Stuart	William Zachs, *Without Regard to Good Manners: A Biography of Gilbert Stuart 1743–1786*, Edinburgh University Press, 1992

Index